PRAISE FOR *OPERATIONAL RISK MANAGEMENT IN FINANCIAL SERVICES*

'Written by a renowned educator, this book is an invaluable resource for both experienced and early-career professionals seeking to enhance their skills and practices to foster value added operational risk management. With a simple and engaging approach, *Operational Risk Management in Financial Services* aptly recognizes the growing complexity of operational risk activities, offering essential tools and practical examples for navigating this evolving landscape.'
Josephine Degaita, Head of Group Operational Risk, National Bank of Greece

'If you are looking for an all-round guide to operational risk management, whether you are an expert who wants to be challenged or just starting out in this field, this book is a must-have! Elena Pykhova seamlessly guides you through all you need to know about operational risk while making it simple to understand. I encourage everyone to read this book to learn from a top expert in this field.'
Inna Schwartz, Chief Risk Officer, Sygnum Bank

'If you can only purchase one book on operational risk management, then I strongly recommend this one. Elena Pykhova's insightful approach makes this book the best choice for those seeking practical, business-oriented solutions.'
Manoj Kulwal, Chief Risk and AI Officer, RiskSpotlight

'Elena Pykhova teaches and writes in simple, clear and engaging language. This book is a brilliant resource for risk professionals, covering all foundational concepts in a practical and easy to follow manner.'
Daniela Biagi, Head of Academy, Euronext Group

'An essential read for all risk professionals and CEOs. This book is the definitive guide to operational risk management in financial services.'
Richard Doe, former CEO, Harpenden Building Society

T0295718

'Operational risk is a topic that is large and complex in both breadth and depth, making it a particularly challenging area for risk managers to get hold of. Elena Pykhova does a masterful job in bringing all the various strands together in a practically valuable yet accessible way. Very highly recommended!'
Moorad Choudhry, Author of *The Principles of Banking*

'Simply, the most practical and educational guide on operational risk management written by an expert. A refreshingly lively read, with useful examples, valuable industry insights, challenges and good practices.
A must-have book for anyone in the industry.'
Susana Gomez Smith, Non-Executive Director, Novo Banco and Leonteq AG

'This is an excellent book. Elena Pykhova writes with passion and clarity, providing the reader with a simple-to-follow, guided journey through all the components of the operational risk framework. This is a great read for experienced risk professionals and non-professionals alike.'
Ellen Brataas, CEO, IIA Norway

'A must for risk management professionals. The book has clear and direct language, very good examples and recommendations to better cope with the heavy burden and great responsibility that comes with operational risk management in the financial world. Very notable are its recommendations at the beginning of each chapter, together with challenges and good practices, which are valuable for those who work to make things happen in operational risk management.'
Esteban Olivares Arellano, Partner, Next Consultores, Adjunct Professor Faculty of Economics and Business, University of Chile and Regional Director, PRMIA

'This book is an essential guide for professionals seeking to understand and manage the complexities of operational risk in today's financial services landscape. Crucially, this second edition provides valuable insights into the future of operational risk management and guides professionals into incorporating ESG into day-to-day strategies. A must-read for anyone in the industry.'
Nigel Boothroyd, Non-Executive Director, British Arab Commercial Bank

Second Edition

Operational Risk Management in Financial Services

A practical guide to establishing effective solutions

Elena Pykhova

Publisher's note

Every possible effort has been made to ensure that the information contained in this book is accurate at the time of going to press, and the publishers and author cannot accept responsibility for any errors or omissions, however caused. No responsibility for loss or damage occasioned to any person acting, or refraining from action, as a result of the material in this publication can be accepted by the editor, the publisher or the author.

First published in Great Britain and the United States in 2021 by Kogan Page Limited
Second edition published in 2024

2nd Floor, 45 Gee Street
London
EC1V 3RS
United Kingdom

8 W 38th Street, Suite 902
New York, NY 10018
USA

www.koganpage.com

Kogan Page books are printed on paper from sustainable forests.

ISBNs

Hardback   978 1 3986 1719 3
Paperback   978 1 3986 1714 8
Ebook   978 1 3986 1718 6

British Library Cataloguing-in-Publication Data

A CIP record for this book is available from the British Library.

Library of Congress Control Number

2024941651

Typeset by Integra Software Services, Pondicherry
Print production managed by Jellyfish
Printed and bound by CPI Group (UK) Ltd, Croydon, CR0 4YY

CONTENTS

LIST OF FIGURES

Figures

ABOUT THE AUTHOR

 Elena Pykhova is an award-winning risk expert, author, international trainer and educator. Based in London, she is the founder of a boutique risk management consultancy, The OpRisk Company, www.theopriskcompany.com, specializing in risk transformation, and in board/executive level advice on effective operational and enterprise risk management strategy, design and implementation. Elena is a renowned educator, who for many years has run public and in-house training courses in the UK and internationally for world-leading organizations including the London Stock Exchange Academy, Euronext, Risk.net, the Møller Centre, Cambridge University and the Institute of Internal Auditors. Elena is also a thought leader, influencer and founder of a prominent industry think tank, the Best Practice Operational Risk Forum. She is a former Director for Education at the Institute of Operational Risk, and chair of the Expert Panel for the Association of Foreign Banks. Passionate about the operational risk discipline, she founded her training and consulting practice after 20 years of experience in senior roles at Fortune 500 companies. She is a regular speaker at conferences and writes articles for Thomson Reuters, Advantage Talent Inc., *Operational Risk & Regulation* and other publications.

PREFACE

Operational Risk Management in Financial Services: A practical guide to establishing effective solutions reflects my passion for the operational risk discipline and the value it delivers to the enterprise. No other domain in financial services is so extensive and all-encompassing, yet at the same time relatively young and still evolving as a discipline. These factors together mean that operational risk is perhaps the most exciting and interesting field to explore in the whole financial services sector. I am delighted to be sharing my passion for this fascinating and important topic, and invite the reader to embark on a journey distinguished by three main features: a practical approach, simplicity and engaging insights.

A practical approach

I came into operational risk from executive leadership roles in operations: running round-the-clock global foreign exchange and money market settlements, processing billions of dollars a day, at American Express; managing busy retail branches with customers queuing at tellers' tills in Citibank Tunisia; and starting up an internal control unit at Citibank Russia, where a dozen initial recruits helped to shape the bank from its inception. My personal experience in these roles taught me to apply a pragmatic approach to operational risk management. When designing and implementing frameworks and tools, I always question whether these tools would have enabled me to *do my job better*. Operational risk management is about the *value proposition* of risk: finding practical ways of embedding risk management into the organization to add value. This has been my personal mantra in group head roles across American Express, Standard Chartered, VTB Capital and Deutsche Bank as well as many executive assignments with a broad range of clients in my consultancy practice.

Simplicity

Simplicity is another essential element. As Albert Einstein is alleged to have said, 'If you can't explain it simply, you don't understand it well enough.'

From an early age I was accustomed to dealing with complexity and translating it into simplicity: my parents are nuclear physicists, my brother studied and worked in the field of laser physics, and for my own degree I chose applied mathematics, admiring the beauty of logic and order. When teaching operational risk classes, I always aim to find ways of relaying complex information in a simple manner, and to communicate in language that is engaging and easily understood. Many of my courses, for example in mainland China, are run with a consequential translator. This construct demands an extra degree of clarity and simplicity when formulating and expressing thoughts. Research demonstrates that our brains can process three chunks of information comfortably. So, throughout the book you will find uncomplicated three-step approaches that help explain the different concepts being outlined: three steps for implementing operational risk practices, three questions for risk identification, the 'Scope–Methodology–Integration' trilogy... and many more besides.

Engaging insights

Another feature of the operational risk journey that is apparent to me is the vital importance of open debate and the sharing of experiences among operational risk practitioners – especially at times when the discipline is actively evolving. To this end, I have been leading industry work in operational risk for over two decades, first as chair of the operational risk expert panel at the Association of Foreign Banks in London, managing round-table discussions and overseeing working groups and papers on good practices. Subsequently I spearheaded the creation of the Best Practice Operational Risk Forum, comprising senior risk practitioners from over 50 diverse and geographically spread financial services firms. One positive development that has emerged from the Covid-19 pandemic is that the Best Practice Forum has expanded even further, as our meetings have moved online. I have been delighted to welcome many new international participants who are now joining the Forum's monthly calls from locations all over the globe. On these calls we share valuable insights – under Chatham House rules to preserve confidentiality – and conduct frequent live polls which enable rapid snapshots of current practices in every single area of operational risk. The Forum's work is reflected in the book, where every chapter contains industry benchmark sections, providing a reader with a perspective of where the industry stands on each particular topic. I also make a point of posting regular insights, reports and briefings on my website www.theopriskcompany.com and on LinkedIn. If these are of interest, you can continue reading them by following my consultancy practice, The Op Risk Company Ltd.

Many friendships emanated from these years of industry work, and I am grateful to every one of my colleagues who has shared my passion for operational risk management over the years.

About the 2nd Edition

What is new in the 2nd edition? There is, of course, an added chapter (14) addressing the integration of environmental, social and governance (ESG) aspects into the Operational risk framework. Without doubt, ESG factors are becoming increasingly important for organizations and their teams. The reader will note my view that the acronym needs to be decomposed into its separate elements: E, S and G, enabling effective assimilation into existing tools and processes.

The operational resilience chapter (15) has been re-written as a number of new publications came out since the first edition, and industry practices have somewhat matured.

There is a new chapter (16) which reflects on the current state and the future of operational risk management. It discusses topical subjects such as Third-party, Cyber risk, and GenAI, and proposes a recipe for risk professionals to remain current and successful to withstand future challenges. This is even more important in the current testing environment, when demands are continuing to increase while budgets and resources (at best) remain at the same level. There is less room for *risk administration* and more impetus for value-added *risk management*. Operational risk professionals must think sharper and act smarter.

Lastly, industry benchmarks at the end of every chapter have been updated to provide the latest snapshots of current practices. Readers will note that industry polls demonstrate gradual and steady progress is many, despite not all, areas, as operational risk discipline continues to mature. One area where deterioration was noted is the Risk and Control Self-Assessments (RCSAs). It appears that the more organizations persist in making the process rigid and complex, with pre-defined and pre-formulated risk and control libraries, the less room is left for free-flowing conversations on what truly keeps the stakeholders awake at night. Thus, a point of reflection: do not overcomplicate the RCSAs: re-inject the energy with expert facilitation, re-engage the stakeholders in meaningful discussions around three simple questions as noted in Chapter 5, and derive value by making the results actionable.

Finally, I wholeheartedly thank all those who made the 2nd edition possible: Charlie Lynn from Kogan Page who worked with me tirelessly, Howard Walwyn from Prism-Clarity who aided in achieving clarity, many inspirational risk experts who took their time to read and comment on the draft chapters, and my family who, second time round, already knew what book writing entails, and were duly patient and supportive. I am hugely grateful to my clients, industry partners and Best Practice Forum members who continue to place trust in me and with whom I am fortunate to work, continuously enhancing operational risk management practices. It's thanks to all of you that this second edition became possible.

I hope that readers will appreciate practical solutions, tips and hints and relate to the challenges highlighted in the chapters. I also trust that the book will help to dispel the myth that operational risk is a boring discipline and inspire more practitioners to apply for roles in the Operational Risk department.

Operational risk 01
Definition and taxonomy

What this chapter covers: This introductory chapter starts with reflections on what risk is, and how to encourage employees to think about risk without viewing it as an alien subject. The chapter provides a definition of Operational Risk and examines its evolution. It then presents the Risk Taxonomy as the essential glue that binds the framework together, laying the foundation for effective operational risk management. It proceeds to emphasize the importance of an appropriate classification system. Finally, the chapter contains an industry study and the results of live polls with industry practitioners.

FURTHER READING

- Operational Riskdata eXchange Association (2019) *ORX Reference Taxonomy*
  Why recommended: The ORX reference taxonomy is the latest positive industry development, presenting a coherent and up-to-date classification system.
- Daniel Kahneman (2012) *Thinking, Fast and Slow*, Penguin Books
  Why recommended: After all, risk management is about decision-making. This international bestseller by Nobel Laureate Daniel Kahneman explores how our minds work and provides practical techniques to help us make better decisions.

Introduction: value-added risk management

Organizations – some more than others, admittedly – take a natural interest in managing their people, systems and processes, and the threats posed by the external environment. Business units and support functions were handling these things well before operational risk was defined in the Basel Accord; and they would continue to do so, even if operational risk practitioners were not part of the equation.

The key question, therefore, is about the value proposition of the risk function. Are operational risk professionals providing end-users with the tools that enable them to do their job *better*? Or do risk frameworks merely add an administrative burden, and hinder employees' experience, rather than enhancing it?

This book is about the *value proposition* of risk: simple, practical ways of embedding operational risk management into your organization to add value.

Helping employees to think about risk

What is *risk* and how do we think about it? Without oversimplifying, risk is an intuitive concept: perhaps without always realizing it, we are managing risk and taking risk-based decisions every day. As individuals, we have an internal compass that guides our risk perception. The tuning of the compass is highly personalized; something perceived as alarming by some may be normal for others, and so our reactions vary. Risk takers may welcome thrilling situations, while other more conservative individuals may prefer to stay as far away as possible from anything remotely threatening.

For over two decades I have been running training courses on operational risk, and I usually start these sessions with a simple exercise: asking participants to exchange stories about something *risky* they have done and getting each group to decide who is the *riskiest* person in their team. This always sets the room in motion: no formal definitions or lengthy explanations are required about what *risk* is. Invariably fascinating stories are told by attendees representing different cultures, nationalities and geographic locations. I consider myself very fortunate to have heard so many of them.

This exercise is particularly helpful because it enables attendees to consider some important concepts as well as draw parallels with the world of operational risk management.

Risk taking for reward

The anecdotes that feature most frequently in these stories are related to extreme sports such as bungee jumping, mountain biking and skydiving. It never fails to fascinate me how many financial services professionals engage fearlessly in activities which are essentially quite dangerous. They illustrate *risk taking* – actively seeking *risk for reward* – doing exciting things while at the same time recognizing that they contain threats.

Risk assessment

It is worth exploring how participants *assessed the risk* and what precautions they took before deciding to (for instance) jump out of a plane with a parachute. These might include:

- researching the service provider to ensure it was a reputable establishment;
- asking to be accompanied by a master instructor on the dive;
- taking out insurance.

These kinds of precautions immediately highlight some important concepts. First, the notion of *inherent risk* – risk without any associated controls. Second, the idea of *risk reduction* via the application of *controls*. Third, the related notion of *residual risk* – the level of risk remaining after the application of controls – which the individual has accepted before choosing to proceed. This example also introduces the concept of a *risk assessment*, which will be outlined in Chapter 5.

Risk mitigation

Many of the courses I run are in countries with different cultures and languages, sometimes alongside a translator. In some languages the word *risk* has a negative connotation and is associated with *danger* or individual participants may attribute this meaning. For them hearing the word *risk* conjures up threats and hazards in their minds. Consequently, their stories sometimes involve snowstorms, floods or explosions. These examples, in turn, illustrate that risk is not always intentionally sought; there is no reward to be gained and therefore the level must be *mitigated downwards*, by any means possible. This summarizes the key dilemma around the nature of operational risk, discussed in Chapter 9, which invites readers to form a view on whether operational risk is taken for return or, akin to a snowstorm, imposed from the outside and not intentionally sought – with reduction or mitigation being left as the only option.

Impact and likelihood

Sometimes, the accounts contain examples of *materialized* risk; perhaps a skiing accident which (thankfully) resulted in only a minor injury. When risk materializes it turns into a *risk event*, as presented in Chapter 4. This illustrates that *risk* is something that has not happened yet and may (or may not) happen in the future; introducing the uncertainty of outcome and the twin dimensions of *likelihood* and *impact*. In the skiing accident example the impact was described as minor; but before the trip took place its outcome was unknown.

Risk appetite

I asked a group of international participants at a course I delivered at Cambridge University to identify the *riskiest* person in their group. They all pointed immediately to the head of the delegation. This was because, on arrival, they had rented a bicycle and gone out exploring the picturesque town on their own. The group perceived this decision as 'very adventurous' due to a lack of familiarity with the layout of the town, not to mention the language barrier, which it was felt would diminish their opportunity to ask for help if needed. The head of the delegation, by contrast, argued that they were well-travelled and used to exploring unknown places, and would continue to do so throughout the stay.

This discussion articulates the fact that people have different individual *risk appetites*, ranging from conservative to expansionary. Similarly, financial services firms have distinct *risk appetites* to suit their size, nature and business model. The example also highlights the importance of *risk conversations*, encouraging people to talk openly about risk, and to compare notes on the magnitude of risk being taken and the quality of controls in place.

Every key concept in operational risk management can be explained via real-life stories of this kind; the list of examples and respective parallels that can be drawn is endless. The main objective of the introductory exercise to the training course is to encourage participants to embrace *risk* and actively converse on the topic. Bringing in examples from personal experience demonstrates that we are already continually reflecting on risk-related matters; and it should be no different when it comes to running a financial services business.

Within a corporate environment, it is essential to find ways of inspiring employees to think and talk about risk, in as many ways as possible.

Defining operational risk

Definition and its evolution

The well-known definition of operational risk presented by the Basel Framework is 'the risk of loss resulting from inadequate or failed internal processes, people and systems or from external events'.[1] Put simply, the regulators concluded that financial services firms could sustain major damage due to risks *other than* credit and market risks. Consequently, a broad range of threats was grouped under the umbrella of operational risk, as depicted in Figure 1.1; and firms were requested, for the first time, to put capital aside to guard against such losses.

Needless to say, the spectrum of the operational risk discipline based on this definition is very wide-ranging, covering deliberate or accidental actions of employees, malfunctions of technological systems and broken processes. The categories of risk covered by this definition are distinct, not homogeneous and require specialist knowledge. This is an interesting phenomenon which has always prompted questions about the identity of operational risk practitioners and the expectation that they need to be masters of all trades. That very breadth of the scope should, however, be viewed as the greatest advantage of the operational risk discipline: no other domain in financial services is so extensive or all-encompassing in scope. Coupled with the fact that it is still a relatively young and evolving discipline, operational risk is perhaps the most exciting and interesting financial services field in which to explore and build a career.

Figure 1.1 Operational risk in a picture

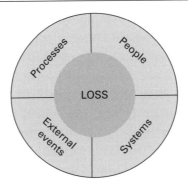

Operational risk, not operations risk

Arguably, the name *operational risk* does not do the discipline justice; whether in English or other languages, it is often mistakenly associated with the *Operations Department* and the potential errors and failures that emanate from operational processing. When my training slides are translated into various languages, I always double-check the definition and frequently have to correct the fact that the word has been translated as *operations*. What was confusing a decade ago is still so nowadays. So it is important to emphasize:

Operational Risk ≠ Operations Risk

The educational journey is far from complete, within both financial services firms and the regulatory authorities themselves. In 2017, the European Securities and Markets Authority (ESMA) issued a pioneering document on the application of distributed ledger technology to the securities market.[2] Under the 'Key Risk' section, however, operational risk still called out only errors and glitches; while other sub-components such as cyber, fraud and money laundering – which should have been mentioned under the same heading – appeared under separate and distinct titles.

In recent years, potential fragmentation was somewhat exacerbated by *conduct risk* being unhelpfully introduced and treated by many firms as a risk distinct from operational risk. To reiterate, in this book operational risk is viewed in its broadest, all-encompassing context. In some organizations, it has even been renamed to *non-financial risk* to emphasize the breadth and remove the confusion with operations.

Just loss no longer works

The roots of the operational risk discipline lay in the Basel *Capital* Accord; the word *capital* relaying the primary focus of prudential regulatory directives on *risk measurement* and the adequacy of internal financial resources. The Basel Committee disclosed, in a study of 30 major banks, that the value of losses crystallizing from operational risk failures between 1998 and 2000 amounted to €2.6 billion;[3] as a result, it became a significant enough concern to warrant an introduction of a capital charge.

In reality there are other important impacts of operational risk failure, in addition to financial losses incurred by the firm itself. These include customer detriment, reputational damage and market instability. Following high-profile mis-selling scandals and significant technology failures, both firms and regulators nowadays are paying close attention to conduct and operational resilience. While the Basel Framework itself is primarily *inwardly focused* on the firm's financial resources, supervisors around the world would argue that organizations also need to have an *outward* view: considering the harm that their wrongdoing may be causing to clients and markets. This friction creates an interesting divergence: a growing number of organizations are coming to the view that the definition which cites only *loss* is no longer fully reflective of today's environment. The universe of operational risk is thus expanded, by amending the first part of the standard Basel definition to:

- the risk of *direct or indirect* loss resulting from…;
- the risk of *actual or potential financial* loss or *client harm* resulting from…; or even more broadly…
- the risk of *not achieving strategic objectives* due to inadequate or failed internal processes, people and systems or from external events.

Link to strategy and value proposition

As a business value proposition, operational risk management has a clear purpose. Its primary goal is to provide tools to business units on the ground to enable them to make well-informed and risk-aware decisions. Even though the Basel description specifically excludes strategic risk from its scope, expanding the definition of operational risk to be more of an enterprise-wide discipline – and specifically linking it to business objectives – makes a lot of sense and immediately bears fruit. Having a conversation with a chief executive and senior managers on what keeps them awake at night inevitably brings more strategic aspects into the discussion. A narrowly defined scope, on the other hand, creates barriers to a free-flowing conversation. It means business-related concerns are expressly carved out and demonstrates clearly that the focus of operational risk should be limited to 'operational' concerns, such as fraud and the like.

The traditional definition of risk cited by the International Organization for Standardization (ISO) is 'the effect of uncertainty on objectives'.[4] This definition purposely focuses on *objectives*; not the whole realm of uncertainties, but rather their specific impact on what needs to be achieved. Similarly, the Committee of Sponsoring Organizations of the Treadway Commission (COSO) stresses the position of risk in relation to mission and strategy.[5]

This may be the missing link in how operational risk is distinguished from other disciplines. At times there is a tendency within the operational risk domain to go its own way, creating lists of all the things that can possibly go wrong due to processes, people or systems, but not always seeing the vital connection to what matters most: the firm's business goals. Expanding the definition to include an explicit link to business objectives elevates the brand and straightaway brings risk practitioners to the strategy table.

In 2018, I conducted a study to understand industry practices around these definition questions, the results of which are presented in Table 1.1. They demonstrate that, while the majority of practitioners are still using the original Basel definition, we are also seeing a positive shift in the industry, re-positioning operational risk where it can help derive the maximum possible business benefit.

As part of the same study, operational risk professionals voted on their presence at the strategy table. The outcome in Table 1.2 reflects a common complaint among practitioners that the operational risk function is not routinely called upon when major discussions and decisions are taking place. This result provides yet more impetus to expand the definition and promote the standing of the discipline.

Table 1.1   Industry study: definition of operational risk

Operational risk definition	% firms
Using Basel definition	56
Expanded to broader than *loss*	13
Expanded to include strategy or link to objectives	23
Other expanded	8

Table 1.2   Industry study: operational risk function at the strategy table

Operational risk function at the strategy table	% firms
Yes	25
Occasionally involved in some strategic decisions	49
Not involved in making strategic decisions	26

To this end, an impressive example of a Governance, Risk and Compliance (GRC) software solution is Corporater (corporater.com), which has adopted a GPRC (Governance, *Performance*, Risk and Compliance) approach. It incorporated *Performance* as a module, enabling alignment of risk management with business performance and strategy execution.

Operational risk taxonomy and its evolution

At the heart of operational risk management is the Risk Taxonomy, which provides further explanation and definition of the scope of what is included in the discipline.

OPERATIONAL RISK TAXONOMY

The taxonomy is a risk classification system which defines and distinguishes different categories of operational risk, enabling it to capture the complete risk universe.

What is the main purpose of this taxonomy? In practice it serves several different uses, as highlighted below.

Common language and areas of focus

Classification introduces a common language of risk, enabling the organization to use consistent terminology. It also allows firms to bring certain themes into the spotlight, by specifically calling them out in separate categories, which helps to focus attention on them during risk identification exercises. There is an additional benefit from the regulatory requirement to map internal taxonomy to standard Basel Committee categories which are described further in the chapter. It means that not only do firms have a common language but there is also an *industry* common language that can be used for benchmarking purposes.

Risk measurement

In the early days, the primary use of the taxonomy tended to be for *risk measurement*. It enables firms to allocate losses – which we can think of as crystallized operational risks, as discussed in Chapter 4 – to a specific named category. This helps firms analyse their loss profile, understand the distribution of loss amounts across the spectrum of possibilities and evaluate the adequacy of their capital.

Risk identification

As the operational risk discipline has matured, the use of categorization for *risk management* purposes has gradually been increasing. For example, during the risk assessment process outlined in Chapters 5 and 6, risk categories provide a helpful reminder that a whole range of themes need to be addressed, from fraud to system failures, ensuring that no material risks are omitted from the review.

Back-testing

The taxonomy is the essential glue that links the framework elements together. If the tools introduced in subsequent chapters all apply the same classification, it is possible to compare and contrast their outputs against each other, which helps to tell a coherent story.

Aggregation and reporting

Following on from this, categorization allows a structure to be imposed on large quantities of operational risk data, allowing the aggregation, analysis and reporting of themes in a meaningful way, and enabling areas of concern to be highlighted.

Introduction of operational risk taxonomy

The Basel taxonomy consists of seven *categories*, or types, described in Figure 1.2. (Note: the terms 'category' and 'type' will be used interchangeably throughout the rest of this chapter.)

Basel classification has been used by many organizations since the very early days of the operational risk discipline, and is now deeply embedded in the core tools of the framework which capture, process and analyse relevant data.

A further nomenclature exists for each of the main (or *level 1*) categories. We can think of these as *level 2* sub-categories (or sub-types) of risk. The Basel Framework, for instance, splits *internal fraud* into more detailed sub-categories, such as *unauthorized activity* and *theft and fraud* (see Table 1.3).

Figure 1.2   Seven operational risk categories, Basel Committee

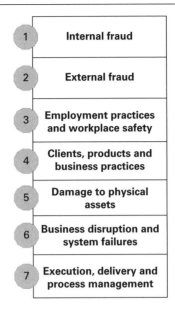

1	**Internal fraud**
2	**External fraud**
3	**Employment practices and workplace safety**
4	**Clients, products and business practices**
5	**Damage to physical assets**
6	**Business disruption and system failures**
7	**Execution, delivery and process management**

Table 1.3   Taxonomy sub-categories

Level 1 category	Level 2 sub-category
1. Internal fraud	1.1 Unauthorized activity
	1.2 Theft and fraud

Typically, firms define a hierarchy with two to three levels, though some organizations go up to five levels, creating a comprehensive catalogue of detailed individual risks. A taxonomy with more than three levels may, however, become too granular and burdensome to use.

Evolution of operational risk taxonomy

While some firms continue to apply the original Basel classification, it is recognized across the industry that it is becoming dated. Increasingly, organizations are taking the opportunity to design a bespoke, fit-for-purpose listing tailored to their own needs. The publication of an updated reference taxonomy by the ORX, summarized in Figure 1.3, has enabled some firms to accelerate progress in adopting a more current categorization system.[6]

Figure 1.3   Sixteen operational risk categories, ORX

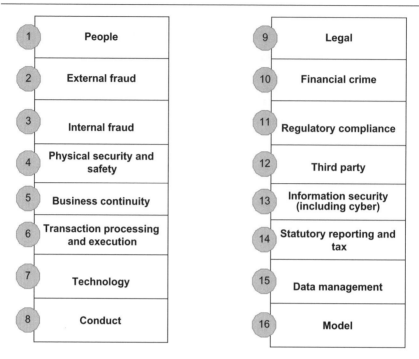

1	People	9	Legal
2	External fraud	10	Financial crime
3	Internal fraud	11	Regulatory compliance
4	Physical security and safety	12	Third party
5	Business continuity	13	Information security (including cyber)
6	Transaction processing and execution	14	Statutory reporting and tax
7	Technology	15	Data management
8	Conduct	16	Model

To create a fit-for-purpose taxonomy, organizations should aim to:

- use simple language which is understood at all levels of the organization;
- shape the categories to reflect the most significant risks in their business;
- create the best possible value for risk identification and management purposes.

Simplifying the language

The Basel Committee naming conventions are not entirely obvious or intuitive to employees on the ground who may be less familiar with operational risk as a discipline. While the term *execution, delivery and process management* is easily recognized by most risk practitioners, it is less meaningful to other departments. To help improve embeddedness, a better value proposition is to deliver the risk framework in the language that people in the business actually use. For example, as seen in Figure 1.3, *employment practices and workplace safety* has been effectively renamed by ORX as merely *people* – a more sensible and intuitive expression of that risk type.

Reflecting the current landscape

Over the years the operational risk landscape has evolved markedly, providing yet another reason for a refresh of the Basel taxonomy. For example:

- *Outsourcing and Supplier (or Third-party risk)* – given firms' increasing reliance on third (fourth and n-th) parties and in view of requirements such as the European Banking Authority's guidelines,[7] this needs to be *promoted* into its own level 1 category rather than displayed as part of *execution, delivery and process management.*

- *Cyber* – for which the Financial Stability Board has developed a whole lexicon of its own – needs to be reflected with adequate language.[8]

- *Clients, products and business practices* is too wide-ranging and includes several distinct topics, including *legal* and *financial crime*. If a firm is assessing its exposure to and appetite for, say, *legal risk* – which is specifically called out by the Basel Framework as part of operational risk – it would be beneficial to have that risk as a distinct category.

- On the other hand, examples such as cheque kiting – a form of unauthorized chequing account activity which Basel lists as level 3 under *execution, delivery and process management* – are becoming less pertinent in the digital age.

Considering best value for risk management purposes

As discussed earlier in the chapter, taxonomy allows firms and practitioners to consciously focus attention on specific themes; it is therefore a powerful risk management tool. For example, where the firm is reliant on a significant number of complex spreadsheets and end-user computing applications (EUCs), it may introduce *model risk* as a level 1 category. This will emphasize the importance of the topic and encourage end-users to identify and assess *model risk*, defined as the risk of incorrect model design or poor implementation. Areas such as trading, finance and market risk commonly use elaborate models, sometimes in the form of spreadsheets, which take assumptions, perform computations and produce critical outputs that are used for decision-making. There are plenty of industry examples of model errors that have caused significant losses and reputational damage to the enterprise, signifying the importance of *model risk* management.

Similarly, if the organization is actively launching new products and value propositions, it may feel appropriate to distinguish a level 1 *product risk* category, as described in Table 1.4.

Product does not appear as a level 1 category in either the Basel or ORX taxonomies; while *model* is present in the ORX but not the Basel level 1 categorization. This discrepancy illustrates that it is useful to refer to industry sources as a guide rather than a rule, and to develop a customized classification scheme. The challenge, of course, is that businesses evolve over time and the scheme has to be meaningful at the moment of creation and yet have the flexibility to evolve in line with business needs.

Cause, event and impact: use of the bow-tie

Generally, the purpose of the operational risk taxonomy is to classify *events*. It is worth discussing this in more detail, highlighting a perpetual operational risk management challenge around *cause*, *event* and *impact*.

- *cause* leads to an event;
- *event* is a specific occurrence, or something that goes wrong;
- *impact* is the consequence of an event.

Staff fatigue may be a *cause* of, for instance, a transactional error or failure to process a payment (an *event*), leading to financial loss, client detriment and other consequences (*impacts*), as outlined in Figure 1.4.

Table 1.4   Taxonomy example: product category

Level 1 category	Subject matter expert	Definition	Level 2 sub-categories
1. Product	Head of Product Development	The risk of product flaws or defects, failure to adhere to specification.	1.1 Product defects 1.2 Failure to adhere to product specification 1.3 Inadequate new/ change product approval process

Figure 1.4   Cause–Event–Impact bow-tie

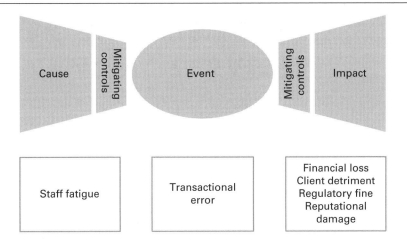

This well-known model, named after its resemblance to a bow-tie, is helpful in differentiating between causes, events and impacts, leading to a neater taxonomy containing *events* (and excluding causes and impacts). The bow-tie model will be further referred to in subsequent chapters of the book. In the earlier example, the event falls under the category *transaction processing and execution*; while staff fatigue, being a *cause*, does not belong in the *event* taxonomy.

That said, it has to be acknowledged that there are endless cause–event–impact chains in operational risk management due to the sheer breadth of the discipline and interconnectedness of various elements. One event can become the cause of another; for instance, miscommunication (cause) can result in an erroneous transaction (event); in turn, an erroneous transaction (cause) may corrupt a system, leading to system failure (event).

PRACTICAL TIP: 'PIN THE BOW-TIE'

To untangle the cause–event–impact chain, practitioners may adopt an approach of 'pinning the bow-tie', whereby the *cause* is ascertained first to distinguish the *event*. Alternatively, employees may choose to 'pin' the *impact* (for example, on the end-customer), working backwards to the *event*. The latter approach is easier and more readily understood by the business units and support functions.

A note on exclusivity, which is a useful design concept when setting the taxonomy. It is important to provide clear guidance to avoid the overlap where a risk or event can easily be placed into two or more taxonomy categories. For example, the *Outsourcing and Supplier (or Third-Party)* category may be designed to capture all events caused by service providers. In this case, *information security* type dealing with data loss, theft or non-deliberate data breaches should clearly denote the exclusion of third-party data-related events, pointing to their coverage under the respective category.

To summarize, when designing the taxonomy, adopt a pragmatic approach, and configure to the extent possible 'clean' event-type categories which are:

- exhaustive;
- mutually exclusive;
- resonant with end-users; and
- aiding the most in risk management.

Importantly, be prepared to invest in the analysis of captured data – and recategorization of it where necessary – accepting that perfection is not feasible in this space. Additionally, maintain mappings to the original Basel categories for industry benchmarking purposes.

Most debated taxonomy categories

There are areas of taxonomy that are actively debated and deserve attention, outlined below.

People

The first one is the *people* category, where both the Basel and ORX taxonomies only count occurrences such as employment lawsuits (*events*). The firms, however, frequently wish to encourage the identification and monitoring of risks related to employees being overstretched, or not having the right skillset. If business functions are urged to record threats to capacity or capability, that might enable the firm to receive signals and proactively act before the problem becomes serious. In this case, the overall employee life cycle from on-boarding to off-boarding – including *well-being*, which became a particular focal point during and post the Covid-19 pandemic – is included in the *event-type* taxonomy to capture the entire range of people-related matters.

Change

Another topic which justifies review, as it often leads to arguments, is the topic of *change*. Inadequate change management is usually a *cause* of events such as errors or failed regulatory reporting obligations. Therefore, it has no place in the original Basel or ORX *event-type* taxonomies. However, due to the increasing change agenda within all organizations, change is often now built into the classification system in its own right; to prompt staff to reflect on the magnitude of corporate transformation and address the pressures of too much change before things go wrong.

Conduct

While *conduct* is sometimes presented in its own right (including by ORX), it is best to treat it as an overarching term to identify the multitude of risks that may result in poor customer outcomes (also see Chapter 12 for further definitions). Arguably, many risks residing in the categories such as *people, financial crime, information security* may have conduct implications. They may, however, also apply to the *technology* category, where for example, underinvestment in systems leading to technology failure is a behavioural matter, as it reflects a lack of customer care: the customer not being at the heart of strategic decisions, prioritization and allocation of budget. Consequently, a conduct *lens* can be applied to almost any risk or event to reflect the fact that it has specific (customer or market) consequences, leading to reporting on conduct risk via consolidation of one or more taxonomy categories.

Operational resilience

Operational resilience according to the Basel Committee is an 'outcome that benefits from the effective management of operational risk'.[9] Similarly to *conduct,* it is best not to shoehorn it into a separate category due to the potential for duplication with other risk types (see Chapter 15 for more details).

ESG

This topical subject has a dedicated chapter describing how E, S and G can be incorporated into the taxonomy. Essentially, E can be treated as a cause, while S (as well as G) as a lens through which traditional operational risks are viewed (see Chapter 14 for more details).

Geopolitical

Geopolitical risk frequently appears as a top operational risk in various industry surveys. As it reflects an external threat landscape, it in fact represents a *driver* of multiple operational risks materializing. Therefore, it is best to view it as a cause; this approach is supported by ORX, where geopolitical/economic/social instability appears in the causal taxonomy among other external causes.[10]

In 2020, I led a comparative analysis of operational risk taxonomies across the financial services sector. Presented in Table 1.5 are examples from six firms, anonymized and slightly modified to preserve confidentiality.

The study demonstrates the expected degree of divergence, and proves that there is no 'right' solution to the taxonomy question. Companies are actively tailoring the nomenclature to suit their needs, splitting or collapsing categories and introducing their own terminology. And while there are some common groupings such as *fraud* and *information technology*, unique types – for example *transparency* or *customer and employee communication* – also appear.

Role of taxonomy in risk management by risk category

A well-defined taxonomy sets the foundation for effective *management* of operational risk not only at the overall level, but also by *risk category*; this is where the naming conventions and appropriateness of the categorization scheme become even more apparent. It is likely that all the risk types decided on are already being managed by the enterprise, and that experts are in place to provide specialist advice. The critical role of the operational risk function, therefore, is to *orchestrate*, *connect* and *coordinate* the various activities, bringing together a wealth of existing expertise while avoiding unnecessary duplication.

A subject matter expert (SME) for a given taxonomy category can be defined as a knowledgeable senior individual who is able to provide expertise and advice on that category, including:

- contributing to its definition and level 2 composition;
- providing expert opinion on operational risk data recorded under the category;
- defining operating policies and standards; and
- contributing to operational risk appetite statement and measures (discussed in Chapter 9).

Table 1.5 Industry study: operational risk taxonomies

Firm 1	Firm 2	Firm 3	Firm 4	Firm 5	Firm 6
Internal fraud	Economic crime	Financial crime	Fraud	Third party liability	Fraud
External fraud	Rogue trading and market abuse		Financial crime		
Unauthorized activity					
Employment practices	Employment practices	People	Staff	Health and safety	Health, safety and security
Personal and physical security	Health, safety and environment Facilities management	Health and safety	Health and safety	Buildings and premises	
Compliance risk	Product flaws Regulatory compliance Legal compliance Customer and employee communication	Model Conduct	Valuation Compliance Legal Tax	Transparency risk Communications	Model governance
Information Technology risk	Information Technology management	Technology and cyber security	Systems	Information technology	Technology

(continued)

Table 1.5 (Continued)

Firm 1	Firm 2	Firm 3	Firm 4	Firm 5	Firm 6
Continuity risk		Operational resilience	Data	Cyber	Business resilience
		Data security		Business continuity	
				Data quality and integrity	
Processing risk	Payments transactions	Execution, delivery and process management	Booking and processing	Estate management	Business process
Control risk	Member service	Change management	Accounting	Reporting	Change management
	Financial, regulatory and critical monitoring and reporting	Supplier	Collateral	Third party risk	Supplier management
			Insurance		
			Project		
			Outsourcing		

Organizational structures often naturally lend themselves to the SME concept, with the head of Human Resources, for example, being the natural SME for the *people risk* category, the Chief Technology Officer for *technology*, the head of the Legal department for legal, and so on. Some organizations utilize the term *risk owner* instead of an SME, which implies more responsibility. Whichever term is used, it must fit well with the accountability regime applied by the organization.

Partnership with SMEs enables operational risk teams to agree each taxonomy category and set the foundation for continuous collaboration in risk management. Operational risk teams must not apply an overly rigid approach, instead consulting with SMEs and incorporating their views. It is better to find the right middle ground to arrive at a sensible and meaningful classification, rather than aiming for a perfect categorization that does not achieve organizational buy-in.

Where a partnership with SMEs is not achieved, operational risk practitioners face a challenge of a high degree of fragmentation – and lack of coordination – of their activities. They will be managing operational risk at an aggregate level, whereas their respective SMEs are dealing with each category individually on the ground. Bringing the framework together and integrating the activities helps greatly in ensuring effective and value-added risk management. That is where governance forums aligned to material risk categories, as described in Figure 1.5, are most effective.

These kinds of forums allow firms to dedicate sufficient attention and perform a deep dive into material risk categories. They also bring together the operational risk function, SMEs, and business units and support functions, enabling much needed coordination. Not all categories are equal; some will require a forum with more frequent meetings, while other less material ones could benefit from either an annual review or coverage as an agenda item at the overall operational risk committee. The benefit of establishing

Figure 1.5   Governance forums aligned to risk categories dedicated forums has to be weighed against the cost of running additional meetings. Some forums may govern multiple risk sub-types, such as an operational resilience forum providing oversight of technology/cyber and third-party risks; or a conduct (or compliance) forum dealing with categories such as conduct, financial crime and regulatory.

While roles may vary from firm to firm, an example of responsibilities is presented in the box below.

The operational risk function is responsible for:

- leading the design and development of the operational risk taxonomy in consultation with SMEs;

- working closely with each respective SME to define each level 1 category and its level 2 components;

- establishing and coordinating governance forums aligned to the taxonomy categories, to provide appropriate depth and quality of risk management discussions for each risk type (Note: the forums may be chaired by the SME or the operational risk function, depending on the firm's approach and governance arrangements);

- analysing operational risk data, validating and reclassifying it as needed;

- leading the definition of the appetite, overall and by risk category;

- reporting on the aggregate level of operational risk and by risk category;

- providing oversight and challenge to first line areas.

First line business units and support functions will, in turn:

- apply taxonomy to identify material risks that may prevent achievement of their objectives;

- involve SMEs as needed in risk and control identification and management;

- participate in governance forums; and

- correctly report and categorize operational risk data.

Common challenges and good practices

Common challenges and good practices when developing an operational risk taxonomy are described below.

Common challenges

No elegance in the solution

I had a discussion with a senior practitioner searching for an elegant operational risk taxonomy, with no cross-overs between causes, events and impacts, and with data falling neatly into allocated places. It is hardly feasible to strive for perfection. But nor is it advisable to have 'dirty data', a term that often applies when events, causes and control failures all end up in the categorization system, creating an entangled and unreconcilable array of data. It is best to apply a practical solution, such as a bow-tie structure, to arrive at a sensible classification that is meaningful to the firm; while accepting that this will inevitably mean some detailed data analysis is required.

Data clean-up and recategorization

Continuing from the first challenge, the importance of continuous clean-up and recategorization of operational risk data is sometimes underestimated. For example, when logging events, employees may erroneously classify payment errors under *people*, reasoning that it is a human error. These operational risk events (OREs) need to be moved to the correct category, such as *transaction processing and execution*. This kind of clean-up is an ongoing activity which has to be factored into the day-to-day responsibilities of risk practitioners (whether first or second line), because invariably they are the firm's main experts in taxonomy. This kind of challenge can be also mitigated, however, by more training of the end-users.

Laborious process of introducing changes

Once classification is embedded into the operational risk software, it takes a substantial effort to introduce any changes. This is because previous data – related to past operational risk events, risks and controls – will need to be re-mapped to the new classification. In large international organizations it may take years to move to a new classification scheme. It is best, therefore, to invest effort up-front into developing a system and classification that is well thought through from the start.

Good practices

Developing expertise

There will be instances where an unusual event may arise which raises questions on how it should be incorporated into the existing scheme. It is crucial to develop expertise on these cases within the Operational Risk department – perhaps even to appoint a taxonomy 'guru' who can interpret arbitrary cases and provide effective guidance.

Creating supplementary classification systems

Some firms use the term 'taxonomy' more widely and create other data categorization structures in addition to *event-type* classification. Most common are classifications for causes and impacts (being the left- and right-hand bows of the bow-tie). For example, a rudimentary causal taxonomy can be based on the definition of operational risk, and include:

- people;
- systems;
- processes; and
- external events.

More developed causal types are expansive, incorporating considerations around lack of staff training; miscommunication; process design failure; system misconfiguration. Reference taxonomies for cause and impact issued by ORX provide a good starting point for organizations.[11]

There may also be a separate classification scheme for control types; for example, by using *Preventative–Detective–Directive–Corrective* categories, as explored in Chapter 5.

Consistent use of taxonomy by other functions

It is good practice to strive for consistent use of taxonomy by other functions; for example compliance and internal audit, as well as specialist areas such as IT and facilities management, who may have separate systems for recording technology incidents or health and safety breaches. Failure to align may result in duplication of effort, varying criteria, confusion for end-users and fragmentation of valuable risk data. In contrast, a unified categorization system utilized by all functions enables data to be compared and contrasted effectively, increasing the quality and depth of analysis.

Industry benchmark

The operational risk taxonomy is the essential glue that binds together all the elements of the framework. Over the years, the Best Practice Operational Risk Forum has kept a constant watch over the state of maturity of this tool, and variations in the way it is applied, recognizing the vital importance of taxonomy and its place in the framework.

As presented in Figure 1.6, organizations are moving away from the original Basel classification, which has become outdated. Only a minority (21 per cent) of respondents are still applying it, which represents a further reduction from the 30 per cent observed in a similar poll in 2020 (see the first edition of the book). Following the publication of the reference taxonomy by ORX,[12] a significant proportion of firms (46 per cent of respondents) have adopted that taxonomy instead. It is clearly a useful guide for those firms considering making changes to this part of their framework. The remaining organizations opted to work with a specific taxonomy tailored to their own needs. This is the optimal solution, because it involves using risk categories that are well understood across the firm, which results in significantly more meaningful risk identification, management and reporting.

Overall, Best Practice Forum members felt more confident with their operational risk classification system in 2022 compared to previous years, with only 17 per cent perceiving that a complete overhaul was needed (see Figure 1.7). The response 'Could be improved' selected by most respondents (70 per cent) implied a lesser degree of required technical re-classification, but actually touched on a more fundamental question; namely, how operational risk could be described in a way that creates a true connection with

Figure 1.6   Industry poll: operational risk taxonomy

What taxonomy are you using?

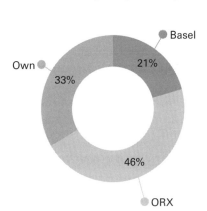

Best Practice Operational Risk Forum, 2022

Figure 1.7   Industry poll: satisfaction with the taxonomy

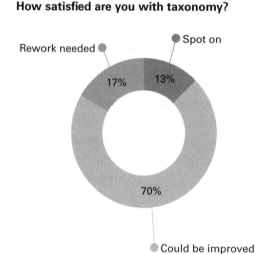

How satisfied are you with taxonomy?

Rework needed ● ● Spot on

17%   13%

70%

● Could be improved

Best Practice Operational Risk Forum, 2022

employees. Since the inception of the discipline, the *language* of operational risk has been somewhat dictated by the Basel Committee, both in the definition of the discipline and in the naming conventions used for taxonomy categories. But organizations are already adjusting and amending that language to suit their own needs. As part of the aim of connecting with *employees* and the things that really *matter to them*, could the taxonomy categories be re-worded around *what people care about*, rather than – as at present – being expressed in somewhat technical, regulatory-driven risk language? This remains an area for consideration.

Another area of continuing challenge is the lack of alignment with areas such as Compliance, Internal Audit and others who tend to employ different categorisation systems. Only a minority of respondent firms achieved full alignment, while others were dedicating resources to improve collaboration in this area.

Practical workplace exercise

Reflecting on the content of this chapter, review the definition of operational risk and the existing classification system used in your firm, considering:

1 Is the definition fit for purpose? Does it position the discipline relative to the firm's business objectives?

2 Is the taxonomy easy to understand, up to date and effective?

3 Are the taxonomy categories exhaustive and mutually exclusive to the extent possible?

4 What works well and should be retained?

5 What can be improved? Note down potential improvements.

MAKE A DIFFERENCE (MAD) ACTION

Note down one action you will take after reading this chapter that will make a positive difference to how the operational risk taxonomy is defined and treated in your firm.

In summary, this chapter introduced operational risk and discussed the importance of the risk taxonomy, as well as challenges related to its development and implementation.

Moving on, the next chapter outlines the framework, and the key tools used to identify, manage and mitigate operational risk.

Notes

1 Basel Committee on Banking Supervision, Basel Framework, www.bis.org/basel_framework/ (archived at https://perma.cc/96FE-VF9B)

2 European Securities and Markets Authority (2017) *The Distributed Ledger Technology Applied to Securities Markets*, www.esma.europa.eu/system/files_force/library/dlt_report_-_esma50-1121423017-285.pdf?download=1 (archived at https://perma.cc/88XL-E6FK)

3 Basel Committee on Banking Supervision (2002) *The Quantitative Impact Study for Operational Risk: Overview of individual loss data and lessons learned*, www.bis.org/bcbs/qis/qisoppriskresponse.pdf (archived at https://perma.cc/CZ7Z-7TV6)

4 International Organization for Standardization (2009) ISO 31000:2009, www.iso.org/standard/43170.html (archived at https://perma.cc/QC2G-Z8WR)

5 Committee of Sponsoring Organizations of the Treadway Commission (COSO) (2017) *2017 Enterprise Risk Management: Integrated framework*, www.coso.org/Pages/erm.aspx (archived at https://perma.cc/RKP9-BZ4Z)

6 Operational Riskdata eXchange Association (ORX) (2019) *ORX Reference Taxonomy*, managingrisktogether.orx.org/operational-risk-taxonomy (archived at https://perma.cc/Z9QC-WC6L)

7 European Banking Authority (2019) *EBA Guidelines on Outsourcing Arrangements*, www.eba.europa.eu/regulation-and-policy/internal-governance/guidelines-on-outsourcing-arrangements (archived at https://perma.cc/4X3C-LZ6Z)

8 Financial Stability Board (2018) *Cyber Lexicon*, www.fsb.org/2018/11/cyber-lexicon/ (archived at https://perma.cc/CWD6-EGUD)

9 Basel Committee on Banking Supervision (2021) *Principles for Operational Resilience*, www.bis.org/bcbs/publ/d516.pdf (archived at https://perma.cc/EA35-62G3)

10 Operational Riskdata eXchange Association (ORX) (2020) *ORX Cause and Impact Operational Risk Reference Taxonomy*, managingrisktogether.orx.org/operational-risk-reference-taxonomy/orx-cause-impact-reference-taxonomy (archived at https://perma.cc/A35M-BNU4)

11 Operational Riskdata eXchange Association (ORX) (2020) *ORX Cause and Impact Operational Risk Reference Taxonomy*, managingrisktogether.orx.org/operational-risk-reference-taxonomy/orx-cause-impact-reference-taxonomy (archived at https://perma.cc/DN4Q-CZN2)

12 Operational Riskdata eXchange Association (ORX) (2019) *ORX Reference Taxonomy*, managingrisktogether.orx.org/operational-risk-taxonomy (archived at https://perma.cc/88N6-8PYP)

Operational risk framework and its implementation

What this chapter covers: This chapter builds a foundation which is then used throughout the book, introducing the Operational Risk Framework and explaining its key components. Each subsequent chapter will commence with a visual diagram of the framework, clearly denoting the element it addresses, and providing a coherent link between all the chapters. The chapter also outlines a structured three-step approach for implementing and embedding operational risk management, presenting a range of practical tools which can help in the deployment process.

FURTHER READING

- Basel Committee on Banking Supervision (2021) *Revisions to the Principles for the Sound Management of Operational Risk*
  Why recommended: Since the early days, the Basel Principles have been the key document to study for operational risk practitioners, and the latest 2021 update forms a solid base for a benchmarking exercise.

- Gerd Gigerenzer (2015) *Risk Savvy: How to make good decisions*, Penguin Books
  Why recommended: An operational risk framework needs to be built out with a simple and pragmatic approach in mind, one that will resonate with the end-users. This mode of thinking aligns with this excellent suggested book, whose author believes that the best decisions are arrived at using common sense and listening to your gut.

Introducing the framework and its components

Every firm embarking on an operational risk journey requires a framework that provides a structure for implementing operational risk management throughout the entire organization. It needs to present a simple yet coherent picture of the essential pieces of the puzzle, and to outline how they join together. The framework should be easy to understand, as it will be communicated to senior management as well as employees at the coal face, serving as an anchor and a key reference point for a whole range of discussions related to operational risk management.

While there is no one-size-fits-all approach, an example of the framework is described in Figure 2.1, and serves as a base for the rest of the chapters in the book. Let's examine these framework components in more detail.

To begin with, each practitioner needs to answer a single question: what tools do I need in my operational risk toolbox? Four core elements are positioned in the middle section of the diagram. They work together in an integrated fashion to ensure the company identifies, assesses and manages the operational risks that it faces. The life cycle of each core element is described in subsequent chapters of the book.

Core tools

Operational risk events

Operational risk events (OREs) are the oldest and the most common of the four core elements. They enable an organization to act promptly following an incident, to minimize the impact from the incident escalating and to derive valuable lessons learnt. Even more, they allow the firm to achieve a clear understanding of its loss profile and evaluate the adequacy of its capital resources.

Risk assessments

Risk assessments are a key forward-looking framework component. They supplement the backward-looking OREs while still taking them into consideration, permitting management to identify and mitigate risks before they crystallize into events. They enable the organization to bring focus to gaps and weaknesses, providing management with a powerful tool for strengthening the control environment.

Figure 2.1 Holistic operational risk management framework

Risk culture

Embedding and maturity assessment

Governance, roles and responsibilities
Establish governance and clear roles across the Three Lines for managing operational risk.

Risk appetite and risk capacity
Define nature and types of risk accepted in pursuit of strategic objectives. Evaluate adequacy of capital resources.

Operational risk events
Record and report risk events, act to minimize future exposure. Monitor trends against RCSAs and KRIs.

Risk assessments
Assess risk exposure in process, business or function via RCSAs. Supplement by evaluating risks emanating from change activities via ORAs.

Scenario analysis
Identify exposure from extreme but plausible events. Mitigate through risk transfer to insurance.

Key Risk Indicators
Monitor risk and control performance through predictive indicators. Act if indicators breach established appetite threshold.

Reporting and decision-making
Review actual risk profile against set appetite, apply active risk management to enable achievement of strategic objectives.

Training and education

Operational risk taxonomy

Scenario analysis

Scenario analysis is an instrument that utilizes proactive risk assessment thinking and applies it to extreme but plausible circumstances. It augments the ORE dataset by adding considered scenarios which – even if they are synthetic – build on the knowledge derived from the other core tools. It is just as valuable for risk management as for measurement purposes.

Key Risk Indicators

Key Risk Indicators (KRIs) are used to monitor the risk and control environment of the organization. KRI information, assimilated and presented in the form of a dashboard, is indispensable for observing the behaviour of the most significant risks identified during forward-looking exercises.

Practitioners can of course change the composition of this toolbox, filling it with the right components to suit the needs of their own organization. For example, they may decide to:

- segregate *external loss data* into a distinct framework element (in this book, it forms part of OREs); or
- add control assurance or process mapping as separate components (here, both are addressed as part of risk assessments); or
- remove KRIs – not all firms adopt this element, although in this book KRIs are viewed as an extremely useful mechanism.

It is up to the second line operational risk team to find the best fit, and the tools most suitable to the nature, size and business model of the firm.

Linking components

Once the core tools have been agreed upon, it is time to link them via *governance arrangements*, *risk appetite* and *risk reporting*, as displayed in Figure 2.1, stretching above and below the main toolset.

Governance, roles and responsibilities

Clear responsibilities are particularly important to operational risk management, where similar roles may be being performed by first line operational risk coordinators as well as by independent second line risk teams. Equally important are the roles of subject matter experts, risk and control owners, and members of the board, senior management and governance committees, all working collaboratively to multiply the power of risk management.

Risk appetite and risk capacity

Operational risk appetite is the most nascent of the framework components. Once it is well developed, however, it converges the core elements and becomes an irreplaceable mechanism for decision-making.

Reporting and decision-making

Reporting is the window through which operational risk teams communicate with management across the organization, the board and senior committees. This is where the results from all the toolbox instruments are consolidated in a meaningful way, answering the vitally important *so what?* question, and supporting a wide range of tactical and strategic decisions.

Supporting elements

Finally, the framework relies on other supporting elements, highlighted in Figure 2.1 on the perimeter around the main components. They include:

- *Risk culture*, given that operational risk is closely linked to and largely dependent on the culture of the organization.
- *Training and education*, without which it would be impossible to embed solid practices firm-wide.
- *Maturity assessment*, which a firm may want to carry out once it has embarked on its risk management implementation journey, to evaluate where it has got to relative to the desired state, and set improvement strategies.
- *Taxonomy*, used for setting the foundation for operational risk management by risk category (covered in Chapter 1).

Three essential steps for implementing operational risk management practices

Where do we start with implementing operational risk management practices in our organization? This question, which was topical at the inception of the operational risk discipline, remains relevant now. There are still plenty of firms starting from scratch for a whole range of valid reasons, perhaps opening a new branch or applying for a new banking licence. But even for a well-established firm, it is equally important to benchmark the framework

Figure 2.2 Three steps for implementing an operational risk framework

that is already in place, to set your direction of travel and define sensible next steps. Whether your firm is in the first category or the second, there are a number of crucial steps to follow, some of which are more challenging while others are easier to accomplish (Figure 2.2).

Step 1: External and internal requirements

Understanding rules and regulations

The first step always consists of identifying the minimum requirements set by relevant regulators, assembling the list of applicable documents and understanding both the *letter* and the *spirit* of the rules. It is worth installing yourself in a comfortable chair and putting on your reading glasses. This stage is key. It builds a solid foundation by forcing firms to actively interpret their fundamental obligations, as well as more nuanced elements, for example:

- Subtle differences in the position of the second line operational risk function, which is expected to provide assertive *challenge* in some jurisdictions but to exhibit helpful *support* in others. These kinds of expectations influence the second line approaches, for instance, scenario analysis and KRIs; whether it oversees the process or assists first line units in completing the tasks.

- Requirements related to control *testing* if, for example, the firm is subject to Sarbanes–Oxley regulation;[1] these rules have a meaningful impact on the risk and control self-assessment (RCSA) methodology, and require a defined approach to testing rather than a purely judgemental assessment of controls.

- The obligation under certain jurisdictions to have a mandatory internal control function, which influences the entire set-up and operation of the Risk department.

KEEPING UP TO DATE WITH REGULATORY REQUIREMENTS

Understanding regulatory requirements for operational risk management is not a one-off exercise. It is critical to achieve clarity as to who is responsible for horizon scanning and picking up changes as they come along. This helps to avoid gaps and grey areas which often exist between compliance and operational risk teams. Sometimes it is assumed that Compliance is performing holistic horizon scanning, and full reliance is placed on their process. In practice, though, the compliance function may be excluding certain topics from its scanning process; for instance, some aspects of prudential regulation, 'best practice' industry guidance, or even selected geographies. Operational risk teams need to ensure agreement on the scope of such processes, and maybe even perform their own reviews of what is a continuously changing regulatory agenda.

For international firms, the most rigorous expectations will usually prevail and be applied across the entire organization. Branches and subsidiaries of international institutions, especially those situated in locations subject to stricter rules, are frequently driving the operational risk value proposition for the whole firm – often including the head office. This can create friction between the head office and the affiliate, whose voice is not always taken into due consideration. In these cases, the local entity needs to take a firm lead in creating any necessary addendums to the group's policies and practices, and in ensuring that it continues to maintain those higher standards locally, withstanding the rigours of regulatory scrutiny.

Developing an internal value proposition

Particularly important at the outset, and at the same time as understanding the external rules, internal requirements also need to be assimilated. Essentially, this process involves analysing the firm's strengths and weaknesses, to determine the key selling points of operational risk management. While undeniably there are many generic advantages of prudent risk management, what *specific benefits* will resonate *the most*? Those particular benefits should be the ones most emphasized during discussions with the chief executive and the business units; they represent cards that will be put squarely on the table in subsequent conversations. Examples of the benefits that operational risk management brings – and the corresponding framework tools that enable their realization – are presented in Table 2.1.

Table 2.1 Benefits and corresponding framework tools

Benefits of operational risk management	Corresponding framework tools to help realize the benefits
Well-developed strategy, risks to strategic objectives are well understood and weighed up	Top-down strategic risk assessment with chief executive and senior management team Scenario analysis to explore the impact of extreme events
Enhancement of internal control environment, revenue protection	Bottom-up risk identification process, prioritizing the controls that need to be strengthened and potentially tested Lessons learnt from OREs, leading to error reduction
Improved decision-making	Risks and opportunities assessment, as described in Chapter 6, enabling the firm to take balanced decisions by weighing up its risks and opportunities Applying risk appetite and Key Risk Indicators to guide mitigation and, at the same time, enable agreement on when to accept the risk and do nothing
Process optimization, efficiency and increased operational resilience	Bottom-up process risk assessment; identifying risks and controls while creating end-to-end process maps, which allow the firm to streamline the entire set of activities and achieve a view based on business processes or services
Strong risk culture	All framework tools; with emphasis on increased transparency, no blame, accountability, risk-awareness and risk reward
Regulatory compliance	All framework tools; regulatory conformance is hugely important yet – rightly – the last element on the list. The organization needs to find the benefits of risk management which lead to compliance, but not the other way around

A word of caution: operational risk loss reduction is frequently seen as a tempting reason for establishing a framework. But this may be a hard sell for a small to medium-sized firm that does not have much history of losses (see Chapter 13 for further details).

Step 2: Conducting benchmarking

Regulatory directives are commonly principle-based and do not prescribe rigidly how to implement the framework or operate the tools. That is where, historically, the Basel Committee Principles for the sound management of operational risk have provided exceptionally useful directional guidance.[2] The Basel Principles, revised several times over the years, with the latest update issued in 2021, succinctly articulate fundamental requirements and remain the primary source for comparative analysis against existing practices. Despite being targeted at banks, they can be applied broadly to insurance, asset management or any other financial services activity, especially in sectors where fewer sources of literature are available compared to banking.

Second line operational risk teams, in conjunction with relevant subject matter experts, must conduct benchmarking analysis against these requirements – at a minimum performing a line-by-line comparison of the Basel Committee's 12 principles and 60+ detailed supporting statements vs the firm's current practices.

The Basel Principles can be supplemented by industry best practice; derived, for instance, from prior experience, from interactions with fellow practitioners, and from specialist industry guidance, such as papers issued by the Institute of Operational Risk.[3] Throughout the book, additional recommended reading of this kind is included at the start of each chapter.

KEEPING UP TO DATE WITH INDUSTRY BEST PRACTICE

Best practices evolve. One of the most important things to do when embarking on an operational risk implementation journey is to create strong links with other practitioners in the industry. There are plenty of forums, discussion groups and professional organizations across the financial services industry, examples of which are outlined in Chapter 11. These kinds of interactions are instrumental for keeping up with peers and closely following good industry practices as they develop.

Part of the purpose of the benchmarking analysis is to judgementally evaluate to what extent the Basel Principles (at a minimum) are already being applied, and to identify gaps and improvement areas. Conclusions can either be presented for each principle individually; or, with a bit more work, structured

Figure 2.3   Example extract from benchmarking study

1. Risk assessments	**2. Reporting**
• RCSAs are used as a 'tick-box' exercise with no resulting actions.They require methodological revision and expert facilitation in order to increase the value-add.	• Operational risk reporting is not comprehensive. The tools are not integrated, making the reports less actionable.
3. Operational Risk Events (OREs)	**4. Risk appetite**
• OREs are recorded and lessons learnt conducted for material events. Data quality is sub-optimal and will benefit from review, and reconciliation with general ledger.	• The basic appetite statement expressed via annual operational risk loss threshold is in place. It requires more comprehensive and meaningful statements and measures.
5. Taxonomy	**6. Training and education**
• The firm utilizes Basel Committee taxonomy. Taxonomy will benefit from refresh and redesign.	• Operational risk training is rolled out for new starters and first line operational risk coordinators. Additional education is recommended to increase risk awareness.

Priority 1: least embedded, in need of enhancement   Priority 2: partially embedded, will benefit from improvement   Priority 3: embedded, consider enhancing

into themes which correspond to the individual components of the operational risk framework, as depicted in Figure 2.1. Results can be documented with the help of round ideograms, often used in qualitative comparative analysis for presenting the degree to which an item meets a particular criterion. An example extract of this kind of analysis is provided in Figure 2.3.

The benchmarking study extract in Figure 2.3 demonstrates that the organization perceives that – relative to other framework elements – it is *risk assessments* and *reporting* that are least embedded and most in need of enhancement. Training and education, on the other hand, has been evaluated as well *embedded* and requires less focus.

Step 3: Planning implementation

The benchmarking exercise outlines the 'as-is' state of operational risk management, effectively defining the point of departure. It constitutes a starting point, enabling the firm to plan its next steps.

Figure 2.4 Swimlane plan: operational risk implementation

	Quarter 1	Quarter 2	Quarter 3	Quarter 4
1. Risk assessments	Develop methodological enhancements	Complete pilot RCSA	50% RCSAs completed	100% RCSAs completed
2. Reporting	Perform assessment of current reporting	Agree template and approach	Train report writers	Implement enhancements
3. OREs		Perform data quality assessment	Agree reconciliation process and approach	Data quality enhanced
4. Risk appetite		Devise plan in conjunction with enterprise risk management	Consult with subject matter experts	Update completed
5. Taxonomy		Propose updated categories	Consult with subject matter experts	New taxonomy agreed
6. Training and education	Develop enhanced training plan	All staff education	Executive briefings	New starter training

Subsequently, the benchmark can be translated into a practical implementation plan, with specific milestones and their timelines agreed and endorsed by senior management. This plan needs to consider the resource requirements to complete each task, and to set a realistic time frame within which it can be accomplished.

An example of a resulting 'swimlane' plan, with the key themes highlighted in Figure 2.3 now split into implementation milestones, is presented in Figure 2.4.

In conclusion, it may be a daunting prospect to start up a new function – and to spearhead the development of operational risk practices within the organization – completely from scratch. If you have landed in such a situation, bear in mind that it will be a very exciting and enriching journey. All operational risk professionals had to start somewhere, and most, myself included, have since grown very fond of what is an outstandingly interesting discipline.

Common challenges and good practices

Common challenges

Insufficient thought given to value proposition

Operational risk implementation can sometimes be triggered by an unsatisfactory audit report or regulatory criticism; regulatory compliance then becomes the primary impetus for developmental activities. A lack of consideration of the internal value proposition – and an absence of explicit articulation or marketing of it – results in operational risk management being perceived as an administrative burden, with unclear value emanating from the function. This leads to first line business units pushing back, and refusing to use the tools or embed the practices. Even when pressed for time, it is crucial for the operational risk practitioner to invest strong effort in developing and articulating their value proposition: with a view to attracting interest and agreement across the board and achieving true engagement from first line units.

Three-step process not followed

In my consulting practice, I occasionally receive questions from practitioners which reflect the fact that Step 1 – namely understanding external and internal requirements – has not been completed properly. For example, a request to determine whether an organization really needs to conduct control testing or can instead adopt a judgemental evaluation of control effectiveness? The short answer to these questions is: it depends. As articulated in the three-step approach, there may (or may not) be a regulatory requirement for control testing, depending on the jurisdictions the firm operates in. Or the firm may actively aspire to perform testing if that will enhance the internal value proposition. Applying a structured three-step approach enables the firm to conduct thorough research and find answers to these kinds of questions before starting its implementation.

Absent or overly complicated framework diagram

Some organizations have developed their operational risk policies and procedures yet have failed to create a single pictorial diagram describing the framework and its key elements. This is challenging for visual learners, who absorb information through pictures. It may also mean that operational risk teams themselves are somewhat unclear how in reality the different pieces join together. At the other extreme, I have seen diagrams that require larger (e.g. A3-size) paper because they are so complicated that they do not fit onto an ordinary (e.g. A4-size) page. An easy-to-understand visual framework is a necessity. As per the classic quote attributed to Albert Einstein, 'If you can't explain it simply, you don't understand it well enough.'

Good practices

Creating a plan

It is good practice in all cases to have an annual plan; whether the framework needs to be designed from scratch or is only undergoing enhancements (in more mature practices). Operational risk is still very much a developing discipline. New guidelines keep emerging, such as the Basel Committee Principles, which were updated yet again in 2021. Board and senior management priorities, new topics such as ESG, Generative AI or Operational resilience, will inevitably require to be considered as part of annual planning. This is an area where simple organization, discipline and rigour will make a difference. Yet, what transpires from my discussions with operational risk professionals is that the plan is rarely well developed. For example, the majority of participants (63 per cent) that attended advanced operational risk management workshops only had *some* targets in place while the remaining 37 per cent did not have a plan in place (Figure 2.5).

Figure 2.5   Industry benchmark: operational risk plan of work

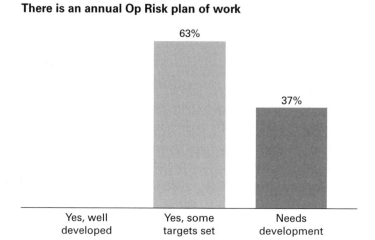

Advanced Operational Risk Management Workshop, 2023

Prioritizing tasks for implementation

Where there are plans in place for implementation, they at times contain unachievable targets, with multiple milestones all falling due at the same time, rather than being spread throughout the year in a more manageable fashion. It is good practice to involve the operational risk team – or even broader business teams – in a ranking exercise, asking them to vote on their top three priority enhancements. Team members can be supplied with pretend tokens and requested to 'put their money' on the three tasks that they believe will generate most value. The votes are then summed and the improvements receiving most support can be scheduled for speedier delivery.

Achieving a balanced plan focussed on value-add

More and more unregulated firms are aspiring to implement solid operational risk management practices. Kudos to these organizations. They approach the implementation straight from an internal value proposition perspective, coupled with industry best practice. This can only make the value-add stronger. However, even with regulatory-driven priorities, the overall plan must be balanced. It should combine key regulatory deliverables with targets that the firm aspires to achieve for itself. From this point of view, it is important to have a constructive dialogue with the supervisors, pushing back on the deadlines and milestones to achieve the right plan, one that first and foremost makes sense to the firm as well as to the supervisor.

Industry benchmark

Amid a continuously evolving operational risk landscape, Best Practice Operational Risk Forum members contemplated whether the current framework and its tools remained fit for purpose. Overall, practitioners agreed that operational risk as a discipline was moving in the right direction, steadily progressing and maturing, though perhaps more slowly than expected. Using the analogy that financial sector organizations are akin to large, powerful cruise ships, getting the cruise ship to change course – that is, to buy in and then fully embrace a wide range of operational risk practices – requires time, plenty of effort and cultural change. A curious finding in this area was a perception that operational risk management has progressed further *in the industry overall* than in the respondents' *firms individually* (as seen in Figure 2.6).

Furthermore, while the overall risk toolkit was seen as effective, a majority of participants (60 per cent, as shown in Figure 2.7) felt that *the way* it operated required some enhancement. The key words were *agility, speed* and *integrity*, with the discussion focusing particularly on technology, data and the need for further speedy progress in a digital world that is relying increasingly and significantly on technology:

- A constantly evolving risk landscape calls for instant access to the firm's current risk profile. In particular, the fast-moving topic of *cyber risk* required interactive dashboards and imminent indicators on the spot, and *third-party risk* necessitated not only internal data but also input from service providers.

Figure 2.6 Industry poll: progress in operational risk management

There has been significant progress

In operational risk discipline in general — 3.5

In operational risk management in my firm — 3.4

Strongly disagree | Strongly agree

1=strongly disagree, 5=strongly agree, ● =average rating

Best Practice Operational Risk Forum, 2024

Figure 2.7 Industry poll: operational risk framework effectiveness

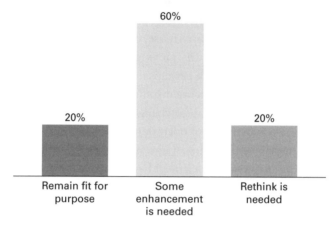

Operational risk framework and tools

Best Practice Operational Risk Forum, 2024

- Practitioners were concerned with some delays in reporting important information. Summary RCSA results were commonly presented with a one to two month time lag, by which time they had often become stale. Members discussed the laborious process required to extract and aggregate the data, and agreed there is a need for investment into operational risk systems, which were not yet generally seen as a top priority investment for firms.

Technological angles (whether related to the use of operational risk systems or the use of technology more broadly within the firm) have been repeatedly explored by the Best Practice Operational Risk Forum over the years. In 2018, against a background of ongoing evolution in the fintech sector, the Basel Committee issued its paper 'Implications of Fintech Developments for Banks and Bank Supervisors'.[4] This is a paper that remains valid to this day, notably in the way it urges organizations to actively extend their risk frameworks to adequately cover technology-related risks. Following the publication of the paper, in 2020 the Operational Risk Best Practice Forum questioned whether the framework and toolset enabled firms to effectively identify, assess, manage and report on fintech-driven operational risks. The results are presented in Figure 2.8.

It is apparent from Figure 2.8 that – at that time – organizations were generally in the early or middle stages of their fintech journey, rather than

Figure 2.8   Industry poll: operational risk and fintech

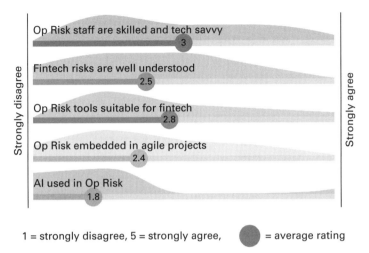

Op Risk and fintech space

Strongly disagree → Strongly agree

- Op Risk staff are skilled and tech savvy — 3
- Fintech risks are well understood — 2.5
- Op Risk tools suitable for fintech — 2.8
- Op Risk embedded in agile projects — 2.4
- AI used in Op Risk — 1.8

1 = strongly disagree, 5 = strongly agree,   ● = average rating

Best Practice Operational Risk Forum, 2020

towards the end. In particular, the use of innovative technologies such as artificial intelligence (AI) for operational risk purposes was still very much at its inception, receiving the lowest score.

The results of this 2020 poll remain just as valid in 2024, in the sense that organizations are still in the middle – rather than towards the end – of their journey towards technological maturity. What this means is that constant careful consideration needs to be applied to all aspects of risk management that involve technology.

Yet to end on a positive note, once a large, powerful cruise ship really gets moving, it is hard to stop. Despite the challenges outlined in this chapter, the overall positive momentum of operational risk management as a discipline is being maintained. And it will continue further as the discipline matures and its practices become ever more effective and embedded.

Practical workplace exercise

Consider key points and ideas presented in this chapter. Obtain and review the operational risk framework used in your firm, questioning:

1 Is there a clear picture of how the framework elements operate together, in an integrated fashion?

2 Has the firm conducted a benchmark against the Basel Committee Principles and other industry documents?

3 Is there a clear implementation plan outlining priorities for the current year?

4 What works well and should be retained?

5 What can be improved? Note down potential improvements.

MAKE A DIFFERENCE (MAD) ACTION

Note down one action you will take after reading this chapter that will make a positive difference to how the firm's operational risk framework is defined and implemented.

In summary, this chapter introduced the operational risk framework and discussed some possible approaches to its implementation.

Moving on, the next chapter starts a deep dive into each of the framework components, commencing with the role of the Three Lines (formerly of defence) in operational risk management.

Notes

1 The Sarbanes–Oxley Act of 2002, www.sec.gov/about/laws/soa2002.pdf (archived at https://perma.cc/9H8R-WXX3)
2 Basel Committee on Banking Supervision (2021) *Revisions to the Principles for the Sound Management of Operational Risk*, www.bis.org/bcbs/publ/d515.pdf (archived at https://perma.cc/TF5P-MAZT)
3 Institute of Operational Risk (2021) Sound Practice Guidance, www.ior-institute. org/sound-practice-guidance (archived at https://perma.cc/L7VE-FNFD)
4 Basel Committee on Banking Supervision (2018) *Implications of FinTech Developments for Banks and Bank Supervisors*, www.bis.org/bcbs/publ/d431. pdf (archived at https://perma.cc/5VQA-88RN)

The Three Lines model 03

Its application to operational risk management

What this chapter covers: The chapter examines how the concept of the Three Lines (formerly of defence) is applied to operational risk management and implemented in practice by individuals that embody the different lines (Figure 3.1). It analyses the role of the first line operational risk coordinators and introduces Problem Solvers, Postmen and Champions. The chapter then concentrates on the second line operational risk function and presents Drifters, Diminishers and Multipliers. The role of internal audit is briefly discussed, recognizing that there is commonly less confusion around the tasks carried out by the third line. The chapter highlights common challenges and good practices and includes an industry benchmark.

FURTHER READING

- Institute of Internal Auditors (2013) IIA Position paper, *The Three Lines of Defence in Effective Risk Management and Control*
- Institute of Internal Auditors (2020) *The IIA's Three Lines Model*

  Why recommended: The first paper is an essential read on the fundamental nature of the original Three Lines of Defence from the Institute of Internal Auditors, for those willing to learn from the source. It is supplemented by the second document issued in 2020, which provides an updated and current position of the Institute, with the word *defence* dropped.

- Dr Simon Ashby, Dr Cormac Bryce and Dr Patrick Ring (2019) *Risk and Performance: Embedding risk management*, ACCA

  Why recommended: A must-read research paper from three acclaimed professors, providing an insight on some of the practical aspects of embedding risk management.

Figure 3.1 Focus of Chapter 3: responsibilities across the Three Lines

Risk culture

Embedding and maturity assessment

Governance, roles and responsibilities
Establish governance and clear roles across the Three Lines for managing operational risk.

Risk appetite and risk capacity
Define nature and types of risk accepted in pursuit of strategic objectives. Evaluate adequacy of capital resources.

Operational risk events	Risk assessments	Scenario analysis	Key Risk Indicators
Record and report risk events, act to minimize future exposure. Monitor trends against RCSAs and KRIs.	Assess risk exposure in process, business or function via RCSAs. Supplement by evaluating risks emanating from change activities via ORAs.	Identify exposure from extreme but plausible events. Mitigate through risk transfer to insurance.	Monitor risk and control performance through predictive indicators. Act if indicators breach established appetite threshold.

Reporting and decision-making
Review actual risk profile against set appetite, apply active risk management to enable achievement of strategic objectives.

Training and education

Operational risk taxonomy

Overview: Three Lines model, its benefits and challenges

The somewhat controversial Three Lines model (formerly known as the Three Lines of Defence model), which had its origins in military planning and sports management, is now firmly engrained into the DNA of financial services firms. It is widely viewed as an important factor in the successful embedding of enterprise risk management, while at the same time attracting a fair share of criticism due to its inefficiencies and challenges. In simple terms, the success or failure of the model depends on how the concept is implemented in practice. And this is particularly relevant to operational risk management, where, as articulated in Chapter 2, fairly similar roles may be performed by the first line operational risk coordinators as well as by independent second line risk teams. An opportunity to work collaboratively? Or to generate conflicts, trip over each other and duplicate tasks?

The original Three Lines of Defence (frequently abbreviated to 3LOD) concept, which is described in the position paper written by the Institute of Internal Auditors (IIA), distinguished between the three groups (or lines) involved in effective risk management:[1]

- functions that own and manage risks;
- functions that oversee risks;
- functions that provide independent assurance.

IIA argued that 'risk management normally is strongest when there are three separate and clearly defined lines of defence'.[2]

A subsequent update issued in 2020 retains the core concepts and the language of 'first line', 'second line' and 'third line', however it advocates for a more collaborative approach de-emphasizing segregation and therefore removing the word 'defence'. Throughout this chapter and the rest of the book, we will therefore refer to the updated 'Three Lines' model.

A typical application of the Three Lines model in financial services is presented in Figure 3.2.

As outlined in the schematic:

- First line business units and support functions are *risk owners* – a term also used by the International Organization for Standardization (ISO) – who have the authority to manage risk and are accountable for doing so.[3] They have primary responsibility for establishing a robust control environment, complying with policies and executing day-to-day risk and control management.

Figure 3.2   Three Lines in financial services

- The second line provides expertise, support, monitoring and constructive challenge, flagging to the board and senior committees if the level of risk is not commensurate with the risk appetite set by the board. Generally, functions such as risk management and compliance are within the second line, although interpretation varies across firms.

- The third line, internal audit, is independent of both business units and supports functions and second line departments. It is responsible for providing assurance about the design and operation of the internal risk and control framework via a programme of risk-based reviews.

The concept of the Three Lines can be illustrated with a picture. France, 1895, the Montparnasse train station in Paris: an iconic photograph of a Granville–Paris train, trying to make up for lost time, entering the station at too high a speed, crushing through the wall of the station and tumbling onto the street. Miraculously, none of the passengers died.[4]

You can imagine a control room engineer sending warning signals to the driver: 'Attention, attention, you are running too fast, please slow down.' The driver increases his speed, ignoring the message from the control room.

The first line, train drivers, own the risks and make choices over whether to control them effectively or not. Front-office staff who sell products to clients, employees processing payments and information technology person-nel maintaining systems all belong to the first line.

Table 3.1   Benefits and challenges of the Three Lines model

Benefits	Challenges
The structure of defined lines provides a level of confidence to the firm's board of directors and senior management.	The model can result in duplication of activities. Who, for example, is performing control testing?
It describes and allocates clear roles to first, second and third lines.	It is debatable what functions form the second line; application across the industry varies.
The model aims to embed enterprise risk management at all levels across the firm and enhance risk communication.	The concept can cause confusion within the organization; do employees know what line they represent?
It serves as a protection mechanism. Functions work effectively together within their line to prevent and/or mitigate significant failures.	One of the key challenges of the model is trust. If lines are fully segregated (especially where the outdated concept of 'defence' is emphasized) trust between them may be low.
Regulators and many professional bodies, including the Institute of Internal Auditors and Institute of Directors, endorse the concept.	The use of the model alone should not be regarded as a guarantee of success.

The second line, control room operators, communicate warning signals, pointing out when the level of risk is too high. Not being in the front line, however, they cannot always stop the train from crashing.

The third line inspect both the train tracks and the set-up of the control room, ensuring that the whole enterprise, comprised of first and second lines, is positioned effectively for delivering on its objectives.

Some of the benefits and challenges of the Three Lines are outlined in Table 3.1.

The Three Lines concept has particular significance to operational risk. To embed good practices, processes and behaviours, first line business units and support functions commonly appoint operational risk coordinators. This practice helps immensely with spreading operational risk knowledge; however, it can also confuse the Three Lines structure.

Figure 3.3 Operational risk personnel in first and second lines

In theory, placing operational risk experts in the first line should double the benefits. It is the same discipline, after all, so operational risk practitioners in both the first and second lines must work together, completely in sync, towards a common goal of augmenting the value of risk management within the organization. In practice, however, models are implemented by people; consequently, a great deal depends on the personalities of the individuals and the way they embody the different lines. The relationship and dynamics between coordinators and the risk department may result in productive outcomes, but they can also lead to unpleasant and avoidable experiences.

It is therefore important to examine operational risk manager roles in more detail, focusing on finding practical solutions to making the spider's web of operational risk professionals across the two lines, depicted in Figure 3.3, work effectively and efficiently. Note that the role of the third line, internal audit, is usually clearly defined and well established, so rarely generates many questions or challenges.

First line operational risk: problem solvers, postmen and champions

An organization's policy will often require all heads of business units and support functions to nominate an operational risk lead: a named individual who serves as both a subject matter expert (SME) on operational risk matters and a key liaison point between the business and the second line Risk department.

Figure 3.4   First line operational risk role types

The theory is well known and understood. Where it becomes interesting is when it comes down to practical implementation. In reality, who are the operational risk coordinators and what is it that they do? Let's review three types of coordinator roles, depicted in Figure 3.4.

The problem solver

Problem solvers, sometimes also called 'risk hunters', are tasked with identifying risks and 'fixing' them, by coming up with action plans, enhancing controls or delivering process improvements. In this model the duty of providing operational risk management for the whole business unit falls on one individual, while the rest of the staff contentedly abdicate their responsibilities. 'How do we manage operational risk? We are very good at it. Please see our colleague around the corner: it is their role and they will tell you all about it.'

Problem solvers also carry the burden of remediation and mitigation activities for the risks that they themselves have identified. They are expected to add value by repairing broken processes and plastering over the cracks of poor controls. The more risks they discover, the more issues they have to solve.

Organizations with less mature risk cultures use problem solvers as a way of ticking the operational risk box, and demonstrating externally that someone is in place performing all the required activities. The problem solvers' approach indicates that the respective heads of business units or support functions are not accepting the accountability they have been allocated for the management of operational risk.

The postman

Postmen see their role as receiving a message from the centre and delivering it to the business unit or function. In many organizations, the first line operational risk coordinator is a part-time role. Coordinators are busy people; throughout the day they are occupied with important tasks within their direct area of responsibility. On top of their regular duties, they will engage with the Operational Risk department as and when the second line calls a meeting, receive the transmitted information, and pass it on to their colleagues and department head. For example:

- 'Operational Risk is implementing a new policy: please find this attached.'
- 'Operational Risk is initiating a firm-wide RCSA refresh: please complete per the stipulated deadline.'
- 'The template for loss reporting has changed: please familiarize yourselves with the new form.'

The second line usually trains coordinators on key tools and processes. Occasionally, therefore, messages will also be relayed in the other direction, from business unit to the second line Operational Risk department. For example, when an event or loss is identified, the postmen will know where to locate the relevant form, and how to fill it in and communicate with the second line.

Given limited time on their hands, postmen are mainly focused on the administrative side of operational risk processes, rather than the actual quality of risk management, which requires more time and thought. They frequently complain that the additional duties of being a coordinator, on top of their daily tasks, are burdensome. I have had many interactions with coordinators via public and in-house training courses that I deliver specifically for first line personnel. Having surveyed over 200 coordinators over the last 15 years, a fair share of them operate as postmen. Generally they spend around 2–15 per cent of their time on operational risk.

The champion

Champions are engaged and passionate operational risk specialists embedded in the first line. They focus on the essence of risk management, ensuring that material risks are identified and mitigated. They take the initiative and spearhead enhancements, with business unit employees giving them proper support while also understanding that risk management is everyone's responsibility.

For example, champions will not only contribute to the Risk and Control Self-Assessment (RCSA) process, but will also consider:

- how to meaningfully engage all employees in risk identification, to ensure their voice is heard – perhaps suggesting a discussion or live poll that can be conducted at the next departmental meeting;

- how to best share the results, so that all employees can consistently articulate the top operational risks of the unit;
- the status and behaviour of material risks, whether actions are being taken to remediate them, and how business units can work collectively with other functions;
- whether RCSA results are used in other initiatives, for example, when developing new products or engaging in regulatory programmes;
- what learnings, whether successes or failures, can be shared with other business units or support functions (also see Chapter 5, Risk and control self-assessments).

(Note: subsequent chapters of the book contain a checklist with proposed champion responsibilities for each of the core operational risk tools – events, RCSAs, ORAs, KRIs and scenario analysis.)

How do organizations step up from using problem solvers and postmen and instead develop an effective and engaged group of operational risk champions? The answer is a combination of contributory factors, which range from very complex (for example, getting the culture right) to very simple (such as having a clear profile of the coordinator role):

- Tone from the top: both across the firm overall and within respective business units or support functions, recognizing the value of operational risk management.

- Understanding the *why* of risk management, integrating risk into decision-making, aligning the effort to better customer experiences and shareholder outcomes.

- Full ownership: it is the role of the first line to manage risks and maintain a sound control environment, and it is a team effort where everyone is accountable for sound risk management.

- Acknowledgement of additional responsibilities allocated to the champion, allowing sufficient time for them to be undertaken effectively.

- Incentives: these can be financial, via increased pay or a reward for significant achievements. They can also be developmental: for example, studying or obtaining a professional qualification in operational risk management; participating in cross-functional initiatives to increase exposure to other departments and disciplines; or joining relevant external forums and committees as a member. This latter incentive is not sufficiently used. Having chaired various operational risk industry forums over the last 20 years, my observation is that typically less than 10 per cent of attendees are from the first line.

- Praise and recognition of good work: this sounds obvious but does not always happen.

- A clear job description: again this sounds basic, but many champions are operating without a clear role profile.

- An appropriate framework and set of tools developed by the second line, which enable and do not hinder the risk management process.

- And another key factor: ample direction, guidance, training and engagement from multipliers in the second line (see below).

Second line operational risk: drifters, diminishers and multipliers

Second line operational risk plays a crucial role in determining the success or failure of risk management. Not only via the design of an appropriate framework and tools, but via the attitude and value proposition represented by the second line, which ultimately matter just as much and have a significant influence on risk outcomes. Different role types are presented in Figure 3.5.

The drifter

Despite working in the second line operational risk function, drifters seem unsure of their role and the definitive risk product that they are expected to be producing. The Operations department is processing payments. Information Technology is maintaining systems. Human Resources is administering payroll. Their output is clear and well understood. Aside from periodic reports to the governance committees, however, drifters are often found deliberating about potential outputs. They understand the objective of providing independent oversight and challenge, but they cannot quite see

Figure 3.5 Second line operational risk role types

how to implement this in practice. Their CV may contain tasks with unclear value, for example:

- attended business unit's meetings;
- requested regular updates;
- collated information from business unit and repackaged for risk reporting;
- communicated RCSA deadlines and monitored completion within schedule.

They drift from meeting to meeting, but rarely contribute, present or provide insights. They are more focused on the administrative side of risk management ('RCSAs completed within the timeline?', 'Operational risk events reported via the right template?') than on the actual management of risks that are important to the business. Over the years, I have conducted job interviews for over 100 second line candidates; and while some came across brilliantly, others struggled to articulate the ways in which they added value to the organization. Which risks have diminished as a result of their role? Which controls have improved? What was their contribution to the firm's ability to achieve its strategy and business objectives?

The diminisher

In her inspirational book about leadership, *Multipliers: How the best leaders make everyone smarter*, Liz Wiseman introduces the concept of diminishers and multipliers. Diminishers, according to Wiseman, 'stifled others and diluted the organization's crucial intelligence and capability', while multipliers 'brought out the intelligence in others and created collective, viral intelligence'.[5] That concept, applied to leadership, can be extrapolated to describe two more types of second line operational risk functions.

Diminishers tend to place emphasis on the role of *independent challenge* entrusted to them by the board and senior committees. They see themselves as advisors to the firm's executives, accentuating the need for the separation between business units and the Operational Risk department. This may include physical segregation, with diminishers located on a different floor or isolated area, which has the effect of widening the gap between first and second lines. They are formal, unapproachable and do not tend to socialize. Diminishers believe that they:

- are *entitled* to attend first line business unit or support function meetings;
- are not here to be liked;

- are independent and therefore cannot discuss, advise or facilitate workshops;
- should be provided with information (for example, RCSAs, KRIs, scenarios) which they will then autonomously challenge.

Under this model the first line, lacking sufficient explanation, education and advice about the context lying behind these processes, ends up producing sub-optimal results and then facing criticism and adverse commentary. This not only strains the relationship but also results in reduced motivation on the part of the first line to manage its own operational risks. Diminishers diminish the work of first line business units and support functions, ultimately creating a negative risk management brand.

It is important to note that the role of diminisher is outdated. It emanates from the original 'Three Lines of Defence' concept which emphasises segregation. The diminisher approach creates blockages and siloed mentality, resulting in bureaucratic and costly processes. Now that the word *defence* has been dropped, the role must change accordingly, embracing the *multiplier* concept.

The multiplier

In contrast, multipliers work in collaboration with the first line, actively positioning them for success. They are informal, approachable, likeable and do not hesitate to work closely with business units and support functions. They also have a clear value proposition and focus on risk management, not risk administration.

> In research published by ACCA, the authors emphasized the importance of informal risk management mechanisms, in addition to formal policies and governance structures, and stressed that the people skills of the risk team are key.[6] They argued that a less formal, integrated accountability approach recognizes distinct roles within the Three Lines, yet still 'allows greater levels of collaboration and cooperation between the individuals responsible for conducting these roles'.

It is of significance that this softer and more integrated approach is also adopted in the revised Three Lines model, where the IIA states that first and second line roles may be 'blended or separated' and emphasizes that the second line provides '*assistance* with managing risk'.[7] The IIA paper came out amid the Covid-19 pandemic, and arguably was not given full attention due to other urgent priorities. Four years after the publication, I still see the original 3LOD model, with *defence* prominently embedded in letter and in spirit, in organizational policies and practices. This signifies that more work is needed to change attitudes and behaviours.

A good way of thinking about second line operational risk responsibilities is by outlining a spectrum of roles and assigning them a RAG (red, amber, green) rating:

- core second line operational risk roles (green zone);
- legitimate second line roles with safeguards (amber zone);
- roles that second line should not undertake (red zone).

Outlining the zones will guide the multipliers to find the right balance, being supportive and, at the same time firm, providing ample assistance yet not doing the job on behalf of the first line.

Green zone

Core second line operational risk multiplier roles:

- Mastermind the framework and design the tools that suit the size, nature and culture of the organization; continuously evolve them based on feedback.

- Analyse information, having the privilege of seeing the overall picture and risk profile of the firm; report to management committees but also circle back to the business units and support functions.

- As a trusted advisor, contribute to the firm's strategy and business plan, scrutinize and influence risk decisions, and provide early warnings.

- Educate, educate, educate. Create engaging, fun and light-hearted training programmes (see Chapter 11, Operational risk training and education).

- Collaborate with business units and support functions to achieve quality outcomes. Workshop facilitation deserves a special mention in this context. Expert facilitation adds great value and does not contradict the Three Lines model. Necessary challenge can be performed during the workshop and subsequently minuted for evidence. Note that it is just as acceptable for first line champions to lead the workshops, as long as they have been fully trained and possess the right skills and expertise to perform this role. On the other hand it is detrimental to ask the first line to undertake this kind of facilitation if they are not ready or do not have the necessary skills; or to require two separate operational risk discussions with the business, one with the first line and a subsequent additional meeting for second line to challenge.

- Invest in developing an engaged network of champions, helping to multiply their capabilities and potential; hold periodic meetings to share successes and challenges.

- Act as a centre of excellence on operational risk; participate in external industry forums and professional bodies, actively seeking to develop more professional knowledge and benchmark one's own practices.

- Be accessible and available for informal advice when needed.

Amber zone

Legitimate operational risk responsibilities, to be performed *as long as* they do not replace the accountability of the first line for risk management (to be adopted with caution):

- Conduct thematic reviews, based on identified trends and themes.

- Perform assurance, carry out periodic or ad hoc spot checks and control tests.

- Provide one-off help to business units or support functions when, for example, assisting with the roll-out of RCSAs; an operational risk expert can be temporarily seconded to the first line in exceptional circumstances.

- Champion the establishment of a risk culture, in close collaboration with senior management.

Red zone

What second line teams should not do:

- Manage operational risks on behalf of the first line; this debate was topical a decade ago, and the industry has moved on since to recognizing the right roles and responsibilities.

- Complete RCSAs (or manage other tools) on behalf of business units or support functions.

- Assume accountability for implementing control improvements and deal with actions instead of first line responsible functions.

- Take decisions on behalf of the business whether to accept or remediate risk.

- Serve as administrative assistants or note takers rather than risk managers.
- Always agree. It is valuable to have an honest second line opinion, regardless of its position; whether it agrees with the first line view or not.

A note about the third line: the Chartered Institute of Internal Auditors has developed a similar spectrum of audit responsibilities with assigned RAG ratings to clearly distinguish and delineate the role of the audit function; a very useful and practical document well worth a read.[8] As it relates to operational risk management, there is rarely confusion around the tasks of internal audit colleagues who execute independent reviews. One area of frequent disputes though relates to the *ownership* of audit findings. At times, all findings related to operational risk management are erroneously attributed to the second line operational risk function, even when the weaknesses arise from the first line business units. It is important to acknowledge the accountability of the first line in the risk management process, and allocate the findings accordingly.

Recipe for success: when multipliers work with champions

The power of risk management is increased when *multipliers* in the second line work with *champions* in the first line.

To begin with, it is essential for the second line Operational Risk department to deliberate, decide and agree on the *what* and the *how* of second line risk management. Often this will be done most effectively using a vehicle such as a strategy day or awayday, to enable a full debate free of distractions.

SECOND LINE OPERATIONAL RISK ESSENTIAL QUESTIONS

- *What* are the products that the second line is producing, apart from policies and periodic reports to the governance committees? Will business units and support functions benefit from these products?
- *How* will the second line work with first line businesses and embedded champions, via what formal and informal interactions? Per ACCA, is the balance of formal and informal mechanisms appropriate?[9] If not, what needs to be done differently and how will second line achieve it?

A similar process, again perhaps via a strategy day, then needs to take place between the second and first line operational risk personnel, who must come to an agreement on the joint plan for success. Some questions to consider in this process may include the following.

JOINT FIRST AND SECOND LINE OPERATIONAL RISK ESSENTIAL QUESTIONS

- Are roles clearly *articulated* and is there a good understanding of each other's responsibilities, to avoid *gaps* and *duplication*? For example, how will the first line operational risk coordinator engage with business units on new products and change initiatives, and what exactly will the second line do?

- Are second line interactions with business units *effective*? For example, if both groups need to review certain outputs – be it a strategy, business plan or RCSA – is it feasible for all concerned to do that at the same meeting rather than conducting separate sessions?

- How is the *output* of the second line *different* to what the first line produces? For example, if the first line creates reports to governance committees, the second line may be able to append their clearly articulated opinion to the report. In this case, governance committees will have the benefit of both views. And finally:

- What does success mean? How will it be measured and what needs to be done to achieve it?

It is also good practice to have periodic catch-ups with other second line functions, for example Compliance, as well as with Internal Audit, to increase collaboration and eliminate inefficiencies to the extent possible.

To summarize, when multipliers work with champions, the collaboration creates great chemistry, leading not only to thoughtful and productive risk management, but also to enjoyable days at the workplace.

Common challenges and good practices

Challenges

Challenges that firms may encounter when implementing operational risk roles and responsibilities across the Three Lines include the following.

Information not shared

The concept of the Lines is also used in sport. In football, players pass the ball to each other to help the team to score a goal. In financial services, employees operating within different lines do not always pass the ball. Information is not always willingly shared by internal audit or risk departments, and business units may be reluctant to provide full disclosure to the second and third lines. Developing the culture of openness and investing in relationship building is essential for the groups to work effectively together.

Operational risk superhero character

In the early years of the millennium another archetypal second line operational risk practitioner – Superman/Superwoman – was responsible for actually managing operational risk on behalf of the organization, stepping way out of their mandate to oversee and challenge the first line. This archetype is now rarely seen, as operational risk practices have matured and roles and responsibilities have matured with them.

Lack of support for champions

Insufficient support is provided to the first line coordinators, who end up doing extra work on top of their daily tasks, without incentivization or recognition. This is a cultural issue and, unfortunately, it sometimes takes a major loss, unsatisfactory audit or regulatory censure to prompt the organization to focus on how they perform risk management.

Duplication of activities

Unnecessary duplication of activities may arise if groups act in an uncoordinated manner. For example, business units developing a new product will often have a risk identification session with the first line coordinator. Subsequently, the second line Operational Risk department will request a separate meeting to provide independent challenge. This kind of duplication only causes confusion ('Another meeting with Operational Risk?'). Joint strategy days, and obtaining agreement on how the lines actually work together, help to minimize this kind of inefficiency.

Confusion over legal department

Questions frequently arise whether the Legal department belongs to the first or second line. The jury is out on this across the industry, and opinion is split. Around half of the firms I have interacted with over the years consider Legal to be within the first line; the other half disagrees and has Legal in the second line.

Criticism of the Three Lines

The Three Lines model is at times criticized for potentially creating slower decision-making, due to the need for sign-offs from first and second lines, which is particularly challenging in an age of technological advancement and revolution. It may be perceived as promoting wrong behaviours, including encouraging employees to rely on someone else to oversee their work ('Two more lines behind me will surely check what I am doing'), rather than accepting accountability themselves.

Good practices

Work in collaboration

There is great power in the model of multipliers working closely and cooperatively with champions. Two lines acting in collaboration go a long way towards shaping good practices and behaviours. Invest in creating a solid champion network and cherish the relationship. It will pay back.

Share experience

Other peer risk disciplines – namely credit, market and liquidity risk – do not have the same issues with the Three Lines model, as there is no need for a credit risk coordinator within, for example, a Human Resources department. Consequently, it is good practice for Operational Risk to regularly confer and share experiences with other functions that use a distributed model, such as business continuity and information security.

Evaluation

First line champions usually have a direct reporting line to the business or function they support. When managers are conducting performance appraisals of first line champions, it is good practice to also solicit feedback from members of the second line Operational Risk department, who can opine on how well the champion performed relative to the first line group.

Discussions with risk takers

Even with first line coordinators in place, it is essential for the second line to have a dialogue with risk takers and decision-makers in business units and support functions. First line coordinators, especially in full-time roles, can sometimes block the second line's access to the business unit. Avoiding blockages like this ensures that communication does not become partial – with risk practitioners talking among themselves – and prevents the decline in the effectiveness of conversations.

Make ownership tangible

A reader of one of my LinkedIn articles commented on the term *ownership*, noting that in their view it is a *care factor*. Aligning risk management efforts to tangible things that employees care about, for example, enhanced customer experiences or more resilient processes, helps to present the case and explain why risk management is so important.

Second line in advisory capacity

Once the framework is embedded and the first line becomes more mature, the second line can take a step back and act in more of an advisory capacity. A measure of success is the number of times the second line is approached for advice; if business units and support functions regularly call on Operational Risk, that demonstrates trust and recognition of value.

Virtual multipliers

In hybrid and working from home environments, risk teams must practice the art of being *virtual multipliers*. Undeniably, being engaging, transmitting good energy levels and *multiplying virtually* is more challenging than in person. When hosting an online meeting, it is useful to utilize check-in routines or warm up activities, tracking what can be seen (body language, facial expressions) and heard (the actual words and the silence), using in-the-moment feedback. If working from home during extended periods of time, it is essential to recognize that an important informal communication line with the business is strained – no chats at the watercooler or quick coffee breaks. In this case, it is recommended to double the efforts to proactively reach out to stakeholders with a *virtual coffee* value proposition, to maintain close contact.

Industry benchmark

Is there a 'right' number of first line risk champions (RCs) in the organization? Over the years firms have tended to increase the number of their RCs, with the aim of increasing first line risk ownership and accountability. Conversely there has been a reverse trend to reduce embedded risk resources – with a view to centralizing, achieving cost savings or building up second line capabilities.

Figure 3.6 Industry poll: % of first line risk champions to total staff

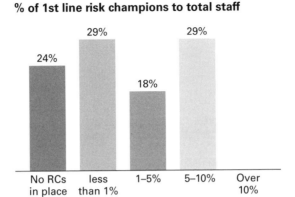

% of 1st line risk champions to total staff

Best Practice Operational Risk Forum, 2022

The results of the live poll from the industry Best Practice Operational Risk Forum highlighted that a range of approaches are still being adopted, as displayed in Figure 3.6:

- Almost one-third of respondents (29%) have extensive first line risk and control departments, representing between 5–10% of total staff, with roles covering a wide range of governance, risk and compliance (GRC) related tasks;

- 18% of respondents opt for a pragmatic approach, with risk champions representing 1–5% of total staff, a combination of full-time RCs in larger businesses and support units and part-time resources in smaller areas;

- A further 29% adopted a minimalist stance, with predominantly part-time RCs operating in a liaison role and as point persons between the second line Operational Risk department and business units;

- Lastly, 24% of voting organizations did not employ RCs at all, deeming it more effective for the Operational Risk department to communicate directly with the business.

It is clear that designing a successful risk champion structure may not be a straightforward process, and may require a number of iterations to get right. Indeed, a majority of forum participants (64 per cent) noted that regardless of the number of RCs in place, further evolution was needed to increase the overall effectiveness of this operating model.

One key area for enhancement was the need to maintain continued engagement, and to provide better support for both full- and part-time champions, to ensure that risk management remains their priority. Operational risk is an exciting discipline, and practitioners need to continue to invest in enhancing its brand and reputation, making the first line champion role a highly desirable and sought-after position. The eventual goal is for champions to really feel that they are enjoying the role and have 'time flies when you are having fun' mentality.

Practical workplace exercise

Reflect on the ideas discussed in this chapter. Obtain role profiles of the second line operational risk function and, if available, first line champions. Review the descriptions, considering:

1 Are the roles sufficiently clear? Do they articulate how the functions will collaborate and avoid gaps and duplication?

2 Are there measures of success for both first and second line operational risk personnel?

3 What good practices exist to support collaboration between first and second line operational risk practitioners; for example, joint strategy days, relationship-building measures, education or similar activities?

4 What can be improved? Note down potential improvements.

A suggested role description for a risk champion is provided in Appendix 1.

MAKE A DIFFERENCE (MAD) ACTION

Please outline the key learnings and note down one specific action you will take after reading this chapter, to enhance your existing practices relating to the Three Lines and its application to operational risk management.

In summary, this chapter discussed the concept of the Three Lines and proposed ways of increasing the power of risk management via effective collaboration of the first and second line functions.

Moving on, the next chapter starts with a deep dive into the first core tool of the framework, operational risk events.

Notes

1 Institute of Internal Auditors (2013) Position paper, *The Three Lines of Defence in Effective Risk Management and Control*, na.theiia.org/standards-guidance/Public%20Documents/PP%20The%20Three%20Lines%20of%20Defense%20in%20Effective%20Risk%20Management%20and%20Control.pdf (archived at https://perma.cc/4AM3-2SEM)

2 Institute of Internal Auditors (2013) Position paper, *The Three Lines of Defence in Effective Risk Management and Control*, na.theiia.org/standards-guidance/Public%20Documents/PP%20The%20Three%20Lines%20of%20Defense%20in%20Effective%20Risk%20Management%20and%20Control.pdf (archived at https://perma.cc/D5HG-PT4G)

3 International Organization for Standardization (ISO) (2018) *ISO 31000:2018, Risk Management – Guidelines*, www.iso.org/standard/65694.html (archived at https://perma.cc/K98D-KUHW)

4 History Daily (2019) Montparnasse Derailment: When a train went through a station walls, historydaily.org/montparnasse-derailment-when-a-train-went-through-a-stations-walls (archived at https://perma.cc/JD72-65B5)

5 Liz Wiseman (2015) *Multipliers: How the best leaders make everyone smarter*, HarperBusiness

6 Ashby, A, Bryce, C and Ring, P (2019) *Risk and Performance: Embedding risk management*, www.accaglobal.com/gb/en/professional-insights/risk/risk-and-performance.html (archived at https://perma.cc/U5QE-V3AU)

7 Institute of Internal Auditors (2020) *The IIA's Three Lines Model*, na.theiia.org/about-ia/PublicDocuments/Three-Lines-Model-Updated.pdf (archived at https://perma.cc/879L-ZZA7)

8 Chartered Institute of Internal Auditors (2017) Position paper, *Risk Management and Internal Audit*, www.iia.org.uk/resources/risk-management/position-paper-risk-management-and-internal-audit (archived at https://perma.cc/U8HK-3KQA)

9 Ashby, A, Bryce, C and Ring, P (2019) *Risk and Performance: Embedding risk management*, www.accaglobal.com/gb/en/professional-insights/risk/risk-and-performance.html (archived at https://perma.cc/VT5A-SEAA)

Operational risk events 04

What this chapter covers: The chapter incorporates multiple industry benchmarks and includes a sample template for operational risk event reporting. Operational Risk Events (including losses) are the oldest and the most common operational risk component, and are now implemented by firms in many countries worldwide (Figure 4.1). The chapter commences with revisiting the basics, including definitions and examples, and then delves into practical matters: examining how to establish an effective collection process, considering the human element of reporting, and ensuring data completeness and accuracy. It addresses the evolution of the tool in the rise of technology incidents, regulatory non-compliance and data breaches; and advocates for broadening the scope of the tool from losses only to operational risk events, moving away from focussing on solely *risk measurement* and capital calculation to active *risk management*.

> **FURTHER READING**
>
> • European Banking Authority (2008) Compendium of Supplementary Guidelines on Implementation Issues of Operational Risk (CP21)
>
> **Why recommended:** Although this document is slightly dated, it is one of the best explanatory guides for those looking for practical examples of losses, boundary events and other concepts.

Overview: importance of operational risk events

Emanating from its original definition, operational risk is the risk of *loss* resulting from inadequate or failed internal processes, people and systems or

Figure 4.1 Focus of Chapter 4: operational risk events

Risk culture

Embedding and maturity assessment

Governance, roles and responsibilities
Establish governance and clear roles across the Three Lines for managing Operational risk.

Risk appetite and risk capacity
Define nature and types of risk accepted in pursuit of strategic objectives. Evaluate adequacy of capital resources.

Operational risk events	Risk assessments	Scenario analysis	Key Risk Indicators
Record and report risk events, act to minimize future exposure. Monitor trends against RCSAs and KRIs.	Assess risk exposure in process, business or function via RCSAs. Supplement by evaluating risks emanating from change activities via ORAs.	Identify exposure from extreme but plausible events. Mitigate through risk transfer to insurance.	Monitor risk and control performance through predictive indicators. Act if indicators breach established appetite threshold.

Reporting and decision-making
Review actual risk profile against set appetite, apply active risk management to enable achievement of strategic objectives.

Training and education

Operational risk taxonomy

from external events. If the firm does not have a clear understanding of its loss profile and has no preview into the common causes of failures, it will be significantly less equipped for managing forward-looking risks effectively.

Historically, losses were the first operational risk component deployed by organizations, while *appetite*, for example, was introduced at a much later stage. For banks, loss data collection was the earliest Basel Committee requirement, primarily as a prerequisite to the development of a credible risk *measurement* system, enabling evaluation of how much capital is needed for operational risk. Early on, banks set up collection processes, striving to accumulate several years' worth of accurate and comprehensive event data. Hence the relative embeddedness of the tool which, according to the Basel Committee, is now reasonably well established and more fully implemented than other operational risk framework components.[1]

The journey, however, is far from complete. The results of multiple industry polls presented in this chapter demonstrate that financial services firms need to persevere in enhancing this seemingly basic instrument. They need to step away from mere regulatory compliance, working in collaboration with other departments to avoid multiple parallel reporting processes. And they need to continue contributing positively to the development of a *no blame* culture that is conducive to staff speaking up and raising incident reports.

Defining scope and thresholds

Operational risk losses occur when operational risk materializes. Examples of operational risk losses include:

- a cashier steals $1,000 from the till;

- a payment of $200,000 is sent to the wrong customer and not returned;

- a bank's ATM is vandalized, and has to be repaired at a cost of $7,000;

- an employee files a lawsuit against the firm, resulting in a court settlement of $70,000;

- late filing of regulatory reports leads to a fine of $10,000.

Further examples illustrate various types of potential *outcomes*:

- a foreign exchange deal is booked with an erroneous amount; correcting the error leads to a *gain* of $37,000 due to a favourable market move (i.e. a fortuitous *gain* instead of a loss);

- technology disruption occurs just outside of trading hours (a *near miss*);
- a duplicate payment of $50,000 is sent by error, and returned within five days (also a near miss, sometimes also termed a *rapidly recovered* loss);
- a payments system outage results in multiple delayed payments to customers (an event which has an *impact on clients* as well as potential future monetary loss to the firm).

These cases demonstrate the complexity of operational risk, which can crystallize into a variety of *financial* as well as *non-financial* (client, reputational, regulatory) outcomes.

The scope of loss data collection depends on the business model of the organization as well as local regulatory guidance and priorities. Some firms concentrate on negative and quantifiable impacts on the profit and loss of the organization – actual operational risk losses. There is, however, a marked drive in the industry towards more active *management* of operational risk, which places increasing emphasis on non-financial outcomes. Adopting this kind of more inclusive approach is beneficial; therefore, the more encompassing term *risk event* (or incident) is adopted – a broader term than *loss*.

> Operational Risk Events (OREs) are transactions/events that arise due to failed processes, people or systems or from the external environment, resulting in actual or potential financial exposure and/or client harm, reputational damage or regulatory censure.

For explanation purposes, it can be stated that an ORE is an event which leads the *actual outcome* of a business process to differ from its *expected outcome*; this emphasizes the erroneous or undesirable nature of the incident.

Recognizing the need for clarity, various regulatory publications have considered different elements as constituting an operational risk loss. They directed institutions towards focussing on the *actual losses*;[2] while acknowledging that recording the other types of incident represents good practice, whether or not their impact is quantifiable.

Table 4.1 Industry study: scope of loss data collection

Element	% of firms collecting
Direct charges	100
External costs incurred as a consequence of the event	80
Provisions	40
Pending losses	40
Near misses	60
Profits/gains	70
Opportunity costs/lost revenue	20
Timing impacts	20

DEFINING THE SCOPE OF OPERATIONAL RISK LOSS

1 Actual losses (including direct charges to P&L, external costs, provisions and pending losses).

2 Near misses.

3 Operational risk profits/gains.

4 Opportunity costs/lost revenues.

5 Timing impacts (financial mis-statements, i.e. negative economic impacts booked in a given fiscal period due to operational risk events, but impacting the cash flows of previous periods).

In 2012, in my role as Chair of the Operational Risk Expert Panel of the Association of Foreign Banks in the UK, I led a group study with branches and subsidiaries of foreign banks to understand what elements were in fact collected by different institutions. The results, presented in Table 4.1, demonstrate the divergence in firms' approaches.

Direct charges and *external costs* are easily recognizable and are captured by most firms, while *gains* and *near misses* are in scope of only some organizations. A minority account for *opportunity costs*, due to the difficulty of estimating the amount; however, there is an increasing desire to capture lost opportunities, especially those incurred by technology downtime. The Basel Committee also acknowledges this variance, concluding that 'only a few banks collect and analyse information relating to *all* internal operational risk events, including losses, near misses and profitable events'.[3]

Further definitions of frequently encountered event types are presented below.

A near miss, or a *nil loss*, is an operational risk event that has occurred but did not ultimately result in a loss. Effectively, in this instance, the firm was lucky. However, as its controls have failed, the next time this event happened it could just as easily lead to a monetary loss or other significant non-financial consequences.

Note the following two alternative definitions used in the industry:

1 An event that could have happened but did not, due to a *secondary* or *supplementary* control preventing it from taking place – for example, a transaction input error was corrected by an authorizer. This interpretation can be administratively burdensome and is not recommended (and, in the end, this is the reason that firms have such controls in place anyway).

2 A possible nuance, to replace *supplementary* with *non-routine* or *out of the firm's control* – for example, a transaction input error was also missed by the authorizer, but was discovered by chance due to a batch failure and the subsequent need to manually re-input all transactions. It is best not to over-complicate. Applied in practice, the definition highlighted in the box is better and easier for end-users to comprehend.

Boundary events touch on our neighbouring disciplines of credit and market risk, with examples below:

• A loan is made to a client based on a fraudulent application via electronic identity fraud (phishing), leading to a loss of $15,000. This is a *boundary* event relating to both operational and credit risks, where both risks have materialized. Another way to describe it is as a lending loss that would not have otherwise occurred, resulting from an internal failure of people, processes and systems.

Table 4.2   Industry study: loss data collection threshold

Threshold	% of firms applying
0	50
£500	10
£1,000	20
£1,250	10
£5,000	10

- A trader position taken in excess of prescribed limits, supplemented by an unfavourable market move, causes a loss of $200,000. This is also a *boundary* event, covering operational and market risk respectively.

Threshold setting

Thresholds for loss data gathering contribute to the deliberations on what should be in scope. Based on the Basel Committee study of 119 banks, 10 respondents applied a *zero* threshold, another 10 set €10,000 while most chose an amount somewhere in between.[4]

In 2012 I led a similar survey of smaller-sized banks in the UK. This study concluded that all participants applied a limit below or equal to £5,000, with 50 per cent setting a *zero* threshold, effectively capturing all OREs regardless of the amount. This result seems to support the view that a low limit is beneficial for smaller-sized organizations.

To develop a fit-for-purpose threshold, consider the following factors:

✓ Size of the organization: a lower amount is suitable for smaller-sized firms which generally have fewer OREs, and typically lower impact values.

✓ History of past events: a lower limit is beneficial for start-ups or organizations that do not have a sufficient history of past data. This allows the firm to gather more events, thus learning from its own experiences of failure and enhancing the internal control environment as it does so.

✓ Capital calculation: losses below the threshold should be immaterial for capital calculation purposes; this may be supported by statistical evidence.

✓ Cost of collection: the ORE collection process is costly, and for larger companies this has to be balanced against the benefits. In these cases usually a higher limit is appropriate. Considerations need to include employees' time, and whether any system or software will be used, as opposed to a manual spreadsheet-based method.

✓ Risk management: active risk management provides impetus for including in scope any material events that have a non-financial impact.

✓ Tone from the top: the set threshold gives an indication of management's expectations of the quality of the ORE process.

Unified impact rating grid

Essentially, regulatory compliance aside, the firm needs to capture incidents that it deems important, without establishing a cottage industry of collecting every minor error and issue. This requires understanding of what, in fact, is meant by *important*. Without written and agreed guidelines this interpretation will inevitably vary from person to person.

To this end, the operational risk function should take the lead in coordinating an aligned Organizational Impact Rating Grid, applicable for assessing OREs as well as evaluating the impact of the risks discussed in Chapters 5 and 6. This kind of grid can also be adopted by compliance and internal audit for rating their issues and findings, and by information technology colleagues for assessing technology incidents. An example of a harmonized grid is presented in Figure 4.2. It guides the end-user to consider a range of consequences, being financial, client, reputational and regulatory. The category with the highest impact determines the overall rating.

A harmonized grid has substantial benefits, including:

- the introduction of a common language and universal meaning of *Low* vs *Very High* across the organization, enabling comparability of events, issues or findings of the same rating;
- help for end-users in prioritizing their focus and actions;
- aid in determining escalation depending on materiality;
- management of risks, events and issues within a set *appetite*.

Figure 4.2   Unified impact rating grid

Impact	Description
Very high	**Financial:** Actual/potential loss greater than $xxx **Client:** Serious client detriment/large proportion impacted **Reputation:** Deep damage to the brand and market value, sustained media coverage **Regulatory:** Formal investigation up to suspension of licence
High	**Financial:** Actual/potential loss between $xx and $xxx **Client:** High level of detriment **Reputation:** Market commentary, serious damage to the reputation, brand and value **Regulatory:** May prompt investigation or regulatory action
Moderate	**Financial:** Actual/potential loss between $x and $xx **Client:** Moderate impact/small proportion or segment **Reputation:** One-off media coverage, minor damage to reputation, brand and value **Regulatory:** Potential enquiry or one-off fine
Low	**Financial:** Actual/potential loss below $x **Client:** Minor impact or complaints **Reputation:** Inconsequential **Regulatory:** Unlikely to result in any regulatory action

Each impact category needs to be agreed and correctly calibrated, with input from compliance, finance, internal audit and other relevant subject matter experts, and approved by the governance committee. To establish what constitutes a material financial consequence, it is helpful to consider the firm's risk appetite (see Chapter 9) and conduct an analysis of internal and external loss data.

In this way, using a unified grid, operational risk can define the scope and threshold for ORE collection of, for example *Moderate* and above. The advantage of this approach is that other impacts, in addition to financial, are accounted for; while minor issues can still be carved out to avoid cluttering the dataset and overwhelming employees with unnecessary administration.

In conclusion, the first rudimentary step of agreeing the scope of ORE in practice requires active thought and strategizing. Some firms continue to struggle to define the scope that is fit for purpose, and end up either collecting minor events or missing out on lessons learnt from important incidents by setting the thresholds too high.

ORE life cycle: from identification to root cause analysis

The life cycle of an operational risk event is described below:

- **Identify and notify:** employee identifies and raises potential event.
- **Escalate:** material events are escalated to senior management.
- **Report:** operational risk event report is completed within set time frame.
- **Resolve and close:** action plan is created; actions tracked until resolution; root cause analysis is performed for more significant events.
- **Analyse:** analysis, trend examination, aggregation and reporting are carried out.
- **Validate:** reconciliation is performed against books and records and other sources to ensure completeness and accuracy.

Identify and notify

Due to the breadth of the operational risk discipline, and the endless possibilities of an event occurring, OREs cannot easily be located in (and extracted from) the organization's books and records. Against this background, other discovery channels can be helpful, including: a) results of day-to-day control and reconciliation checks; b) source documents for passing accounting entries related to fines, penalties, compensations and write-offs; c) customer complaints; d) technology incident reports; and e) the results of quality assurance and inventory reviews.

However, the primary mechanism for capturing OREs when things go wrong is to rely on employees. Business units and support functions operating at the coal face need to be able to:

- understand what an ORE is, visualize examples and recognize an event when it occurs;
- know how to report it once discovered and have the means to do so;
- know who to ask in case of doubt.

The completeness of event reporting remains a challenge for many firms, for multiple reasons:

- employees not wanting to draw attention to their own failure;

- arguments as to who owns the ORE;
- the consequence of having to manage the follow-up root cause analysis and remediation efforts; and
- a lack of understanding, with an unclear ORE definition possibly leaving too much to judgement.

To address the latter point, it is useful to compile a list of possible ORE examples, to provide clarity and assist employees in recognizing an incident.

Potential events for a Human Resources department may include:

- payroll calculated incorrectly; employee underpaid;
- delivery of payslips to the wrong address by an outsourced provider;
- spreadsheet containing employee personal data placed on a public drive and accessed by unauthorized personnel;
- disgruntled member of staff threatens a lawsuit, resulting in an out-of-court settlement (Note: it is important to remember that out-of-court settlements count as operational risk events);
- failure of payroll system results in delayed salary disbursement.

The list of possible incidents for a trading business may comprise:

- wrong trade amount (fat-finger error);
- an error in model design, leading to incorrect valuation of the deal;
- erroneous valuation of a position due to a failure in updating prices;
- trading system upgrade, causing errors in transaction reports made to the regulatory authorities;
- client order taken on an unrecorded mobile phone; client subsequently claims not to recognize the order; trade reversed at a loss.

Similar lists can be prepared and discussed with each business unit and support function. Continuous, tailor-made employee training and education is essential to keep up a solid level of understanding.

In 2023, Best Practice Operational risk Forum participants discussed their level of confidence that events were indeed being reported by staff as required. Six per cent of respondents exhibited high confidence that over 90 per cent of incidents were identified and escalated; while 67 per cent believed that over 70 per cent were collected, as illustrated in Table 4.3. This is an improvement from a similar poll in 2020 (see first edition of this book), reflecting increased employee familiarity with the event logging process which is becoming 'the norm' within financial services firms.

Table 4.3   Industry study: confidence in completeness of ORE reporting

Confidence level	% Firms
High: 90% and above	6
Medium high: over 70%	67
Medium low: over 50%	17
Low: less than 50%	10

Escalate

Material events need to be escalated promptly. Escalation is becoming more important over time, involving rapid alert to senior management at the very early stages of an incident, to enable customer and stakeholder communication and speedy resolution. Especially with technology downtime, impacted clients may turn to social media to flag service unavailability; the very last resort in finding out about your own event should be from the customer themselves. Major incidents may necessitate swift assembly of the crisis management team, who will take the lead in coordinating follow-up action.

Some OREs also have to be notified to the regulators, depending on local supervisory guidelines, which vary by jurisdiction. Supervisors frequently set an amount above which they have to be informed of a loss within a given period of time; or outline types of impacts, for example, involving customer harm, which require to be promptly escalated.

The definition of what is *material* is also changing. A decade ago, materiality was mostly expressed in financial terms.

DEFINITIONS OF MATERIAL

Example 1

Material OREs are events where actual or potential loss ≥ $500,000. These events need to be immediately notified to the head of Finance, head of Risk, chief operations officer and the head of respective business or function.

When you add in client harm, reputational damage and regulatory censure, significance can be expressed via a combination of financial and non-financial impacts.

Example 2

Material OREs are events with *High* or *Very High* impacts in any of the categories (financial, client, reputational or regulatory) defined in the unified rating grid. They need to be immediately notified to the Operational Risk department, which will, in turn, inform relevant stakeholders and escalate to the chief operating officer, chief risk officer, head of Compliance and the head of respective business or function. The chief operating officer may initiate a crisis management process and will ascertain the need for client and regulatory communication.

Depending on the nature of the event, there may be other participants in the chain. Cases of fraud or financial crime will be routed to Human Resources, Fraud Prevention, Legal or some combination of the above. There are advantages in directing all events via the operational risk function, which can serve as a central point to determine subsequent escalation.

Report

The Operational Risk department usually develops a reporting template. A standard form is useful to stipulate minimum requirements, including important dates – the dates of occurrence, discovery and accounting – and an example template has been provided in Appendix 2. Reporting needs to be completed within a set timeline, which can vary significantly from firm to firm, from 24 hours up to 90 days. Rapid recording is encouraged, to relay the essence of the issue, rather than waiting for all facts to come to light. It is best to just get the record in, and if necessary add to it as new details emerge.

In many instances, the area that discovers the event is not the one that caused it; for example, the Finance department identifies an incorrect booking made by Operations. Who is responsible for filing the ORE? To avoid a heated debate, it is good practice for the *identifying business unit or support function* to report the incident, regardless of whether or not they are at fault. This helps speed up the process and prompts departments to work in collaboration. The operational risk function can assist in moderating complex cross-functional events where multiple areas are involved.

A reporting process can be established in one of two ways:

- Reporting is made available to all employees, for example, via a chat line, a link to a form on the firm's intranet site, or a paper template. Any member of staff can then complete a report and submit it directly to required recipients, ensuring swift notification. Investing in automation and streamlining the process via built-in menus and predefined distribution lists enhances the end-user experience and makes the tool straightforward and easy to use. All-staff reporting of this kind requires a higher level of maturity of the organization, where employees have reasonable knowledge and understanding of OREs. The approach works best in firms where the culture is conducive to accepting bad news and reacting constructively, focusing on resolution rather than pointing fingers.

- Reporting is accessible only to a smaller group of nominated first line operational risk champions within each business unit and support function. These risk champions are usually trained on various aspects of OREs and other operational risk tools, which enables a significant increase in the quality of the reports, and a weeding down of false alerts. This approach may, however, slow down the reporting process because the risk champion becomes a key dependency.

It is possible to combine both options in a two-step process, allowing all employees to flag an event which is then routed to the champion for subsequent review.

An industry study conducted in 2020 revealed a definitive move towards simplifying the reporting process. As many as 50 per cent of respondents had a short and simple online incident reporting form available to all staff, either via the firm's intranet portal or as part of the operational risk system. Another 25 per cent used paper templates and the remaining 25 per cent limited access to first line champions, in order to increase the quality of submissions (see Table 4.4).

Table 4.4   Industry study: operational risk event reporting process

ORE reporting	% firms
Paper template available to all employees	25
System or online intranet module available to all employees	50
Reporting by champions only	25

Resolve and close

Until now, we have been discussing the event identification and reporting process. One of the fundamental challenges faced by operational risk professionals is ensuring that OREs are not merely seen as a *reporting exercise*. Even the name given in the Basel Accord, *internal loss data*, invites the use of the word *collection* next to it. A lot of focus is placed on the gathering aspect – scope, template, timeline – to the extent that sometimes the most important element, *active risk management*, is underemphasized.

Essential learnings can be derived from OREs when thought, time and effort are invested in understanding what controls have failed and why. *Material* OREs necessitate an exhaustive root cause analysis, sometimes called a *deep dive* or *lessons learnt*. The operational risk function can facilitate this process, lend guidance and expertise, and provide a standard template to ensure consistency in the approach. Analysis can be completed via a workshop with subject matter experts (SMEs), and with the right stakeholders in the room a discussion will usually suffice. The firm may also apply techniques such as 5 Whys or fishbone (Ishikawa) diagrams, which are widely employed in the Six Sigma process improvement methodology:[5]

- 5 Whys prompt continual asking of the *why* question, to drill down into the problem and get to its true origin;
- a fishbone diagram is useful in exploring distinct groups of causes; for example, what are the people-, system- or process-related causes of the incident.

> Where a deeper analysis of root causes and failed controls is not completed, the firm will end up merely *counting* the loss occurrences, their volume and value; without understanding *why* they happened and *how* to prevent the next event from materializing.

Following the in-depth study, action plans must be created, with owners and target dates, to prevent future reoccurrence. The second line Operational Risk department usually monitors the progress of these plans and escalates to the relevant governance committees any OREs which have not closed by the target resolution date. Operational Risk can also take a more active role and sign off on the actions, to confirm that the intended control enhancements actually address the risk.

Lastly, OREs can serve as a trigger to consider revision of other tools, such as RCSAs, KRIs and scenarios.

Analyse

Analysis, trend examination, aggregation and reporting are crucial activities which bring value to the organization. Correct event classification using the risk taxonomy category, and tagging it against the primary responsible business unit and legal entity, help build a solid foundation for the analysis.

The second line Operational Risk department has a view of the entirety of the firm's ORE data and is best placed to conduct the analysis. The questions to consider include:

- What is the overall story – has there been an increase/decrease in the number or value of OREs? It is helpful to analyse incidents relative to transaction volume: if a business unit doubles its transaction processing but OREs go up by only 10%, that could be interpreted as positive news.

- What can be said about the firm's risk profile? Are there certain risks that are continuously materializing?

- Are OREs occurring in different areas but with the same root cause? Another useful tool borrowed from Six Sigma, Pareto analysis, can be applied to the ORE data, with a view to finding a few key drivers which contribute to the majority of failures.[6]

- Is there a particular day of the month when events take place (e.g. month-end)?

- What are the weak spots, where controls appear to fail repeatedly? This is particularly a concern if prevention measures have already been implemented.

- What is the rate of near misses to actual monetary losses? This reflects the strength of preventative controls.

- What is the length of time between the date of event occurrence and the date of discovery? This provides insight on the performance of detective controls.

- Is there a cluster of events that occurred during a short period of time, which may be connected?

- Are OREs being reported within the timeline set by the policy? This provides a good reflection of the firm's culture.

- Integration with other tools – are the reported OREs consistent with the outputs of other tools, such as RCSAs (see Chapter 5) and KRIs (Chapter 7)?

In short, a meaningful story around the OREs needs to be relayed to senior management and appropriate governance committees (see Chapter 10, Operational risk reporting).

Another powerful technique is to present trends and findings back to first line business units and support functions, who can sometimes feel that their reported OREs seem to disappear into a black hole without any follow-up feedback. This kind of reporting back can be done, for example, in a quarterly review session with each business unit, where the department's own events are discussed and additional firm-wide analysis is shared by the second line operational risk team.

Validate

The validation stage focuses on data accuracy and completeness. Sound data collection, and the quality and integrity of the collected data, are crucial – for risk management purposes as well as measurement – to generate capital outcomes that are aligned with the firm's operational loss exposure. The Basel Framework requires banks to 'have processes to independently review the comprehensiveness and accuracy of loss data'.[7]

Validation steps may include regular reconciliation of OREs recorded in the operational risk system or spreadsheet to the firm's accounting records. This ensures that losses are correctly reflected in the general ledger; and in the opposite direction, checks that the respective general ledger entries correspond to what is captured in the system.

An additional *certification* mechanism can be used, where business units are asked to attest to the completeness and accuracy of OREs in the reporting period. To facilitate this process, it is good practice to provide departments with the OREs they have submitted, and to seek written confirmation from the department head that no other incidents have taken place.

Firms may find it useful to open a separate general ledger account for recording OREs, ensuring transparency and ease of reconciliation. As an example, in a trading business all gains and losses commonly end up in the same profit and loss account. This makes it very difficult to extract entries related to operational risk events from the normal day's P&L; a dedicated account helps in this process.

External loss data

External events provide excellent case studies and enable a firm to proactively consider the question *could this happen to us?*. Data can be obtained from various sources, including newspaper articles or a paid subscription to external loss data consortia. It is the role of the operational risk function, both second line personnel and first line champions, to institute a disciplined approach for examining external events, selecting those cases that are most relevant, and following up by facilitating workshops on the events with subject matter experts.

Addressing the human element

Another key ORE challenge is linked to the culture of the organization: ensuring that employees feel comfortable and empowered to speak up when things go wrong. Fostering a *no blame* environment and emphasizing the value of lessons learnt will encourage staff to raise issues. The operational risk function is often a catalyst of positive change in this direction; providing training to employees on the value of OREs, as well as requesting senior management to avoid reacting to events with negative comments or an immediate demand for the responsible employee's name. The operational risk function can also be a mediator, especially when transmitting bad news up the chain of the organization, focusing constructively on addressing the cause rather than naming and shaming members of staff. Needless to say, the second line operational risk should not have a role in any post-event disciplinary proceedings.

Operational risk helps transition from a *who did this?*-style comeback from management to a *how do we solve this?*-type reaction. Alas, this is a broader cultural challenge that cannot be solved by operational risk alone, even if mammoth efforts are made. In some organizations, the fear of reprisal significantly impedes the firm's ability to make effective reports and hence to derive true value from the lessons learnt.

Unfortunately, OREs are always 'bad news'; with the rare exception when an incidental gain is incurred instead of a loss. Over time, this can create a negative brand to the process, and if not managed, can spread to affect the reputation of the whole operational risk discipline. Positive energy needs to be consciously injected by:

- focusing on lessons learnt;
- presenting the results of deep dives which demonstrate process enhancements implemented as a result of the incident;

- sharing details of events between departments, to promote common learning and help avoid similar problems in other areas;

- celebrating success, highlighting any positive employee or customer feedback that relates to improved processes.

Treatment of technology-related events, data breaches and conduct failures

As discussed in the first chapter, the operational risk discipline is moving away from solely focusing on regulatory capital calculations, and the definition of operational risk as the risk of just *loss* is no longer truly reflective of today's environment. Following cyber-attacks, significant technology incidents and failures of third-party service providers, firms' operational resilience is being brought into the spotlight, as highlighted in Chapter 15. Supervisors are constantly asking organizations to assess how their failures are impacting *their clients* and the *markets* they operate in. This conflict between the letter of the earliest Basel Committee requirement and the evolution of the financial services environment has created a divergence; either firms need to expand their treatment of operational risk losses to incorporate other non-financial impacts, or they need to create alternative parallel processes which capture events with client, reputational and regulatory outcomes.

Specifically, there are three areas of challenge: technology-related events, data breaches and conduct failures.

Technology-related events

These are subject to continual debate between operational risk, information technology and now additionally operational resilience colleagues, due to the lack of integration between the ORE process and IT helpdesk incident management. Major (not all) technology incidents usually turn into operational risk events, and a mechanism needs to be in place to guide decision-making: at what point does system failure or an attack become an ORE? As one example, the criteria can be agreed by instituting a unified rating grid as discussed earlier in the chapter. But end-users also need to be educated as to what notification route they should follow, be it via the IT helpdesk or an operational risk *material* event escalation channel. Equally, incidents may emanate from a failure on the part of a third-party provider of outsourced

IT services. Those kinds of failures should be logged as OREs, and the firm must both oversee resolution of the incident and ensure that the supplier introduces measures to prevent reoccurrence.

Technology-related events may not immediately translate into a clear financial loss to the firm. However, with increased reliance on technological solutions they are becoming more and more impactful to clients. As discussed in Chapter 15, the resilience dialogue evolves primarily around technology, and hence operational resilience colleagues are now firmly involved in these kind of events. The speed of escalation, customer and regulatory communication and event resolution is vital, especially where enhanced incident management requirements are introduced by regulation such as the Digital Operational Resilience Act (DORA). Who steps up to the challenge and assumes the role of incident coordinator? This varies between operational risk, IT and operational resilience teams, and at times all of the above aim to hold a central position and orchestrate the activities, including any necessary liaison with required stakeholders from various disciplines. The need for integration, collaboration and clarity when it comes to roles and responsibilities is also discussed in Chapter 15.

Data breaches

The EU Global Data Protection Regulation (GDPR) introduced a dramatic increase in penalties for poor data management. Prompt identification and reporting of actual and potential violations is now part of every firm's priorities. Good practice is to use an existing operational risk event reporting channel for data-related issues. This requires an update to the ORE policy to clarify the scope. But it also relies on an increase in the speed of ORE submission, to comply with GDPR timelines, as well as good coordination between operational risk and data protection officers, to ensure prompt circulation and actioning of the report. In a similar way to a technology failure, a data breach may not generate an immediate and obvious loss, but does have an impact on the customer (or employee if it is an employee-related event). It can also emanate from a third-party failure.

The alternative to using one incident reporting process is to create a separate data breach reporting one, with a different (yet another) template for the end-user, a separate policy, training and education. Unfortunately, many organizations choose this route; but it is confusing for the employees at the coal face, who already have multiple templates to complete for different purposes.

Conduct-related events

This is another field where the ORE process can be a conduit for capturing and escalating material breaches, rather than creating an equivalent compliance reporting mechanism. For example, an incident where a new product is traded with a client prior to formal sign-off from the new product approval committee. Although it has zero financial impact, this represents a severe misconduct and internal policy breach. Similarly, an account opened for a client prior to customer due diligence (CDD) verification, where the CDD is completed 10 days later with no exceptions, epitomizes a lucky escape. There could have been significant consequences for the firm if the new client was subject to sanctions, or was operating outside the firm's target market and ended up not being approved. Even if a financial penalty was avoided, from a risk management perspective it is beneficial to examine the causes of this event and derive lessons learnt.

The operational risk function needs to work closely with compliance to agree on a joined-up approach. End-users will always favour having a single channel for raising all types of exceptions, which are then routed to respective SMEs, whether compliance, operational risk, IT or data protection.

In terms of reflecting events that have conduct implications, an ORE template can include a flag or a field which addresses behavioural elements. This enables any conduct-related events to be easily extracted from the overall database and subjected to subsequent analysis.

Roles and responsibilities

It is the responsibility of first line business units and support functions to identify, escalate and report OREs in compliance with the requirements stipulated by the policy. Business units agree on and fund control improvements to prevent incidents reoccurring, and track the enhancements until they have been fully implemented. They also need to use OREs as a trigger to consider any necessary updates to other operational risk tools – risk and control self-assessments and Key Risk Indicators.

First line operational risk champions, embedded in the business, play a crucial role as risk coordinators, ensuring that OREs are used effectively to improve risk management.

An ORE checklist for first line risk coordinators is presented below.

FIRST LINE RISK COORDINATOR CHECKLIST: ORES

✓ All staff in the department are trained on operational risk events.

✓ Employees understand the importance of learning from incidents and are encouraged to raise them.

✓ Root cause and trend analysis are performed, actions are taken to improve control environment.

✓ Completeness of events is ensured through validation or attestation.

✓ Risk coordinators share lessons learnt from OREs.

✓ Relevant external events are examined: can they happen to us?

The second line Operational Risk department is responsible for establishing policy requirements, providing training and education to end-users, conducting overall trend analysis and providing insights to help derive the maximum value out of past events. The second line back-tests OREs against other tools in the framework, to ensure consistency, and derives key views on risk measurement and capital adequacy.

Operational risk specialists are often catalysts of cultural change, especially in firms where speaking up and raising incidents may be challenging. The function works in close partnership with first line business units, promoting and facilitating cross-functional learning.

Common challenges and good practices

Common challenges

Potential challenges related to operational risk events can include the following.

Reluctance to raise OREs

This is a very real hurdle especially in organizations characterized by a blame culture, where the first question is usually *who did it?*. The operational risk function plays a key role in positively influencing the culture and encouraging transparency and no blame; but there are limits to what a single department can accomplish. Using data analytics and artificial intelligence can help to surface incidents automatically, placing less reliance on personnel and removing the emotion from the process. This is an embryonic area but one definitely worth exploring further.

Lack of action following the event

The necessary improvements are identified but are not completed on time due to other priorities, insufficient budget, apathy or for other reasons. In these cases, actions turn overdue and target dates are extended multiple times. To avoid this scenario a pragmatic approach needs to be adopted, differentiating between minor and material matters. For insignificant events, improvements may be too costly and risk acceptance is the optimum solution. If the event and corresponding actions are material, however, they need to be treated with the same rigour as internal audit action plans.

Lack of ownership of cross-functional incidents

Where multiple areas are involved in an event, none of the business areas are willing to step up and lead remediation, passing the accountability around: *this is not my event.* In such instances the Operational Risk department can moderate the resolution, facilitating conversations and agreeing the right steps forward.

Over-engineered ORE framework and template

Simply put, business units hesitate to use the ORE mechanism. If the form is too complicated and appears to provide no value then the reporting hurdle may not even be attempted. Simplifying the process ensures that, from an end-user perspective, it adds value compared to the time and effort invested.

Administration instead of risk management

There is some risk that the whole ORE exercise can become solely about form completion; especially if thresholds are inappropriately low, combined with over-zealous employees in the Operational Risk department who duly chase each event, action and target date regardless of materiality. While it is important to have a disciplined approach to logging and analysing events, it is equally essential to apply a risk-based perspective and common sense when it comes to minor issues.

Unbalanced operational risk engagement

Criticism is sometimes directed towards the Operational Risk department to the effect that it is only visible when there has been an operational risk event. And while the business unit is determinedly focusing on investigating and resolving the incident, operational risk is unhelpfully following up every hour demanding submission of the ORE report. It is true that the second line needs to be actively involved at all stages of the event management process; but this should not be the only time it ever engages with end-users. Relationship building, understanding each other's roles and working in partnership throughout the whole risk management life cycle are key to effective risk management.

Good practices

Training and education

Engaging and interactive training sessions, which are tailored to reflect examples relevant to business units and support functions, increase understanding about OREs and make the process more accessible. Educational programmes need to be continuous, to account for new joiners.

Trend analysis

It is good practice to invest time in conducting trend analysis at firm-wide level, to really understand the story that OREs present. To some extent, the loss profile reveals a firm's strengths and weaknesses, and this valuable knowledge should guide the organization when taking key decisions – for example when it is considering major business changes, expansion or investment in new product lines.

Examination of decline in OREs

While any increase in the value and number of events is concerning and should be investigated, a sharp drop is equally worrying. This can occur due to process improvements that the firm has implemented; but it can also occur as a result of a new leader stepping in and propagating *no errors/no losses* type objectives, instilling fear in any employees who deliver unpopular messages. Consequently, the absence of OREs may not necessarily be good news, and the operational risk function needs to keep its ears to the ground, evaluating the situation and understanding what has caused it.

Sharing learning

The second line Operational Risk department can lead a forum with first line champions to share relevant events, learnings and success stories. This process encourages debate and prompts champions to develop their own network, enhancing their ability to reach out to each other and compare notes. Is it worth mentioning that event sharing is particularly valuable in large organizations with the same activity being undertaken in various geographical locations. Fraudsters may identify a weakness in a firm's system and undertake the same fraud in different jurisdictions and locations. Sharing of incidents can prevent this from happening.

Data confidentiality

Organizations need to ensure that customer or employee names and personal details are removed from the text of all event reports. Litigation, fraud and financial crime events contain sensitive details, so it is important that only a respective loss amount is recorded in the ORE report, supplemented by a reference number for the respective file which contains full details and is retained in the Human Resources or Legal department. This is particularly important when capturing sensitive data like pay-offs to staff.

In jurisdictions where firms are subject to bank secrecy or data privacy laws, client and transaction information should be relayed outside the jurisdiction only to the degree permitted by local privacy laws.

Celebrating success

This is particularly important given that OREs intrinsically have a negative connotation embedded in their name (*incidents, losses*). Operational risk needs to emphasize improvements, focusing on lessons learnt, and to encourage first line business units and support functions to adopt the same attitude. Recognition of timely and disciplined reporting, reward for process enhancements and, especially if available, client feedback related to perfected processes turn the focus from *what went wrong to what works well and has been improved*. This tool is not used nearly enough in most firms.

Knowledge of the second line operational risk function

Due to their direct use in *risk measurement*, OREs require in-depth knowledge and proficiency with definitions and attributes. To name a few, these attributes include gross and net amounts, reference dates and timing impacts (which, for example, should be captured when they span more than one financial accounting period and give rise to legal risk).[8] As described in

Chapter 11, which covers training and education, operational risk policy setters must be able to not only articulate how the ORE process works but also explain: *why* a particular approach and scope was selected; what considerations went into the decision; which home and host supervisory guidelines have been examined; what cost/benefit analysis has been conducted; and whether cultural aspects have been considered.

Industry benchmark

The Best Practice Operational Risk Forum, which comprises practitioners from a wide range of financial services firms, conducted a deep dive into the topic of operational risk events.

Addressing the cultural aspect: a marginal improvement

As described in Figure 4.3, the majority of respondents (58 per cent) perceived that their firms contained different pockets of culture, which was largely due to different managers encouraging right – or wrong – behaviours and attitudes in their respective areas. This tendency generated a mixed re-

Figure 4.3   Industry poll: first line attitude to reporting OREs

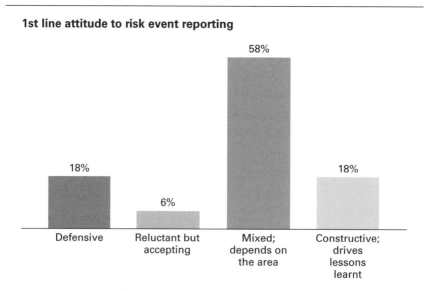

1st line attitude to risk event reporting

Best Practice Operational Risk Forum, 2023

sponse to the topic of OREs; some areas were supportive of the ORE construct, and happy to focus on lessons learnt, while others' attitudes were defensive or even blame-orientated. On a positive note, there was an improvement in the number of respondents pointing to a consistently constructive approach, from 8 per cent in 2020 to 18 per cent in 2023 (see first edition of the book for details of 2020 poll results); in these cases leaders across the whole organization were prepared to accept that mistakes happen, and to devote their energy to finding solutions. This is a promising result, which is a tribute to firms' leadership setting the right tone, as well as the event logging process becoming more of a norm across the industry.

Celebrating success

It is crucial to consciously inject positive energy into OREs, not only to avoid the negative brand of this important tool but to create an environment of psychological safety. The premise of 'there is no improvement without openness about mistakes and failures' was discussed, with focus on encouraging constructive reaction to bad news, and a thorough lessons learnt process. Members noted that while, previously, psychological safety was an HR-led area, the Operational Risk department is increasingly stepping in to lead or co-lead the efforts.

Nevertheless, practitioners acknowledged that, in general, positive reward and recognition mechanisms were not being applied sufficiently. The majority of respondents (61 per cent) felt that they had limited time on their hands, and that just as one ORE was investigated and closed, another one came in and the busy cycle continued, leaving not enough time to celebrate

Figure 4.4 Celebrating success using OREs

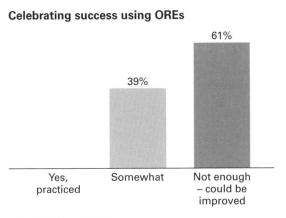

Best Practice Operational Risk Forum, 2023

the benefits and positive ramifications of the event. However, in those cases where rewards were given, forum members shared how much the positive affirmation truly mattered to recipients. It seems that much more emphasis on the constructive aspects of OREs – such as transparency, learning and meaningful enhancements – is both desirable and needed. In short, practitioners need to take stock and dedicate time to congratulating and encouraging employees and teams that exhibit the right attitudes and behaviours.

Practical workplace exercise

Reflecting on the content of this chapter, examine a sample of operational risk events recorded within your organization over the last year, and consider the following questions:

1 Have a scope and thresholds been set for OREs and are they fit for purpose?

2 What analysis has been undertaken to support the scope and thresholds?

3 Is there evidence of active risk management of events, with analysis of the root cause and actions to prevent reoccurrence?

4 Is the culture of the firm conducive to employees speaking up and logging incidents without fear of reprisal?

5 What are the strengths of the process?

6 What can be improved? Note down possible enhancements.

MAKE A DIFFERENCE (MAD) ACTION

Please outline the learnings and note down one action that you will take after reading this chapter to enhance your existing practices related to operational risk events.

In summary, this chapter addressed operational risk events, historically the first tool deployed by organizations, where many challenges still remain; from complex ones such as getting the culture right, to more simple ones such as setting the correct threshold.

Moving on, the next chapter will focus on forward-looking risk identification.

Notes

1 Basel Committee on Banking Supervision (2014) *Review of the Principles for the Sound Management of Operational Risk*, www.bis.org/publ/bcbs292.pdf (archived at https://perma.cc/X9UQ-5ZAB)

2 European Banking Authority (2008) *Compendium of Supplementary Guidelines on Implementation Issues of Operational Risk (CP21)*, www.eba.europa.eu/sites/default/documents/files/documents/10180/37070/8bfec18c-2de6-4436-ae28-2f1b044bd385/CEBS%202008%20230%20Final.pdf? (archived at https://perma.cc/F2V4-B35T)

3 Basel Committee on Banking Supervision (2014) *Review of the Principles for the Sound Management of Operational Risk*, www.bis.org/publ/bcbs292.pdf (archived at https://perma.cc/XBW2-27EM)

4 Basel Committee on Banking Supervision (2009) *Results from the 2008 Loss Data Collection Exercise for Operational Risk*, www.bis.org/publ/bcbs160.pdf (archived at https://perma.cc/24GS-MXYN)

5 George, ML, Maxey, J, Rowlands, D and Price, M (2004) *The Lean Six Sigma Pocket Toolbook: A quick reference guide to 100 tools for improving quality and speed*, McGraw-Hill

6 George, ML, Maxey, J, Rowlands, D and Price, M (2004) *The Lean Six Sigma Pocket Toolbook: A quick reference guide to 100 tools for improving quality and speed*, McGraw-Hill

7 Basel Committee on Banking Supervision, Basel Framework, www.bis.org/basel_framework/ (archived at https://perma.cc/3JNV-5BB8)

8 Basel Committee on Banking Supervision, Basel Framework, www.bis.org/basel_framework/ (archived at https://perma.cc/3JNV-5BB8)

Risk and control 05 self-assessments

What this chapter covers: Risk and Control Self-Assessments (RCSAs) are used by many organizations, yet the instrument attracts its fair share of criticism. This chapter draws attention to methodologies that have proven effective over time; suggests an approach to risk identification based on three simple questions; and emphasizes the importance of engaging with stakeholders via personable and meaningful conversations (Figure 5.1). While covering the main fundamental concepts, it also focuses on overcoming pitfalls and proposing measures of success that help evaluate whether the RCSA has delivered desired outcomes. The chapter contains case studies, examples and an industry benchmark.

FURTHER READING

- Committee of Sponsoring Organizations of the Treadway Commission (2017) *Enterprise Risk Management: Integrating with strategy and performance*

  Why recommended: One of the many strengths of the COSO approach is its emphasis on the value of enterprise risk management in relation to the setting and carrying out of strategy, positioning it in the context of the firm's performance rather than as an isolated exercise. This useful guide aids in building a business case when considering RCSA roll-out.

- Theodore Zeldin (1998) *Conversation: How talk can change your life*, The Harvill Press

  Why recommended: Perhaps a rather unusual choice for the chapter, this book brings out the art of conversations. The aim of including it is to stress the fact that RCSA is not a checklist or a mechanical task, but a meaningful – and potentially even enjoyable – interaction of minds.

Figure 5.1 Focus of Chapter 5: risk assessments

Risk culture

Embedding and maturity assessment

Governance, roles and responsibilities
Establish governance and clear roles across the Three Lines for managing operational risk.

Risk appetite and risk capacity
Define nature and types of risk accepted in pursuit of strategic objectives. Evaluate adequacy of capital resources.

Operational risk events	Risk assessments	Scenario analysis	Key Risk Indicators
Record and report risk events, act to minimize future exposure. Monitor trends against RCSAs and KRIs.	Assess risk exposure in process, business or function via RCSAs. Supplement by evaluating risks emanating from change activities via ORAs.	Identify exposure from extreme but plausible events. Mitigate through risk transfer to insurance.	Monitor risk and control performance through predictive indicators. Act if indicators breach established appetite threshold.

Reporting and decision-making
Review actual risk profile against set appetite, apply active risk management to enable achievement of strategic objectives.

Training and education

Operational risk taxonomy

Rethinking the approach: essential ingredients of the perfect recipe

Risk and Control Self-Assessments (RCSAs) are a key forward-looking component of the operational risk framework, and one of the most interactive and engaging tools available to risk practitioners. While widely used by many firms in financial services, RCSAs typically generate a mixed response, not only from business stakeholders but also from practitioners themselves. Sceptics question whether they bring any benefits; critics suggest that they are a waste of time. A study of industry practices published by the Operational Riskdata eXchange Association (ORX) in 2020 even reflected the view that RCSAs were seen as simply not delivering enough value, and were perceived as a tick-box exercise rather than truly influencing business decisions.[1]

By this stage of evolution of the RCSA tool, firms are likely to have developed detailed procedures, predefined templates for what needs to be captured in a software or spreadsheet solution, and a library of commonly phrased risks and controls. Could it be that the methodology has become too prescriptive and that the process has trumped the business value-add? Whether starting from scratch or rethinking an existing approach, it is important to bear in mind that the essential ingredients of the perfect RCSA recipe are quite basic: the right stakeholders participating in the process, personal and meaningful engagement, a high degree of preparedness and an expert facilitator.

Heightened focus on proactive risk identification

Firms are subject to growing interest in their operational risk profile. Nowadays, boards, internal and external auditors, as well as regulators, frequently focus discussions towards the most material operational risks the firms face. And this is not surprising, as over the past decade operational risks have arguably surpassed financial risks in order of magnitude. This is demonstrated by the shift in the risk profile of the annual Global Risks Report published by the World Economic Forum. In 2024, it is the operational risks – AI-generated misinformation and disinformation, extreme weather events and cyber – that topped the risk chart,[2] with increasing interconnectedness among the risks themselves.

The growing ask for clear articulation of *top operational risks*, in addition to well-established routine loss reporting, demonstrates very effectively the shift of focus in the industry: from being merely an operational risk regulatory capital calculation towards more active risk management. To this end, RCSA is a core tool that encourages proactive thinking, provides boards and management with a detailed view of the firm's risk and control environment, and leads to prudent decision-making. Coupled with the big drive towards increased personal accountability, RCSAs are instrumental in helping senior management to demonstrate and evidence that they have taken reasonable steps in understanding and managing their risk and control environment. There are plenty of reasons to make the most of the exercise.

Top-down and bottom-up assessments and their features

Defining RCSAs

In Chapter 4 we discussed OREs, the events of the past. RCSAs, in contrast, encourage firms to consider the areas where they are exposed and where things *could* potentially go wrong for them in the future; thereby enabling them to invest in preventative as well as detective measures.

Terminology varies widely between firms. The risk assessments may also be called Risk and Control Assessments (RACAs), Control Self-Assessments (CSAs) or Own Risk Self-Assessments (ORSAs). Going forward, throughout this chapter and the rest of the book, we will refer to these assessments collectively as Risk and Control Self-Assessments, or RCSAs.

RCSA is a process of the identification and assessment of risks faced by the firm and review of the control environment, in order to highlight areas where controls are ineffective or insufficient to mitigate the risk and take appropriate action.

Despite the RCSA concept being rather straightforward and necessarily simplistic, it generates multiple questions that all require answers. As with any process, one of the fundamental steps in carrying out a successful RCSA is deciding on the right way of doing it. With no standard industry design, it is imperative that each firm selects an appropriate methodology and approach, process and level of granularity that is suitable given its own circumstances.

Methodological questions that need to be considered include:

- How to structure a *bottom-up* approach, gathering intelligence from the employees at the coal face as well as how to obtain a *top-down* view from the senior stakeholders; *both sets of discussions* are needed;
- What assessment scales should be adopted;
- Whether controls will undergo judgemental evaluation or need to be actively tested;
- How to add value and measure the success – or failure – of the exercise.

Presented below are examples of selected RCSA approaches, their key features, advantages and weaknesses.

Granular assessments

Detailed bottom-up assessments help a firm to achieve greater understanding of its risk and control profile. One methodology in this category is process risk self-assessment (PRSA) which aims to map a particular process end-to-end, and to identify the key risks and controls within it. Activities are selected based on certain criteria. For example, if the driver is Sarbanes–Oxley (SoX), a regulation which historically gave rise to many internal control evaluation programmes, the focus would be on the processes that impact the company's most significant general ledger accounts.[3]

Where the driver is operational resilience – as has been the case more recently – the organization identifies the critical operations which are most important for its clients or the financial markets it operates in.

Organizations that have historically applied a PRSA methodology driven by SoX are also better positioned when it comes to satisfying operational resilience demands. This is because the fundamental yet very time-consuming task of mapping the process, and understanding its interdependencies, would have already been accomplished in the first stage of analysis. (See also Chapter 15, Operational resilience.)

A PRSA schematic is described in Figure 5.2.

Examples of processes or services that may be selected for PRSA include:

- Client deposits: these are mapped end-to-end, from the point of establishing a client relationship and performing due diligence checks, through to the client depositing the money which results in accounting entries on the balance sheet.

Figure 5.2 Process risk self-assessment

- Foreign exchange: similarly this process is mapped from the point of a new corporate/institutional client being set up, to agreeing the deal with the trader, confirmation, settlement and general ledger accounting entries.

PRSA is a *bottom-up* assessment, resulting in relatively granular risk identification, for example:

- risk of money laundering resulting from missed or poorly executed client due diligence at the account opening stage;
- risk of incorrect foreign exchange transactions due to trader 'fat finger' error.

The key features of this approach are outlined below.

- Advantages:
  - Process mapping is a robust technique which in itself generates immediate benefits, including process optimization, as redundant steps are identified and eliminated.
  - A cross-functional methodology brings together participants from the front office, operations, finance, technology and other functions, encouraging fruitful dialogue and increasing overall understanding of the risk and control environment; and improving collaboration between business units and support functions.
  - Due to end-to-end mapping, the impact of failure on the external customer becomes transparent and measurable. This is essential learning for non-client facing departments and a key differentiator of the approach.

○ Often process controls are actively tested (rather than judgementally evaluated), making the assessment more factual and objective.

- Challenges:
  ○ It takes a lot of thought, and sometimes some trial and error, to set the right boundaries around the process; and to obtain agreement on where it starts and ends and what is (and is not) included. It may be equally challenging to find an owner for a particular process, due to its cross-functional nature. Organizations are rarely structured *by process*, but usually rather by department.

  ○ The approach is labour intensive and requires rigorous work creating maps and keeping them up to date; it is most likely to succeed where a firm is already in the habit of process mapping as part of its culture.

  ○ The approach requires consideration of how the broader risks of, for example, poor governance or conduct can be addressed; as well as how the granular results are aggregated and presented to the board and senior management at the top of the house.

An alternative detailed form of assessment is the *departmental* RCSA, focusing on the risk and control environment of a particular department, business or function. This approach fits well with firms' organizational structure, with clear *units of measure* – departments – already established and operating, and an obvious RCSA owner, the respective unit head. It also aligns closely to senior management accountability and therefore can be used in personal attestations to satisfy certification and accountability regimes where they exist. The approach is, however, siloed by nature as each business unit is evaluating its own setting without considering interdependencies and reflecting on the overall impact of the risk or control on the client or the balance sheet. Overall, therefore, PRSA is a stronger and more rewarding approach. But if you are conducting the assessments at departmental level, aim to maximize the exploration of linkages and interdependencies.

High-level assessments

Top-down assessments are essential for engaging with senior management and arriving at an enterprise-wide view. Strategic risk assessment (SRA) focuses on the identification of risks which may prevent the firm from achieving its strategic objectives, and the formulation of controls to mitigate those risks. The starting point is the high-level business plan, which usually translates into the goals of business heads. This gives rise to an immediate value

Figure 5.3 Strategic risk assessment

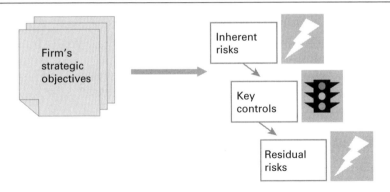

proposition: the conversation starts with an offer from the risk practitioner to help the business identify and mitigate the risks that could impede the successful realization of *their own* objectives and business plan. It sounds so much better than a bald statement of the type 'You need to complete your RCSA'.

Operational risk practitioners often complain that they are not invited to the strategy table. In this context the SRA is a sound tool which not only generates value but also elevates the brand and profile of risk professionals. The assessment is best conducted at the start of the year, to *coincide with strategy setting*, arriving at robust objectives given risks that have been well understood and evaluated. This timing is important to ensure that the SRA does not represent an isolated exercise but is linked to the need to *make a decision* – namely to discuss and adopt the strategy given the risks to it. As noted by COSO, enterprise risk management and these kinds of exercises enrich the 'dialogue by adding perspective to the strengths and weaknesses of a strategy' and allow management 'to feel more confident that they've examined alternative strategies'.[4] This is described in schematic form in Figure 5.3.

SRA is a top-down assessment resulting in the identification of high-level risks which stretch beyond purely operational, actually entering into enterprise risk territory.

CASE STUDY 5.1

An investment bank sets one of its objectives as being 'to create an extensive range of competitive products that meet client requirements', with a plan to significantly increase its client value proposition during the coming year. During the SRA, in discussing what issues might prevent the business heads from executing on this objective, three risks are identified:

- inadequate product design leading to poor customer outcomes;
- inability to identify and implement new regulatory requirements on a timely basis;
- new product approval process too slow.

The last risk is considered a real blocker to delivering on the strategy. A multimillion improvement programme is launched, to recruit additional resources in support functions and invest in a parallel system testing environment. Metrics are agreed as to what constitutes an acceptable new product review and approval time frame, and each new product is measured against the timeline.

Arguably, reasoning such as this ('new product approval process too slow') does not belong in the operational risk domain. In the above example, however, this is clearly a very important risk for the business; and the methodology needs to be flexible enough to accommodate what truly matters to stakeholders, rather than what can be neatly fitted into the standard taxonomy.

The key features of the SRA approach are presented below.

- Advantages:
  - SRA is a vital tool for understanding the most significant risks that underlie the business. This is an essential step for subsequently setting the firm's risk appetite (see Chapter 9, Operational risk appetite).
  - The exercise is directly relevant to business heads as it is closely linked to their goals and strategic objectives. This kind of value proposition helps to build a convincing case for participants.
  - SRA promotes *risk conversations* at the senior management level, increases awareness, elevates the value of the risk assessment process and drives the need and appreciation for resulting management information and reporting.
  - By its nature, SRA is broader than operational risk and evaluates the risk and control environment on a holistic basis, considering both gaps and areas that might be overcontrolled.
- Challenges:
  - By design, the SRA does not delve deep into the details of individual controls.

o It is not easy to organize and requires robust planning given the busy diaries and preoccupations of the participants.

o Controls are evaluated judgementally, not tested, making the assessment less factual.

The organization needs to conduct assessments that are both granular and high level. They complement each other, enabling a deep dive as well as considering the firm-wide profile, which cannot be arrived at via mere aggregation. The risks are *key* at the level where they are raised; so a PRSA will capture process-related risks, but is not expected to reflect executive committee concerns (for example, around failed governance arrangements or strategic business risks).

Whichever approach is applied, an RCSA has a number of distinct steps that need to be followed.

Risk identification and assessment

Identifying risks

Risk identification aims to highlight material risks for the area covered by the RCSA, potential failures that may impact key business activities and prevent respective business unit or support functions from meeting *their objectives*.

To achieve a robust outcome, it is essential to involve the right stakeholders – usually the heads of the respective departments, their direct reports and selected subject matter experts (SMEs) – and for strategic risk assessment, the chief executive and their management team.

While there is no agreed universal approach, risk identification lends itself well to individual interviews with the appropriate participants, facilitated by an experienced operational risk practitioner. This can be followed by a follow-up workshop, discussed later in the chapter. One-to-one discussions allow inputs to be gathered effectively and efficiently. A good start can be achieved via a conversation centred around three basic questions, described in Figure 5.4.

The open question

Open questions explore participants' concerns about the area in scope, to obtain an understanding of *what keeps them awake at night*. The

Figure 5.4   Three questions for risk assessments

question is broad and posed in the language of the participant (rather than risk-type language such as 'what are your inherent risks?'). Stakeholders understand their business; the answer should provide a good feel for their key areas of focus.

Various elements may arise from this process which are not necessarily risks; the aim is to listen, probe and turn the information into desired output. Many accomplished operational risk managers see themselves as *translators*, interpreting regulation into day-to-day practices, converting stakeholders' input into risk language and complexity into simplicity.

Slightly digressing from the discipline of operational risk into the art of leading a conversation: to quote Theodore Zeldin, 'Real conversation catches fire. It involves more than sending and receiving information.'[5] A risk practitioner is not an administrative note-taker, but a knowledgeable and equal partner in the dialogue, orchestrating the conversation. A relationship of mutual trust helps bring about a good debate.

Back to risk identification, an alternative open question might explore *what could go wrong, or what might prevent stakeholders from achieving their annual objectives?*. Linking every risk assessment to objectives brings much needed connection to the business plan and what needs to be achieved. Or, *if they were building this process from scratch, what would they be concerned about?*.

The intention is to talk about risk in language the stakeholder can easily understand, even better without using the actual word *risk* itself.

Failure of a control is *not* a risk.

Potential hurdles to watch out for include participants raising, for example, *failure of account reconciliation* as one of their concerns. Account reconciliation is a control that detects occurrences of multiple risks, including the risk of transactional error or internal fraud, as highlighted in Figure 5.5. In

Figure 5.5 Use of the bow-tie model in RCSA process: risks

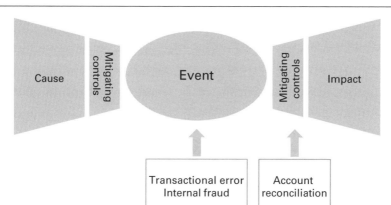

this case the facilitator needs to bring the focus back to the risk: one way of achieving this is via the use of the bow-tie model outlined in Chapter 1. This model, yet again, helps us to visually differentiate between materialized risks (events) and their causes and impacts, as well as the controls discussed later in this chapter. Skilled operational risk practitioners operate the bow-tie model subconsciously, automatically converting inputs into the right formulation of risks.

Often the answers to the open question will cover most of the necessary ground, but a few remaining risks will emerge from the second question.

The leading question

The second, follow-on question is about completeness. Simply put, it comes down to what else *should* be keeping the stakeholder awake at night. This is where the risk taxonomy – whether the Basel version, ORX or internally developed – is particularly handy, helping the discussion to become leading, or 'menu-based'. The risk practitioner encourages the stakeholder to consider relevant topics not brought up previously; for example, considering the possibility of future technology failures and their impact on the business; probing whether their exposure to money laundering is increasing; or whether internal fraud is more or less likely to happen than previously.

Facilitating free-flowing stakeholder conversations does not mean arriving at the meeting unprepared. On the contrary, the more skilled and equipped with information the risk expert is, the more confidently they will hold their ground at the session.

Before the meeting, the risk professional must have formed their own view on what risks they expect to come up, based on their understanding of the business and its environment. A pre-reading pack with supplementary information is an essential aid for the assessment. Pack materials might include:

- strategy and business plan, financials, minutes of governance committee meetings, planned material change programmes;
- operational risk data, including a history of operational risk events, Key Risk Indicators, and outputs from previous RCSAs if they exist (Note: these are certainly useful, but it is important not to allow them to limit the scope of the current assessment);
- output from other control disciplines, for example, compliance assessments and internal audit reports;
- data from external sources, including external loss data for peer firms, information on the regulatory landscape and priority areas for home and host state regulators.

Detailed preparatory work, including close examination of the pack, enables the risk practitioner to be an equal partner in the discussion, effectively providing *oversight and challenge*.

The prioritization question

The third part of the conversation needs to concentrate on *how much* the raised concern is keeping the stakeholder awake at night. In practical terms, what monetary loss do they expect to sustain next year as a result of the concern? What level of customer harm, reputational damage or regulatory censure is anticipated? This line of questioning helps to evaluate the risks relative to each other; some being more significant than others in terms of impact. Which brings us neatly to risk assessment.

Assessing risks

Risk assessment needs to be carried out on both an inherent and a residual basis.

Residual risk

Residual risk is the risk remaining after the application of controls, and is quite intuitive. Stakeholders are asked to articulate – even given the current control environment – what still *keeps them awake at night*. This kind of questioning reflects the existing state of the environment, 'as is', and participants are usually easily able to perform the assessment.

Inherent risk

Inherent risk is the risk before the effect of the existing controls. It is a less intuitive concept, as it can be very challenging for business units to try to imagine their environment without controls. It is also a very specific form of risk jargon, whether expressed in English or other languages. Depending on the maturity and level of risk knowledge of the audience, at times it may be best, therefore, to start the risk assessment by evaluating the level of residual risk first, followed by inherent risk; perhaps using the more intuitive wording *how much worse could it be if the primary controls failed?*.

Risks are commonly assessed in two dimensions: the likelihood of their occurrence and their impact.

Likelihood means the possibility of the risk materializing in the future, expressed using a range of values. While the methods used by organizations to articulate likelihood vary considerably – with time horizons that may stretch from 12 months out to 100 years – RCSAs are typically confined to the current business cycle and thus focus primarily on the near term (one–five years). The tool is not intended to analyse worst-case or catastrophic events – for example, a 1-in-100-year flood. Those are generally addressed through a separate scenario analysis, as discussed in Chapter 8. Some firms do, however, find it useful to highlight extreme risks as part of the RCSA exercise; noting them down as *potential candidates* for scenario analysis and developing them further at a later stage.

The second dimension, risk *impact*, evaluates the consequences, both financial and non-financial, of risk materializing. The unified impact rating grid has already been introduced in Chapter 4, in Figure 4.2.

While the most common non-financial impacts consist of client, regulatory and reputational consequences, firms may also add other categories; for example *people* impact – perhaps evaluating the scope for physical and psychological injury to staff; *resilience* impact, which is particularly relevant for payment service providers, central banks and other organizations where stability of service delivery is crucial to the operation of the firm, its customers, or even the economy more widely.

These two dimensions, impact and likelihood, when combined, reflect the overall exposure of the firm to the identified risk. This finds its place on a *heat map*, an example of which is presented in Figure 5.6.

Figure 5.6 Risk grading matrix

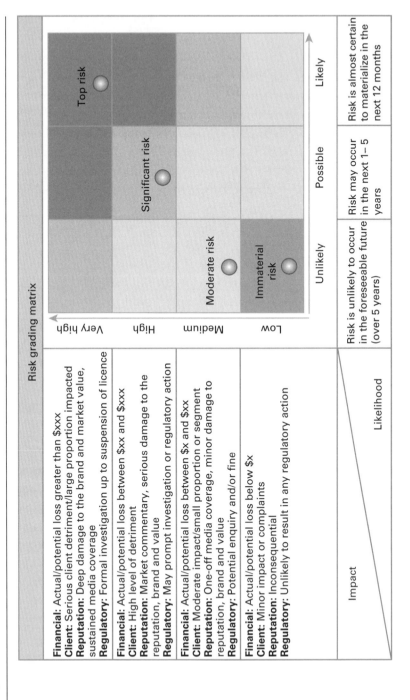

Risk grading matrix

		Unlikely	Possible	Likely
Impact	Very high			Top risk
	High		Significant risk	
	Medium	Moderate risk		
	Low	Immaterial risk		
	Likelihood	Risk is unlikely to occur in the foreseeable future (over 5 years)	Risk may occur in the next 1–5 years	Risk is almost certain to materialize in the next 12 months

Very high
Financial: Actual/potential loss greater than $xxx
Client: Serious client detriment/large proportion impacted
Reputation: Deep damage to the brand and market value, sustained media coverage
Regulatory: Formal investigation up to suspension of licence

High
Financial: Actual/potential loss between $xx and $xxx
Client: High level of detriment
Reputation: Market commentary, serious damage to the reputation, brand and value
Regulatory: May prompt investigation or regulatory action

Medium
Financial: Actual/potential loss between $x and $xx
Client: Moderate impact/small proportion or segment
Reputation: One-off media coverage, minor damage to reputation, brand and value
Regulatory: Potential enquiry and/or fine

Low
Financial: Actual/potential loss below $x
Client: Minor impact or complaints
Reputation: Inconsequential
Regulatory: Unlikely to result in any regulatory action

Heat maps attract criticism due to their imprecision and the high level of human judgement involved in the assessment process. And it is important to recognize these limitations. The value of the exercise is more to compare risks relative to each other, to understand which ones are more material and need to be prioritized for remediation. The aim is not to find a *perfect risk position* on the grid. Understanding these constraints helps the tool to be used appropriately as a visual aid supporting the exercise.

Assessment scales often start out as compact 3×3 dimensional matrices, with some more extensive versions being as large as 20×20. A more sensibly sized matrix of 4×4 is usually sufficient, preferably with an even (rather than odd) number of cells, to discourage any tendency for participants to aim for a mid-point and 'sit on the fence'.

Potential methodological enhancements for the risk grading tool are described below.

More on risks: velocity, killer risks, risk acceptance

Risk velocity

An additional third dimension, *risk velocity*, is useful to understand how quickly a given risk is expected to change its position on the matrix. Some risks may develop rapidly and start posing a threat which was not evident before, and therefore require more focus at an earlier stage. Where velocity is not used, *risk direction* (e.g. increasing, decreasing) can be outlined.

Killer risks

One of the key learnings that came out of the Covid-19 pandemic is the danger of deprioritizing material risks which are deemed *unlikely* to happen. The threat of infectious diseases was in fact identified in the January edition of the 2020 global risk report by the World Economic Forum, rated as significant but with relatively low likelihood.[6] This was an interesting finding which has been extensively discussed by the risk community, including questions as to what the risk profession could have done better to ensure pandemic preparedness. One possibility, therefore, for enhancing the risk matrix is to take the probability out of the equation for risks with a *very high* impact. As a result, the *entire row of very high* risks can be viewed as *top* or

Figure 5.7 Risk grading matrix: extending top risks

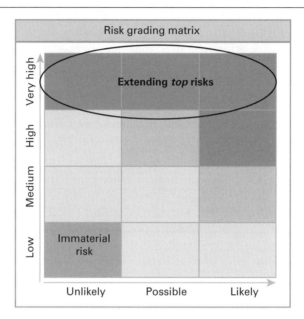

killer risks as described in Figure 5.7; prompting to concentrate on their mitigation regardless of the likelihood score. In fact, this approach has been adopted by multiple regulatory bodies in terms of *operational resilience*, where it is assumed that disruptions *will occur*. Therefore, the firms are requested to focus on mitigating the impact only, building strength, and maintaining continuity.

Escalation, appetite, acceptance

Heat maps are very useful in helping to guide end-users on subsequent action. For example, the level of *escalation* required for residual risks, depending on their magnitude, can be articulated with the help of the heat map, with more material risks needing to be brought to the attention of the board and senior committees. Similarly, the heat map can be used to define which risks lie outside the firm's appetite, will not be tolerated and require mitigation. Rules can also be set around *risk acceptance*, determining what authority is required to accept each risk level. For example, *moderate* risks can be accepted by the head of the business or support function if mitigation is not cost-effective; *significant* risks require appropriate committee sign-off, while *top* risks will be considered in exceptional circumstances only, and with the approval of the board. It is useful to instil a structured process, whereby risk acceptances for *significant* and above risks are logged and reviewed at least annually. This is important in ensuring that decisions remain valid with the change in strategy and business environment.

Documenting risks

What is the right way to document risks, and how prescriptive should the format be? The documentation methodology will vary depending on the type of the exercise:

- Allow stakeholders, aided by risk practitioners, to phrase their risks in their own language (free style). This approach is suitable for strategic risk assessments with a senior audience.

- Provide guidance language, based on the premise that risk is a negative statement. This approach will typically make use of words such as *inability*, *inadequate* and *failure of*. For example: *Inability to identify and implement new regulatory requirements on a timely basis, resulting in fines, regulatory censure and reputational damage.* This approach is not overly prescriptive hence appropriate for most assessments.

- Establish a format along the lines *there is a risk of... due to... resulting in... .* For example: *There is a risk of data breaches due to inappropriate data usage by staff, leading to fines, client harm and reputational damage.* This is a sensible structure but should be used with caution. The *due to* element can inadvertently lead to a proliferation of identified risks, by exploring multiple causes which all lead to the same risk materializing.

- Develop a library of risks, where the stakeholders can select pre-populated risks that specifically relate to them.

The more prescriptive the approach, the more consistent the documentation of the risks. However, some of the nuances and real concerns may be lost, and the value of the exercise diminished accordingly. After all, when elaborating the firm's strategy, the chief executive and their team do not select strategic objectives from a predefined list of objectives. It is better for the risk practitioner to help the stakeholders articulate their risks in the required format while capturing as closely as possible the true meaning of what was said.

Identified risks need to be mapped to the firm's taxonomy, which allows for cross-comparison with other framework elements. Usually, RCSAs in the operational risk space lead to the identification of risks aligned to the Basel or ORX categorizations or the firm's internal classification. However, high-level strategic RCSAs – dealing with the risks that may prevent the firm from achieving its objectives – will usually highlight a broader spectrum of risks, including strategic and business risks.

Control identification, categorization and assessment

A control is an activity or process established to mitigate the risk and, as noted by COSO, is 'designed to provide reasonable assurance regarding the achievement of objectives'.[7]

Every risk is typically mitigated by a multitude of controls. For RCSA purposes we are looking for *key* controls, or the controls which mitigate the risk *the most effectively* – and thus cannot be left out of the assessment. In arriving at the determination of whether or not a control is *key*, it is useful to consider what the impact would be if the control was removed.

There is no prescribed number of controls to mitigate each risk. But the suggestion is to identify at least one primary control, and no more than three to five in total.

Control identification

In a similar way to risk identification, controls can be defined during one-to-one interviews with SMEs.

As with risks, approaches vary when it comes to documenting controls and deciding on how rigid the format should be:

- Provide minimum guidance to ensure the process referred to is known and understood, for example, *account reconciliation, client due diligence, employee recruitment*; this approach should certainly be used in high-level assessments.

- Prescribe the format, requesting a description of both the process and its results, and noting, at minimum, *what, who* and *when*. [what?] Pre-employment screening is conducted for all staff [by whom?] by HR [when?] prior to employment. This is a useful format which results in controls being described quite specifically, with allocated accountability for control performance and a defined *control owner*.

- Develop a library of controls, where participants can select existing controls that mitigate their risk.

A helpful way of thinking about controls is by categorizing them into *Preventative*, *Directive*, *Detective* and *Corrective* types, as described in Figure 5.8.

Preventative and *Directive* controls reduce the likelihood of risk materializing, by establishing processes which preclude the threat from happening, and clearly instructing employees to do the right things.

Detective and *Corrective* controls decrease the impact, via prompt identification of deficiencies and speedy remediation, not allowing the impact to spread.

The distinction described above is reflected pictorially in Figure 5.9.

There is a clear relationship between the inherent and residual risk levels, which is directly dependent on the controls in place. If an inherent risk (say Risk 1, as depicted in Figure 5.10) is mitigated only by preventative or directive controls, that will reduce the likelihood of its occurrence, i.e. move the risk horizontally (left) along the heat map to assume residual position 1.1. Conversely, controls which are solely detective or corrective will only allow the risk to move vertically (downwards), decreasing its impact to a residual level of 1.2.

Figure 5.8 Control categorization

	PREVENTATIVE	DETECTIVE	
Reduce likelihood	Prevent risk from happening **Examples:** Segregation of duties User access rights Client due diligence	Help to identify if risk has materialized **Examples:** Reconciliation Control testing and assurance Reviews	Reduce impact
	DIRECTIVE	**CORRECTIVE**	
	Provide guidance and direction on tasks and duties **Examples:** Policies and procedures Training	Ensure continuous improvement **Examples:** Implementation of internal audit recommendations Actions from OREs	

Figure 5.9   Use of the bow-tie in RCSA process: controls

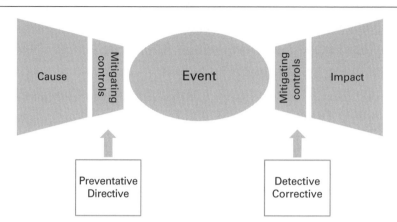

In order for the risk to move diagonally (to position 1.3), both types of controls have to be present and effective.

This point is important as sometimes inherent and residual risk levels are assessed independently and placed on the heat map in almost random positions; not substantiated by mitigating controls.

RCSA encourages users to directly evaluate the controls that they operate. If one of the key controls is owned by another function, it can still be included and relied on (with the agreement of the respective function). This is a good practice which prompts employees to collaborate and explore risk and control interconnectedness. For example, a business may own the risk of *inability to identify and implement new regulatory requirements on a timely basis*; and include its own controls as well as an additional regulatory horizon scanning control owned by the compliance function.

Control assessment

Assessment of controls establishes how effectively they are being implemented in practice, and therefore to what extent they reduce the level of inherent risk. There are two main methodologies for this form of assessment: either judgemental evaluation or factual testing.

Judgemental evaluation

Evaluation involves SMEs opining on control effectiveness based on their knowledge and experience. The rating can be one-dimensional, for example

Figure 5.10 Residual risk dependency on controls

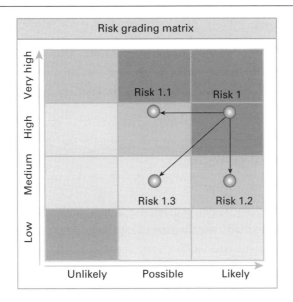

'effective', 'somewhat effective' or 'ineffective'. Or it can be carried out on a two-dimensional scale:

- *Control design*: this considers how well the control has been built to mitigate the risk; is it automated or manual, and does it mitigate the risk fully?

- *Control performance*: this considers how the control operates in practice, including the human element; whether employees are appropriately skilled and execute the task correctly, on the required frequency and to the expected quality standard.

Following evaluation of each control individually, it is beneficial to assess the *overall suite* of controls, considering whether in aggregate they provide a sufficient level of risk reduction. An ineffective overall control suite may reveal a missing control which needs to be considered in addition.

Testing

Testing is a process which involves selecting a representative sample of control performances to establish how effectively the control is operating.

CASE STUDY 5.2

A private bank develops a control testing programme to periodically check the key controls that mitigate its most significant inherent risks. An example test programme plan is created, describing the risk, the control, the test plan and its frequency.

Risk to appropriateness and suitability

Selling products that do not fit clients' risk appetite or investment profile, resulting in sales-related complaints.

Control

Prior to conducting any trading or investments on a client's behalf, an investment risk profile is established, reflecting the client's investment objectives and risk appetite. This is agreed with the client and updated with the frequency required by policy.

Test plan

Select a sample of 25 accounts opened during the last quarter, and ascertain the date of the first investment transaction from the system:

- review whether or not the investment risk profile is present in the client file and has been approved by the appropriate investment specialist;

- check that investment specialist's sign-off precedes the date of the first transaction, as identified above;

- select a sample of 15 existing customer account relationships and confirm that their investment profiles have been updated according to the frequency established by policy.

Test frequency: quarterly

The testing programme is approved and operated effectively by the institution. Use of test scripts with clear control objectives and defined sample sizes allow staff with no audit or risk background to perform effective testing in line with internal audit practices.

In 2023, I ran a LinkedIn poll for my network of risk professionals to ascertain their view on control evaluation vs testing. The results are presented in Table 5.1 and demonstrate that almost all respondents employed at least some testing activity.

Table 5.1 Industry poll: should firms move away from judgmental evaluation of control effectiveness to conduct more testing?

Response	% of responses
Yes, more testing is needed	46
No, evaluation is sufficient	1
A good balance is best	53

RCSA workshops

RCSAs lend themselves well to workshops, which provide an opportunity to build on collective intelligence, debate ideas and challenge assessments. Workshops are usually arranged as a follow-up to individual interviews, where participants have already considered their risks and controls, thus laying a foundation for the joint meeting. They are, however, an expensive tool as they collect multiple senior people in the room for a period of time. Consequently, they require maximum preparedness, with clear messages on what is expected to be achieved, how the meeting will be run and how long it will take. Good workshop organization includes inviting the respective *risk owners* for the whole duration of the meeting, while allocating specific time slots to discuss particular controls. Using this approach, *control owners* or SMEs – such as Human Resources for people-related controls or Technology for information technology-related matters – need only join for their allocated time slot. This saves SMEs time, makes the meeting more focused and moves it along. Facilitation is a key skill which needs to be mastered by the workshop leader; this is discussed further in Chapter 11. Short, targeted meetings facilitated by expert operational risk teams are typically well received by attendees and this helps to achieve the desired outcomes.

RCSA life cycle and measures of success

The RCSA life cycle is presented below: the first two components, identification and assessment, have already been covered in this chapter:

- **Identify:** significant risks which may prevent the achievement of objectives are identified, together with the controls that mitigate them.

- **Assess:** risks and controls are evaluated using a defined methodology.
- **Conclude and act:** results are presented to achieve formal sign-off and agreement of action plans for any areas where controls are ineffective or insufficient to mitigate the risks.
- **Refresh:** RCSA is updated periodically or based on particular trigger events.

Conclude and act

To finalize the exercise, the executive owner is required to sign off that the RCSA is a true and fair reflection of the risk and control profile of their respective area; and most importantly, to consider the 'so what?' question, confirming actions and next steps. Presenting the results in a clear manner, with key messages and actions outlined, supports the conclusion. A meaningful three-page report will contain:

- Page 1: an executive summary explaining the overall risk profile, whether it is elevated, has decreased or remained stable and articulating key changes since the last assessment. This summary needs to be supported by key facts, such as OREs, issues, audit and compliance findings, which should correlate to key messages in the summary.
- Page 2: visual aids that support the narrative: for example, a heat map drawing attention to the most significant risks, or a radar chart which is effective in pointing out risk and control relationships, highlighting risks as well as areas that may be overcontrolled.
- Page 3: a list of actions and/or risk acceptances, with target dates and owners, for the approval of the executive owner.

The executive owner signing the report must be the direct report of the Chief Executive Officer, possessing the required authority, budget and resources to act on the results. One of the reasons RCSAs are perceived as not truly influencing business decisions is the fact that the results are not presented to individuals with decision-making powers.

Refresh

RCSA is a living document which needs to be kept current. This has historically been a challenge, and remains so. As noted by the ORX industry study, 'RCSAs are often out of date'.[8] Usually a periodic – e.g. semi-annual – refresh is combined with trigger-based updates. The trigger can be a material change to the business model, product set or organizational structure; anything that creates impetus to revisit an area's capability to continue delivering on its objectives given the change. A significant ORE that raises a question on control effectiveness, an external event or a major regulatory change can also serve as triggers. In the periodic refresh, it is worth following the same structure adopted in the main RCSA process: three questions, starting with seeking an understanding of what keeps the stakeholder *awake at night* at any given moment; aiming to elicit material changes since the last update.

The usual risk management life cycle is comprised of the components identify–assess–manage–report. So the valid question may arise: what about reporting? Monitoring and reporting of *top risks* is undertaken via Key Risk Indicators (KRIs), which are a suitable way to address these key components of the overall life cycle. This is discussed further in Chapter 7.

Marketing the benefits and measuring success

RCSA is a significant value-added activity, and known benefits of a well-executed RCSA programme include the following:

- process optimization, enhanced operational resilience and a well-developed customer-centric mentality (where the PRSA methodology is used);
- sound strategy setting with a good understanding of risks (where SRA is used);
- prioritization for budget and resource spend;
- evidenced support for senior management certifications and attestations;
- an improved control environment, through the identification of weaknesses and implementation of adequate corrective actions;
- documented agreement where risk is accepted and no further action is needed;
- positive cultural impacts: *risk conversations* encouraging risk thinking and elevating risk and control consciousness at all levels of the firm.

However, RCSA *marketing* is rarely consciously undertaken, and all the positive points described above are rarely publicized and drawn attention to. The commencement of the programme is commonly announced via an email stating that departments are required to complete an annual RCSA refresh by a certain date. This creates a sense of a *task* added to the to-do list rather than something that business units *want to do* due to its benefits. Therefore, investing efforts into *marketing* the tool, finding all the salient points and positioning them upfront is essential.

To support the value proposition of RCSA, it is also a good practice to develop specific *measures of success*. These can include:

- RCSA as a driver of change: any actions emanating from the RCSA – ideally with the monetary value of any improvement projects initiated as a result of the programme – are good measures of how useful the exercise has been.

- RCSA as a driver of transparency around the risk and control environment. RCSA should minimize surprises in subsequent internal or external audit reviews, as material risks are already known and addressed. In view of this, the number of new or unknown significant risks identified by internal audit (perhaps as a percentage of the total number of risks), can be used as a tangible measure of RCSA effectiveness. Some firms use a Management Awareness Rating System (MARS), where internal audit provides two ratings, one on the audit result and a separate one on the effectiveness of self-identification of risks and issues.

- RCSA as a robust risk management tool: surveys can be used to gauge stakeholders' feedback, especially after the RCSA is introduced for the first time or following a change in approach. The questions can be centred around the value RCSA delivered, asking for an outline of the most significant benefit. They can also enquire about the overall stakeholder experience, as well as collect views on what has worked and what can be improved.

An industry study I conducted in 2018 demonstrated that very few organizations explicitly measure the success of their RCSAs, as outlined in Table 5.2.

Table 5.2   Industry study: measuring success of RCSAs

RCSA measures of success	% firms
No formal measures of success	72
Actionability (number of emanating actions)	10
Risk awareness (no surprises in audits)	22
Other measures	5

Institute of Operational Risk (IOR), 2018, webinar

Roles and responsibilities

The role of the second line Operational Risk department is key to the success of the RCSA programme. The department is responsible for developing the approach and methodology; educating stakeholders on the process and expected benefits; completing pre-work and being fully conversant with the area's environment; mastering facilitation skills; as well as providing the usual oversight and challenge on whether the outcome reflects and correctly represents the environment. Ultimately, the operational risk team is largely responsible for the success (or failure) of the initiative.

As *risk and control owners*, first line business units and support functions are accountable for the robust identification and management of risk. It is to their benefit to ensure that the exercise is taken seriously, that the right stakeholders are at the table and that the RCSA generates meaningful results. First line functions must develop action plans to address weak controls, and track them through to resolution. Where business units have embedded operational risk coordinators, they can take on the role of risk experts, interviewers and workshop facilitators – leading the whole RCSA exercise – as long as the right level of knowledge and skills have been transferred to them by the second line team.

Below is a risk coordinator checklist.

FIRST LINE RISK COORDINATOR CHECKLIST: RCSAS

✓ Management and staff can consistently articulate top risks of their area.

✓ OREs and other relevant data are used to inform RCSA.

✓ Action is taken to manage the risks and improve poor controls.

✓ There is process and governance around decision-making. (What level of risk can be accepted? By whom?)

✓ RCSA is a living document and is refreshed with frequency set per policy and upon major change.

✓ RCSA results are used in decision-making.

Common challenges and good practices

Common challenges

Challenges that may be encountered when designing and deploying RCSAs are outlined below.

Stakeholders not engaged

RCSA is an up-front investment in understanding and improving the control environment to prevent potential risks materializing in the future. It is not always obvious to stakeholders why they should spend time *now* when nothing bad has happened (and may never happen). It is somewhat easier to spearhead the remediation of operational risk events, where the firm has already experienced unpleasant consequences; but more challenging to achieve the same level of engagement and interest in risk assessments. It is essential to have senior management, who are personally accountable for failures, fully involved in the process and fully conversant with the value proposition and the time commitment required. They should also ensure the scope of the exercise is explicitly agreed at the appropriate governance committee.

Underinvestment in risk expertise

As can be seen from this chapter, it is the author's opinion that risk teams play a crucial role in the whole RCSA process. Although RCSA has the word *self* in its name, business units rarely, if at all, have the maturity and understanding to conduct self-assessments on their own, without expert support. They need guidance on the level of granularity to adopt; the correct formulation of what is a risk (and what is *not* a risk); assistance on how to approach impact-likelihood assessment; and a general understanding of what good looks like. Forms, questionnaires and requests to complete Excel spreadsheets are not effective: RCSA needs to be *facilitated by a knowledgeable individual*. Perhaps the tool needs to be renamed to RCFA, risk and control *facilitated* assessment.

To provide the required level of support, risk teams, both second and first line, should have extensive experience not only in the risk discipline itself but also in the softer skill of facilitation. Underinvestment in this skillset will lead to a situation where neither the leaders nor the followers really know what they are doing. The whole enterprise will undergo an expensive exercise that only results in sub-optimal outcomes.

Disproportionate effort

If the approach is too granular (which is the case in many organizations), RCSAs may end up with hundreds and sometimes thousands of entries – emphasizing *quantity over quality* and quickly leading to organizational fatigue. After all, no firm will be actively managing 500+ risks. While there is no accepted standard number of risks, a departmental RCSA will probably generate a range of 10 to 15 risks, with three to five key controls per risk. Not all risks need to be recorded; the focus should be on material items, as smaller risks are less damaging. It is good practice to work this guidance into the assessment, for example, recommending the capture of only *top* and *significant* inherent risks (see Figure 5.6) and carving out less important entries.

RCSA not actionable

The RCSA is completed and filed, but no action emanates from the exercise due to an inability to draw conclusions, apathy, poor communication of the results or pitching to the wrong audience of non-decision-makers. A study of industry practices conducted by ORX concluded that RCSA is 'not sufficiently influencing business decisions' and 'not enabling institutions to be as proactive on risk management as intended'.[9] A lack of tangible outcomes leads to questions about the value of the programme, and major effort should be put in to deriving clear, well-worded actions and next steps.

Good practices

Correct approach

RCSAs are typically applied across the whole organization and remain the most demanding, laborious and time-consuming of all the tools in the operational risk framework. Therefore, it is worth investing time and thought up-front into developing the right approach. It is recommended that the exercise only commences after a detailed research review of relevant literature; benchmarking against the industry and discussion with fellow practitioners to draw out good practices; and conversations with senior management on the desired outcomes. Allocating enough budget to obtain external consultancy advice and provide the necessary training for facilitators helps considerably in achieving the right outcomes.

Identification of overcontrolled areas

As part of the RCSA exercise, it is good practice to focus on any areas that might be overcontrolled, in addition to searching for gaps and weaknesses. This not only provides a more balanced view on the control environment but also results in potential cost savings where unnecessary controls can be reduced or eliminated. This is a valuable activity that is not undertaken enough in the industry; control reduction may be an uncomfortable subject for both senior executives as well as for some risk practitioners.

Reflection of outsourced activities

In cases where the organization outsources activities to a third party or another group entity, the risk is still owned by the entity and this should be fully recognized in the RCSA. For example, if the process of developing and maintaining credit models is performed by a third-party provider, the organization will need to reflect *outsourcing risk* (including third-party failure and inadequate oversight) as well as *model risk* (inaccurate design or implementation of models).

Aggregation

One of the common questions around RCSAs relates to aggregation. As articulated in this chapter, both *bottom-up* and *high-level* assessments are needed. High-level assessments are, effectively, judgemental summaries of more detailed results, using the collective intelligence of senior leaders across the organization. Executives arriving at the top-down workshops may take their existing granular RCSAs into consideration, enabling them to arrive at the entity- or firm-wide view, which will inevitably be more elevated and thematic. If the firm is not in the habit of conducting high-level assessments, the second line Operational Risk department can take on the role of aggregating RCSA outcomes itself. This process also needs to be judgemental, with due consideration of key themes and using the firm's taxonomy to report on the results.

Embedding risk thinking

To ensure that risk assessments are properly embedded, business units and support functions can be encouraged to add a quick 'top of mind' risk identification exercise as part of their periodic departmental meetings. This can be accomplished by splitting employees into groups, with each group being asked to use a heat map to discuss what *keeps them awake at night* and comparing notes afterwards. Not only does this highlight true concerns, it also generates good risk conversations and exchanges of knowledge between employees. Similarly, an important activity that I lead every year via the Best Practice Operational Risk Forum is to benchmark top and emerging operational risks across the financial services industry. Practitioners from various firms are split into groups and use a simple heat map which invariably generates a lively debate and important outcomes.

Industry benchmark

The perpetual topic of RCSAs always causes a debate on the ways to increase their value. In 2023, half of Best Practice Operational Risk Forum members believed that RCSA effectiveness could be improved (50 per cent, Figure 5.11), although some were in a better place, with 22 per cent evaluating the tool as 'effective'. The poll reflects a challenge the firms are continuously facing in keeping the high level of business engagement and generating outputs that are used by senior management in decision-making.

RCSAs were primarily seen as a time-consuming exercise (53 per cent, Figure 5.12). The overall perception of business units has deteriorated as compared to previous years, as the results of a similar poll taken in 2019 reflected that employees seemed to have embraced RCSAs and accepted that

Figure 5.11   Industry poll: RCSA effectiveness

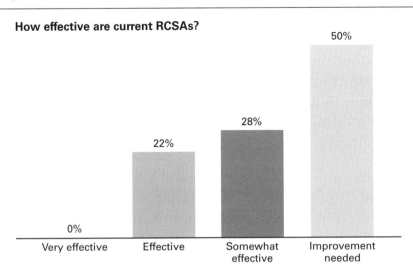

Best Practice Operational Risk Forum, 2023

Figure 5.12   Industry poll: first line perception of RCSAs

1st line perceives RCSAs as

Best Practice Operational Risk Forum, 2023

they were a necessity, with 22 per cent noting that the process was adding value. In contrast, in 2023 no respondents chose value-added option (see first edition of this book for further details of 2019 poll results).

What are the reasons for this deterioration? While operational risk management is still a developing discipline and a gradual evolution is expected year-on-year, the progress to maturity is not linear, but rather goes through peaks and troughs. The decline is attributed to multiple factors, including:

- Challenging macroeconomic and geopolitical environment, recession and rising interest rates, pushing firms to revisit the resilience of their business models and thus impacting people, their workload and priorities. In stressed environments, first line business units concentrate on pressing matters with less time left for quality RCSAs discussions.

- Operational risk digitalization not keeping up with the pace of automation within the firm. While many first line units benefit from instant access to information and use of AI and data science for decision-making, operational risk RCSA are at times stored in multiple spreadsheets, or if systems are in place, they are cumbersome to use, making RCSA a rather laborious process.

- Chosen methodology: it appears that the more organizations persist in making their RCSA process rigid and complex, with predefined and pre-formulated risk and control libraries, the less room is available for free-flowing conversations on what actually keeps stakeholders awake at night.

- Cultural aspects, significant change in personnel – both within Risk departments as well as first line business units – have also influenced the scores.

Figure 5.13   Industry poll: maturity of control testing and assurance

Maturity of control testing and assurance

Best Practice Operational Risk Forum, 2023

Even so, risk professionals were confident that RCSA as a tool will continue to generate benefits. Targeted control testing programmes supplemented the value proposition, and were utilized by the majority of firms, with 13 per cent rating their assurance process as 'mature' and the rest at various stages of development (Figure 5.13), with a combination of testing carried out by first and second line units.

In conclusion, while there is no simple recipe, more positive outcomes can be delivered by applying situational awareness, which at times means reducing the scope of RCSA exercises to focus on material risks only (rather than performing a complete refresh); or re-balancing the use of core tools with more emphasis on scenario analysis. Replacing templates with meaningful facilitated discussions, applying risk acceptance and focusing more clearly on actionability will also bear fruit.

Practical workplace exercise

Consider key concepts and ideas examined in this chapter. Obtain an example of the firm's RCSA, and review it, considering:

1 Is the organization conducting both top-down strategic and more granular assessments?

2 Considering the most significant operational risk events of the past year, were the risks that the event may occur identified *before* the event?

3 If risks were identified, were they documented in the RCSA?

4 How is the exercise perceived by stakeholders and are there formal measures of success in place for the RCSA exercise?

5 Make notes of RCSA features that you particularly like.

6 What can be improved? Note down potential enhancements.

MAKE A DIFFERENCE (MAD) ACTION

Please outline key learnings and note down one specific action you will take after reading this chapter, to enhance risk and control self-assessments within your organization.

In summary, this chapter introduced RCSAs, a forward-looking tool for identifying and assessing risks that may prevent threats to the achievement of the firm's objectives.

The next chapter will focus on a supplementary assessment methodology for change initiatives.

Notes

1 Operational Riskdata eXchange Association (ORX) (2020) *Optimizing Risk and Control Self-Assessment*, orx.org/resource/rcsa-practice-benchmark (archived at https://perma.cc/GK3T-7AL7)

2 World Economic Forum (2024) *The Global Risks Report 2024*, www3.weforum.org/docs/WEF_The_Global_Risks_Report_2024.pdf (archived at https://perma.cc/ART5-T3RN)

3 The Sarbanes–Oxley Act of 2002, www.sec.gov/about/laws/soa2002.pdf (archived at https://perma.cc/CK4A-P6K3)

4 Committee of Sponsoring Organizations of the Treadway Commission (2017) *Enterprise Risk Management: Integrating with strategy and performance*, www.coso.org/enterprise-risk-management (archived at https://perma.cc/UC2D-TCLA)

5 Zeldin, T (1998) *Conversation: How talk can change your life*, The Harvill Press

6 World Economic Forum (2020) *The Global Risk Report 2020*, www.weforum.org/reports/the-global-risks-report-2020 (archived at https://perma.cc/7JAY-YYWB)

7 Committee of Sponsoring Organizations of the Treadway Commission (2013) *Internal Control: Integrated framework*, www.coso.org/guidance-on-ic (archived at https://perma.cc/3P9A-Q6XZ)

8 Operational Riskdata eXchange Association (ORX) (2020) *Optimizing Risk and Control Self-Assessment*, orx.org/resource/rcsa-practice-benchmark (archived at https://perma.cc/J7T3-6EHG)

9 Operational Riskdata eXchange Association (ORX) (2020) *Optimizing Risk and Control Self-Assessment*, orx.org/resource/rcsa-practice-benchmark (archived at https://perma.cc/J7T3-6EHG)

Operational risk assessment of change initiatives 06

What this chapter covers: This chapter continues discussion on the topic of risk assessments, outlining an approach to evaluating the risks associated with change initiatives (Figure 6.1). It is centred on the *Scope–Methodology–Integration* trilogy: defining the range of activities that benefit from further scrutiny; presenting techniques for conducting a *risks* and *opportunities* assessment; and considering how to effectively transition residual risks to a 'business-as-usual' (BAU) environment. The chapter analyses specific features of new product and system launches, projects and regulatory programmes; and highlights the value of post-implementation reviews. It includes examples, case studies and an industry benchmark.

FURTHER READING

- Helen Winter (2019) *The Business Analysis Handbook: Techniques and questions to deliver better business outcomes*, Kogan Page

  Why recommended: This book is valuable for learning about project management, including tools and techniques such as RAIDs (risks, assumptions, issues, dependencies) and process mapping, as well as waterfall/agile methodologies, in language that is engaging and easy to understand.

- Dr Spencer Johnson (1999) *Who Moved My Cheese? An amazing way to deal with change in your work and in your life*, Ebury Publishing

  Why recommended: An old-time favourite, this entertaining book on the crux of change management is a must-read for every risk practitioner. It is still widely read, by both individuals and teams, and especially during major corporate transformations.

Figure 6.1   Focus of Chapter 6: risk assessments

Embedding and maturity assessment

Risk culture

Governance, roles and responsibilities
Establish governance and clear roles across the Three Lines for managing operational risk.

Risk appetite and risk capacity
Define nature and types of risk accepted in pursuit of strategic objectives. Evaluate adequacy of capital resources.

Operational risk events	Risk assessments	Scenario analysis	Key Risk Indicators
Record and report risk events, act to minimize future exposure. Monitor trends against RCSAs and KRIs.	Assess risk exposure in process, business or function via RCSAs. Supplement by evaluating risks emanating from change activities via ORAs.	Identify exposure from extreme but plausible events. Mitigate through risk transfer to insurance.	Monitor risk and control performance through predictive indicators. Act if indicators breach established appetite threshold.

Reporting and decision-making
Review actual risk profile against set appetite, apply active risk management to enable achievement of strategic objectives.

Training and education

Operational risk taxonomy

Trilogy: Scope–Methodology–Integration

'Nothing is permanent except change.' This quote is attributed to Heraclitus, a Greek philosopher famous for proclaiming that change is the essence of the universe, and author of a well-known saying about not stepping into the same river twice. Financial services as an industry is characterized by an enormous amount of transformation, driven by technological advancements and new regulation. In this dynamic environment, are the risks inherent in change activities identified and managed consistently and effectively?

One of the Basel Principles for the sound management of operational risk evolves around assessments of operational risks for all 'material new products, activities, processes and systems'.[1] According to the Basel Committee's survey, only two-thirds of respondents conducted such assessments; a rather meagre uptake given the importance of this principle.[2]

Indeed, the sheer breadth of firms' change agenda often hinders the implementation of a uniform approach. The most common challenges include:

- a struggle to come up with a *holistic definition* of change, which results in the governance framework not covering all types of initiatives;
- decentralized management of change activities, resulting in *inconsistent treatment* across initiatives;
- sub-optimal transition to a *business-as-usual* state, with a lack of monitoring of risks emanating from the initiatives and an absence of formal *post-implementation reviews*.

Recognizing these potential weaknesses, Basel Committee purposefully strengthened the requirements in its latest 2021 update, demanding that senior management ensures that 'change management process is comprehensive, appropriately resourced and adequately articulated between the relevant lines' [of defence].[3]

Whether challenging or not, conducting operational risk assessment of change initiatives is simply and intuitively the right thing to do. Drawing parallels with credit risk, a firm is unlikely to lend money to a client without evaluating their creditworthiness: any governance committee would look in disbelief if such a proposal were presented. Similarly, major change to a process, system or product is prone to a wide spectrum of operational risks, and simply must not be implemented without the full understanding of the underlying risks it may pose.

Figure 6.2   Trilogy: Scope–Methodology–Integration

The role of the Operational Risk department in this area is instrumental. The function must take the lead in enabling the firm to apply a risk lens to change programmes, raising questions centred around three main topics, presented in Figure 6.2.

> **OPERATIONAL RISK FOCUS ON CHANGE INITIATIVES INCLUDES:**
>
> - *scope*: how to identify those activities that require an operational risk assessment (ORA);
> - *methodology*: what tools are best suited to assess the risks emanating from the initiative; and
> - *integration*: how to transition risks and their ownership into a business-as-usual environment on completion of the programme.

Identifying risky change activities

Change activities consist of a vast variety of events, including, for example:

- new product launches;
- system upgrades;
- relocation to a new building;
- payments process optimization;
- reorganization leading to offshoring of tasks to another location;
- implementation of a new regulatory requirement.

Every business/function within an organization will inevitably be managing a pipeline of projects. Among this sea of initiatives there could be a handful of potentially *riskier* programmes which could have significant impact outside the firm's appetite, and therefore would really benefit from increased scrutiny.

The role of the operational risk team is to develop criteria that enable a wide net to be cast to capture those activities that are more material and potentially more risky, ensuring that they undergo an ORA. This process is more powerful if done in close collaboration with project management functions (where they exist), to jointly agree on the most suitable approach.

Criteria for material and therefore *riskier* change initiatives can be expressed via a set of parameters that are centred around:

- *criticality* of business processes impacted by the change (see Chapter 15, Operational resilience);
- *novelty*, e.g. whether the activity is business-as-usual or a new market or product; the less familiar the territory, the higher the risk;
- *scale/magnitude*, e.g. duration, resources, spend, number of impacted areas;
- *urgency*, considering whether implementation is being rushed through and therefore poses higher risk; and
- *complexity* of requirements, e.g. a new regulatory directive.

As an alternative, the determination can be also made using a more guided scorecard approach. This consists of developing a set of questions with predefined responses that have a score assigned to them. The overall sum of individual scores serves as a guide to suggest what category the change falls under – whether minor or material – thereby providing a triage mechanism. Examples of questions that can appear in the scorecard are presented in Table 6.1.

In any approach, it is not possible to cover all the idiosyncrasies of every change. Business units and support functions need to apply common sense to identify activities that may have material impact on the risk profile of the organization.

Table 6.1   Scorecard approach for assessing materiality of change initiative

Theme	Criteria	Score
Operational Resilience	Will the change pose a threat to operational resilience?	Score 1: No new system development; a minor process or people change in a non-critical business process
		Score 3: Limited system development, use of spreadsheets or other user-developed applications (also called *end-user computing* (EUC) applications); moderate process or organizational change in a non-critical business process
		Score 5: Significant system development, reorganization or process transformation; any change activity impacting a critical business process; or one requiring new or amended business continuity arrangements in a non-critical business
Outsourcing	Does the change involve outsourcing of all or part of the activities?	Score 1: No outsourcing
		Score 3: Limited change to the scope of existing outsourcing arrangement
		Score 5: Material new third-party or inter-group relationship
Data	Does the change involve processing of personal or sensitive information?	Score 1: No change to data processing
		Score 3: Moderate impact to a limited scope of internal use data only
		Score 5: A change to processing personal and/or sensitive information
Regulatory Compliance	Is there a risk of regulatory non-compliance?	Score 1: No regulatory impact
		Score 3: Potential limited fines for non-conformance
		Score 5: Regulatory-driven initiative with substantial fines or other penalties for non-compliance

Methodology: risks and opportunities assessment

ORA DEFINITION

The operational risk assessment (ORA) of change activity evaluates the risks emanating from the activity; which enables the relevant governance committee to take an informed Go/No-Go decision on its implementation.

Unlike RCSAs, as discussed in Chapter 5, ORAs are temporary and valid only for the duration of the initiative, leading to its implementation. After this they cease to exist, with any remaining risks being transitioned to business-as-usual. They are also linked directly to a specific decision requiring action. Therefore, while ORAs have some similarities with RCSAs, they also possess distinct features, as discussed in this chapter.

ORA IS A SHORTENED FORM OF RCSA:

- inherent risks are identified and evaluated in a similar manner;
- no control assessment takes place due to the activity being in a *transitional/project* mode; instead, actions to reduce the level of inherent risk throughout the duration of the programme are noted; and
- residual risk levels, anticipated after the completion of intended actions, are recorded.

Analogously to the RCSA, the ORA is ideally conducted via a cross-functional workshop with subject matter experts, facilitated by a skilled operational risk professional. The facilitator leads the discussion, drawing out the significant risks of the change activity. To ensure a consistent approach across the organization, the same risk grading matrix introduced for RCSAs (see Chapter 5, Figure 5.6) should also be applied for ORAs. This familiar matrix prompts consideration of impact and likelihood, providing uniformity not only to the approach, but also to the meaning of the risk levels, from *low* to *high*.

Two potential methodological enhancements are described below:

1 First, some initiatives, for example new products, are prone to credit, market, strategic, business and other risks. The coverage of the assessment can be *expanded* to a broader universe of threats, beyond operational, providing a rounded, all-encompassing view. This provides a perfect opportunity for operational risk professionals to exhibit their facilitation skills and, at the same time, increase their exposure to a wider universe of risks.

2 Second, the evaluation can be enriched by supplementing the 'risks' view with the mirror view of 'opportunities'.

Risks and Opportunities assessment aims to create a balanced view of threats and benefits, emphasizing the positive aspects of risk management.

EXAMPLE ORA

The firm is evaluating a new proposition which includes the use of narrow artificial intelligence (AI) for providing personalized insights to clients based on their transactional history.

Identified risks include:

- AI displacing workforce;
- software failure or glitches impacting performance;
- risk of poor machine conduct, resulting in inadequate or discriminatory advice;
- inappropriate use of data leading to potential privacy breaches;
- cyber risk: the probability of cyber incidents occurring and their impact.

Opportunities include:

- speed and efficiency;
- availability of advice 24/7;
- enhanced quality of insight based on data analysis;
- cost reduction.

Figure 6.3 Risks and opportunities matrix

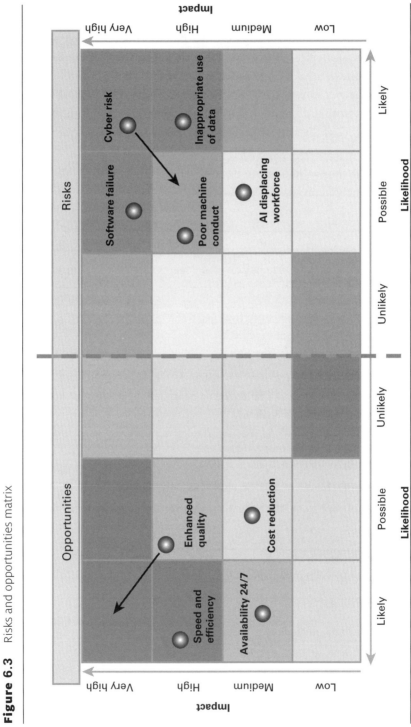

Risks and opportunities are plotted on a double-sided heat map (see Figure 6.3) for an assessment of the threats and opportunities landscape and to help prioritize areas of focus. Can opportunities be maximized? Risks reduced? The purpose of the workshop with subject matter experts is to establish a consistent approach to the risk assessment and build on combined knowledge.

Following the exercise, detailed focus groups are established to further explore material risks, as well as opportunities.

The opportunity assessment can be undertaken when evaluating business prospects, products, ventures and processes. In fact, it is suitable for a balanced appraisal of any change activity. It reinforces *positive risk management*, an enabler not a show stopper, assisting business units to arrive at an honest picture of threats and benefits in order to weigh them up and take a prudent, risk-aware decision. In reality, the view that recognizes both risks and opportunities is not given enough airtime. The Risk department, like a gloomy critic, is often in the habit of highlighting the negatives and missing the positives. In a live poll conducted by the Best Practice Operational Risk Forum in 2020, less than half of respondents admitted to having a structured approach to identifying and evaluating the upside of risk.

When is the best time to perform an ORA? Ideally, at the inception of the product/process development, enabling valuable conversations around risks and opportunities to take place in a structured manner. This remains an industry challenge. On occasions, business units work on a new proposition for months before reaching a decision, with the operational risk function neither aware of the proposal nor present at the table. The risk assessment is then hastily completed at the end, to satisfy governance requirements, which devalues the process.

What steps should be followed to enact the ORA more meaningfully, ensuring that it takes place at the right time and in a disciplined manner?:

- Start with senior management education: outline the value of a clear articulation of risks and opportunities to help them reach a Go/No-Go decision.

- Provide broader education for relevant staff and first line champions: to help embed the use of the ORA tool, list examples and illustrate successful programmes where evaluation helped to identify significant risks.

Table 6.2   Example change landscape

No	Type of change activity	Materiality threshold?	Governance committee?	Committee name	Policy in place?	Policy name
1	New Products	Yes	Yes	NPA Committee	Yes	NPA Policy
2	System Changes	Yes	Yes	IT Change	Yes	IT Change Management
3	Projects	No	No	–	Yes	Project Management
4	Regulatory Programmes	No	Yes	Regulatory Programmes Oversight Committee	No	–
5	Process Changes	No	No	–	No	–

- Where change activity is overseen by a central governance committee, work in close partnership with the secretariat responsible for assembling committee papers; this will ensure that requests submitted without a completed ORA are caught on a timely basis and returned to the respective business/function.

- For decentralized activities – for example, process changes and reorganizations – collaborate with first line champions to facilitate implementation within their respective areas.

It is also useful to understand the overall landscape of change activities within the organization. The result can be documented in an inventory, an example of which is presented in Table 6.2.

This inventory will demonstrate that some initiatives, for example, new products, may already have set criteria to define *new* or *materially different* products, and are executed in a structured manner, with a dedicated policy and a governance committee. Others, for example, process changes, do not apply any notion of materiality, and are completely decentralized and implemented by each department in its own way.

To further illustrate the point, various types of change activities and their specific features are analysed below. (Note, the final part of the trilogy Scope–Methodology–Integration is covered later in the chapter as part of the change life cycle.)

Change activities and their features

New products

New Product Approval (NPA) is a process through which an organization channels new products or customer propositions, ensuring that rigorous review and sign-off take place prior to the product launch. In many organizations this process is relatively well-established and contains the following features:

- *Clear scope*: a definition of what constitutes a *new* and/or *significantly modified* product, thus capturing all initiatives that fall under the policy and providing a perfect trigger for an operational risk assessment. Where this is the case, no additional criteria or scoring are needed.
- *Central governance committee* that ultimately makes a Go/No-Go decision.
- *Defined roles* of product sponsor and *cross-functional reviewers* from operations, technology, finance, compliance and other functions, enabling a comprehensive and multifaceted product evaluation.

Compared to other change activities, NPA usually works like a well-oiled machine, with propositions going through defined steps, one of which is an ORA. Stakeholders are bound and energized by the same goal of getting the product launched. They have interest in achieving success, and a risk assessment to help the team identify and mitigate the risks of their *own* initiative is usually well received. A real measure of success is to have product owners *want* their projects to be evaluated, demonstrating their understanding of the value and benefits of prudent risk management.

System changes

System enhancements deserve special attention because of the fact that change management is cited as the number one root cause of technology outages and a threat to operational resilience.[4] To strengthen industry practices, as an example, the European Banking Authority specifically articulated ICT (information and communication technology) projects and change management principles, noting that 'financial institutions should appropriately monitor and mitigate risks deriving from their portfolio of ICT projects'.[5]

Information technology (IT) departments commonly have their own change management processes and categorizations of activities. The challenge is one of alignment. It is imperative for operational risk experts to work closely with IT colleagues to agree on what constitutes a material change. The criteria should not be skewed towards purely system considerations but should also extend to financial, client, regulatory and reputational impacts.

In contrast to new products, system enhancements employ a fair amount of technical jargon; this can result in stakeholders who are less IT-savvy becoming disengaged and the change being typically assessed and implemented by the Technology department itself. In contrast to NPA governance, this means that at times there is either no or minimal cross-functional review and sign-off of IT changes, despite the undoubted value in involving business units and support functions – the actual users of the technological solutions. Successful IT functions present their initiatives in simple language, explaining potential implications, encouraging dialogue and maximizing input from other departments.

CASE STUDY 6.1

In close collaboration with a business unit, the IT department is planning a system upgrade which will result in superior product features to the benefit of the clients. The change is regarded as *material* and triggers an ORA.

The operational risk team is facilitating a cross-functional workshop, and in addition to more common risks of *significant system failure* and *inadequate business continuity arrangements*, the risk of *unfair customer treatment* is raised. This emanates from an exception included in the small print of the product documentation. A particular customer segment has been excluded from the proposition, and the group questions whether as a result these customers may unfairly lose out on the service. This scenario has simply not been considered: the main reason provided is the clients' accounts of the excluded segment reside on a different, older platform which is becoming obsolete and therefore any upgrades are out of scope.

As a result of the discussion, the programme objective is amended to find appropriate solutions and make the offer available to all client groups.

This case study demonstrates the value of proper cross-functional risk conversations. Accomplished operational risk practitioners thrive on facilitating workshops with varied audiences, thinking out of the box and pulling out key risks, including the less obvious risks as well as the more common ones. Workshop facilitation is also addressed in Chapter 11, Operational risk training and education.

Additional challenges with system changes are related to the firm's culture, especially in matrix organizations where the IT department is set goals on a different basis than the rest of the organization. In an agile environment, this translates into IT work prioritization being at variance with the project manager's needs and expectations. Operational Risk has a role to play in ensuring that the ordering principles applied in the technology pipeline are appropriate; and that there is adequate governance in prioritizing, for example, regulatory requirements and business growth initiatives. Where the ranking of IT change activity conflicts with project requirements, it is important that the organization has effective conflict resolution mechanisms, with quick escalation so that decisions can be made by senior management.

Emergency upgrades deserve a special mention. In these cases, urgency is already embedded in the name, and consequently these implementations are risky by nature. There may not be time for a fully documented ORA, but a formal recognition of material risks, followed by a post-upgrade review, is essential for emergency upgrades. This ensures that the Technology department will not flick the switch without citing approvals from the key stakeholders.

Projects

Project managers may argue that they are already managing risks by using the RAIDs (risks, assumptions, issues and dependencies) concept which is a core part of project management methodology. However, operational risk management can still bring distinct value to this domain. The two disciplines are complementary. Experts running change initiatives are, naturally, mostly focused on the risks to the programme itself: the risks of not being on time or within budget, or of not delivering to the required specification. This is consistent with the definition of project risk used by the Project Management Institute: 'An uncertain event or condition that, if it occurs, has a positive or negative effect on one or more project objectives such as scope, schedule, cost and quality.'[6]

ORA will supplement this by bringing out the operational risks *inherent in the programmes.*

CASE STUDY 6.2

Due to a change in its business model, a corporate bank is planning to transition multiple customer accounts from one entity to another. A multi-year project is initiated, led by the central Programme Office.

Throughout the duration of the project, the risks of not delivering on time, on budget or failing to execute client transition seamlessly are rigorously identified and tracked via a central RAID log. Due to the magnitude of the programme, an ORA is also carried out and facilitated by the Operational Risk department. The assessment examines a range of risks and highlights an increased risk of external as well as internal fraud. Clients may be targeted by fraudsters during a mass change in account numbers; while employees may find the environment prime for unauthorized activity.

The ORA triggers further examination of these risks and a review of the overall internal control environment.

This case study reflects the complementary nature of the ORA and project RAIDs. And yet again, it highlights the significance of risk conversations facilitated by expert facilitators.

The traditional project methodology, also sometimes known as a waterfall approach, involves a sequential process of 'defining requirements before design starts, then design being completed before development starts'.[7] From a risk management perspective, these projects are easier to manage due to the fact that they involve robust governance, impact assessment and sign-offs at each stage prior to proceeding to the next stage.

More and more organizations are, however, moving to an agile environment. Agile projects apply an iterative approach, with teams working in parallel, delivering in increments and collaborating to evolve the design over time. This flexible methodology is based on self-organized teams, motivated individuals and face-to-face conversations, welcoming 'changing requirements, even late in development'.[8] From an operational risk perspective, agile projects pose more challenges compared to waterfall projects, simply due to their fluidity.

> Embedding operational risk specialists into agile teams is the ideal way of ensuring that *risk conversations* take place throughout an agile programme.

This does, however, place a high demand on risk resource, be it first or second line.

Agile environments also embrace the concept of a minimum viable product (MVP), a product which meets the basic design features and requirements but does not have all the bells and whistles that may be developed subsequently. By definition, an MVP may have limitations which create risks. It is essential that these risks are appropriately assessed to determine whether the limitation is acceptable against the overall risk appetite. For example, perhaps an MVP does not have a reporting capability which limits the performance management of a product; or regulatory reporting must be completed manually, leading to impacts (including errors and penalties) which are potentially outside the firm's appetite.

Regulatory programmes

JWG, a pioneering market intelligence company, performed the interesting exercise of counting the total number of pages of new regulation and estimating the height of the pile if they were stacked on top of each other. They noted that 'since the financial crisis, we have been gifted over two Eiffel Towers high worth of complex and costly financial regulation, ever increasing in quantity and intricacy'.[9] Needless to say, then, a large proportion of transformation is driven by regulation.

These regulatory change programmes are inherently risky. Countless examples of substantial supervisory fines demonstrate how easy it is to end up with inadequate implementation.

The key challenge of regulatory programmes evolves around the interpretation of voluminous technical texts, spanning hundreds of pages, into practical implementation. Among other things this interpretation process needs to point out which specific field in the system needs to be amended and how. Is the organization crystal clear on who is taking this decision? It may be assumed that this is the role of the compliance function. Compliance, however, will argue that they can recite the letter and the spirit of the regulation, but that it is up to business users, with their in-depth knowledge of the business process, to take the right decision. Assumptions will be made, and the best judgement of project participants will be accepted as the way forward. In these situations, ORAs are needed more than ever, to articulate the risks, including any uncertainty around the correctness of the application together with an assessment of the magnitude of its impact. However, this requires a level of maturity where *all* employees are sufficiently conversant with risk management concepts and tools to pause the discussion at the right point, in order to recognize and document the risks. Rarely is an organization this advanced. The path to success is in firm-wide education; and in the meantime, yet again, in embedding operational risk practitioners into major regulatory programmes, to facilitate *risk conversations*. Even this is often challenging, due to the scarcity of resource.

As an example, the Markets in Financial Instruments Directive (MiFID II), a complex piece of legislation, led to big changes in the structure and operating model for trading, treasury and support functions, and involved significant decisions being taken by project teams. In 2017, prior to the directive going live, I led an industry study to understand the extent to which operational risk professionals were party to the programme. This study revealed that in the majority of firms the project was run by compliance; and over half of operational risk practitioners admitted to having little or no involvement. A third of the group were members of the relevant governance committees, providing oversight at a high level; but only a minority were actively engaged facilitating ORAs. As part of the study, the group concluded that it was key for operational risk staff to get more involved in major initiatives of this kind; however, this inevitably clashed with other priorities.

For complex regulatory directives, multiple ORAs may be executed for logical sub-parts of the programme. As an example, MiFID II and the Global Data Protection Regulation (GDPR) generated a range of 10 to 20 separate ORAs, allowing the assessments to cover a wide range of the programme. In complex cases the process is iterative for each ORA, with an assessment conducted at inception and subsequently amended in the event of significant change to any of the parameters.

Process changes

This is the least homogeneous of all the change areas, and the one where clear criteria on what constitutes a *material* change is most needed. One way of handling process transformations is by extending existing governance – for example, NPA – to accommodate a broader set of initiatives, thereby ensuring the same rigour is applied to process changes, organizational changes, restructuring and others. In this way the NPA committee upgrades itself to NPCA – the New Product and *Change* Approval committee. In other cases, organizations create a separate material change committee. Most firms, however, do not apply consistent governance in this area. The lead from the Operational Risk department is absolutely essential, initiating the development of a set of parameters and embedding the discipline of risk assessing process changes.

Change assessment life cycle

The change risk assessment process life cycle is described below:

- **Scope:** a clear set of parameters is agreed in order to capture activities that require an operational risk assessment.

- **Assess:** a practice of risk assessing material change initiatives is adopted firm-wide.

- **Integrate:** a hand-over process is set up to transition residual risks into the BAU environment.

- **Check:** post-implementation reviews are conducted to evaluate success and derive lessons learnt.

- **Aggregate** and **Monitor:** the overall impact of multiple transformations on the risk profile of the firm is assessed and monitored via Key Risk Indicators.

The first stage (scope), describing the parameters which differentiate significant initiatives, was covered at the beginning of this chapter.

Assess

As outlined earlier, ORA is a simple yet effective way of evaluating the risks of change initiatives, using the already-familiar risk grading matrix. Are there alternatives to ORAs, and what other approaches exist for dealing with change risks?

- Where ORA is not used, the change may serve as a trigger to revisit an existing risk and control self-assessment. While this approach is plausible, it does not lend itself well to the transient nature of the change.

- Scenario analysis can be conducted to examine extreme outcomes. This tool is supplementary rather than primary as it does not deal with volume – it is neither feasible nor necessary to run scenarios for each material change.

- There may be no specific assessment, but instead stepped governance, implemented based on the scale of the activity. This increases the level of scrutiny, but does not provide a structured approach to identifying and assessing risks.

Integrate

Integration is another key step in the *Scope–Methodology–Integration* trilogy. While change programmes are live, they attract attention, energy and rigour. We have all witnessed the decline that is triggered when project teams are disbanded, people leave and in-depth knowledge departs with them. It is vital to ensure transition not only of the relevant expertise, but also of any residual risks that have been flagged and not closed during the risk assessment stage.

Material residual risks not mitigated during the change programme must be formally handed over to the new business-as-usual owner, with the transfer being cemented by a sign-off from the recipient. The change activity cannot be considered complete without this sign-off.

The hand-over of risks is executed via transitioning a completed ORA to the now-accountable head of the business unit or support function. Challenges may arise at this stage if, during the programme, identified risks were assigned to a project resource – potentially not the owner who is best placed to understand, mitigate and treat them holistically. It is always advisable to involve BAU teams in the change activity from the beginning. Engagement and regular updates will ensure full proficiency in and agreement with the amended processes and controls; as well as the risks that the BAU team may need to manage in the future.

One possible solution is for the BAU risk owner to formally accept the residual risks of the initiative prior to going live, thereby acknowledging that these risks will now be managed as part of the business's overall portfolio of risks.

Check

Post-implementation reviews (PIRs) have multiple aims. Firstly, a PIR evaluates how effectively the project, programme or activity was run and what lessons can be derived for the future. Secondly, it determines whether initial objectives were met; for example, for new products, it allows comparison of actual volumes to forecasts, and an assessment of profitability and customer feedback. And finally, PIRs provide a great opportunity to do a *deep dive* into the control environment. If significant risks were identified during the initial risk assessment, the reviewer can cast a critical eye over the performance and quality of the controls that mitigate these risks. The latter element is rarely in scope and not considered nearly enough; yet, for regulatory programmes, for example, it provides an opportunity to ensure that controls are still operating as originally intended and that the operating environment has not deteriorated subsequently.

Post-implementation reviews are commonly conducted within three to nine months of the change. Sometimes they can be followed by an additional long-term review, within two years of completion of the change. PIRs can also be triggered by an increased incidence of operational risk events, signalling that transition to a BAU state has not been smooth.

Not all activities require a PIR. New products, system changes and regulatory programmes, however, are among those that most benefit from the look-back and re-evaluation that a PIR provides. It is also worth testing a sample of change initiatives that were not in scope of the initial risk assessment, to determine whether they actually should have been included. This acts as a deterrent against change owners understating the scale of the change to avoid review.

Aggregate and monitor

The aggregation step aims to assess the overall impact of multiple simultaneous initiatives and to evaluate whether the firm's *change risk* is elevated beyond its appetite. Various approaches are possible to achieve this:

- The most common consolidation is based on an inventory of initiatives in flight, prepared by a central change management function (if such a function exists within the organization). An appropriate governance committee reviews the list noting pressure points, including dependencies on key personnel, to weigh up whether the firm can cope effectively with the change portfolio. This results in a judgemental assessment of whether the overall impact of multiple transformations is tolerable.

- Another option is to add a *change risk* category into the operational risk taxonomy. As discussed in Chapter 1, the question of whether *change risk* is a distinct risk type or a cause of other risks crystallizing is an active debate, which has split opinion in the industry. If a separate category is used, functions can highlight the raised risk levels in their respective RCSAs, which can then be aggregated later.

- A final option is to perform a trigger-based review, via analysis of operational risk events and their root causes. An increase in the number and/or value of risk events with the same root cause (i.e. an excessive change agenda) will signal that immediate focus is required. While this kind of review is somewhat beneficial, it is a rather reactive approach.

Presented below are examples of Key Risk Indicators that can be useful for evaluating various aspects of change:

KRI1: *Change risk* – the percentage of overdue and at-risk projects within the active project portfolio. The KRI reflects on the overall health of the portfolio, monitoring the ratio of struggling programmes vs those that are on track.

KRI2: *Transition to business-as-usual* – the number of change activities where post-implementation reviews highlighted material issues. PIRs are used to measure the success of project discipline and the metric tracks unsuccessful and poorly implemented projects.

KRI3: *Risk assessments* – the number of material change activities in scope without a completed ORA. This metric is related to cultural aspects of the firm, and monitors compliance with the set process to ensure that change projects undergo a risk assessment.

Further KRI examples are discussed in Chapter 7, Key Risk Indicators.

Roles and responsibilities

Second line Operational Risk departments are the masterminds behind the change risk assessment methodology, working closely with relevant stakeholders – be they project, product or other teams – to ensure that ORA is integrated into business practices. Effective collaboration enables a firm to find the right solutions that are appropriate to the size, nature and culture of the organization. The Operational Risk department provides training and education for first line business units and support functions, and facilitates workshops. It is also the role of the department to oversee and challenge material initiatives, ensuring that the level of risk is commensurate with the activity, and reporting on the aggregate level of change risk to the relevant governance committees.

First line business units and support functions own the risks and are ultimately accountable for the success or failure of their initiatives. They are responsible for identifying material projects and programmes that fall within the set criteria, and for conducting ORAs as required. Where there are embedded first line operational risk champions, they help considerably in spreading knowledge and can serve as advisors and facilitators when it comes to ORAs.

A first line risk coordinator checklist can be found in the following box.

FIRST LINE RISK COORDINATOR CHECKLIST: ORAS

✓ Staff are aware of policy and governance for change activities.

✓ Change initiatives are evaluated according to the set criteria to define their materiality.

✓ ORA is completed for *material* change initiatives.

✓ Risks and opportunities are considered to arrive at a balanced view.

✓ Upon completion, remaining residual risks are transitioned to business-as-usual state in a disciplined manner.

✓ Post-implementation reviews are conducted.

Common challenges and good practices

Common challenges

Potential hurdles when dealing with change risk assessments are presented below.

Unbalanced goals and objectives

Cultural challenges may arise when business goals are weighted so heavily towards growth and efficiency that product and change owners are not incentivized to ensure that the control environment is appropriate to the risk that is being taken on. They may not necessarily see the review process as beneficial, rather as a necessary stage or even a hindrance to their project, and may refuse to jump through the approval hoops. The right tone at the top and balanced business goals that reflect the risk appetite of the organization help to address this challenge.

Lack of transparency from change sponsor

By the same token, if a risk-based approach is adopted for conducting ORAs for *riskier* initiatives, it is important to ensure that the sponsor provides a full perspective on the proposition so that it is not understated and as a result falls below the review threshold. This is a concern particularly if the owner does not see the review as beneficial or adding value.

Reluctance to complete the ORA

Business units and support functions may be reluctant to complete an ORA, reasoning that they do not have capacity and in any case that the review is a bureaucratic step which will not highlight anything new. The best way to convert the sceptics is to identify true risks that were missed or not thought of. Presenting past success stories, demonstrating that the Operational Risk department can skilfully lead discussions, facilitating workshops and lending your own expertise also help to change sceptical attitudes.

Incorrect roles and responsibilities

It is widely deemed to be the role of the operational risk team to complete the ORA. The Basel Committee noted this paradox in its survey,[10] emphasizing that actually first line business units and support functions are responsible for identifying and managing their *own* risks. Operational risk is a powerful facilitation partner but is not the owner (see also Chapter 3 highlighting roles and responsibilities of the Three Lines).

Criteria not fit for purpose

When the criteria for what constitutes a *material* change initiative are set too low, the exercise becomes a formality, a tick-box template. This can cause the business, as well as the Operational Risk department, to be overwhelmed by numerous unnecessary assessments. Using sound judgement helps to correctly calibrate the parameters and align the ORAs with the risk appetite of the organization.

Sub-optimal transition to business-as-usual

Sometimes, transition from the programme to a BAU state is sub-optimal; the project is closed without formally transferring the remaining risks, or the newly identified owner is not willing to accept accountability. Involving the right stakeholders and teams from the start – and ensuring they are part of the risk conversation – helps avoid failures down the line.

Lack of operational risk involvement

There are instances of major change activities with no participation or involvement from either first or second line operational risk employees. This creates a gap in understanding of the overall risk profile of the change; as well as missed opportunities for operational risk professionals to be at the decision table and help implement a structured approach to evaluating risks and opportunities. It is recommended that first and second line operational risk functions hold periodic catch-ups to ensure adequate coverage and awareness of the most material change activities.

Good practices

Embedded use of ORAs

Organizations with a well-embedded risk culture recognize the value of risk assessments. Executive committees and boards rely on ORAs accompanying material change initiatives, because a clear picture of risks and opportunities is simply indispensable for decision-making. They will reject a new business proposition without an ORA; this is a sign of maturity and sends a powerful message in support of robust risk management practices.

Risks and opportunities assessment

Use of a *risks and opportunities* matrix brings a positive sentiment to risk management and enhances the brand of the operational risk function. In developing approaches and leading conversations, it is important to balance out the words that have a negative connotation – *losses, threats, risks* – with more optimistic and upbeat terminology – *opportunities, benefits, lessons learnt.*

Finding the right approach

If a template is used for conducting ORAs, it is good practice to have the operational risk taxonomy built into the template, as a reminder of areas that need to be covered. The sponsor can then select relevant risks from the menu and add commentary, evaluate estimated inherent and residual risk levels, and outline known mitigating actions at an early stage of the programme. However, to the points raised in Chapter 5 on RCSAs, while templates do provide a framework to encourage consideration of a full range of risk pillars, they can also limit the risk identification mindset. In this case the template becomes a tick-box exercise. Often assembling a meeting with the right stakeholders and starting with a blank page asking *what are the risks here?* can draw out top-of-mind themes more effectively. The template can then be used as a basis for documenting the discussion in a disciplined way.

Using system or software

Unlike RCSAs, risk assessments of change initiatives are short-lived (and even, for longer regulatory programmes or projects, have an end of life). They are usually documented via manual Word or Excel documents. If operational risk software has a *change* module, it enables the loading, tracking and storage of ORAs in one place. Evaluating how many live ORAs exist at any point in time, and what their risk level is, helps operational risk to oversee the overall transformation landscape and increases transparency. As highlighted in the industry benchmark further on, this technique is rarely used, and only by a minority of organizations.

Celebrating success

The Operational Risk department commonly has a preview of all ORAs, given their role in facilitation, review and challenge. Consequently, operational risk staff gain an enormous amount of experience and insight, and can use that knowledge to draw out relevant lessons learnt and share them with business units and support functions. Celebrating success is once again an important topic. Discussions that focus on cases where assessments were particularly impactful really reinforce the value of risk management.

Retaining evidence

In the age of evidence, it is important to retain solid documentation of ORAs, demonstrating how risk decisions were taken. Assessments can be referred to in the future, especially in cases where personnel have moved roles or left the organization.

Industry benchmark

Change risk is on the increase, and since 2022 has appeared as one of the top three operational risks across the financial services sector, as assessed by

Figure 6.4   Industry poll: maturity of operational risk approach to change

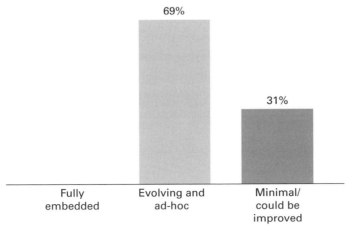

Maturity of Op Risk approach to change

Best Practice Operational Risk Forum, 2022

the Best Practice Operational Risk Forum. Practitioners evaluated the maturity of the operational risk approach to change initiatives, with 69 per cent of respondents considering that their firm's practices were still evolving and ad hoc, while the remaining 31 per cent noted that improvement was needed (see Figure 6.4). No respondents at all considered that the approach to change in their firms was already fully embedded.

By contrast, in a similar poll carried out four years earlier (2018), 40 per cent of professionals had been confident that *significant* or *riskier* activities were consistently identified and risk assessed in their firms, demonstrating a pattern of good embeddedness (also see first edition of the book for further details). Overall, then, this rating deteriorated from 2018 to 2022, and the pace of progress in implementing robust change management practices now appears slower than expected. This setback is largely attributed to an understandable focus on other urgent priorities during the pandemic years and the subsequent challenging economic environment. These factors have often resulted in change programmes being underfunded and lacking sufficient attention from boards and senior management. An increase in organizational fragmentation, greater reliance on third parties and a siloed operating environment may have also contributed to these challenges.

On a positive note, however, a majority (76 per cent) of risk professionals are involved in change projects, with 46 per cent being engaged throughout the duration of the initiative, as reflected in Figure 6.5.

Figure 6.5   Industry poll: operational risk involvement in change projects

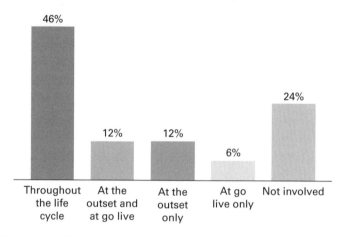

When is Op Risk involved in change projects?

Best Practice Operational Risk Forum, 2022

Figure 6.6   Industry poll: tools used to measure change risk

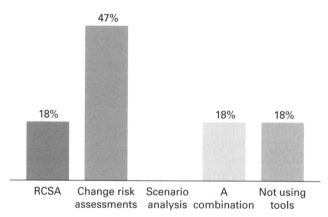

What tools are used to measure change risk?

Best Practice Operational Risk Forum, 2022

Change risk assessment was considered as a core mechanism to measure and manage *change risk*, enabling increased levels of scrutiny and sign-off where needed. RCSAs and other tools, in combination, were also used for this purpose (see Figure 6.6). Change assessments continued to be recorded largely manually, with only a few firms developing and using a change risk assessment module within their operational risk systems.

Overall, Best Practice Forum members yet again concluded that change management remains a focus area. Operational risk professionals could serve as effective *connectors*, reaching across the silos, and teaming up with colleagues from various areas to jointly produce better outcomes. The reason for this is the ongoing intensity of change agenda and its impact on business models. In turn, this is inspiring operational risk professionals to remain at the heart of the process, continually embedding robust risk management practices with energy and enthusiasm.

Practical workplace exercise

Obtain a sample of various change initiatives completed within the last year, and consider the following questions:

1 Are there set criteria for defining *material* change activities that would benefit from an ORA?

2 Is there an ORA process; or if not, how are the risks emanating from change initiatives identified, assessed and managed?

3 What is the role of the Operational Risk department in the change process?

4 What is working well?

5 What can be improved? Note down possible enhancements.

A template for the ORA process has been provided in Appendix 3.

MAKE A DIFFERENCE (MAD) ACTION

Please outline key learnings and note down one specific action you will take after reading this chapter, to enhance your existing practices relating to the risk assessment of change initiatives in your organization.

In summary, this chapter discussed the approach to identifying and assessing risks in change initiatives, supplementing Chapter 5, RCSAs.

Now that risk identification is complete, the next topic is dedicated to risk monitoring via Key Risk Indicators.

Notes

1 Basel Committee on Banking Supervision (2021) *Revisions to the Principles for the Sound Management of Operational Risk*, www.bis.org/bcbs/publ/d515.pdf (archived at https://perma.cc/3AW7-3S2D)

2 Basel Committee on Banking Supervision (2014) *Review of the Principles for the Sound Management of Operational Risk*, www.bis.org/publ/bcbs292.pdf (archived at https://perma.cc/3V88-VK6R)

3 Basel Committee on Banking Supervision (2021) *Revisions to the Principles for the Sound Management of Operational Risk*, www.bis.org/bcbs/publ/d515.pdf (archived at https://perma.cc/FX66-VY83)

4 Financial Conduct Authority (2018) *Cyber and Technology Resilience: Themes from cross-sector survey 2017–18*, www.fca.org.uk/publication/research/technology-cyber-resilience-questionnaire-cross-sector-report.pdf (archived at https://perma.cc/LUV7-G6FZ)

5 European Banking Authority (EBA) (2019) *EBA Guidelines on ICT and security risk management*, www.eba.europa.eu/sites/default/files/document_library/Publications/Guidelines/2020/GLs%20on%20ICT%20and%20security%20risk%20management/872936/Final%20draft%20Guidelines%20on%20ICT%20and%20security%20risk%20management.pdf (archived at https://perma.cc/46HX-HYW8)

6 Project Management Institute (2013) *A Guide to the Project Management Body of Knowledge*, 5th edn, Project Management Institute (PMI)

7 Winter, H (2019) *The Business Analysis Handbook: Techniques and questions to deliver better business outcomes*, Kogan Page

8 Manifesto for Agile Software Development, agilemanifesto.org/principles.html (archived at https://perma.cc/9LYB-K57R)

9 JWG (2017) Preparing for the regulatory flood: standards getting us to high ground!, jwg-it.eu/article/preparing-for-the-regulatory-flood-standards-getting-us-to-high-ground/ (archived at https://perma.cc/8UUS-XAHV)

10 Basel Committee on Banking Supervision (2014) *Review of the Principles for the Sound Management of Operational Risk*, www.bis.org/publ/bcbs292.pdf (archived at https://perma.cc/N6YE-95JV)

Key Risk Indicators

07

What this chapter covers: Key Risk Indicators (KRIs) score the lowest rating in operational risk implementation surveys, and remain a challenge for practitioners. This chapter examines KRIs from a practical perspective, focusing on their purpose, design and benefit to the business (Figure 7.1). It discusses what is really important when implementing KRIs; provides a framework for assessing whether a metric is *useful* or *useless*; and reviews examples of effective (and not so effective) indicators. It also includes an industry benchmark and a list of 50 suggested KRIs (see Appendix 4).

FURTHER READING

- Institute of Operational Risk (2021) *Operational Key Risk Indicators*

  Why recommended: A short supplementary read, containing several examples of Key Risk Indicators.

- Michael George, John Maxey, David Rowlands and Mark Price (2004) *The Lean Six Sigma Pocket Toolbook: A quick reference guide to 100 tools for improving quality and speed*, McGraw-Hill

  Why recommended: This excellent handbook is one of many on Six Sigma methodology and is useful for those wishing to obtain a broader perspective on the importance of measurement and how it fits into the overall process improvement cycle.

Definition, examples and key attributes

A primary monitoring mechanism, usually referred to as Key Risk Indicators (KRIs), is a core component of the operational risk framework and a powerful risk management tool.

Figure 7.1 Focus of Chapter 7: Key Risk Indicators

Risk culture

Governance, roles and responsibilities

Establish governance and clear roles across the Three Lines for managing operational risk.

Risk appetite and risk capacity

Define nature and types of risk accepted in pursuit of strategic objectives. Evaluate adequacy of capital resources.

Operational risk events	Risk assessments	Scenario analysis	Key Risk Indicators
Record and report risk events, act to minimize future exposure. Monitor trends against RCSAs and KRIs.	Assess risk exposure in process, business or function via RCSAs. Supplement by evaluating risks emanating from change activities via ORAs.	Identify exposure from extreme but plausible events. Mitigate through risk transfer to insurance.	Monitor risk and control performance through predictive indicators. Act if indicators breach established appetite threshold.

Reporting and decision-making

Review actual risk profile against set appetite, apply active risk management to enable achievement of strategic objectives.

Training and education

Embedding and maturity assessment

Operational risk taxonomy

The secret of success with KRIs is in channelling energy and thought into designing the right, targeted metrics and setting suitable thresholds, without overburdening the business or support functions with terminology and definitions. In terms of practical application, the *usefulness* test matters most: have the KRIs resulted in better business decisions?

In 2014, in a survey of regulated banks, Basel Committee found that KRIs scored the lowest implementation rating out of all operational risk framework tools.[1] Either they were not used as part of the framework at all; or, in most banks surveyed, they were still under development and not yet fully implemented. In 2019, Best Practice Operational Risk Forum was encouraged to see some progress, whereby KRIs, despite not yet scoring full marks for their usefulness, were being deemed a helpful tool in decision-making. Fast forward five years, in 2024 the topic of KRIs remains very pertinent. In my extensive experience of running public and in-house training courses, it is often the KRI module that still attracts ample discussion and debate – and sometimes even light-bulb moments. Furthermore, at the end of each course when I ask participants to call out the most useful takeaways, many mention points related to KRIs.

It would be fair to note that there remains some divergence and confusion with the definition. As the Basel Committee noted, some banks considered *Key Risk Indicators* and *Key Performance Indicators* to be the same set of metrics; while others differentiated between *Key Risk Indicators* (metrics designed to measure inherent risk) and *Key Performance Indicators* (focusing on the adequacy of underlying processes and controls). Other firms use *Key Control Indicators* for controls and *Key Performance Indicators* to measure business performance. It is not surprising, then, that, for simplicity, some firms find it easier to replace the term KRI altogether, with the label *monitoring metrics*.

The challenge goes deeper than definition, however. It extends to the role of the KRIs and their place in the broader operational risk framework.

Let's start by defining KRIs and discussing their role and place in the broader operational risk framework.

KRI DEFINITION

- A Key Risk Indicator (KRI) is a metric or measure used to monitor the state of a *key* risk, indicating whether it is increasing or reducing.
- The KRI can be linked to the risk itself or to a key control that mitigates the risk.
- The KRI should be a well-chosen, targeted metric that helps the firm to take decisions (*usefulness test*).

In Chapter 5, we covered Risk and Control Self-Assessments (RCSAs). An RCSA is effectively a snapshot, at a point in time, of the firm's risk and control environment. The assessment is true and valid on the day it takes place; but what can happen tomorrow, next month or next quarter? The control environment may deteriorate due to, for example, experienced members of staff, with knowledge of information technology systems, leaving the firm. Inherent risk may increase due to the firm starting to trade new products. While it is important to periodically refresh RCSAs, it is not cost-effective to do this on a continuous basis.

That is where KRIs come in.

Once the most important (*top* or *key*) risks have been identified, the purpose of KRIs is to monitor them. As part of the RCSA process, business units or support functions have already agreed that the key risks are more significant than other risks; and therefore, they are now selected for special treatment. They are worthy of the time and effort involved in monitoring them and KRIs are defined for each *key* risk, to allow us to keep an eye on its behaviour.

> The word *key* in 'Key Risk Indicators' relates to the risk and signifies the *risk* being key, not the *indicator*.

When KRIs are selected to monitor key risks, the advantages include:

- clarity on why the metric is being collected – it monitors the behaviour of a risk which is known to be significant to the firm;

- reduced number of indicators – it enables a small sub-set of key risks to be monitored, which is more efficient and ensures focus on what is important.

CASE STUDY 7.1

A medium-sized firm acquired by a larger organization identifies one of its key risks as *Loss of staff, causing inability to meet business requirements*. During the 12 months of integration after the acquisition, senior management has to ensure continuity of high-value, high-volume transaction services, while recognizing that inevitably, there will be attrition. Management decides that in this situation it is crucial to monitor the risk via a KRI, *Predicted attrition* – defined as the number of employees expected to leave in the next month, as a percentage of the total number of staff. Each leader is requested to maintain an honest dialogue with their staff discussing future plans, and report the *Predicted attrition* KRI on a monthly basis.

While accepted to be not very scientific, this KRI, based on the leader's knowledge and informal estimates, proves very useful. It provides a basis for management to act, proactively recruiting temporary workers and a consultancy firm to fill identified potential gaps, and the integration is successfully completed.

Attributes of the *Predicted Attrition* KRI:

- It is directly relevant to the risk *Loss of staff causing inability to meet business requirements.*

- It measures the level of risk, indicating whether that is increasing or reducing, and is helpful in decision-making.

- Although not precise, it is at least measurable: to quote the British philosopher and logician Carveth Read, 'It's better to be approximately right than exactly wrong.'

In normal circumstances, though, the practice of asking employees whether they are planning to resign in the near future is neither feasible nor recommended. So, what are the alternatives?

Risk: loss of staff causing inability to meet business requirements

KRI1: *Absenteeism* – this can be narrowed down by cause, e.g. stress-related absenteeism; an increase may be a sign of poor staff health, leading to future attrition. The opposite – *Presenteeism* – equally became a concern during and post the Covid-19 pandemic, where working hours have stretched with employees spending extended time behind the screen, potentially leading to fatigue and burnout.

KRI2: *Use of employee helpline* – if this kind of facility is available, spikes in usage may signal a broader issue and require investigation.

KRI3: *Employee satisfaction survey rate* – decreased staff satisfaction with the role, manager or the company may lead to resignations.

KRI4: *Exit interview analysis: number of identified concerns* – if the Human Resources department interviews leavers and analyses trends (a very valuable activity), they will be able to flag if there is a recurring theme or concern.

KRI5: *Salary benchmark*, showing the number or percentage of positions not benchmarked or below the industry benchmark – uncompetitive pay may prompt employees to look elsewhere.

KRI6: *Key staff without succession plan* – this will not prevent employees from leaving, but will reflect how well the impact can be mitigated if they do.

Depending on particular aspects of risk that are of concern to the firm, additional indicators can be designed, for example, ones that help understand *who* is leaving:

KRI7: *High performance (regretted) turnover* – highly rated leavers as a percentage of total number of leavers.

Or *how quickly* people are leaving:

KRI8: *Permanent staff leavers* – left within six months of joining.

CASE STUDY 7.2

In a highly dynamic start-up firm, indicator *Permanent staff leavers, left within six months of joining* was instrumental in helping management to monitor a pattern whereby employees either stayed for a long time, or joined and left very quickly. Following further investigation, it was revealed that the vibrant and entrepreneurial environment was either loved or hated by the members of staff. As a consequence, Human Resources enhanced the employee on-boarding process to explain the culture to prospective new joiners at the interview stage, allowing them to decide up-front whether it suited them, and reducing the number of speedy departures.

What attributes are we looking for when selecting KRIs?

ATTRIBUTES OF GOOD KRIs

✓ relevant, targeted – specific to the risk or control;

✓ predictive, forward-looking – provide an early warning;

✓ useful – help the firm to take decisions;

✓ available for collection;

✓ measurable.

Some organizations use the KRI *Staff attrition rate*. While factual, this KRI is backward-looking (i.e. employees have already left); and it provides no insight into why the departures happened or whether people are more or less likely to leave in the future. It is difficult for management to act on the information and therefore, from a risk management perspective, the KRI is not very helpful. The recommendation is to select more predictive and targeted metrics that can provide an early warning when the level of risk is increasing.

Another example of risk worth reviewing is the *Unauthorized/rogue trading*, which is a key risk for firms with markets or trading business. Direct measures of the risk (in this case, the number of employees expected to turn rogue in the next month) rarely exist, if at all. If there are no risk indicators as such, KRIs can be set to monitor the control environment in order to alert management to any deterioration, thus allowing them to promptly implement corrective measures.

Indicators can be established for a *risk* as well as for a *control* that mitigates the risk.

Risk: Unauthorized/rogue trading

Example of a KRI dashboard for the risk of *Unauthorized/rogue trading*, containing control indicators.

KRI1: *Unconfirmed deals over 20 days* – highlighting aged trades that have not been agreed to by the trade counterparty for a long time (e.g. over 20 days), flagging a potentially erroneous or fraudulent deal.

KRI2: *Trades executed at off-market rates* – identifying 'unusual' trades that require further explanation.

KRI3: *Late deals* – counting exceptions where trades have been concluded after the close of the business day.

KRI4: *Unresolved profit and loss (P&L) differences as of month-end over the threshold* – monitoring discrepancies between a trader's position and the books and records of the firm.

KRI5: *Cancel & amends* – showing the number of deals that were cancelled and/or amended after being agreed with the counterparty, potentially requiring further investigation.

KRI6: *Trader mandate breaches* – monitoring instances where trades were executed outside of the prescribed mandate, either due to an error or deliberate non-compliance.

Risk: Money laundering/financial crime

Finally, examining the risk of *Money laundering/financial crime*, which can be measured using a combination of risk and control indicators:

KRI1: Percentage of *high risk accounts vs overall accounts* – a risk indicator which provides a view of the overall portfolio.

KRI2: *Client due diligence (CDD) reviews past due over 30 days* – highlights delay and/or non-completion of CDD refresh, a control indicator.

KRI3: *Open activity monitoring alerts not properly actioned* – monitors investigation and resolution of alerts of suspicious activity, a control indicator.

Market abuse and financial crime are growing concerns in the financial services industry, with some firms moving to automated real-time trader surveillance to detect manipulation, and use of artificial intelligence to identify suspicious patterns. This is an area of continuing enhancements and a great opportunity for operational risk practitioners to lead the way in transforming manual KRI monitoring into state-of-the art real-time indicator dashboards.

Defining thresholds and mastering aggregation

Once KRIs have been identified, thresholds (or tolerance levels) need to be established for each indicator. The levels define tolerance for error or failure with respect to the specific risk or control that the KRI is intended to monitor, effectively outlining what is acceptable and what will not be tolerated.

Thresholds are essential for escalation and action, and are commonly set on a Red/Amber/Green (RAG) basis:

Red: Unacceptable: immediate action needed

Amber: Tolerable: attention, explanation, monitoring and/or plan to bring to green

Green: Acceptable: no action needed

RAG status may also be defined in more detail. For example, red metrics may require escalation to an appropriate governance or a board-level committee.

The following steps are recommended when setting the thresholds.

SETTING RAG THRESHOLDS

✓ Establish data collection process.

✓ Observe values internally.

✓ Benchmark with industry (if available).

✓ Present a proposal to the governance committee.

Thresholds outline what the firm considers acceptable, effectively establishing the firm's operational risk appetite (see Chapter 9, Operational risk appetite). They need to be approached with a high level of rigour, including review and approval by the relevant governance committee(s). Group-wide or *top of the house* indicators and their thresholds are usually approved by the board.

Collecting the data and observing current values helps greatly in understanding the existing risk and control environment, although should not be used for guidance in setting the thresholds. External benchmarks are rarely available in financial services, but are worth checking if a relevant study has been published.

EXAMPLE 1

Risk: Payment errors/poor transaction execution, leading to customer detriment, financial loss and reputational damage.

KRI: *Number of aged reconciliation breaks* – a control indicator, monitoring volume of discrepancies and speed of resolution.

Thresholds:

Green: Less than 20 breaks outstanding >30 days at month-end AND zero breaks outstanding >60 days

Amber: Less than 50 breaks outstanding >30 days at month-end AND zero breaks outstanding >60 days

Red: Over 50 breaks outstanding >30 days at month-end OR any breaks outstanding >60 days

The same KRI can be turned into a composite measure, combining both volume and the monetary value of reconciliation breaks,

KRI: *Strength of reconciliation process* – combining volume and value.

Green: Less than 20 breaks outstanding >30 days at month-end AND zero breaks outstanding >60 days AND overall value of unresolved discrepancies <$50,000

Some indicators can be binary, turning from *acceptable* directly to *unacceptable*, i.e. by-passing the *tolerable* level.

EXAMPLE 2

Risk: Incorrect financial/regulatory reporting, resulting in penalties and regulatory censure.

KRI: Number of high-risk spreadsheets or end-user computing (EUC) applications with policy exceptions – a control indicator, already narrowed down to critical spreadsheets/EUC applications where the firm has no tolerance for exceptions to policy requirements (protecting the content, restricting access, performing back-ups and validating the formulas).

Thresholds:

Green: zero

Red: >= 1

Aggregation

At both group-wide and business unit level, there are usually multiple KRIs, each reported with its own RAG rating. Hence the need arises for aggregation of the measures, to enable an understanding of whether the risk overall is within or outside the firm's risk appetite.

Aggregation can be rule- or judgement-based. In rule-based aggregation:

- Conservative/cautious: the overall rating is based on the worst value KRI, i.e. if at least one indicator is at an *unacceptable* level, the overall RAG rating becomes *unacceptable*.

- Moderate/modest: the result is *unacceptable* if a set percentage of KRIs is flagging red (e.g. over 20 per cent).

In judgement-based aggregation, the KRI owner – namely the responsible first line head of business unit or support function who owns the KRI – decides on the overall rating using their expert knowledge. To ensure the process is robust and avoids gaming, the reasons for the rating need to be articulated in writing, which enables the second line operational risk function and respective governance committees to provide effective challenge.

CASE STUDY 7.3

A global financial markets business unit, trading out of multiple locations, is monitoring the risk of *Unauthorized/rogue trading*. One KRI (*Unconfirmed deals >20 days*) is flagging Red in one location (Figure 7.2). When presenting the dashboard to the risk committee, the head of financial markets confirms that an investigation into the Red KRI has commenced and argues that, overall, the risk is within the elevated but tolerable Amber level. This is due to the good performance of mitigating controls in place (namely other KRIs flagging Green), which were recently reviewed and tested by the Quality Assurance function.

The committee accepts this argument but requests to see the results of the investigation. On further analysis, it transpires that all unconfirmed trades are with the same small-size corporate client, with a single authorized signatory whose frequent business travels result in a significant backlog of unsigned confirmations.

Given the increased risk of fraudulent and erroneous trades that this represents, the firm decides it has no appetite to continue dealing with the client unless they appoint an additional signatory and regularize the backlog. The client complies and the KRI returns to Green within two months.

Figure 7.2 Example Key Risk Indicators dashboard

Operational risk dashboard	WHEM		EMEA	APAC		Global
KEY RISK INDICATORS	NY	Miami	UK	Sing	HK	GFM*
RISK of ROGUE TRADING						
B-1: Unconfirmed deals >20 Days	○	●	○	○	○	
B-2: Trades executed at 'Off-Market' rates	○	○	○	○	○	
B-3: 'Late deals'	○	○	○	○	○	
B-4: Unresolved P&L differences as of month-end >threshold	○	○	◐	○	○	◐
B-5: Cancel and amends	○	◐	○	○	○	
B-6: Mandate breaches	○	○	○	○	○	

● = Red ◐ = Amber ○ = Green

In the above example, judgement-based aggregation was used. If a rule-based conservative/cautious approach was applied, the overall RAG rating would have turned Red, flagging that the overall risk of *Unauthorized/rogue trading* for the global financial markets business is outside the firm's risk appetite.

KRI life cycle and checklist: useful or useless?

The KRI process cycle is described below:

- **Select:** A key risk that requires monitoring is selected (from RCSA);
- **Design:** A workshop is run with subject matter experts to define KRIs;
- **Collect:** A data collection process is established;
- **Propose thresholds:** Subject matter experts conduct the study to propose thresholds;
- **Approve thresholds:** KRI and thresholds are presented to the relevant governance committee for approval;
- **Monitor:** KRI is monitored with agreed frequency; actions are taken if the level becomes 'unacceptable';
- **Validate:** Data accuracy is periodically reviewed (e.g. by Internal Audit).

Selection

KRIs are commonly established at multiple levels throughout the organization, including at group-wide and individual business or support function level. Respectively, the starting points are key risks at the top of the house which are most significant to the firm; and more granular individual business- or function-level risks. The selection process involves deciding on what constitutes key risks that require monitoring. These can be, for example, inherent risks with the highest impact and likelihood rating; or residual risks that are outside the firm's risk appetite; or a combination of both. Less is more – narrowing down is important to ensure that reviewing the KRI dashboard is manageable.

Design

This stage is best achieved via a workshop with respective subject matter experts from the business or support functions, led by operational risk. Design is a creative, stimulating and enjoyable process, where participants collectively define the best metrics that possess the right attributes – relevant, targeted, predictive, useful, measurable and available for collection – for each of the key risks. Business units and support functions are already engaged as the value proposition is clear – let's find ways to monitor those significant risks that may prevent the *business* from achieving its *own* objectives.

In preparation for the workshop it is worth examining existing metrics, as some may already be collected. If this stage proves difficult, and the team is running out of ideas, external help is also available. Some organizations provide a library of Key Risk Indicators (via a paid subscription service), as well as guidance on where and how each indicator can be used.[2] A collaborative approach of second line operational risk professionals, who have a solid understanding of the framework and desired outcomes, working together with business units and support functions, ensures that identified metrics will provide an insight into the level of risk and present a true and fair reflection of the risk profile of each unit or function.

Data collection

This stage is usually manual, because KRIs are the most manually intensive of all operational risk tools. Data accuracy is key, and KRI owners need to establish verification procedures to ensure the correctness of information which is used for decision-making. This may involve review and sign-off by department heads.

Thresholds

These were discussed in the previous section.

Monitoring and mitigation using KRIs

Breaches of KRI thresholds need to be explained, acted upon and notified to the appropriate governance committees. Especially the unacceptable Red level which, if correctly calibrated, cannot be ignored. The firm has already agreed what outcomes would not be tolerated and needs to follow through with investigation, resolution and if needed, monetary investment. Clear account-ability helps to achieve desired results, so it is good practice to have an owner for every KRI. This may be the respective risk or control owner, who takes the lead in resolving the breach and bringing the metric back to acceptable level.

Validation

As highlighted in the data collection step, beware errors in the dataset. Many organizations end up having to go back to the risk committee and/or the board explaining why the KRI was mis-reported for the previous month(s). Maintain data quality with spot checks, period assurance and internal audit reviews.

Periodic updates

KRIs should be subject to periodic review following the RCSA refresh, trig-gered by a major change or significant operational risk event, or at least annually. During the review, it is recommended to consider the *usefulness test* (see box below).

KRI USEFUL

✓ clearly linked to a *key* risk;

✓ targeted, relevant metric;

✓ demonstrable decisions;

✓ drives improvement, replaced with a better KRI.

In many instances, once KRIs become visible and continuously monitored, they lead to enhancements. To quote H James Harrington, the US perfor-mance and quality guru, 'Measurement is the first step that leads to control and eventually to improvement.'

Six Sigma, an effective problem-solving methodology for improving busi-ness performance, is centred on the DMAIC concept: Define, Measure, Analyse, Improve and Control.[3] In my career I have been fortunate to man-age Six Sigma green and black belts, working with the methodology and seeing first-hand evidence of the value that the projects delivered. Robust Key Risk Indicators fit into this overall improvement cycle; and if used correctly can take a firm a long way towards advancing its processes and performance.

CASE STUDY 7.4

A firm experiences a failure of a third-party technology service provider, where it transpires that the supplier had facilities in a flood prone area, with sub-optimal disaster recovery and business continuity capabilities. In addition to remediation activities, a programme of work commences to carry out a review of all critical third-party suppliers to ensure robust climate risk assessment (the *E* component of ESG) has been completed, and BCP/DR plans and test results are available and fit-for-purpose.

Management selects an interim measure to monitor the risk of *critical third-party failure*: *The number of Critical third parties with missing climate risk assessment or BCP arrangements*. The KRI reflects the progress of the programme; and measures the population of critical suppliers where robust information has not yet been obtained or is not available (for example, in cases where service providers have not evaluated their own exposure to climate-related risk drivers), hence flagging an unknown potential areas of exposure.

The firm sets a zero tolerance for the KRI as it has already been narrowed down to *critical* suppliers, resulting in *unacceptable* Red RAG rating for the duration of the project. Stringent governance is thus required, with updates from the chief operating officer, responsible for coordinating the Supplier management programme, to the governance committees and the board.

Following project completion, as the required information has been collected, the KRI becomes redundant and is replaced by a better indicator – *Critical suppliers with inadequate climate risk exposure or BCP arrangements*, for continuous monitoring of any negative (or positive) changes to the risk profile.

KRI NOT USEFUL

✓ not linked to a *key* risk;

✓ difficult to explain why collected;

✓ no decisions taken;

✓ constant Green;

✓ if it turns Red, it is argued that it is not a real Red: no action needed.

In some firms, KRIs are not linked to any particular risk. A dashboard is created from scratch (perhaps based on the question *what shall we monitor?*) or assembled using data that is already being gathered. KRIs are subsequently monitored in case they collectively flag a developing risk. While this approach is feasible, it is also laborious and ineffective, as the firm ends up collecting more indicators than it needs (not all related to *key* risks), and struggles to justify why a particular metric is being monitored. When working with clients, I always recommend identifying the *key* risks first, and selecting the KRIs subsequently.

In terms of decision-making, examples of less useful KRIs include those backward-looking, or lagging, indicators that reflect risk having already materialized. Among them is the earlier-mentioned *Staff attrition rate* (employees have already left) as well as *Number of system failures*, *Number of cases of internal fraud*, and *Number of reported operational risk losses*. In short, it is good practice to select predictive, rather than backward-looking metrics, where possible.

KRIs – and their thresholds – may also need to be examined in case they persistently report *Green* for a prolonged period of time (e.g. over a year), including in periods of stress. This pattern may signify that the department is overstaffed or has extra capacity, or that the threshold has been set incorrectly.

Even worse is when KRI turns *Red* and the importance of the event is downplayed. For example, an explanation is provided that it is not a true exception and that there is no reason to be concerned. This situation warrants a review. The threshold may have been incorrectly set, or, more likely, it is recognized that investment is required to resolve the issue, but there is neither budget nor appetite among management to progress this further.

Appendix 4 provides some example KRIs.

Roles and responsibilities

First line business units or support functions are responsible for most of the KRI cycle: developing indicators which monitor their risk and control environment; proposing the thresholds; establishing a data collection process; monitoring and providing commentary; and then acting when indicators breach the threshold. This is common sense risk management, and if indicators are correctly selected to monitor significant risks that may prevent the business or support function from achieving *their own* objectives, there should be no pushback.

An Operational Risk department works in partnership with first line functions, facilitating KRI workshops and adding its expertise and knowledge of the KRI tool and the desired outcomes. Oversight and constructive challenge are provided as part of the discussion at the KRI workshop. The second line usually has the right to add or alter indicators or thresholds. If the firm has first line coordinators embedded into its business units or support functions, those individuals will play a crucial role in achieving the right outcomes.

Below is an example checklist for a first line risk coordinator.

FIRST LINE RISK COORDINATOR CHECKLIST: KRIs

✓ KRIs are set to monitor *key* (top) operational risks.

✓ Collected data is accurate and reliable; data quality is validated.

✓ KRI thresholds are defined and approved by the relevant governance committee.

✓ Dashboard is used in decision-making – if KRI breaches the threshold, action is taken.

✓ KRI outputs are compared and contrasted against other core operational risk tools.

Common challenges and good practices

The following challenges may be encountered when designing and deploying Key Risk Indicators.

Common challenges

Business units disengaged

At times, employees may perceive KRIs as a pointless exercise and refuse to engage in their design. It is crucial to build a value proposition and make a case for monitoring what is important to the *business*, namely those significant risks that may prevent the business from achieving *their own* objectives.

Threshold manipulation

Business units or support functions may attempt to game the threshold, proposing ranges that will always exhibit a Green KRI (in particular in firms which are characterized by a blame culture, i.e. to avoid the consequences of being Red); or, on the contrary, purposely setting a threshold to display Red in order to substantiate a request for more people or better systems. Independent second line operational risk opinions (referred to earlier as *challenge*) can be helpful in resolving these tendencies.

Lack of action

A dashboard with Red flashing indicators is presented month-on-month but with no action taken to resolve the matter and bring the metric within the tolerable level. This pattern should be avoided at all costs, as it simply devalues the whole process.

Manual data collection

KRIs are the most manual tool in the operational risk framework. When starting the project, allow sufficient time and resource not only for the design phase but for the future manual and possibly labour-intensive collection process. Consider automation where possible – firms investing in technological solutions are ahead of the game, using the best practice of inviting IT and data specialists to the initial KRI workshop and thus ensuring that potential automation is considered from the outset.

Too many KRIs

It can be challenging to identify the correct number of KRIs for a given firm: usually there are too many (the challenge is rarely in the opposite direction, namely too few). Some organizations monitor hundreds (or even thousands) of indicators. I am frequently asked what is the right number. While there is no absolute correct answer, a range of around 30 good KRIs at the top of the house is appropriate.

Good practices

Review what already exists

While it is unrealistic to rapidly turn existing departmental metrics straight into a KRI dashboard, it is valuable to review what is already being collected.

Frequently, current indicators serve as a base for the conversation. Business units and support functions naturally manage their people, systems and processes and will often have a good set of measures that help them take decisions. This can be supplemented by blue-sky thinking, to consider what KRIs should ideally be used, and if felt important, time and technical capabilities invested to put them in place. If risks are the starting point, that narrows down the scope and creates a much better case for agreeing what is essential to monitor.

Define a healthy portfolio

Evaluate the proportion of predictive metrics vs backward-looking measures in the overall KRI set. A healthy set of indicators will contain predominantly predictive measures that aid in decision-making. In 2024, I ran a LinkedIn poll for my network of risk professionals to ascertain their view on what constitutes a healthy portfolio, and was pleased that almost half of respondents favoured forward-looking KRIs, while the other half opted for a balance of predictive and lagging indicators (see Table 7.1). This is a positive sign, as organizations should be moving away from dashboards merely filled with historic data.

Translate KRIs into a story

Ensure KRIs tell a story to the governance committees and especially when presented at board level. The context helps in escalating Red KRIs and ensuring they are acted upon. Measure and highlight the length of persistency of Red KRIs, which demonstrates apathy and unwillingness to deal with issues.

Apply the usefulness test

Apply the *usefulness* test and revisit KRIs after major changes, aiming to continuously evolve them. Review KRIs in search of better, more targeted

Table 7.1 A healthy portfolio of KRIs contains

Response	% of responses
Mostly forward-looking KRIs	43
Mostly backward-looking KRIs	3
An equal proportion of each	54

metrics, avoiding stale indicators. Additionally, review the thresholds periodically to make sure that they are still appropriate and fit for purpose.

Share learnings and celebrate success

Share good examples of KRIs between first line risk coordinators. It is good practice to run periodic workshops where coordinators present their best indicator of the year, substantiated with reasons why. Group discussions and the exchange of practical hints and tips injects positive energy into risk management. Report on cases where KRI monitoring has resulted in improvements, emphasizing the value of risk management. This practice is not done nearly enough.

Appreciate the bigger picture

The operational risk team needs to be involved and fully on-board with the firm's strategy and business objectives, to ensure that the data collected and monitored aligns with the bigger picture and is truly important to the firm.

Industry benchmark

In 2024, the view on KRIs remains consistent with previous years: firms are constantly searching for targeted, predictive and useful indicators. Some 73 per cent of risk professionals taking part in an Advanced Operational Risk workshop were aiming to enhance their KRI set, as presented in Figure 7.3. Around 8 per cent were working to decrease their number of KRIs (especially if the number ran to hundreds), while others intended to start or increase KRI reporting if the tool was somewhat new.

Risk professionals mentioned that KRI dashboards still contained many backward-looking indicators such as staff attrition, transaction errors, compliance breaches and system failures. While they were factual and available for collection, they did not provide a perspective on the future areas of risk or shed a light into underperforming controls. Therefore, the overall satisfaction with the KRI portfolio remained rather low (see Figure 7.4).

Despite not yet at the point of arrival, KRIs were actively used in measuring the level of operational risk against risk appetite, thus aiding in decision-making. To advance the use of this excellent tool, operational risk professionals were planning to invest time into facilitating workshops with the first line units, to identify more targeted, relevant and predictive metrics.

Figure 7.3   Industry poll: next steps for Key Risk Indicators

What are your plans/next steps for KRIs?

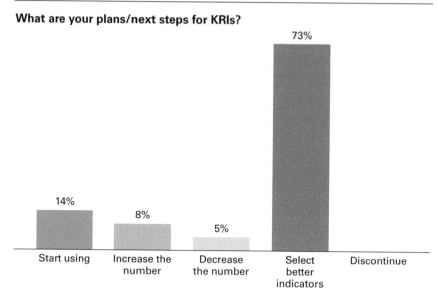

Advanced operational risk management workshop, 2024

Figure 7.4   Industry poll: usefulness of Key Risk Indicators

Key Risk Indicators

1 = strongly disagree, 5 = strongly agree,   = average rating

Advanced operational risk management workshop, 2024

This will, in turn, enhance important board and senior management conversations centred around risk appetite, leading to better decisions.

Practical workplace exercise

Reflect on the content of this chapter. Obtain a copy of the RCSA or a list of your firm's top/key risks. Select three risks and practise creating three or four Key Risk Indicators for each risk, taking into account the attributes of good KRIs.

Obtain a copy of your firm's KRI dashboard. Review it, considering the following questions:

1 Are the KRIs clearly linked to a key risk? Are they reported together with the risk?

2 Do they have the right attributes?

3 Are decisions taken when the KRI breaches the threshold?

4 Which KRIs are most useful? Make notes of the features that you particularly like.

5 Which ones are less useful and can be replaced? Note down potential 'better' KRIs.

MAKE A DIFFERENCE (MAD) ACTION

Please outline the key learnings and note down one specific action you will take after reading this chapter, to enhance your existing practices relating to Key Risk Indicators.

In summary, this chapter discussed the ultimate monitoring tool, KRIs, used for observing the behaviour of *key* risks and aiding in decision-making.

The next topic is dedicated to the final core tool of the operational risk toolbox – scenario analysis.

Notes

1 Basel Committee on Banking Supervision (2014) *Review of the Principles for the Sound Management of Operational Risk*, www.bis.org/publ/bcbs292.pdf (archived at https://perma.cc/ECZ3-KB9N)

2 RiskSpotlight, www.riskspotlight.com (archived at https://perma.cc/7YCJ-5NPH)

3 George, M L, Maxey, J, Rowlands, D and Price, M (2004) *The Lean Six Sigma Pocket Toolbook: A quick reference guide to 100 tools for improving quality and speed*, McGraw-Hill

Scenario analysis

08

What this chapter covers: This chapter explores Scenario Analysis, a tool that historically was used solely for risk measurement purposes; and advocates for the strengthening of its use, given its benefits for risk management (Figure 8.1). The chapter provides an overview of the process by exploring three different scenario workshop case studies. The chapter outlines examples of good practices, lists common pitfalls and provides suggestions on how to avoid them. It also includes an industry benchmark containing the results of a live poll with industry practitioners.

FURTHER READING

- Basel Committee on Banking Supervision (2009) *Observed Range of Practice in Key Elements of Advanced Measurement Approaches*

  Why recommended: The document contains a valuable benchmark on the various aspects of scenario analysis, for those interested in exploring a wide range of practices.

- Nassim Nicholas Taleb (2008) *The Black Swan: The impact of the highly improbable*, Penguin Books

  Why recommended: Simply the best book on the subject of the unpredictable.

Definition and purpose: for risk management and measurement

As mentioned in the Preface to this book, in my role as chair of various industry bodies I regularly lead operational risk meetings with practitioners.

Figure 8.1 Focus of Chapter 8: scenario analysis

Embedding and maturity assessment

Risk culture

Governance, roles and responsibilities

Establish governance and clear roles across the Three Lines for managing operational risk.

Risk appetite and risk capacity

Define nature and types of risk accepted in pursuit of strategic objectives. Evaluate adequacy of capital resources.

Operational risk events	Risk assessments	Scenario analysis	Key Risk Indicators
Record and report risk events, act to minimize future exposure. Monitor trends against RCSAs and KRIs.	Assess risk exposure in process, business or function via RCSAs. Supplement by evaluating risks emanating from change activities via ORAs.	Identify exposure from extreme but plausible events. Mitigate through risk transfer to insurance.	Monitor risk and control performance through predictive indicators. Act if indicators breach established appetite threshold.

Reporting and decision-making

Review actual risk profile against set appetite, apply active risk management to enable achievement of strategic objectives.

Training and education

Operational risk taxonomy

For these meetings, we typically select a topic and conduct a study of how it is being addressed by member firms. Risk and Control Self-Assessments (RCSAs) and Key Risk Indicators (KRIs) are among the most popular subjects, and usually manage to create engagement with all participants.

In contrast, whenever scenario analysis (SA) comes up as the study topic, a third of the audience will invariably skip the meeting. The reasons given often include the fact that the tool is too quantitative, and that many operational risk practitioners – especially if working in a foreign branch of an international organization – are not closely involved in the process. The tool is usually administered by a select group of experts in the organization's head office, where scenarios are run for capital calculation purposes; or by insurance industry practitioners who generally favour quantitative approaches.

In a similar way to operational risk losses, scenarios were historically required and used primarily for risk *measurement* purposes.

The tool was utilized with a single intent – to come up with numbers which could be put into a statistical model in order to produce a capital charge. The overall dataset for the model was reasonably solid. Many firms made significant progress in collecting internal loss events (usual, or *expected losses*), and additionally many subscribed to external loss data consortia to supplement their internal data. However, at the end (or tail) of the impact scale – covering rare, severe or *unexpected losses* – the loss data was sparse, as over time the industry simply had not experienced that many extreme operational events, as described in Figure 8.2.

That was where scenario analysis came in: a tool for generating synthetic data not yet observed, by imagining hypothetical events and estimating their corresponding impact.

Putting aside the need to satisfy a regulatory objective – deriving numbers for capital calculation purposes – the design and examination of scenarios is actually one of the most interesting, interactive and intellectually challenging activities in the operational risk toolset. It is also great fun. Scenario analysis is as useful for risk *management* as it is for risk *measurement*; it can be used for both, or for risk *management* only (also see Chapter 15 for articulation of *operational resilience* scenarios).

The chapter aims to illustrate practical ways in which a firm can establish and maintain scenario analysis as part of its overall operational risk framework.

Figure 8.2   Loss distribution curve

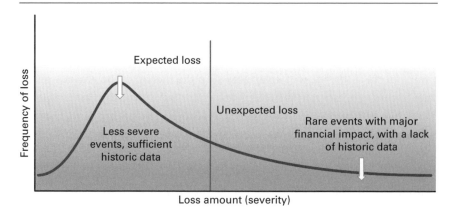

Figure 8.3   OREs, RCSAs and scenario analysis horizon

Aim of scenario analysis

Scenario analysis is the continuation of risk assessment, as pointed out in Figure 8.3, with a specific focus on events at the more extreme end of the spectrum. Each scenario is also a deep dive into a particular theme, allowing focus on a detailed story line.

The two main differences between scenario analysis and RCSAs, described in Chapter 5, are the time horizon and the magnitude of considered events. While RCSAs concentrate on the business cycle and business-as-usual risks (high frequency, low severity), scenarios focus on rare but major occurrences (low frequency, high severity). The two tools are complementary in helping to build the overall risk profile of the firm. Some organizations have separate RCSA and SA processes; while others combine them by stretching the time horizon of the risk assessment matrix (discussed in Chapter 5) to a lengthy period, for example up to 100 years. The firm can adopt either approach, as long as they are fully integrated into the risk management framework and serve to enable the best decision-making.

A note on terminology. In previous chapters, we discussed *impact* and *likelihood*:

- When working with scenarios, the terms *impact* and *severity* are often used interchangeably. The term *severity* has been historically applied by quants to model severity distribution – a statistical distribution of the amount of loss incurred in each risk event. But the word also handily emphasizes the extreme nature of scenarios and their position on the impact scale.

- *Frequency* reflects how often the event occurs – as opposed to how large it is – and is used when talking about modelling *frequency distribution* – a statistical distribution that displays how often (i.e. frequently) various outcomes occur.

Terms such as severity, frequency and probability are mathematical concepts that are common in scenario analysis; where often we are asked to estimate a 1 in X year event – an event which has both a defined impact (i.e. 'severity') and a 'frequency' that it will only occur once in every X years. But for most audiences it is advisable to use the softer, more intuitive terms and language, as described in the good practices section, and a simplified way of approaching these mathematical concepts.

The main aims of scenario analysis are to:

- consider the worst outcomes of risks materializing and evaluate their impact on the organization;

- examine the control environment and the firm's preparedness for extreme events;

- create a consolidated, forward-looking view of the firm's most material exposures by examining a portfolio of scenarios;

- enable the firm to develop a horizon-scanning capability for emerging risks, based on an understanding of the drivers of potential extreme, low-probability events;

- raise awareness among senior management of the severe, but plausible types of events they could experience;

- use the outcome for operational risk management and reduction;

- review the adequacy of the firm's insurance coverage and identify whether any specific form of insurance is needed; and

- calculate regulatory and economic capital, and support the internal capital adequacy assessment process.

Scenario selection process

Examples of scenarios are significant events such as major cyber attacks or rogue trading, extreme weather leading to a flood in the data centre, sustained regulatory non-compliance resulting in a supervisory intervention and fine, an employment discrimination lawsuit or a pandemic. While these are relatively common story lines, the exact scenarios depend on the nature of the firm, its business model and risk profile.

The strategic RCSA (at the top of the house, reflecting risks for the whole entity or a business line) is a good starting point for thinking about scenarios, as the firm has already used this tool to consider its key, strategic level risks. Story lines can then be developed for each of the *most significant inherent risks*, pushed to their extreme. Or several risks can be assumed to have *simultaneously materialized*. The firm's taxonomy categories provide a helpful reminder of the whole range of themes to be addressed via scenarios.

External newspaper articles describing significant operational risk events – along with industry *top operational risks* surveys – can also be used to generate ideas. External events are incredibly powerful to counteract the inevitable challenge from participants that this could never happen to us and this could never cost that much. Keeping in touch with the industry and leveraging incidents also reflects very well on the organization.

Alternatively, it is possible to start from a blank page and just think the unthinkable, contemplating for example, a complete destruction of the data centre. The firm's operational risk taxonomy provides a useful checkpoint of the completeness of coverage, ensuring that scenarios have been considered for the key categories of the taxonomy.

For the scenario to materialize, controls – sometimes several of them – are assumed to have failed. This is a challenging aspect for those participants who operate the daily controls and may have high confidence (and a vested interest) in their performance. But in extreme scenarios, business-as-usual controls may turn out to be less effective simply because the environment prevents one or more component, such as people or systems, from functioning properly.

As described in Figure 8.4, scenarios usually bounce between business-as-usual known experiences and *lights-out, end-of-the-world* thinking. The hard part is developing and cultivating an *extreme but plausible* mindset that the firm can actually work with as a basis for credible testing.

Figure 8.4 Scenario analysis spectrum

Business-as-usual	Extreme but plausible	'Lights out'
Benign, not severe enough	*Right mindset for scenarios*	*Too extreme*

Examples: Payments transaction error; late product launch	**Examples:** Major data breach or failure of the critical provider of outsourced services	**Examples:** Meteorite falling on the data centre; nuclear war

Scenarios in practice: three case studies

Let's review three case study examples of different scenario approaches, to articulate the range of practices used in the financial services industry, and highlight their strong points and areas for improvement.

CASE STUDY 8.1

A newly established financial markets equities and fixed income business examines a *Rogue Trader* scenario, which it sees as its most significant potential risk. This is done via a workshop with the following participants:

- head of Operational Risk (workshop *facilitator*);
- head of Trading (scenario *owner*), joined by a trader;
- chief risk officer;
- head of Market Risk;
- head of Operations;
- head of Finance;
- representatives from Compliance and middle office/product control.

The head of Operational Risk sets the scene and introduces the purpose of the workshop. Given the business line is newly established, the specific aim is to deliberate exactly *how* a dishonest trader might approach unauthorized trading and what strategies they may adopt. It is also to evaluate the firm's control environment, and to test its resilience and ability to withstand a worst-case event. The outcomes will also feed into the firm's capital adequacy process, though this objective is secondary.

The trader describes three potential rogue trading strategies, which are reviewed in detail by the participants:

- *deliberate skimming*, including collusion between the trader and their counterparty (to share the profits);
- *excessive intra-day position taking*, a foolish bet whereby the trader believes they can make major profits during the day and establishes large positions which they subsequently liquidate by the end of the day; and
- *concealing positions*, whereby large positions are created by over-the-counter (OTC) deals being intentionally not entered into the trading system.

The group scrutinizes key preventative and detective controls:

1 Trader supervision, relying on the head of Trading to be constantly aware of all traders' dealing activities. It is assumed that this control fails and fraudulent activity is overlooked.

2 The confirmations process, administered independently by Operations. This is a primary detective control ensuring that each deal is matched with a corresponding counterparty's trade. Upon close examination, a gap is identified. It transpires that the process involves several counterparties signing a short form confirmation which is received by the trader rather than an independent operations unit. An action to remediate the deficiency is taken jointly by the head of Trading and head of Operations; this should include re-evaluation of the relevant risks and controls set out in the RCSA.

During the workshop, the overall maximum amount of loss for each of the three scenarios is estimated by reviewing trading volumes, considering the nature and number of counterparties, and external limitations set by exchanges and correspondent banks.

Following the meeting, the head of Operations and head of Finance state that they found the study very useful, and ask Operational Risk to facilitate similar workshops within their respective areas. Their request is to replicate the thought process of the rogue trading workshop, examining possible ways in which unauthorized or fraudulent payments can be executed, and trying to find potential loopholes. These workshops are subsequently run for risk *management* purposes only – it is known a priori that the financial outcomes will be lower than *rogue trading* and therefore are unlikely to be used for capital assessment purposes.

What are the positive features of this process?

- An approach with a strong sense of purpose, which engages the participants and establishes scenario analysis as a valuable risk management tool that subsequently becomes in demand.
- An explicitly defined executive level scenario owner (the head of Trading).
- A value-added control review leading to remedial actions.

What can be improved?

- The estimation of the amount at risk, considering different elements that might contribute to a loss; including, for example, regulatory fines and remediation costs.

CASE STUDY 8.2

A medium-sized regulated subsidiary is subjected to a review of its internal capital adequacy assessment process (ICAAP), with unsatisfactory results. One of the regulator's criticisms is around scenarios, which are deemed too benign and not sufficiently extreme. As part of the remediation, senior management agrees to start running multifactor scenario analysis. Despite the process being regulatory driven, the head of Operational Risk is aiming to derive maximum value out of the exercise.

The 10 most significant (top) inherent risks are extracted from the subsidiary's risk and control self-assessment and noted down on Post-it Notes, one risk on each note. Five members of the senior executive team consisting of the CEO, head of Corporate Banking, head of Risk, chief operations officer and head of Finance are asked to each pick two Post-it Notes at random and to come up with a scenario where their two chosen risks materialize at the same time. This approach is useful because in real life an extreme unexpected loss often arises from a combination of unrelated events which, when combined, place intolerable stress on the control environment.

The head of Finance selects *Poor change management process* and *Significant data breach* and develops a plausible story line combining two failures:

- the subsidiary is planning to migrate customer accounts to a new system;
- the deadline is fast approaching and corners are cut in the testing phase;
- once the transition goes live, a major issue is highlighted, and migration has to be stopped and rolled back to the pre-transition stage;

- an employee participating in the project, who has worked significant overtime over several months, is frustrated with this result and uses the opportunity to print out and anonymously leak confidential details of multiple client accounts;

- the leak is not discovered until later due to key personnel being occupied with the roll-back.

Other participants introduce their respective scenarios before the two-hour workshop concludes. The workshop generates lively debate among senior management participants, resulting in agreement about several areas that need further exploration and possible enhancement of processes and controls. Proposed story lines are subsequently supplemented by a study of relevant internal and external loss data, and a financial value for each scenario is estimated at follow-up meetings with a broader audience of subject matter experts (SMEs).

What are the positive features of this process?

- Multifactor scenarios, assuming that multiple risks crystallize at once.

- Senior stakeholder engagement.

- Several improvement projects emanating from the workshop.

What can be improved?

- A disciplined approach to the creation of a preparatory pack; this should contain supporting materials with internal and external loss data and other information to facilitate the assessment of scenario amounts.

CASE STUDY 8.3

An institution using a statistical model to calculate its operational risk capital is running a scenario analysis workshop. (Note: the firms in the earlier case studies were not using statistical models.) The workshop is led by the first line operational risk coordinator, with middle management from relevant business lines in attendance. The operational risk coordinator explains that scenarios need to be created due to key gaps in the relevant loss data. In the future, these scenarios could be decommissioned if they are replaced by real events, either internally or externally sourced.

Figure 8.5   Cause–Event–Impact approach to scenario analysis

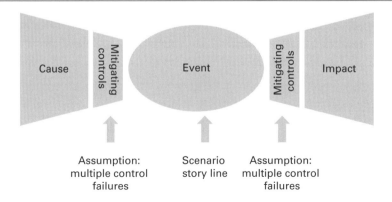

As preparatory work, operational risk has distributed a reading pack containing internal loss data, external loss data and an analysis of the risk and control environment relevant to the story line. A training session has also been offered to participants prior to the workshop, which some of the attendees have opted to take.

The scenario story line is a major regulatory breach. The group discuss the cause, the event itself and its consequences, using the already familiar bow-tie approach, as per Figure 8.5.

Causal factors include prior regulatory criticism of the lack of first line ownership, poor change management and rushed implementation of a new regulatory initiative. Assumptions are documented around a generally deteriorating business environment and a series of minor reportable breaches which preceded the main event. This combination of factors then culminates in a major regulatory non-compliance incident, whereby the firm fails to identify, understand and implement an important new regulatory directive before its effective date.

The consequences of the event include a fine and investigation, disciplinary actions against the firm and its managers, and a loss of client business due to damaged brand and reputation.

To assist scenario quantification, participants use the checklist in Table 8.1 which contains different categories of possible impacts.

The overall loss amount is estimated as a sum of applicable sub-components. Participants are asked to consider three scenario frequencies – a 1 in 10-year event, 1 in 25 and 1 in 40 – and to come up with an estimated loss number in each category, giving rise to three points to model as the basis of a loss curve.

Table 8.1   Scenario quantification

Loss category	Description	Applicable? Yes/No	Amount
Direct loss	Impact of the loss on the P&L account		
Fines and penalties	Regulatory, compliance, taxation or other penalties as a result of non-compliance		
Expenses	Consultancy costs or other unbudgeted expenses		
Legal liability	Legal fees, legal judgement and/or settlement		
Indirect costs	Overtime paid to staff due to extra hours worked in resolving the loss, short-term rental of additional premises, travel and other indirect expenses		
Risk of life	Danger or loss of life of an employee		
Reputational impact	Reduced sales and lost revenue due to brand damage		

The workshop lasts for one and a half hours and concludes with no further actions.

What are the positive features of the workshop?

- Structured approach to generating pre-reading materials and providing training.
- Consistent format for estimating the amount, resulting in well-reasoned evaluations.
- First line operational risk in the lead.

What can be improved?

- The value proposition, use of a workshop for risk management purposes, ownership and agreement of actions, senior stakeholder engagement.

Life cycle: from pre-reading packs to mitigating bias

The scenario process life cycle is described as:

- **Define:** A theme or topic for a scenario and a detailed story line are developed.

- **Prepare:** Relevant data is researched and assembled into a pre-reading pack.

- **Explore and Assess:** A workshop is run with SMEs to discuss the scenario and arrive at the estimated numbers.

- **Extract Learnings and Actions:** Identified control gaps and actions are noted down, with owners and target dates.

- **Validate:** Scenario outcomes are scrutinized by relevant SMEs and governance committees.

Define

As mentioned above, the most significant inherent risks from RCSAs can be a good starting point to generate scenario ideas. It is good practice to examine simultaneous multiple failures, for example, by combining two to three *top* risks from the RCSAs, for example *Significant system failure* and *Internal fraud*. In the event that the firm is anticipating an acquisition or expansion into a new market, this kind of strategic initiative also needs to be taken into consideration.

> When defining story lines, it is important to ensure that scenarios are *forward looking* and correspond to the organization's strategy. Scenarios can examine plausible events that may crystallize as a result of a chosen strategic direction, thus aiding good decision-making.

Scenarios can be established at multiple levels of the organization, including at group-wide and individual business or entity level. The selection process involves deciding on what constitutes a key risk which would benefit from further exploration. There may be a need to run the same scenario – for example *Internal fraud* – several times to ensure all business units are included. Systemic risks impacting any number of control processes operating in business units also need to be considered.

It is good practice to agree an *executive sponsor* at the outset, a senior executive who owns and is accountable for the content and the story line. The owner plays a key role in the whole life cycle, from defining the story line to providing sign-off as part of the later validation stage, and finally ensuring any follow-up actions are actually completed.

Prepare

Pre-reading packs help to structure the workshops. Typically, the operational risk team researches, prepares and analyses relevant materials. These will often include internal losses, a selection of pertinent external events experienced by peer firms, and RCSA data reflecting the firm's risk and control environment, as well as the results of compliance monitoring and internal audit reviews. Applicable operational and financial data, containing transaction volumes, values and profitability, help to make the discussion more factual and to arrive at accurate loss estimates. It is useful to outline the inherent risk exposure from the RCSAs up-front; as well as noting if the scenario involves breaches of the firm's appetite. A consistent and uniform approach to the preparatory packs helps to achieve reliable outcomes.

Generally, the more time spent in preparation, the shorter the required length of the workshop. Foundational activity may involve working with the scenario owner and relevant business experts to define a story line. The workshop can then be used, in effect, as a validation activity.

Alternatively, a shorter preparation time can result in a longer workshop where the story line itself is debated and developed in detail. This can be done using, for example, a technique such as a Bayesian tree scenario, commonly used in the insurance industry. In simple terms, this approach allows a mapping of the scenario journey by workshop participants all working together. This might involve a starting point: for example, the new normal of *working from home* which has emanated from the Covid-19 pandemic. The story line is then progressively developed, exploring potential for a data loss, cyber attack and internal fraud. The strength of this approach is its ability to explore the interconnectivity between various different causes.

Explore and assess

The Basel Committee notes four possible approaches to scenario analysis, namely workshops, individual interviews, questionnaires and voting.[1] In the 2020 poll I ran with industry experts, 100 per cent of respondents were using workshops: no other mechanism was deemed nearly as effective, though the duration of workshops differed sharply, as illustrated in Table 8.2.

As part of the workshop, an estimation should be made as to the frequency and severity of the losses occurring in different timelines; usually in normal situations as well as worst or stressed cases. The quantification is then completed by business experts based on their subjective judgement. This process involves a risk of partiality or unfairness (bias) in the assessment; driven by common bias factors such as overconfidence, motivational bias, availability or anchoring. Consequently the firm needs to have measures in place to address those biases, for example as described in Table 8.3.

Based on the 2020 industry study mentioned earlier, only 50 per cent of respondents explicitly addressed biases in their scenario analysis process.

Extract learnings and actions

This is a critical part of SA, which in practice is underemphasized or entirely overlooked. The workshops need to answer both questions: *how much?* (capital calculation, or a risk *measurement* question) and *so what?* (a risk

Table 8.2 Industry study: scenario workshop duration

Workshop duration	% respondents
1 hour	30
1.5–2 hours	20
3–4 hours	30
Half-day or longer	20

Table 8.3   Mitigating bias

Bias	Explanation	Mitigation
Overconfidence	Attendees overestimate the robustness of controls	Pre-reading pack containing factual data on past internal events Stress testing controls: exploring what will make them fail
Motivational	Participant is conflicted/ interested in influencing the outcome of the workshop (to, for example, reduce the estimated loss amount)	Consistent and robust facilitation to manage conflicting interests Use of anonymous voting polls or obtaining estimated numbers beforehand Challenge and validation by SMEs
Availability	Increased focus on recent events as they can be easily recalled	Pre-reading pack containing factual external event data Encouragement to think about possible events that have not yet occurred
Anchoring	Different starting points (anchors) will yield different results	Use of neutral open questions Avoidance of leading questions containing a number (anchor) Training for participants to explain different terms; and what should or should not be included into estimates Request to submit quantifications ahead of the workshop Use of ranges instead of specific values

management question). A key aim of scenario analysis is to use the outcomes for risk reduction. Risk mitigating measures need to be considered when:

- a specific control weakness is identified as a result of the exercise; or
- assessment reveals that insurance cover is insufficient or inadequate; or
- the measurement results of the analysis exceed a certain threshold level, bringing it outside the firm's appetite (also see Chapter 9, Operational risk appetite). This may happen when a specific scenario highlights significant risk exposure and consequences that are deemed unacceptable for the organization.

The actions need to contain a target date and an owner, and the Operational Risk department usually monitors progress until they have been fully implemented.

At times, the purchase of insurance is a standalone activity which is not coordinated with the firm's risk management efforts. Evaluating the degree and scope of insurance coverage is a great opportunity for operational risk to work closely with the department responsible for procuring the firm's insurance: for example, assessing proposals obtained in the market, considering the types of cover offered and analysing whether they are appropriate. This is the opportunity to consider gaps in cover as well as any ambiguity on whether a particular loss is or is not included in the policy. Insurance needs to be both commensurate with identified exposure and in sync with the story lines examined in the workshops. Furthermore, given the nature of the insurance market, both corporate insurance buying functions and external brokers can be good sources of credible but extreme scenario suggestions.

Finally, the scenario workshop can also trigger a revision of RCSAs, to sense check the inherent risk assessment; as well as amendments to/introductions of new Key Risk Indicators, discussed in Chapter 7.

Validate

Based on the Basel Committee study, four challenge functions are used to maintain the integrity of scenario analysis: review by a risk control function (93 per cent); review by internal/external audit (83 per cent); comparisons by experienced or expert staff (76 per cent); and comparisons with other data elements (62 per cent).[2]

The second line Operational Risk department is usually the first point of validation. To enable this to occur, it is critical that the team does not contribute to the quantification, to avoid marking its own homework.

Scenarios can be assessed for consistency of outcomes, ensuring that:

- the scenario is correctly classified using the firm's usual operational risk taxonomy;
- financial impact is not lower than that experienced from internal loss events;
- if different frequencies are used, the financial impact with the lower frequency is smaller than the higher-frequency event;
- story lines and related assumptions are comparable with related external events;

- there is consistency in the documentation and rationale around the outcomes, to ensure 'a clearly defined and repeatable process'.[3]

Further evaluation is usually undertaken by a wider group of stakeholders, either at the risk committee or the capital and stress testing committee; or by the appropriate governance committee responsible for the operational risk capital calculation.

How are the reviewers determining whether the story lines are extreme enough and the amounts plausible?

The construct and extremity of scenarios is in part a cultural matter, reflecting how cautious and well capitalized the firm aspires to be. The approach is often tested in practice at times of crisis, resulting in some conservative firms having sufficient reserves while others find themselves operating to the wire and perhaps in need of external help. During the early stages of the Covid-19 pandemic, Nassim Taleb relayed thoughts on this topic when discussing the concept of bail-out, stipulating that bail-out (of banks in particular) is encouraging the wrong behaviour, favouring those firms that do not have an adequate buffer, and pointing out that 'not having a buffer is irresponsible'.[4]

Therefore, in practice, scenario validation can be a tenuous activity. By definition, scenarios are made-up events with imaginary story lines that have been allocated a potential loss amount by workshop participants. The cultural element in firms often manifests itself in haggling over the numbers. One of three things can happen: reduce the estimate, increase the estimate or enhance controls.

Call to reduce the estimate

Reviewers will state that estimated amount is abnormally high, resulting in a greater than expected capital requirement; workshop participants must go back and re-evaluate the amount, ideally bringing it lower. This eventuality can be due to incorrect workshop attendees, poor methodology or excessive confidence in the ability of the control regime to respond to the event. However in many cases there is an additional cultural aspect: a refusal to tolerate any buffer that increases the cost of running the business (this links back to motivational bias). This attitude also creates a danger of losing the operational value of the risk management points raised by the scenario, simply due to over-consideration of the costs of the final number.

Call to increase the estimate

The estimated amount can also be perceived as too low, with a similar request to re-work it. This, again, can occur because of procedural elements, but in most senses is a positive sign: the firm would rather be too cautious than overly optimistic. This happens far more rarely and is a credit to any firm whose leaders raise this kind of challenge.

Call to enhance controls

The scenario amount is assessed as unacceptably high; however, rather than changing the number, there is a request to improve the control environment, so that if the scenario materializes, the impact is reduced. Participants walk away from the process committing to develop, agree and implement mitigating actions. This is the preferred outcome, which not only demonstrates the use test but also does not devalue the efforts of workshop participants and does not over-ride their judgement. A sign of risk maturity is to learn from the expertise in the room but as a consequence of the scenario analysis to seek to reduce its impact or likelihood.

Periodic updates

Many organizations factor trigger-based scenario updates into their policies. In practice, however, where scenarios are run mainly for risk measurement purposes, they are more usually updated annually, to coincide with the update of the ICAAP. Ideally, scenarios are management's first choice when it comes to exploring or anticipating the impact of major changes or disruptions to the firm's business. These can include:

- changes in business model, including a new line of business, service or geography, acquisition, or divestiture;
- material changes in the external environment, be it new regulations, a material external loss event, or wider social or political behaviour;
- a large unexpected internal loss or significant deterioration in the internal control environment.

The outbreaks of avian flu in 2003 and Covid-19 during 2020 prompted many organizations to run a pandemic scenario, exploring the readiness of the firm and considering actions (risk *management*) as well as evaluating their potential impact on the capital position (risk *measurement*). Similarly, large industry rogue trading events served as a trigger for scenario revision. If a scenario owner is engaged and has enjoyed a good experience with the workshop, they will be more inclined to rely on the tool as a first point of call in the event of a major shift in the day-to-day environment – as a way to explore the consequences of the event. This can be one of the clearest measures of the success of the tool: to have the owners *want* to use the SA process.

Other softer factors are also recognized as a foundation for good decision-making; including situational awareness, which refers to perceptions about the wider environment and a good comprehension of the meaning and projection of the future state. Indeed, what transpired during Covid-19 is that while most firms had the scenario analysis tool at their disposal, it was those firms with a situational awareness mindset who promptly applied it in practice and showed maximum responsiveness.

Emerging risks

Scenario analysis plays a key role in the management of *emerging risks*. The insurance industry is more advanced in this area compared to banking and asset management, as insurers typically seek to understand as much as possible about the emerging risks potentially impacting their portfolios. These emerging risks have the characteristic of being less familiar than the existing risk portfolio. They are not fully understood but still perceived to be potentially significant. As an example, the International Risk Governance Council (IRGC) defines an emerging risk as 'a risk that is new, or a familiar risk in a new or unfamiliar context or under new context conditions (re-emerging)'.[5]

> In the operational risk context, *emerging risk* can be defined as a new or increasing operational risk which has the potential to become a *top risk*.
> In turn, *top risks* are those inherent risks which, if not well controlled, will result in the most significant impact to the firm.

This is an interesting subject in its own right, and not just for insurers. Public sector bodies have a considerable interest in emerging risks, while a number of think tanks and academics have produced research and guidance on the topic. For the financial services sector, regulators have continually urged organizations to adopt a forward-looking approach. The BIS's Corporate Governance Principles for Banks emphasize the need for ongoing 'identification of new or emerging risks';[6] while the Principles for the Sound Management of Operational Risk insist that Operational risk reporting should include 'a discussion and assessment of key and emerging risks';[7] and the Risk Data Aggregation Principles underscore the focus on 'risk exposures, concentrations and emerging risks'.[8]

Against this background, it is important that organizations have a meaningful process in place from horizon scanning for emerging themes to risk quantification via the use of scenario analysis. The operational Risk department can implement a structured approach of monitoring internal and external sources in order to develop a watchlist of emerging risks. This can be further discussed at the Operational Risk or other relevant governance committee, and *candidate risks* can subsequently be selected for further scenario analysis. Depending on the outcomes of examination and quantification via scenario workshops, significant candidate risks could be *promoted* to top risks, with subsequent actions, a statement of appetite, and enhanced monitoring. An example of this kind of process is presented in Figure 8.6.

To expand on the process of monitoring internal and external sources, in other words *risk horizon scanning*. This is different to compliance horizon scanning which usually focuses on the presentation of a regulatory radar of new and forthcoming directives applicable to the firm. Instead, risk horizon scanning involves:

- A scan of major external operational risk losses or regulatory fines incurred by peers;

- A review of external sources that publish top and emerging risks;

- A scan of characteristics and changes in the firm's external operating environment;

- An examination of the firm's internal environment, to identify potential emerging risks emanating from within the firm, such as *change fatigue*;

- Employee surveys to gather internal intelligence on emerging risks, considering questions along the lines of, perhaps, 'risks you are aware of that are not being actively mitigated'.

Emerging risk horizon scanning maturity varies significantly among organizations, as presented in Figure 8.7. Some firms are inwardly focused and do

Figure 8.6 Emerging risk management cycle

Figure 8.7 Emerging risk horizon scanning maturity

not dedicate risk resources to reviewing the environment for emerging risks. Others perform ad hoc analysis, as and when a prominent industry event materializes. In turn, the mature stage of this practice involves continual scanning of external and internal sources, followed by further examination and quantification of identified risks via scenario analysis. In my consultancy experience, most firms lack a robust forward-looking process in this area, and would benefit significantly from putting more emphasis on emerging risks. In addition, this process provides an excellent opportunity to become a trusted board advisor.

Roles and responsibilities

The second line operational risk team sets the tone and determines whether the SA exercise will be used for measurement and regulatory compliance purposes only, or whether it will have a true value proposition. It goes without saying that key building blocks need to be in place. These include robust policy and guidance for participants; close oversight, ensuring that story lines are clearly defined with sufficient level of detail; the right stakeholders being involved; a strong validation and challenge process; and, last but not least, a trigger-based refresh process. It is far more difficult, and yet at the same time essential, to invest time and effort in turning the scenario exercise into a tool that stakeholders are truly keen to use; because of its clear benefits to them. The actions and behaviours of the second line, whether consciously or subconsciously, define the brand and reputation of scenario analysis. How will it be seen? Is it 'this needs to be done for capital purposes; but apart from that it's not very useful'? Or is it 'a valuable exploratory exercise; our first point of call when considering significant internal and external changes which also, by the way, generates inputs into the capital calculation'?

First line business units and support functions own and operate the controls and therefore, the scenario process examines *their* exposure to extreme risks. They are responsible for owning the story lines, evaluating the environment, identifying and agreeing actions and following them up until resolution.

Below is an example checklist for a first line risk coordinator.

FIRST LINE RISK COORDINATOR CHECKLIST: SCENARIO ANALYSIS

✓ Staff are aware of the SA tool and its benefits.

✓ There is a nominated senior executive, *the scenario owner*, for each scenario owned by the department.

✓ Material change in the environment triggers a consideration of scenario refresh or a need for a new one.

✓ Actions emanating from the SA are followed up until resolution.

✓ Post-SA, other core tools, including RCSAs, KRIs, OREs and where separately used, *emerging risks*, are considered for revision.

Common challenges and good practices

Common challenges

The following challenges may be encountered when dealing with scenario analysis.

Challenges of the operational risk discipline

Within the operational risk discipline, historically there existed a disconnect between the quantitative community of modellers who designed statistical models for the capital calculation, and generalists who focused more on the qualitative aspects of embeddedness, helping to implement good practices within, for example, the Human Resources or IT departments. Modellers and generalists not working together often led to risk *measurement* and *management* not being in sync. This is a very specific challenge to operational risk. In contrast, credit and market risk disciplines are more homogeneously quantitative – they do not have to work hand-in-hand with, say, Human Resources. On the other side, the compliance function – which is perhaps akin to operational risk in that it works with all the different units across the firm – does not typically design or run its own statistical models. It is crucial for both communities to work together. The generalists who have a natural curiosity about the quantitative aspects and take the time to understand the model assumptions and limitations often play a key role in bridging the gap between the quants and the business.

Participants dismissive of the story line

Workshop participants are dismissive of the scenario, taking the viewpoint that *this can never happen to us*. This is a common challenge from attendees who operate controls and understandably take pride in their robustness. Participants need to be pushed to think outside their comfort zone, by being educated and informed about the purpose of the SA process. It should be emphasized that it is not a test of the BAU control environment but a stressed, extreme environment enabling the firm to build shock-proof controls; and bringing to the fore relevant case studies of external events which prompted failures.

Terms hard to understand

Attendees struggle to understand the notion of frequency, questioning what exactly do the statements *1 in 40 years* or *1 in 100 years* actually mean.

Operational risk teams need to provide an explanation, comparing it more intuitively to, for example, a *once in a career event* or a *once in a lifetime event*. Some practitioners run workshops using softer terminology, keeping the probability numbers and concept in the background. One approach that should definitely be avoided is to invite attendees to *assess the 95th percentile loss amount*, or other similar statistical measures; as these are mathematical concepts which may take considerable time to explain. (Note: another common misunderstanding is that a *1 in 40 year* event will not occur with the prescribed impact for the next 40 years; while it could happen tomorrow!)

Difficulty in arriving at a number

From a *measurement* viewpoint, scenario analysis relies heavily on expert judgement to produce a rather extreme number. It is important to recognize that participants from business and support functions, as knowledgeable as they are in their areas, are not really experts in predicting the future, and consequently may be only partially effective in providing loss estimates. It often helps to allow people to express ranges, even for a single event or component of it.

Lack of action

A rather bureaucratic exercise is run and quickly forgotten. After the numbers are obtained, no actions emanate from the workshop and its value rapidly diminishes. It is essential to acknowledge the value of SME inputs; to share outcomes with senior management; to keep participants informed on uses of the output, and to highlight real-life internal and external events when they happen (helping to demonstrate the reality of the scenarios); as well as to ensure that the SA exercise includes a thorough control examination. All these features should be a mandatory part of the process.

Overall number of scenarios

The number of scenarios varies significantly from firm to firm. Similar to KRIs, some organizations design and run way too many scenarios, running to hundreds, purely for *risk measurement* purposes. While there is no right target number and it is often determined by the firm's risk taxonomy and footprint, a range of around 15–30 scenarios with solid *risk management* outcomes is appropriate. This comes with a caveat, however, of what is meant by scenario and what value is derived from the process. For management purposes, cyber war games, crisis management and incident response table-top exercises are also labelled as scenarios by some organizations, even though they do not generate a capital number. Some firms differentiate 'big S' Scenarios used for capital calculation purposes and 'small s' scenarios run to identify and remedy control weaknesses.

Models drive the exercise

Sometimes organizations applying less quantitative, formula-based approaches to capital calculation are not driven and *constrained* by the statistical model and consequently do better with scenario analysis from the value proposition point of view. This, however, does not have to be the case; business benefits need to come first regardless of the approach, with regulatory compliance a secondary, not primary outcome.

Good practices

Ensuring value proposition

The secret of success with scenario analysis is in ensuring it has a clear value proposition *for the attendees* and does not become an operational risk number-generating exercise. When running workshops, it is important to consider what benefits *participants* will derive from the meeting. A clear purpose ensures that the scenario process is integrated with business decisions. The purpose can be, for example, to examine preparedness for a particular event that is relevant to the business owner and keeps them awake at night; to assess the impact of a major change, including a new product, service or geography, or wider social and political shifts. Scenarios are there to help first line business units and support functions to examine *their own* exposure to extreme risks, and to mitigate them so eventually they are able to meet *their own* objectives.

Workshop facilitation

Good workshop facilitation, discussed in Chapter 5, is even more critical for scenarios. The Basel Committee notes the need for 'qualified and experienced facilitators with consistency in the facilitation process'.[9] This is important for the brand and value proposition of the exercise as well as for achieving reliable outcomes. Facilitation can include the use of aids such as live polls which can help mitigate, for example, motivational bias by requesting participants to anonymously vote on a scenario estimate. Expert guest speakers, YouTube clips and functional presentations also make the workshop more engaging for the attendees.

Stress testing controls

It is good practice to challenge each control in turn, finding ever more extreme situations in which a control may fail. This can be thought of as *stress testing* each control. In real-life situations one or more controls fail to operate due to what are often unforeseen circumstances, thus proving that the improbable is actually more probable in practice than in theory.

Rigour and documentation

Regulatory focus is often on the rigour of the process used to obtain inputs into any capital model. That process needs to be systematic and to generate good-quality documentation. The output pack needs to contain the scenario description and rationale for its selection, assumptions, a chronology of events, and robust loss estimates with justification of the amounts; as well as any other scenarios considered and discounted. Scenarios are rarely loaded into the operational risk system/software. Instead, the evidence is commonly kept in an Excel or Word format. Maintaining the library to a good standard ensures accessibility and evidenced decision-making. Actions emanating from the workshops can be uploaded into an *action* module, to enable tracking of progress until full resolution.

Measures of success

One of the measures of success is the number of actions that emanate from scenario workshops; even better if they lead to monetary investments in improving the control environment. This outcome is, unfortunately, underused. The Basel Committee notes that 'overall, few banks develop action plans from their scenario analyses'.[10]

Industry benchmark

Best Practice Operational Risk Forum members participated in a live poll to examine the use of scenario analysis in operational risk management. Overall, this meeting revealed a positive story. The majority of participants considered that the added value of this core tool has been gradually increasing as firms have developed better practices, with 38 per cent of respondents noting significant improvement, as shown in Figure 8.8.

Firms were selective with their scenarios, with the majority (78 per cent) having fewer than 20 scenarios and the rest between 20 and 30. These numbers have remained largely consistent over the years, usually ranging between 10 and 40, with organizations generally planning to reduce the number of scenarios if it exceeded 30 (Figure 8.9).

Limiting the number of scenarios (as compared to RCSAs, for example) enables firms to do a better job of developing meaningful story lines, producing preparatory information packs and leading effective workshops with participants. Good practices in this area included:

- Senior management engagement, and ownership from the executive sponsor. The majority of organizations agreed that senior management and the board took great interest in scenario outcomes.

- A thorough review of detailed story lines by workshop participants; at times this prompted further reflection and amendment to the narrative, to address a more urgent and pertinent topic more in the forefront of business participants' minds.

Figure 8.8   Industry poll: scenario analysis value-add

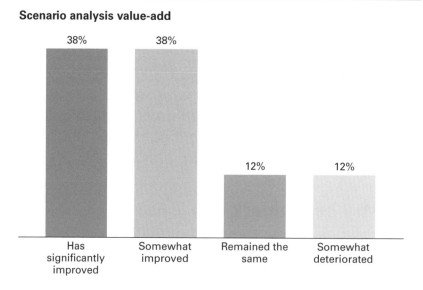

Scenario analysis value-add

38%	38%	12%	12%
Has significantly improved	Somewhat improved	Remained the same	Somewhat deteriorated

Best Practice Operational Risk Forum, 2023

Figure 8.9 Industry poll: number of scenarios considered

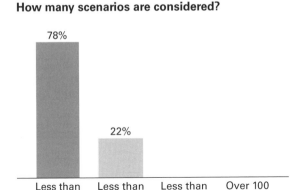

How many scenarios are considered?

Best Practice Operational Risk Forum, 2023

Despite the historic use of scenario assessment for risk *measurement* purposes only, gone are the days of pure number generation. The industry seems to have had success tackling this challenge, with the majority of firms using the tool for both risk *management* and risk *measurement* purposes. However, actionability remained a challenge, and many firms ran workshops which did not lead to any further follow-up actions. This needs to remain an area of continued focus in the future.

Practical workplace exercise

Obtain a copy of the firm's set of scenarios from the scenario library. Review it, considering the following questions:

1 What is the firm's approach to scenario analysis? Is it driven by capital considerations and run primarily for risk measurement purposes, or risk management, or both?

2 Are scenarios clearly defined? Is the story line documented and does the documentation contain assumptions, a clearly described workshop rationale and justification of the resulting loss amount?

3 What actions have been considered following the workshop? Did the scenarios covered include an examination of the control environment and did any improvements result from the process?

4 Is there a comparison of scenarios with the firm's insurance coverage?

5 What works well? Outline the strength of the process.

6 What could be improved? Note down potential areas of enhancement.

MAKE A DIFFERENCE (MAD) ACTION

Outline the key learnings and note down one specific action you will take after reading this chapter, to enhance your existing practices relating to scenario analysis.

In summary, this chapter discussed scenario analysis, an instrument that utilizes proactive risk assessment thinking and applies it to extreme but plausible circumstances.

Now that all the core tools of the operational risk toolbox have been examined, the next chapter considers mechanisms that converges the core elements, commencing with the operational risk appetite.

Notes

1 Basel Committee on Banking Supervision (2009) *Observed Range of Practice in Key Elements of Advanced Measurement Approaches*, www.bis.org/publ/bcbs160b.pdf (archived at https://perma.cc/5FBU-QM9S)

2 Basel Committee on Banking Supervision (2009) *Observed Range of Practice in Key Elements of Advanced Measurement Approaches*, www.bis.org/publ/bcbs160b.pdf (archived at https://perma.cc/5FBU-QM9S)

3 Basel Committee on Banking Supervision (2009) *Observed Range of Practice in Key Elements of Advanced Measurement Approaches*, www.bis.org/publ/bcbs160b.pdf (archived at https://perma.cc/5FBU-QM9S)

4 Bloomberg (2020) Interview with Nassim Nicholas Taleb, www.bloomberg.com/news/videos/2020-03-31/nassim-taleb-says-white-swan-coronavirus-pandemic-was-preventable-video (archived at https://perma.cc/F6PJ-WXWH)

5 The International Risk Governance Council (IRGC) *IRGC Guidelines for Emerging Risk Governance* (2015), irgc.org/risk-governance/emerging-risk/a-protocol-for-dealing-with-emerging-risks/ (archived at https://perma.cc/RCX9-CNGV)

6 Basel Committee on Banking Supervision (2015) *Corporate governance principles for banks*, www.bis.org/bcbs/publ/d328.pdf (archived at https://perma.cc/G325-V5BG)

7 Basel Committee on Banking Supervision (2021) *Revisions to the Principles for the Sound Management of Operational Risk*, www.bis.org/bcbs/publ/d515.pdf (archived at https://perma.cc/FX66-VY83)

8 Basel Committee on Banking Supervision (2013) *Principles for effective risk data aggregation and risk reporting*, www.bis.org/publ/bcbs239.pdf (archived at https://perma.cc/46HX-HYW8)

9 Basel Committee on Banking Supervision (2011) *Operational Risk: Supervisory guidelines for the advanced measurement approaches*, www.bis.org/publ/bcbs196.pdf (archived at https://perma.cc/66QD-MLSQ)

10 Basel Committee on Banking Supervision (2014) Review of the Principles for the Sound Management of Operational Risk, www.bis.org/publ/bcbs292.pdf (archived at https://perma.cc/H6CY-SUT5)

Operational risk 09 appetite

What this chapter covers: The chapter discusses Operational Risk Appetite, a topic which continues to pose challenges for firms due to its essentially qualitative nature (Figure 9.1). The chapter considers two divergent opinions, examining whether operational risk is consciously taken for reward or is merely mitigated downwards. It then proceeds to practical implementation, proposing a three-stage process to developing a risk appetite that is meaningful and used for decision-making. It goes on to present an approach for the expression of risk appetite using particular tools, and provides an assessment scale to help analyse the maturity of the approach. The chapter also provides examples and contains an industry benchmark.

FURTHER READING

- Financial Stability Board (2013) *Principles for an Effective Risk Appetite Framework*

  Why recommended: Although slightly dated, this is an essential guide covering the risk appetite framework and definitions of capacity, tolerance and profile.

Risk reward equation and its application to operational risk

Financial services firms are in the business of taking risk and have been doing so for hundreds of years. When it comes to the neighbouring disciplines of credit and market risk, the risk–reward equation is well understood: conservative lending is less profitable while loans to riskier sectors

Figure 9.1 Focus of Chapter 9: operational risk appetite

Embedding and maturity assessment

Risk culture

Governance, roles and responsibilities
Establish governance and clear roles across the Three Lines for managing operational risk.

Risk appetite and risk capacity
Define nature and types of risk accepted in pursuit of strategic objectives. Evaluate adequacy of capital resources.

Operational risk events	Risk assessments	Scenario analysis	Key Risk Indicators
Record and report risk events, act to minimize future exposure. Monitor trends against RCSAs and KRIs.	Assess risk exposure in process, business or function via RCSAs. Supplement by evaluating risks emanating from change activities via ORAs.	Identify exposure from extreme but plausible events. Mitigate through risk transfer to insurance.	Monitor risk and control performance through predictive indicators. Act if indicators breach established appetite threshold.

Operational risk taxonomy

Reporting and decision-making
Review actual risk profile against set appetite, apply active risk management to enable achievement of strategic objectives.

Training and education

attract higher interest rates and generate better returns. This is described in Figure 9.2.

The same formula becomes less obvious when applied to operational risk. There are two main schools of thought on this subject.

The first one differentiates operational risk from credit and market risks, using the word *contrary* in explaining its nature.

Contrary to credit and market risk, operational risk:

- has no material upside in terms of return or income generation;
- cannot be capped; and therefore
- must be mitigated downwards.

This view is somewhat echoed by the European Banking Authority, who wrote that operational risk is by nature 'unavoidable and it is neither willingly incurred nor is revenue driven. Moreover, it is not diversifiable and thus it cannot be fully eliminated.'[1]

This attitude of risk mitigation can be illustrated by examining sub-category 4 of the Basel operational risk taxonomy *clients, products and business practices*:

- Events in this contentious sub-category include unlicensed activity, breaches of regulation, inappropriate sales practices and unsuitable products.

- There is no upside in consciously choosing to contravene the regulation or offer ill-designed products. In fact, it is unethical and unlawful.

- The risk will inevitably materialize into incidents as a result of human errors, poor training or wilful misconduct. It is not possible to put a hard limit on the level of risk in terms of the number and value of losses as they cannot be completely eradicated – unless the firm chooses to exit the business altogether.

Figure 9.2   Risk–reward relationship

- Consequently, organizations revert to a risk reduction approach, implementing policies, providing training and enhancing detective mechanisms for early identification of non-compliance.

There is, however, a second viewpoint that uses the word *similar* instead of *contrary*.

In a *similar* way to credit and market risk:

- operational risk has to be looked at on a risk–reward basis;
- the reward aspect may include revenue from engaging in specific activities or cost reductions; and therefore
- the right level of risk is consciously taken in pursuit of strategic objectives.

When running training courses, I usually ask the audience to come up with examples where operational risk is taken for return. This commonly proves to be less familiar territory for participants, and it is typically more difficult for them to contemplate the 'risk–reward' concept compared to 'risk mitigation'.

CASE STUDY 9.1

A client of an investment bank makes a request to trade a new product. To satisfy this demand, the bank develops a value proposition and carries out an operational risk assessment (ORA). While credit and market risks are within the firm's appetite, product booking and accounting cannot be accommodated systematically and will need to be processed via manual workarounds. The firm acknowledges that the level of operational risk is high; but so is the reward being offered by the client. The proposal is discussed further in the light of the firm's appetite, and is agreed with acceptance of the risk commensurate with the return.

The risk–reward philosophy applied to operational risk leads to a more commercially astute position, balancing the risk with just the right amount of mitigation. Too few controls will result in fines, client detriment and reputational damage; but overdoing them, introducing excessive processes and procedures may render the proposal non-viable. The latter reasoning is generally underused by firms; not only senior managers but even some risk practitioners themselves can feel quite uncomfortable talking about 'letting go of controls' and accepting even a small level of errors and losses. This is an area where the operational risk function can increasingly add value, introducing a risk–reward equation to assist in arriving at balanced, sensible decisions. As discussed in Chapter 6, with the Risks and Opportunities assessment, this approach reinforces positive risk management, encouraging appropriate risk taking while protecting the firm from an overly aggressive attitude.

This more entrepreneurial style also reflects the position expressed in the Financial Stability Board (FSB)'s guidelines on risk appetite; and therefore will serve as a base for the definition of operational risk appetite:[2]

DEFINITION: OPERATIONAL RISK APPETITE

Operational risk appetite represents an aggregate *level* and different *types* of operational risk that 'a financial institution is willing to assume in order to achieve its strategic objectives and business plan'.[3]

The FSB document is a helpful guide for any risk practitioner. It nevertheless recognizes that operational risk appetite is a more difficult summit to conquer due to the qualitative nature of the topic, and therefore goes no further into outlining what good looks like for this particular area.

Deliberations of this kind, on the nature of operational risk and the chosen attitude, be it *mitigated downwards* or *taken for reward*, are important. They define the firm's overall stance towards risk, and the language that will be used to describe it. They also stretch into more cultural aspects, namely whether the firm perceives itself as rather conservative or more entrepreneurial.

Three steps for developing an effective appetite statement

As is the case with most operational risk tools, there is no prescriptive or universally accepted operational risk appetite framework which perfectly suits every organization, sector or jurisdiction. In fact, it is perhaps the most embryonic element in the entire operational risk discipline.

Risk appetite is inextricably linked to *measurement*, which in itself remains a process that is still to be fully mastered by the industry. Those in favour of quantitative approaches – and thus seeking a definitive number to express the appetite – may find that a risk appetite framework does not lend itself well to purely numeric limits and thresholds. In fact, as we will see from this chapter, many descriptors are primarily qualitative.

Also, creating an appetite is not about merely writing a set of statements: it involves providing a decision-making tool to enable prioritization and the deployment of resources, and to drive considered, risk-based decisions. The hardest part of it is fulfilling the *use test* and achieving *embeddedness* throughout the organization. Appetite development is an iterative process where less is more; it is better to have an unsophisticated framework which is well embedded and understood, than a state-of-the-art appetite statement which does not translate into actions and behaviours.

Proposed below is a three-stage process for building an operational risk appetite, outlined in Figure 9.3.

It is suggested that the three steps below are followed when implementing an operational risk appetite:

- define the desirable risk level on a spectrum – both overall and for principal operational risk sub-types;
- develop qualitative statements at an aggregate operational risk level and for each principal risk sub-type;
- establish qualitative and quantitative limits and triggers.

Step 1: Defining desirable risk level on a spectrum

In the first instance, it is valuable to understand the overall types and levels of risk the organization is willing to take in pursuit of its objectives. In

Figure 9.3 Three steps for developing an operational risk appetite simple terms, this step explains how the company intends to remain profitable (i.e. by taking a given level of risk or accepting a particular level of reward), considering return requirements and the specific idiosyncrasies of the firm's business model. This is an enterprise risk exercise which should be led by Operational Risk, jointly with other risk colleagues, to encompass all risk categories and create a consolidated framework. Desired risk levels can be expressed with the help of a qualitative scale, which provides a useful point of reference for future discussions. The scales can be absolute or relative.

An example of an absolute four-point scale is presented in Figure 9.4 below:

Figure 9.4   Risk appetite: absolute scale example

Minimal	Low	Moderate	High
Avoid; take as little risk as possible	*Reduce; adopt conservative approach*	*Take risk commensurate with return*	*Actively accept exposure to risk to maximize reward*

The risk range can also be expressed using a relative scale. An example of a four-point scale is included in Table 9.1:

Table 9.1   Risk appetite: relative scale example

Risk-averse	Avoid or minimize risk; the firm is willing to accept below market risk return/incur losses significantly lower than peers
Neutral	Adopt a balanced approach; control risk to achieve returns/incur losses in line with industry norms
Risk-tolerant	Take a measured amount of risk; the firm is willing to accept some risk if the circumstances include reward in line with or above industry norms
Expansionary	Actively pursue risk; the firm is willing to accept superior risk-adjusted reward/accept losses if reward is significantly above industry norm

The use of ranges and postures such as these enables a sensible conversation with the board; summarizing in a nutshell what kinds of risk the firm will actively pursue vs the ones it will aim to control or avoid. For example:

Risk type	Risk appetite
Strategic risk	*high* – actively accept exposure to risk to maximize reward
Operational risk	*moderate* – take risk commensurate with return
Market risk	*low* – reduce; adopt conservative approach
Credit risk	*low* – reduce; adopt conservative approach

And positioned on the scale (Figure 9.5):

Figure 9.5 Positioning principal enterprise risks on the scale

The attitude to operational risk taking, whether *mitigated downwards* or *taken for reward*, will define the position it occupies on the scale.

Ancillary to this discussion is the concept of risk tolerance; the words *appetite* and *tolerance* are often used interchangeably when applied to operational risk. Organizations that adopt a *mitigate downwards* attitude towards operational risk frequently give preference to the term *tolerance*, signifying that the risk has to be (unwillingly) endured as it cannot be eliminated.

However, approaches vary:

- Tolerance in some firms can be *greater* than appetite. To use an example, the police's appetite for speeding is set by the speed limit assigned to a road (30mph, for example) but the officers will often tolerate a higher speed (which may be 33mph) before they prosecute.

- Other firms adopt a stance that tolerance is *lower* than appetite. For instance, appetite will be set at a 33mph limit which should not be exceeded at any cost; consequently, tolerance is set below the appetite at 30mph to provide an early warning sign.

Once the principal risk types have been placed on the appetite range, the same exercise needs to be conducted for the next level *top* or *principal* operational risks, which were discussed in Chapters 1 and 5. *Top* or *principal* risks are those inherent risks which, if not well controlled, will result in the most significant impact to the firm.

Due to the huge variety of possible risk sub-categories, considering risk appetite solely at an aggregate operational risk level – for example, lumping together *financial crime, third party, people* and other risk sub-types of an entirely different nature – is simply inadequate.

It is better to elaborate appetite statements for each principal operational risk sub-type that underlies the firm's business thus addressing 'the nature, types and levels' of operational risk the firm is willing to assume.[4]

Figure 9.6 provides an example of a firm that identifies five principal operational risk sub-types and expresses their desired risk level on a spectrum.

Figures 9.5 and 9.6, presented to the board simultaneously, should generate some discussion. If the firm has a *high* appetite for strategic risk and is planning to significantly expand, on-boarding clients from new businesses and geographies, how does this tie in with the fact that it accepts only a *minimal* level of financial crime risk? This may be more suitable for a conservative, mature organization which is mostly maintaining an existing client base; since it has to be recognized that growth will inevitably generate an increased level of exposure to financial crime. If the board is not comfortable with that formulation, perhaps the firm's strategic aspirations and business plans need some revision. Alternatively, maybe the firm needs to double its investment in controlling financial crime risk, to maintain its minimal appetite level given expansion. Is the money on the table? This is the exact purpose of the scales, to generate debate on anticipated risk levels and the relationship between different elements of risk.

A question that frequently arises when working with risk ranges evolves around the exact meaning of terms, e.g. *minimal, risk-averse, expansionary.* To provide more colour and help define boundaries, the scale can broadly be based on the operational risk unified impact rating grid discussed in previous chapters. Accordingly, as illustrated in Figure 9.7, risk-averse appetite translates into tolerating low financial, client, regulatory and reputational impacts; while an expansionary stance assumes acceptance of at least one (usually *financial*) of the stated *very high* consequences.

Figure 9.6 Positioning principal operational risks on the scale

Minimal	Low	Moderate	High
Avoid; take as little risk as possible	*Reduce; adopt conservative approach*	*Take risk commensurate with return*	*Actively accept exposure to risk to maximize reward*

Figure 9.7 Aligning appetite scale with the unified impact rating grid

	Impact	Description
Expansionary *Actively pursue risk for superior reward*	Very high	**Financial:** Actual/potential loss greater than $xxx **Client:** Serious client detriment/large proportion impacted **Reputation:** Deep damage to the brand and market value, sustained media coverage **Regulatory:** Formal investigation resulting in action and fines
Risk tolerant *Take a measured amount of risk*	High	**Financial:** Actual/potential loss between $xx and $xxx **Client:** High level of detriment **Reputation:** Market commentary, serious damage to the reputation, brand and value **Regulatory:** May prompt investigation or regulatory action
Neutral *Adopt a balanced approach*	Moderate	**Financial:** Actual/potential loss between $x and $xx **Client:** Moderate impact/small proportion or segment **Reputation:** One-off media coverage, minor damage to reputation, brand and value **Regulatory:** Potential enquiry or one-off fine
Risk-averse *Avoid or minimize the risk*	Low	**Financial:** Actual/potential loss below $x **Client:** Minor impact or complaints **Reputation:** Inconsequential **Regulatory:** Unlikely to result in any regulatory action

Some firms prefer to use the ALARP principle as an alternative to appetite ranges.

> The ALARP Principle – *As Low As Reasonably Practicable* – encourages the mitigation of identified risks by balancing the cost of mitigation with the benefits, and formally enabling acceptance of the residual operational risk.

ALARP is applied as a decentralized decision-making model and operates by placing accountability on individual senior managers and executives. They assume risks and defend the position of what is practicable in terms of mitigation in each individual case. This can generate inconsistencies in application. If this thinking is adopted, it is important that the second line operational risk function reviews and challenges decisions, to ensure process reliability and robustness of outcomes. It is also recommended to supplement the ALARP approach with clear direction on desired appetite levels, via the use of qualitative ranges.

In summary, while qualitative scales are somewhat imprecise, they help to set the scene and provide soft guidance for better understanding the approach to risk taking within the organization. These scales are widely used by non-financial services firms, as they explain the appetite, at a high level, in pictures and language that are easy to comprehend. At times financial services firms, especially those applying more quantitative approaches to the operational risk capital calculation, favour numerical expressions and statistical probabilities – perhaps losing the softer explanatory element as well as the opportunity for honest board discussions. Perhaps this is something that can be learnt from non-financial services industries?

Step 2: Qualitative appetite statements

The second stage of the process involves assigning a qualitative risk appetite statement for operational risk overall and for principal risk sub-types.

The statement is a more detailed explanation, in written form, supporting the position of each risk on the spectrum. It aims to rationalize whether the risk will be actively pursued, controlled or avoided; and provides the reasons for the chosen approach. Yet again, due to the qualitative nature of operational risk, descriptive statements are essential, and may include cultural and behavioural nuances, which cannot be measured in numbers.

Starting from the overall level, the attitude to operational risk taking, *mitigated downwards* or *taken for reward*, will be explained further. Compare the following statements.

EXAMPLE 1

The firm's tolerance for operational risk is minimal. It is not possible to eliminate operational risk, but the firm aims to reduce it. Operational risk tolerance is defined via a limit of $25 million on aggregate operational losses, which is then broken down to lower limits across sub-categories of operational risk including, among others, fraud, legal, compliance and money laundering.

This is a very basic outline which nevertheless appears in the annual reports of many financial services firms in some form or another. It is good practice to develop more elaborate statements; and challenge whether the firm indeed intends to apply a *risk avoidance* attitude to the entirety of its operational risk, as a blanket approach, or whether it is prepared to differentiate between sub-categories. Note, the term *tolerance* is used here, instead of *appetite*, to emphasize the desire to mitigate the risk downwards.

EXAMPLE 2

The firm takes operational risk consciously in pursuit of its strategic objectives. It believes that risk acceptance is often necessary to foster innovation and that it is neither possible nor necessarily desirable to eliminate all the operational risks inherent in its activities. The firm's overall appetite is neutral, with a maximum loss appetite threshold of $10 million. For certain sub-categories, such as *financial crime, conduct* and *regulatory compliance,* the firm assumes a more conservative risk-averse attitude. Eight principal risk categories have been identified, namely *financial crime, technology and information security, execution, conduct, regulatory compliance, change, people* and *third party* and each has been assigned a qualitative risk appetite statement supplemented by various risk metrics. Each principal risk is owned by a named senior executive, who is accountable for devising appropriate controls and presenting the overall level of risk to the board. The board is ultimately responsible for agreeing the appetite for each risk. Breaches to the risk appetite must be escalated and actioned.

FEATURES OF OPERATIONAL RISK APPETITE STATEMENTS

✓ Easy to understand; this is crucial for subsequent embedding of risk appetite in the organization.
✓ Provide a definition of the risk sub-type; important to avoid second-guessing of what is included.

✓ Contain a link to strategic objectives; this sounds like an obvious point, but unfortunately it is still rare that operational risk statements are displayed with direct reference to strategy and business plans.

✓ Outline accountability, which may include a risk owner, subject matter expert or relevant committee.

✓ Contain a response framework, stating the consequences of breaching the appetite.

This expanded statement has several helpful attributes; specifically, it refers to accountability and response. Further features are outlined in the box above.

Considering these features, an example of an appetite statement for a sub-type of operational risk is provided in Table 9.2.

This statement for the *third-party* sub-type of operational risk follows the recommended format. It provides a definition, outlines the link to strategy and points to the executive owner as well as delivering an explanatory narrative.

Similar statements need to be developed for the remaining top/principal operational risk sub-types.

Let us expand on two rather challenging aspects: accountability and response frameworks.

Accountability framework

Accountability assumes that each of the key risk areas has clear ownership; either by a dedicated senior executive or a joint group or committee (depending on the governance arrangements) responsible for devising appropriate controls and risk mitigation activities. This is challenging to achieve in practice as it requires a well-defined allocation of responsibilities within senior executive teams. Also, some risks span across multiple business lines and geographies.

As an example, *technology risk* is usually the responsibility of the chief technology officer (CTO) as the majority of controls reside with the IT function; alternatively it can be co-owned by the heads of the business, the primary users and drivers of technological solutions, and the CTO. *Financial crime risk* is *not* owned by Compliance, despite the fact that compliance is usually tasked with designing and owning the framework. Rather, it is the

Table 9.2 Example operational risk appetite statement

Principal operational risk sub-type	Definition	Linked to strategic objective	Risk owner	Risk appetite	Risk appetite statement
Third-Party Risk (Outsourcing & Supplier)	The risk emanating from reliance on third parties, including incidents or failures of third parties to deliver on their obligations.	Confident customer experience	Chief operating officer (COO)	Moderate	The firm relies on third parties in delivering core business activities and services to its clients. It is willing to accept moderate level of risk working with contracted third parties to gain access to new technological platforms, improve flexibility and efficiency. Clients and regulators expect the firm to manage these arrangements effectively. The firm aims to limit disruptions by conducting robust third-party due diligence and performing monitoring and oversight by a dedicated Outsourcing team. The firm has identified single points of failure and, where feasible, developed a substitution plan in case of critical provider failure or unavailability. Where substitution is not viable, the firm has enhanced oversight and actively takes part in third-parties' testing of their resilience and recovery capabilities.

Elevated level of risk and breaches to appetite are escalated to the board and require action according to the firm's Response Framework.

The firm accepts that occasional minor disruptions may occur. |

duty of each and every employee and hence all senior executives to instil appropriate practices and behaviours within the organization to combat fraud and crime. Similarly, accountability for *People risk* is shared across all business units and support functions, while Human Resources provides policies and guidance. These kinds of risks should typically have joint owners in the first line, being the heads of major business units; or alternatively, the firm's chief executive.

Discussions on ownership can be heated and contentious; to the extent that the *risk owner* column is sometimes removed altogether. Cultural aspects play a significant part in this area, and firms that have a collaborative, honest and risk-aware ethos commonly excel in agreeing their accountability framework. With increasing supervisory focus on culture and conduct, and the introduction of personal accountability and certification regimes, the ownership of risks at the top of the house should align and conform to the broader accountability statements.

Response framework

In turn, the response framework deals with mechanisms to treat appetite breaches seriously and trigger robust action. One way of bringing this framework to life is by ensuring that significant breaches result in monetary penalties for the responsible owner or senior executive who is accountable to keep the risk within the limit; or perhaps a shared penalty for the whole senior executive team if they are jointly accountable for the risk sub-type which has caused the breach. This approach makes the instrument tangible and less of a theoretical exercise; but its success depends significantly on the firm's ability to agree on the accountability framework described above. It is worth noting the Basel Committee's view that 'compensation policies should be aligned to the bank's statement of risk appetite and tolerance'.[5]

Step 3: Limits and triggers

The final step consists of translating the appetite statements into limits and triggers that will help to measure actual risk exposure against established levels, indicating when the appetite has been – or is about to be – breached.

What tools are used to measure the appetite?

Common tools to measure operational risk appetite include:

- qualitative and quantitative – Key Risk Indicators;
- quantitative – losses and scenarios.

We have already examined these instruments in their respective chapters. Let's review them in more detail in the context of the operational risk appetite.

Key Risk Indicators

KRI metrics are important because they define what is acceptable (and, respectively, unacceptable), thus setting standards and guiding behaviours. They are inextricably linked to the culture of the organization. As described in Chapter 7, indicators are developed for the *key/top* risks, which is exactly what we have at hand when it comes to the expression of appetite.

Quantitative measures are equally significant as they warn about potential capital erosion. The firm is only able to assume any given amount of risk *within its risk capacity*.

> *Capacity* is the overall resource or, in other words, *the budget*, that the firm has at hand reflecting the maximum level of risk it is able to assume; and is inseparably linked to economic capital. The firm will not be able to sustain losses beyond its capacity, as it will become insolvent.

The FSB definition of risk appetite includes risk taking within the firm's *capacity*,[6] which – in the context of financial risk types such as credit and market risk – is represented by an amount of capital. For operational risk, strictly speaking, the definition is broader and includes, for example, the supply of people and systems; meaning that the firm will not be able to process more transactions than humanly possible given the number of employees it recruits and the systems it operates. These factors are harder to incorporate into appetite considerations; therefore, where the term *capacity* is used, it usually refers purely to financial resource.

Operational risk losses

Actual operational risk losses reflect the instances where risk has materialized. Organizations would not be able to absorb an unlimited amount of losses; and therefore, a threshold on the *expected* annual amount is an adequate and the most commonly used quantitative measure. Its purpose is to signal when the level of crystallized events may pose a threat to the broader corporate objective of remaining profitable.

This threshold can be absolute or relative, as illustrated in the following examples:

- absolute: the losses must not exceed $5 million;

- relative: the firm is prepared to tolerate a potential loss of 1% of recurring revenue.

It is important to note that these measures do not put a cap on losses; even if the firm is not willing to exceed a set amount, that may still happen. Rather, they serve as triggers for action. When the appetite is breached – or even better, before the breach, when approaching the limit – this warrants an immediate review and investigation of why the negative financial impact has exceeded the level that was agreed as acceptable; and requires the relevant risk owner to come up with a plan of action. This may, at times, include drastic measures, for example having to discontinue a product or exit a business line/geography if it is not a viable, cost-effective proposition.

Scenario analysis

Scenarios supplement the loss threshold by measuring the level of *unexpected* operational risk losses that the organization is able to withstand. As discussed in Chapter 8, scenarios help a firm to explore and anticipate the impact of major changes or disruptions to its business. Setting an appetite for scenario outcomes – which in truth is rarely explicitly defined by firms – can help to guide the enterprise during, for example, a major change to its business model. It could signal, for instance, that the level of unexpected losses incurred from a given scenario may be above the acceptable level. In the case of outsourcing and supplier risk cited in Table 9.2, this could happen if, for example, further critical activities were outsourced to the same service provider, creating an intolerable dependency on a single third party.

Limits and triggers are a double-edged sword: while they are essential, they can also drive inappropriate behaviours. If an executive is set a quantitative loss and/or scenario limit for which they are personally accountable, this could result in the executive being incentivized to hide or under-report losses, or to wilfully underestimate scenario outcomes. In a similar way, as described in Chapter 7, business units may attempt to game KRI thresholds in order to present a more positive picture.

Continuing to build on the example in Table 9.2, appetite measures for a sample sub-category of operational risk are presented in Table 9.3.

Table 9.3 Example: defining appetite measures

Principal operational risk sub-type	Appetite measures	Board approved threshold: AMBER – elevated; define path to GREEN	Board approved threshold: RED – unacceptable; immediate action needed
Third-Party Risk (Outsourcing & Supplier)	**Losses:** maximum total financial loss from third-party failures	> $1.5 million	>$2 million
	Scenario analysis maximum estimate	>$25 million	>$30 million
	KRI1: Percentage of critical providers with service below expected SLA levels for 2 consecutive months, without an action plan	>1%	>5%
	KRI2: Percentage of critical providers without resilience arrangements or with material failures identified during testing	> 5%	> 10%
	KRI3: Percentage of critical providers without defined succession plan/ not easily substitutable	> 20%	> 30%

The measures highlighted above are used to monitor the level of risk in the following dimensions:

- actual amount of materialized losses, a backward-looking but factual measure;
- scenario estimate, a forward-looking metric;
- predictive *control* indicators (KRI1 and KRI2), which closely monitor performance levels against service level agreements (SLAs) and resilience capabilities; and

Figure 9.8   Appetite maturity ladder

QUALITATIVE ONLY	QUANTITATIVE ONLY	QUALITATIVE AND QUANTITATIVE
➢ Ranges or scales (e.g. low/medium/high)	➢ Limits or triggers (e.g. single and aggregate losses)	➢ Overall and by Top Risk
➢ Provides direction, however vague	➢ Capital focused	➢ Qualitative and quantitative
➢ Not measurable – no quantitative metrics	➢ Not actionable – not driving behaviours	➢ Linked to strategy
		➢ Descriptive and easy to understand
		➢ Accountability framework
		➢ Response framework
		➢ Communicated to staff and embedded
RED ZONE: *ineffective*		GREEN ZONE: *effective*

- a predictive *risk* indicator (KRI3), reflecting the level of exposure to critical suppliers which have no identified alternative and therefore may in future represent a single point of failure.

The same process of designing and agreeing limits and triggers needs to be repeated for the remainder of top/principal operational risk sub-types.

A simple scale to assess the quality and maturity of the operational risk appetite is presented in Figure 9.8.

Monitoring risk profile and taking action

Risk appetite expresses the *desired* level of risk that an organization should be taking in pursuit of its objectives. In reality, the firm may be assuming less or more risk than intended; hence the need to monitor the actual exposure, or the firm's *risk profile*, against the pre-agreed parameters.

This assessment is performed on a monthly or quarterly basis at the respective governance committees, where actual values are reported against the appetite. An example of a risk profile report is presented in Figure 9.9.

Embedding the appetite

The risk appetite needs to be 'used as a tool to promote robust discussions on risk', and as a basis for decision-making.[7] Undoubtedly, though, embedding it is often difficult to achieve in practice.

Figure 9.9 Monitoring risk profile against the appetite

Principal operational Risk sub-type	Definition	Risk owner	Risk appetite	Risk level relative to appetite	Trend
Third-party risk (outsourcing and supplier)	The risk emanating from reliance on third parties, including incidents or failures of third parties to deliver on their obligations.	Chief Operating Officer (COO)	Moderate	○ Elevated, define path to GREEN	⬆

Expected losses	Unexpected losses	Key risk indicators
○	○	◉
GREEN	GREEN	AMBER

The appetite is first developed at a corporate, firm-wide level. To enable it to really be used effectively, appetite needs to:

- be understood, debated and approved by the appropriate governance body, commonly the board;
- have regular and formal monitoring arrangements, via, for example, monthly or quarterly reviews by the risk committee and the board, where the actual risk profile is evaluated against the desired appetite levels;
- have effective limits and trigger points enabling escalation and action;
- have assigned owners at the executive level, ensuring accountability and requiring them to act;
- be appropriately documented and reviewed on a periodic basis.

For small to medium-sized organizations where the same senior executives sit at the table taking most of the relevant business and operational decisions, a single top-of-the-house appetite is sufficient. For larger international firms with multiple lines of hierarchy, the appetite needs to be disseminated and translated at lower levels of the organization, or strata; for example, based on entity or business line:

- Business lines, usually at a global level, require an appetite statement which is cascaded from the corporate statement. Quantitative limits are then *allocated* to the business based on various parameters including their revenue share. For example, the threshold for the overall expected loss amount can be split into lower sub-component limits attributed to various businesses. Qualitative indicators may apply in exactly the same way (for example, conduct, people or fraud-related indicators); with business units being given identical or more restrictive thresholds. Some measures may be relevant to a specific area only; for instance, rogue trading metrics will be monitored by the markets business only and will not apply to other business lines.

- Material group entities, in particular, subsidiaries or legal entities that operate with their own board of directors, will also need to develop their own appetite, for approval by their board. The entity's appetite statement will represent a hybrid cross-over between the business lines operating out of that entity alongside a cascade of the corporate statement.

- Statements need to operate consistently at a consolidated level and at sub-strata level.

- A response framework needs to be in place within both the business lines and the entities.

The ultimate responsibility for approving the appetite lies with the board of directors of the organization. The second line operational risk team plays a crucial role in developing the approach; articulating the firm's position; working with subject matter experts (SMEs) and risk owners to make sense of the framework; and proposing statements and thresholds. It is an exciting opportunity to work with risk owners and senior executives to arrive at a meaningful appetite framework.

Common challenges and good practices

Common challenges

Challenges that practitioners may experience when developing and embedding an operational risk appetite are as follows.

Losses only

A decade ago, operational risk appetite was defined via a limit on aggregate losses; sometimes additionally broken down to lower limits across principal sub-categories. While this is a good start, quantitative measures alone are insufficient as they are backward-looking (i.e. the losses have already crystallized) and do not provide guidance on behaviours. They need to be supplemented, as discussed in this chapter, with descriptive statements and qualitative Shading of circles should be consistent with figure 7.2 - medium dark =Amber, lighter = Green (ie reverse the shading).

Zero tolerance

A declaration of *zero tolerance* frequently features in the narrative. While this may work well in internal policies developed by Human Resources that articulate the firm's position towards, for example, internal fraud committed by employees, it does not work well when applied to the appetite. If the firm has *zero tolerance for fraud*, it may as well consider exiting the business, because some instances of fraud will inevitably occur. While a 'zero fraud' expression may be tempting to use, a better approach to the language would be to state that the firm has a risk-averse approach to financial crime, and aims to mitigate the risk by maintaining a robust control environment, while recognizing that occasional instances of fraud may occur.

Use of distributions and percentiles

Bringing statistics into this domain is not always helpful either. Poor examples include statements that 'operational risk appetite is defined by the operational risk loss value using a 99.5 per cent confidence level on the statistical aggregate loss distribution'. Such statements will not be easily understood by all staff, are not actionable and – similarly to *zero tolerance* – should be avoided.

Stakeholders not engaged

At times, operational risk faces lack of engagement from business units and subject matter experts, to the extent that it becomes, as articulated by one frustrated risk practitioner, like *getting blood out of a stone*. The best way forward is to find the correct *risk owner*, to whom the management of relevant risk, and therefore its appetite, matter. This is not easy in organizations with vague accountability frameworks. The challenge may also arise at the board of directors' level if the directors do not think they have any responsibility for or involvement in the risk appetite process, which is a rather worrying sign. Director education and executive briefings can somewhat mitigate the challenge.

Wordsmithing exercise

Appetite may be approached as an exercise to contribute to the annual report. Statements are developed by report writers in risk management or finance teams, in silos, without collaboration, discussion or agreement. In this case the stated appetites do not carry weight and are not embedded in the organization. It is important that the whole appetite cycle is followed, including essential value-add board conversations.

Significant effort

Operational risk appetite, although not an embryonic topic, is still not studied carefully enough in most firms. Because of the difficulty deriving a meaningful statement and metrics, people may give up on the effort. It is better to approach the topic as an iterative process, starting with simple statements and measures and enhancing them over time and as experience is gained, not aiming for perfection up-front.

Good practices

Overall and by top risk

As discussed in the chapter, operational risk appetite needs to be established at the overall operational risk level as well as for sub-categories of risk. The correct taxonomy plays a critical role and helps with the definition of the sub-categories. If the organization is using the Basel Committee taxonomy, it can make this process somewhat more difficult – for example the *execution, delivery and process management* risk sub-type – due to the sheer breadth of the category. It is good practice to develop more intuitive and fit-for-purpose categorizations as described in Chapter 1. The taxonomy will split the risk universe into principal risk sub-types for which appetite statements can then be developed.

Benchmark with industry peers

In addition to developing appetite frameworks, every year I research and analyse the appetite statements of both financial and non-financial services firms, to observe industry progress in this nascent area and extract good examples. These statements are publicly available as part of firms' annual reports and can be easily located on the internet. This is a very useful exercise, recommended for all those working on developing an appetite framework. The research proves that, overall, steady progress is being made in this area, despite drastic divergence in the chosen approaches and the variable quality of outputs.

Language easy to understand

As mentioned earlier, firms outside the financial services industry commonly achieve more clarity using simply worded statements, compared to financial services firms, some of which are *constrained* by statistical models, appear to favour probability-based measures and underestimate the importance of qualitative aspects. Statements do not have to be over-complicated; on the contrary, if they can be explained simply enough for every employee to understand, then the employees *may* in fact read them. It is even better if highlights of the appetite can be presented to all staff as part of management town halls or educational campaigns, helping larger numbers of staff to better understand their own organization.

Industry benchmark

Put simply, operational risk appetite is not easy to get right, and whenever the topic comes up it invariably ends in debate and split opinions over what constitutes an effective appetite statement. Nevertheless this remains an exciting subject for discussion.

Presented below is a snapshot of the current landscape taken at the Advanced Operational risk training workshop in 2023.

Nature of operational risk: similar or different to other risk disciplines?

As shown in Figure 9.10, around a third of participants took a stance that operational risk is not willingly incurred and is expected to be *mitigated downwards*. On a more positive note, the remaining 67 per cent of respondents were prepared to adopt a more entrepreneurial approach and to embrace risk-reward thinking for at least some of the sub-categories of operational risk in their firms, perhaps enabling more balanced conversations on risk appetite to take place. The result is almost identical to a similar poll taken in 2019; and demonstrates a split in views on the nature of operational risk across the industry.

Expression of appetite

It is encouraging to see a high number of practitioners (66 per cent, as demonstrated in Figure 9.11), expressing their risk appetite via both qualitative

Figure 9.10   Industry poll: approach to operational risk

Approach to operational risk

Advanced Operational risk training workshop, 2023

Figure 9.11   Industry poll: expression of appetite (qualitative vs quantitative)

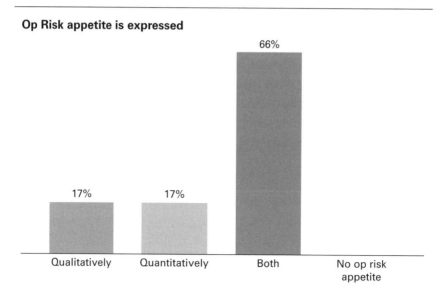

Op Risk appetite is expressed

Advanced Operational risk training workshop, 2023

and quantitative measures. Both are needed given the complex and broad nature of operational risk. This is a significant step forward from the 2019 poll, where only 39 per cent of respondents had reached this level of maturity; while others were either still in the process of developing an appetite statement or had just one type of metric in place.

Figure 9.12   Industry poll: operational risk appetite features

Operational risk appetite

Linked to strategy — 3.5

Helps in decision-making — 3.5

Drives behaviours — 3.3

Communicated to staff — 3

Strongly disagree — Strongly agree

1= strongly disagree, 5= strongly agree, ● = average rating

Advanced Operational risk training workshop, 2023

Appetite features

Overall, despite not yet being perfect, operational risk appetite was seen to be driving decision-making, risk levels were continuously monitored and breaches were being taken seriously, investigated and acted upon. This has become feasible as a result of the growing focus on *top risks*, those that were recognized by boards as potentially harmful to the achievement of firms' strategic objectives. This link to firms' wider business strategy has enabled more meaningful senior management conversations, and encouragement of the right behaviours within the firm as an outcome. As for staff communication, participants agreed that a simple summary of the operational risk appetite would be beneficial, and could be useful for employees to better understand their firm's approach to risk taking (see Figure 9.12).

Practical workplace exercise

Reflecting on the content of this chapter, obtain a copy of the firm's operational risk appetite and review it, considering:

1 Is the appetite easy to understand and does it articulate the *types* and *levels* of risk the firm is willing to accept?

2 What approach has been adopted, *mitigated downwards*, *taken for reward* or a combination of both?

3 Are principal risk sub-types distinguished and have statements been set for them?

4 What qualitative and quantitative measures are used?

5 What works well? Make notes of the features that you particularly like.

6 What can be improved? Note down potential appetite enhancements.

MAKE A DIFFERENCE (MAD) ACTION

Please note down one action that you will take after reading this chapter that will make a positive difference to the development of operational risk appetite.

In summary, this chapter proposed an approach to creating an operational risk appetite framework and statement, defining measures, and ensuring it remains a useful tool for decision-making.

Moving on, the next chapter focuses on operational risk reporting and combines elements from all the tools examined in previous chapters.

Notes

1 European Banking Authority (2019) *The EBA Methodological Guide: Risk indicators and detailed risk analysis tools*, www.eba.europa.eu/sites/default/documents/files/documents/10180/1380571/343e01d7-0c8f-4d7f-b59e-cc23a7b-9dd9d/Revised%20EBA%20Methodological%20Guide%20%20Risk%20Indicators%20and%20DRAT%20%2820%20March%202019%29.pdf (archived at https://perma.cc/6LFW-9GV5)

2 Financial Stability Board (2013) *Principles for an Effective Risk Appetite Framework*, www.fsb.org/wp-content/uploads/r_131118.pdf (archived at https://perma.cc/E9S4-F5KZ)

3 Financial Stability Board (2013) *Principles for an Effective Risk Appetite Framework*, www.fsb.org/wp-content/uploads/r_131118.pdf (archived at https://perma.cc/9XFB-46D5)

4 Basel Committee on Banking Supervision (2021) *Revisions to the Principles for the Sound Management of Operational Risk*, www.bis.org/bcbs/publ/d515.pdf (archived at https://perma.cc/E45Y-GK3N)

5 Basel Committee on Banking Supervision (2021) *Revisions to the Principles for the Sound Management of Operational Risk*, www.bis.org/bcbs/publ/d515.pdf (archived at https://perma.cc/E45Y-GK3N)

6 Financial Stability Board (2013) *Principles for an Effective Risk Appetite Framework*, www.fsb.org/wp-content/uploads/r_131118.pdf (archived at https://perma.cc/F7TL-3EKU)

7 Financial Stability Board (2013) *Principles for an Effective Risk Appetite Framework*, www.fsb.org/wp-content/uploads/r_131118.pdf (archived at https://perma.cc/2LTZ-M6DB)

Operational risk reporting 10

What this chapter covers: The chapter stresses the significance of Reporting as the window through which Operational Risk communicates with the outside world and sends important messages to stakeholders (Figure 10.1). It discusses how results from the tools and instruments examined in previous chapters can be consolidated in a meaningful way for consumption by board and senior committees, without being excessively lengthy and verbose. It highlights practical ways of presenting an operational risk profile, getting right to the point and answering the vitally important *so what?* question, making reports succinct, punchy and actionable. The chapter includes examples and an industry benchmark.

FURTHER READING

- Basel Committee on Banking Supervision (2013) *Principles for Effective Risk Data Aggregation and Risk Reporting*

  Why recommended: a key regulatory document on the subject, outlining requirements on risk aggregation and reporting.

- Trevor Bentley (2002) *Report Writing in Business: The effective communication of information*, CIMA Publishing

  Why recommended: A perfect read for those interested and willing to improve their report-writing skills.

Reporting: its role and its challenges

Operational risk reporting is a key activity. It is the culmination of all the hard work invested in designing framework tools which represent the best fit for the firm; and many days and weeks spent on embedding, training and

Figure 10.1 Focus of Chapter 10: operational risk reporting

Risk culture

Embedding and maturity assessment

Governance, roles and responsibilities

Establish governance and clear roles across the Three Lines for managing operational risk.

Risk appetite and risk Capacity

Define nature and types of risk accepted in pursuit of strategic objectives. Evaluate adequacy of capital resources.

Operational risk events	Risk assessments	Scenario analysis	Key Risk Indicators
Record and report risk events, act to minimize future exposure. Monitor trends against RCSAs and KRIs.	Assess risk exposure in process, business or function via RCSAs. Supplement by evaluating risks emanating from change activities via ORAs.	Identify exposure from extreme but plausible events. Mitigate through risk transfer to insurance.	Monitor risk and control performance through predictive indicators. Act if indicators breach established appetite threshold.

Reporting and decision-making

Review actual risk profile against set appetite, apply active risk management to enable achievement of strategic objectives.

Operational risk taxonomy

Training and education

educating the business. It is the end-result of analysis, discussions, debates and sometimes arguments with colleagues to resolve issues, find solutions and agree action owners. It is the opportunity to package up all this content, so it is well worth investing in the best quality packaging – it will reap benefits in the long term.

But caution: it also comes with a warning. Underinvestment in reporting will devalue the whole framework. Even when operational risk tools are operating effectively, if the reports are unclear, not well structured or not actionable, the readers – mostly senior executives who only see the final product – may not appreciate or make sense of the importance of the operational risk management process and information.

When starting an assignment with a new client, I usually ask for a set of the operational risk reports that are submitted to governance committees. They provide an invaluable insight on the quality and maturity of the framework. If the reports do not meet the expected standard, I tend to investigate from the end-product back to the beginning. Does the policy mandate the use of the right tools? Are the elements of the framework calibrated correctly, embedded and generating meaningful outputs? If there are challenges, they usually lie with the design or calibration of the tools, or their embeddedness. It is a real pity if in practice everything is working well but when it comes to the last step – packaging the content – the author did not do the content proud.

From the outset, writing and structuring operational risk reports to the board and senior committees is a demanding activity. More generic hurdles on report writing are compounded by the immense challenges emanating from the breadth and complexity of the operational risk discipline.

Generic challenges

Over the years, I have participated in and led many exercises to help committees self-assess their effectiveness. This is good governance practice. Members rate important aspects of their own practice, including committee composition; the manner in which meetings are conducted; the allocation of time to various topics on the agenda; the quality of information received; and other attributes which help them to evaluate whether the committee is effectively discharging its duties. Inevitably, reporting receives its fair share of feedback. The most common criticisms from committee members – who are after all the report recipients – include:

- papers being too lengthy (board and committee packs are rarely just in the hundreds – more likely thousands – of pages in length);

- not outlining the *ask* clearly – for example, is the paper for approval, opinion or information only;
- not providing an overall perspective;
- being backward- rather than forward-looking;
- not being timely;
- being too vague and unfocused.

And the list goes on.

When speaking to report writers – individuals or teams within departments tasked with drafting committee papers – they are also vocal on this topic, and raise plenty of reporting challenges, including:

- The absence of any brief from the board or senior executives on what they would like to see in the report. Are there any particular areas of interest? Authors frequently complain that no one has ever sat down with them to clearly explain what the recipients are looking for.
- The lack of a standard reporting template, leaving the writer to decide which style and format to use.
- A lack of training for report writers. What does good look like? How long, how detailed, structure, language, format? Word or PowerPoint?
- No feedback loop – after being written, reports usually disappear into a black hole. Authors rarely receive feedback on whether the information met recipients' expectations, whether any actions emanated from the discussion and how they could do better next time.

Operational risk reporting challenges

All these challenges are relevant when it comes to operational risk report writing. In addition, operational risk faces some specific considerations:

- the breadth of the discipline, where every risk sub-type is important in its own right and deserves attention;
- multiple tools that generate significant output – losses, RCSAs, KRIs, scenarios – can all be presented using their own individual narratives, charts and graphs; and
- the fact that the discipline has both qualitative and quantitative components.

The objective of reporting is to present the overall operational risk profile, highlight pressure points, articulate whether the level of risk is within or outside the appetite and drive decision-making. For example, the UK Corporate Governance Code provides guidance by stating that directors should receive '*accurate, timely and clear information*', reinforcing that the board should always ensure that it has 'the policies, processes, *information, time and resources it needs in order to function effectively and efficiently*'.[1]

Or, simply put, they need to know if there is a problem; and if so, what action needs to be taken to resolve it.

What makes a good report?

Three steps for effective report writing

Three steps for effective report writing, proposed in Figure 10.2, are described in detail in this chapter.

Step 1: Data gathering

The first step in report writing consists of gathering accurate, timely and meaningful data. This involves extracting the outputs from operational risk tools – hopefully from the systems or, if not, from Excel spreadsheets or other sources – and collecting relevant inputs from first line business units. The industry faces continued focus on the quality and integrity of its data following the Basel Committee's publication of its principles on risk data aggregation and reporting: these require firms 'to generate accurate and reliable risk data' which is 'aggregated on a largely automated basis so as to minimize the probability of errors'.[2] This task is, however, mainly dependent on the firm's IT capabilities and remains a challenge, as is recognized by the Basel Committee in their 2020 progress report. While firms had clearly 'made improvements to their data architecture and IT infrastructure', there is 'still much work to do in this area'.[3] A subsequent 2023 progress report by the Basel Committee yet again notes the delay in achieving compliance,

Figure 10.2 Three steps for report writing

'seven years after the expected date of compliance'.[4] And so remediation programs continue as organizations strive to upgrade their processes and tools to overcome risk data challenges.

Once the information is collected, a pause to contemplate: whose role is it to make sense of the data and interpret what it means? If the Operational Risk department perceives that it is the role of senior executives – the report recipients – to answer the *so what?* question, then the activity stops here. This is especially true if there is a fast approaching deadline for the paper to be submitted to the committee. The collected *raw data* is then pasted into the report, inviting the readers to decide for themselves what they make of it. Let's review an example of such a report.

EXAMPLE 1

Extract from an operational risk report

1 Operational risk events: This month, there have been 11 operational risk events, totalling $18 thousand. The largest loss of $9 thousand occurred in the Markets Division; further details are presented in Appendix X. There is a downward trend: overall ORE value is decreasing month on month since the beginning of the year, although the number of occurrences has increased from 7 to 11 a month in the last quarter.

2 RCSAs: There are four *high* residual risks in departmental RCSAs.

3 KRIs: There are no *Red* Key Risk Indicators this month.

This narrative is supplemented by:

- bar chart: operational risk events – actual losses, rolling 12 months;
- bar chart: operational risk events – number of events, rolling 12 months;
- pie chart: operational risk events split by Basel (or internal taxonomy) category;
- pie chart: operational risk events split by business unit;
- RCSA results table – total number of *very high*, *high*, *moderate* and *low* risks by business unit;
- KRIs – a table with Green, Amber and Red indicators.

In reading this extract, inevitable questions arise. What does this mean? Is this good or bad? What, if any, action is needed? The burden of analysis is passed on to the reader. While the bare facts may be somewhat interesting, without any interpretation from subject matter experts (SMEs) this report is difficult to digest, is not actionable, and ultimately will not allow board or committee members to function *effectively and efficiently*.

Therefore, we move on to Step 2.

Step 2: Analysis and interpretation

Typically, a substantive manual effort – or perhaps semi-automated if systems permit – is required to review the data and translate it into a *story* that answers the *so what?* question. This is, after all, the essential value-add of the Operational Risk teams, who are the SMEs best placed to interpret the data. They need to analyse it from all perspectives, considering, for example, the following questions:

- What are the key changes in the risk profile since the last report?
- Is the level of risk within or outside the stated appetite?
- Is there any evident deterioration – an increase in OREs (value or numbers), significant risks or *Amber/Red* KRIs? If so, why?
- Are the operational risk tools telling a consistent story?
- Are there common themes across different business units or support functions?
- Is there a common root cause of various OREs?
- Are there any controls that seem to keep failing repeatedly (for OREs), or controls that are poorly assessed by multiple departments (RCSAs)?
- Are there any indicators which have been *Amber* for more than two consecutive months? If so, why?

Practitioners must search for trends, themes and a story where every piece of data is adding to the narrative. In practice, this kind of in-depth research, with a list of rigorous investigative questions, is rarely discussed or agreed among the operational risk team. Use of sophisticated data analysis tools and application of data science and AI would be of immense help with this process. Basel committee notes that 'new technologies such as artificial intelligence have not yet materially impacted banks' risk data aggregation and risk reporting processes'.[5] Despite being quite embryonic in operational risk space, some organizations are including exploration of techniques that offer future potential into the list of their priorities.

As a concept, operational risk appetite, as discussed in the previous chapter, can also assist. If well defined, it ties the various tools together, reducing the need for a separate coverage of RCSAs, OREs, KRIs and scenarios. Even so, a diligent analyst will investigate beyond the appetite considerations. Actual financial losses may be within the appetite, but could have been prompted by a common control failing in different business units – providing a great opportunity to call the problem out and discuss any necessary action.

In sizeable operational risk teams, it is essential to agree the role of the report writer relative to the rest of the department.

> The report writer is the *executive advocate*, stepping into the shoes of senior executives – the report recipients – and examining the document from their perspective.

The writer needs to challenge and refuse any raw data dumps provided by colleagues. If the data provides no insight and no story that answers the *so what?* question, the report writer should simply reject the input, explaining how it needs to be improved for subsequent submissions.

An additional important governance role is that of the report sponsor.

> The *report sponsor* is a senior executive member of the respective committee whose role is to review the paper for fitness and quality prior to its final submission.

For risk reports, the sponsor is usually the chief risk officer, who reviews credit, market, operational, liquidity and other relevant papers. This process creates another opportunity to sit down and actively challenge the material. So it is good practice to mandate this kind of sponsor review for all senior committee and board papers.

Compare the following extract from a risk report after this kind of in-depth analysis has been completed.

EXAMPLE 2

Extract from an operational risk report, after in-depth analysis

This month there have been 11 operational risk events, totalling $18 thousand. Analysis of root causes and comparison with the RCSA and KRI data reveal that 8 out of 11 occurrences are due to the failure of the same control, namely segregation of duties. This control is rated as ineffective in three business units that use system X, due to manual workarounds required to operate it.

After this second step, the report is likely shorter, and outputs from the ORE, RCSA and KRI frameworks have now been integrated into the analysis.

Step 3: Opinion, call for action

The third step takes us to the next level, aiming to provide an opinion and call for action. It reflects *behind the scenes* activity which happens *in between the reporting cycles*: the Operational Risk department acting on the story that emerged from the investigative analysis undertaken in the previous step. This step involves arranging meetings, discussing and agreeing actions and action owners. If applied to the earlier example, the report will be further enhanced as seen in the following example.

EXAMPLE 3

Extract from an operational risk report, after further activity

This month, there have been 11 operational risk events, totalling $18 thousand. Analysis of root causes and comparison with the RCSA and KRI data reveal that 8 out of 11 occurrences are due to the failure of the same control, namely segregation of duties. A cross-functional working group facilitated by operational risk examined relevant cases and concluded that there is a significant risk of errors and future losses. A proposal to invest in enhancing the segregation of duties is presented for the committee's approval: see agenda item X.

After this third step, as more time is spent on the analysis, with key messages being summarized for the recipients, the depth and quality of the paper is enhanced while the overall length is decreased; some of the individual appendices can now be removed as they have been integrated into the narrative.

The increased accountability of senior executives, as a result of the various regulatory regimes, is driving a desire to move away from ambiguous charts, graphs and appendices to succinct and clearly worded, actionable content that can be revisited, if necessary, months or even years after being written. As we will see from the industry benchmark at the end of the chapter, some operational risk reports are 20 to 30 pages long. There is a real danger of information overflow, with directors and senior managers missing vital pieces of information hidden in the voluminous reports.

The ideal length of value-add papers is under five pages, while being able to summarize this kind of content into one–two pages is an outstanding feat, bordering on brilliance.

'If I had more time, I would have written a shorter letter' is a quote attributed to many, including Mark Twain and Winston Churchill. Spending more time on the analysis, key messages and storytelling increases the quality and decreases the length.

Helpful format and templates

While operational risk reporting diverges significantly across firms, a golden rule is to have an effective executive summary. Let's examine an example of a page, presented in Figure 10.3, which frequently appears in some shape or form in operational risk reports.

Positive features of this example include:

- a quick preview, in a summarized format, of what is to follow on subsequent pages;
- focus on actionability with separate sub-section dedicated to actions;
- outline of prior month status, reflecting on dynamics.

What could be improved, as discussed at the beginning of this chapter, is the integration of separate elements – RCSAs, KRIs, losses and audit issues – into one story answering the holistic *so what?* question.

Figure 10.3 Example of executive summary

Operational Risk dashboard

Executive summary

Section A: Operational Risk events

Current month assessment   RED ●

Actions taken or to be taken

Prior month assessment (summary): ●

SECTION C: Audit issues

Current month assessment   AMBER ●

Actions taken or to be taken

Prior month assessment (summary): ●

SECTION B: Risk and Control self-assessments

Current month assessment   GREEN ○

Actions taken or to be taken

Prior month assessment (summary): ○

SECTION D: Key Risk Indicators

Current month assessment   GREEN ○

Actions taken or to be taken

Prior month assessment (summary): ○

Having written, read and helped to design hundreds of papers over my career, out of the many possible approaches I favour the CQC concept of good report writing, also advocated by Board Intelligence.[6]

> **CQC**: Context–Questions–Conclusions provides a solid structure for a board or committee paper.

This kind of report often starts with a short explanation of *why* the recipient is reading the paper (Context). For example:

- This is a quarterly operational risk update provided to the committee in line with its terms of reference; or
- The purpose of this ad hoc operational risk report is to brief the committee on a significant operational risk event, and outline actions taken to resolve it.

Context is important, as it helps the reader to answer the question which is frequently on their mind: *why am I reading this?*.

The next phase is Questions, providing opportunity for the writer to outline the scope of the paper and articulate what issues it will be addressing. The choice of questions is key. As an example, 'good' questions include:

- What are the key changes to the operational risk profile since the last report?
- Is the level of risk within the appetite?
- What actions are proposed for the committee's approval?

The Conclusions then provide short answers to the above questions, for example:

- Since the last report there has been a moderate increase in the overall risk profile. Operational risk levels are elevated for *Technology and Information security* (same as last quarter), *Outsourcing and Supplier* (new) and *People* risk (new), resulting from the pandemic and working from home (WFH) arrangements.
- While the level of operational risk remains within the appetite, there are six new early-warning Amber indicators for the three risk categories outlined above. Actions are on track for a path to Green in *Technology and Information Security* risk.

Figure 10.4 Example operational risk report format

Quarterly Operational Risk update for the Risk Committee of the Board, per Committee's Terms of Reference	
Prepared by: head of Operational Risk	**Executive Sponsor: Chief risk officer**

Questions this paper addresses:

		Conclusions:
1	What are the key changes to the operational risk profile since the last report?	Conclusions:
2	Is the level of operational risk within the stated appetite?	Conclusions:
3	What actions are proposed for Committee's approval?	Conclusions:

Input received

	Input sought
In producing this paper, input has been received from the following departments...	The committee is requested to agree proposed plan of action...

Main part of the report

Conclusions are expanded with a broader narrative, and supporting charts and graphs included. Main part of the report can be 2–3 pages long.

Summary

Previous quarter: AMBER	⬤	Current quarter: AMBER	⬤	Expected next quarter level: GREEN	◯
Movement	⇦	Moderate increase in risk profile		Justification is included...	

- The committee is requested to review and agree actions proposed to mitigate the *People* and *Outsourcing and Supplier* risks, bringing exposure within the desired appetite level.

Summary questions to avoid include:

- Individual questions on operational risk events, RCSA results or KRIs; analysis needs to be conducted integrating the outputs from these tools to extract a story, rather than presenting them separately.

- What is the operational risk profile? (as opposed to 'what are the key changes since the last report?'). If there are no noteworthy changes for several quarters in succession, the paper runs the risk of becoming repetitive. If the profile is stable, the opening line can say so up-front, leaving room to focus instead on a particular risk sub-type, and perhaps do a deep dive into, for instance, *legal* risk or *financial crime* risk.

- What has the Operational Risk department been doing? For obvious reasons, boards and committees are more interested in outcomes than in the specific activities of employees.

An example reporting template is provided in Figure 10.4.

Common challenges and good practices

Common challenges

Challenges that firms may encounter when compiling board or committee operational risk reports.

Never-ending reporting cycle

Significant effort goes into the preparation of reporting documents, with hours spent compiling, drafting and redrafting them. One of the rather unfortunate implications of the personal accountability and certification regimes is an even longer set of reports to boards and senior committees, prompted by a desire on the part of accountable individuals to document everything to the nth degree. By the time the reviews have been completed and approvals obtained, the next reporting cycle has already commenced and papers are due again. To avoid being caught up in a never-ending reporting saga, provide shorter updates on a monthly basis, and more complete reports with detailed deep dives quarterly or semi-annually.

Discipline too broad

As described earlier in the chapter, every operational risk sub-type is significant in its own right and deserves attention. This makes it challenging to cover a broad spectrum of sub-categories succinctly in a single report. It is good practice to spread deep dives into different risk sub-types throughout the course of the year; covering, for example, *Outsourcing and Supplier* risk in the first quarter, followed by *Technology and Information Security* risk in the second. The schedule can be discussed with the committee chair, and dates for the presentations agreed in advance. This planning provides ample time to develop a value-added paper, after engaging with relevant SMEs. It also shortens the regular operational risk report and makes it less repetitive. This approach can also help to address the perpetual topic of various reports not being integrated. Often the Compliance function presents on financial crime, Information Security develops its own set of papers and the Legal department reports on legal risk. Additionally, the operational risk function presents on all of the above topics, given that they are also sub-sets of operational risk. This can create duplication or even confusion if there are discrepancies between two datasets. Working in collaboration and producing a joint report is an excellent initiative, though rarely done in practice.

Report writer removed from the front line

In larger operational risk departments, the reporting unit is usually separate from the framework and oversight teams, who are in the front line talking to business units and support functions. This creates a challenge for report writers who do not have the full picture themselves and are dependent on colleagues to submit intelligent insights. In this kind of structure, reporting team members need to take it upon themselves to educate their colleagues on what good looks like, and to push back on inputs of suboptimal quality.

Software not producing expected outcomes

Whether off-the-shelf or developed in-house, operational risk software is unlikely to deliver a finalized committee paper at the touch of a button. It can be very useful in the analysis and interpretation stage, allowing interrogation of the data from different angles. But expert knowledge, time and effort is still required to produce the report, so it is best to avoid expectations of the software that are unrealistic.

Reports internally focused

Most organizations are largely internally focused and do not provide enough external perspective. It is good practice to actively engage with industry forums and trade associations, and to read external and regulatory reports to obtain a view of how the firm compares with its peers and the industry more broadly. What emerging risks are on the horizon? What are your peers focusing on? In this context another good question to add to the set of Questions highlighted earlier is 'How does the firm's profile compare to industry peers/external trends?'.

Data lacks integrity

As repeatedly highlighted by the Basel Committee, data integrity remains a challenge for most firms.[7] Many of the standard operational risk instruments are manual, or even where software is used the outputs are not easy to aggregate. Some pieces of data quickly become out of date. Self-assessment of data quality, integrity and timeliness, with follow-up actions if needed, is a robust practice.

Good practices

Create a reference library

We have all been on the receiving end of a report that is poor and does not answer the *so what?* question. Generally, these will go straight into the bin, allowing us to move onto the next urgent task on our list. On the other hand, every time we come across a clear, concise report – where every piece of data is adding to the narrative – we can add it to a reporting 'reference library', to store ideas and give us a head start when producing the next document.

Know your audience

Knowing your audience helps greatly in delivering reports that are fit for purpose. For example, some recipients may be colour blind; worldwide there are approximately 300 million people with colour blindness.[8] For these people, a typical risk heatmap, filled with Red, Amber and Green KRIs, will not be well received and is better replaced with descriptive narrative. Alternatively, both colour and a descriptor (e.g. the word *Amber*) can be used simultaneously. Furthermore some senior executives may favour high-level summaries while others will be highly detail orientated and will want to search for supporting data. To manage this problem effectively, aim to solicit feedback proactively, initiating a dialogue with the committee or board to really understand their expectations and discuss what went well in the last report and what might be improved. This kind of feedback is rarely forthcoming if not asked for; it is best to take the initiative and seek it out.

Address report writing basics

As obvious as it sounds, it is important to address generic report-writing challenges, including developing a template, and providing training to report writers and other team members who are tasked with submitting inputs. Ideally, appoint a person with excellent language skills in addition to operational risk expertise. Ensure that all graphs are annotated with explanatory notes, so the audience is not left guessing as to their meaning.

Write steering and supervising papers

Boards and senior committees – some better than others, admittedly – balance their time between *steering* and *supervising* kinds of discussions. Steering the organization requires challenging whether the firm has the right strategy, risk appetite and risk culture, and if there are smarter ways of working. In turn, supervising evolves around monitoring if the agreed strategy is on track, targets have been hit and level of risk is within the appetite.

Consequently, the Operational Risk department – and indeed all risk disciplines – write both types of papers to aid senior committees to exercise their dual role. Examples of *supervising* papers include the more common risk profile updates, risk appetite reports and escalation of material operational risk events. Steering papers are often more reflective and may involve external comparative benchmarks, such as comparison of own operational risk appetite with peers (risk appetite of peer firms can be easily extracted from publicly available disclosures); external view on top operational risks in contrast to internal risk profile; suggestion to introduce a new emerging risk horizon scanning process in line with industry best practice. Based on the live poll conducted by Best Practice Forum members, the majority (87 per cent) of produced papers were of *supervisory* nature; and more *steering*-type reports would be beneficial.

Append opinion to first line business units' reports

First line business units and support functions should also produce or contribute to committee and board papers. It is good practice to ask the risk owner in the first line to present on their own risk profile. This approach is especially effective in cases where the first line is asking for investment to mitigate a material risk. It is also beneficial for celebrating success; if, for example, an area has been found to have significant flaws and subsequently took remedial actions, deriving meaningful lessons learnt which are worth sharing.

When first line business units and support functions are authoring reports, the second line Operational Risk department can append its independent opinion to the first line reports. This is a powerful technique that allows senior committees and the board to have the benefit of both sets of views.

Add value

Reporting is a start of the process, not the end of it. Every paper has its purpose, be it, for example, to *initiate further action or request input*. When producing a document, ask yourself the question 'Is it adding value?'. Inevitably, committee and board meetings run out of time, and papers *for noting* are usually taken as read and therefore skipped. This makes it even more important to develop reports that appear at the front of the pile, generating discussion and helping in decision-making. Some firms actively prohibit papers that are *for information only* or *for noting*.

Industry benchmark

Operational risk practitioners from various financial services firms of different sizes and geographical spread participated in a live poll to examine different aspects of operational risk reporting.

How long are operational risk reports?

There has been a positive change in this area: by 2023, reports to risk committees, executive committees and the board had somewhat decreased in length compared to previous years (also see 1st edition of the book). The majority of respondents (65 per cent) produced reports of around 10–12 pages, while 29 per cent wrote more detailed papers of 20–30 pages (see Figure 10.5). In 2019, 7 per cent were producing voluminous papers over 50 pages long; this practice was no longer observed in 2023.

Figure 10.5   Industry poll: length of operational risk report

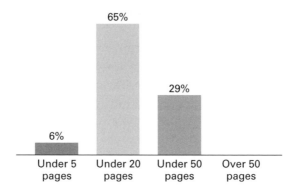

What is the length of Op Risk report?

Best Practice Operational Risk Forum, 2023

Have operational risk reports improved over the years?

A large majority of respondents (94 per cent) agreed that firms have grad-ually evolved their ability to create shorter, punchier operational risk re-ports which help boards and committees to take the right decisions. Of these, 12 per cent noted a substantial enhancement. This has been achieved predominantly via improved risk commentary, creating a meaningful nar-rative to answer the *so what?* question. Structurally, a combination of a clear and succinct executive summary and a more developed risk appe-tite – enabling reporting of the level of risk against an agreed appetite – have also aided the positive transformation. Experience gained over the years and understanding what boards view as a *good report* has also helped. There is no 'one size fits all' when it comes to board expectations of reporting. Some boards prefer succinct summaries while others like the report to go into substantial detail.

What are the key reporting challenges?

Reporting improvements were largely achieved at the expense of employees working longer and harder to process an ever-increasing volume of manual data. Arguably, the challenges around report writing have intensified in line with increased digitalization. In ranking order, time and capacity constraints came first, coupled with poor data and sub-optimal risk tools (see Figure 10.7). Participants lacked instant access to an up-to-date risk profile

Figure 10.6 Operational risk report maturity

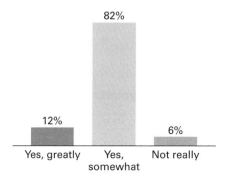

Op Risk report has matured and improved

Best Practice Operational Risk Forum, 2023

Figure 10.7 Industry poll: operational risk reporting challenges

Rank Op Risk reporting challenges in order of significance

Best Practice Operational Risk Forum, 2023

which could be generated at a click of a button. Considering we are in a digital age, risk professionals spend a notable amount of time assembling risk reports, manually extracting data from Excel spreadsheets and other sources, to create an aggregate view of the risk profile. On this basis the Basel Committee's comments on the need for continued investment in technological tools in the risk arena remain valid to this day, reinforcing the strong case for advancement.

Practical workplace exercise

Reflecting on the content of this chapter, obtain copies of operational risk reports submitted to the risk committee, board or other governance committee over the last year, selecting at least three reports for comparison purposes. Review the reports, considering:

1 Has the report writer followed all the three steps outlined in this chapter?

2 Is there an opinion and call for action?

3 Is the report clear and well structured?

4 What works well? Make notes of the features that you particularly like.

5 What can be improved? Note down potential improvements for future reports.

MAKE A DIFFERENCE (MAD) ACTION

Please outline the learnings and note down one action that you will take after reading this chapter that will make a positive difference to operational risk reporting practices in your workplace.

In summary, this chapter discussed the crucial role of operational risk reporting, proposing an approach for developing concise, actionable and value-add reports.

Now that we have covered the core elements of the operational risk framework, subsequent chapters move to describing supplementary aspects, starting with training and education.

Notes

1 Financial Reporting Council (2018) *The UK Corporate Governance Code*, www.frc.org.uk/getattachment/88bd8c45-50ea-4841-95b0-d2f4f48069a2/2018-UK-Corporate-Governance-Code-FINAL.pdf (archived at https://perma.cc/47XG-5UUA)

2 Basel Committee on Banking Supervision (2013) *Principles for Effective Risk Data Aggregation and Risk Reporting*, www.bis.org/publ/bcbs239.pdf (archived at https://perma.cc/Q3XQ-467P)

3 Basel Committee on Banking Supervision (2020) *Progress in Adopting the Principles for Effective Risk Data Aggregation and Risk Reporting*, www.bis.org/bcbs/publ/d501.pdf (archived at https://perma.cc/F9BM-7FXA)

4 Basel Committee on Banking Supervision (2023) *Progress in Adopting the Principles for Effective Risk Data Aggregation and Risk Reporting*, www.bis.org/bcbs/publ/d559.pdf (archived at https://perma.cc/B8NE-QYVE)

5 Basel Committee on Banking Supervision (2023) *Progress in Adopting the Principles for Effective Risk Data Aggregation and Risk Reporting*, www.bis.org/bcbs/publ/d559.pdf (archived at https://perma.cc/B8NE-QYVE)

6 Board Intelligence, www.boardintelligence.com/product (archived at https://perma.cc/MET9-MZM7)

7 Basel Committee on Banking Supervision (2023) *Progress in Adopting the Principles for Effective Risk Data Aggregation and Risk Reporting*, www.bis.org/bcbs/publ/d559.pdf (archived at https://perma.cc/B8NE-QYVE)

8 Colour Blind Awareness, www.colourblindawareness.org/colour-blindness/ (archived at https://perma.cc/KA7G-M8C4)

Operational risk training and education 11

What this chapter covers: The chapter focuses on the importance of investing in upskilling colleagues across the organization on operational risk; and embedding further knowledge about the responsibilities across the firm (Figure 11.1). In an age of training fatigue – when employees can easily be overwhelmed by the number of mandatory training courses they need to complete – the chapter suggests useful hints and tips for deploying best-in-class training programmes that employees will find educational, engaging and memorable.

FURTHER READING AND RESOURCES

- Becky Pike Pluth (2021) *Webinars with WOW Factor: Tips, tricks and interactive activities for webinars*, Creative Training Productions

  Why recommended: This practical book covers the need-to-know of effective virtual training, and features activities that create connection, energize learners and keep the life in your training programmes.

- Additionally, there are very useful resources including free guides and trainer kits, as well as excellent courses to upskill your training capabilities available on the website www.bobpikegroup.com. These can be supplemented by books on specific topics:

  o Facilitation:

  Becky Pike Pluth (2018) *Training Difficult People*, Creative Training Productions

- o Public speaking:

  Viv Groskop (2018) *How to Own The Room: Women and the art of brilliant speaking*, Bantam Press

- o Influencing:

  Thomas Harris (2012) *I'm OK, You're OK: A practical guide to transactional analysis*, Arrow

  Eric Berne (2016) *Games People Play: The psychology of human relationships*, Penguin Life

Advocating for continuous risk education

Education is one of the most powerful things in life. As a professional trainer with over 20 years' experience in delivering public and in-house courses, I feel passionate about this subject and always advocate for profound investment in learning. Education is particularly important when it comes to operational risk management as it is vital for embedding the practices in the organization. The discipline is still relatively young and has not yet fully bedded down; therefore, there is a continuous need for managers and practitioners to keep constantly raising awareness, delivering impactful and relevant messages to ensure that all employees are conversant with and apply key risk management principles and concepts. Over the past decade, the need for risk education was repeatedly emphasized. A review conducted by the Basel Committee in 2014 noted that most firms 'indicated that some form of operational risk training has been established but had plans to enhance existing training'.[1] An update to the sound practices issued by the Basel Committee in 2021 since strengthened the educational requirements, directing organizations to ensure that an 'appropriate level of operational risk training is available at all levels throughout the organisation'.[2] Yet in 2024, banks' non-financial risk training was slammed as 'inadequate',[3] with a patchwork approach, lack of a minimum standard and employees left on their own to find training opportunities. Therefore, risk education requires ongoing investment in terms of time, thought and resources to maintain – and even excel – in delivering high quality learning.

Figure 11.1 Focus of Chapter 11: training and education

Risk culture

Embedding and maturity assessment

Governance, roles and responsibilities

Establish governance and clear roles across the Three Lines for managing operational risk.

Risk appetite and risk capacity

Define nature and types of risk accepted in pursuit of strategic objectives. Evaluate adequacy of capital resources.

Operational risk events	Risk assessments	Scenario analysis	Key Risk Indicators
Record and report risk events, act to minimize future exposure. Monitor trends against RCSAs and KRIs.	Assess risk exposure in process, business or function via RCSAs. Supplement by evaluating risks emanating from change activities via ORAs.	Identify exposure from extreme but plausible events. Mitigate through risk transfer to insurance.	Monitor risk and control performance through predictive indicators. Act if indicators breach established appetite threshold.

Reporting and decision-making

Review actual risk profile against set appetite, apply active risk management to enable achievement of strategic objectives.

Training and education

Operational risk taxonomy

Building blocks for upskilling risk professionals

The educational journey must begin with the second line operational risk function. As discussed in Chapter 3, second line *multipliers* are tasked not only with engaging with the first line *champions* but also with passing on their own knowledge and inspiring the entire organization. Consequently, the skills and abilities of the second line team are a core factor in successfully implementing risk management tools and processes across the firm. The development of deep second line expertise leads to the department being perceived as a centre of excellence and each team member becoming an ambassador of good practices.

While specific training requirements may arise based on individual need assessments, there are several key skills that all team members should possess in order for them to become all-round role models. This key skillset consists of three essential building blocks proposed in Figure 11.2, and a number of bonus add-ons.

Operational risk framework and tools

The first learning objective is to achieve full proficiency with the framework and tools. It is difficult to educate others when one's own knowledge is only partial. To excel, every second line employee needs to master all individual components of the framework – RCSAs, KRIs, appetite and others – as well as having a clear grasp of how the components relate to each other. In larger teams, employees may be split into sub-units, focusing on a particular aspect of operational risk management which they are practising continuously and in which they consequently develop deep expertise. These focused employees can (and should) be requested to routinely share their knowledge with

Figure 11.2 Three educational building blocks for the second line teams the rest of the group. Instil the discipline of dedicating part of regular departmental meetings to an overview by one of these specialists, covering their particular subject. Over time every component of the framework can be covered in a series of sessions, increasing everyone's familiarity with the multifaceted framework and equipping the whole team with broad and cohesive knowledge. After this process, personnel will be well positioned to transfer skills to the rest of the organization. In fact, for staff working in the Operational Risk department there is simply no excuse for operating in silos or displaying limited know-how.

External perspective and industry acumen

Integrated framework knowledge allows employees to answer the *how* question: how do we manage operational risk in our organization? Practitioners also need to be able to articulate *why* the tools have been designed in a particular way. This is a more difficult challenge to surmount. Ideally it requires heuristic experience of working in multiple companies, enabling the practitioner to compare practices first hand, to reflect on what works and tailor the appropriate solutions. Knowledge of the *why* can, however, also be acquired by consciously seeking a perspective on how the firm's operational risk management compares with industry best practices. As discussed in previous chapters, these practices are not set in stone; there is great divergence among financial services institutions in the use of the different framework elements. Successful professionals have their finger on the pulse. They are perceptive about where the industry is headed, conversant with regulatory priorities and areas of focus, and aware of how their own tools and processes relate to the benchmark.

Practical suggestions on how this wider perspective can be achieved are listed below:

- Researching, finding and joining practitioners' forums. Nothing replaces the value of conversations between fellow professionals, performing comparative analysis and sharing real life successes and challenges.

- Subscribing to news feeds and magazines. Plenty of free subscriptions are available, including Operational Riskdata eXchange Association (ORX)[4] and Risk Channel[5] which provide thoughtful insights that anyone can benefit from. Examples of paid platforms include: Thomson Reuters,[6] an industry leader in regulatory intelligence; Risk.net,[7] which includes events, conferences and a magazine; and RiskSpotlight,[8] which offers a horizon scanning portal.

- Obtaining membership in professional organizations such as the Institute of Risk Management which enables access to seminars, a network of practitioners and an opportunity to obtain a qualification (Certificate in Operational Risk Management – CORM).[9,10]

- Attending external operational risk training courses. These are run by multiple organizations, Risk.net and Euronext[11] being good examples.

- Inviting external guest speakers or trainers to share their views on particular topics.

- Asking first line colleagues to attend second line team meetings and talk about their risks.

Use all the means available to you to continuously gather and share intelligence and stay abreast of industry developments.

Interpersonal: facilitation, speaking, influencing

Even with exceptional framework and industry knowledge, practitioners will not be successful if they are unable to relay it effectively. The importance of softer skills was emphasized when discussing *multipliers*, who communicate, collaborate and build strong relationships (see Chapter 3). Consequently, enhancing the ability of risk employees to engage with an audience and energize their stakeholders is crucial. As will be seen from the industry benchmark later in the chapter, firms tend to underinvest in the development of softer skills, and more focus is needed in this area.

Operational risk *multipliers* should be already spending a significant proportion of their time out there talking to their audience; whether educating, making presentations or facilitating RCSAs, KRIs or scenario workshops.

Facilitation

> Workshop facilitation involves leading a group of participants to success and providing them with the necessary resources and opportunities; it is the art of making meetings more effective.

Facilitation is a key skill which needs to be practised and mastered. It can be mistakenly assumed that anyone can step in and competently lead a workshop with any type of audience, instantly achieving the desired outcome. On the contrary, sufficient thought and planning is needed on the prerequisites and capabilities required by the facilitator. Audiences can be unruly; and trying to facilitate a meeting or workshop without sufficient know-how or dexterity in handling problems can be a recipe for disaster. So important is this attribute that the outcome of a group session often depends significantly on the talents of its leader. At the other end of the spectrum, regrettably, I have witnessed poor workshop management being a major contributor to a sub-optimal RCSA programme.

Facilitation training prior to leading any RCSA, KRI or scenario workshop needs to include:

- The basics, covering organizational matters such as creating an agenda, setting expectations, managing time and delivering an outcome.

- Advanced components, including various workshop structures, agreeing ground rules, use of tools (Post-its and flipcharts for face-to-face workshops, interactive features of online platforms for virtual meetings), and a range of approaches to engaging participants and shaping group discussions, with particular focus on hybrid meetings which require more thought and preparation.

- Core and vital – but nevertheless frequently omitted – is an understanding of the different types of personalities attending the workshop, and a range of tactics for managing them. Tailored approaches can be used to handle disruptive participants such as *the domineering*, who overrules everything that is said; *the sceptic*, who constantly questions the value of the meeting and doubts whether anything useful will come of it; and *the introvert*, who holds valuable information but never speaks; among many others.

- Additional useful techniques for dealing with latecomers and distractions (for example, phones and laptops), disengagement (such as cameras switched off during virtual meetings), managing conflicts and drawing on the collective intelligence of the room.

If budget permits, invest in external facilitation masterclasses and/or certifications. Alternatively, assemble a library of essential books and online resources as recommended in the beginning of the chapter.

CASE STUDY 11.1

A large international financial services firm launches operational risk assessments which it plans to execute via a series of workshops. Over the years, the company has successfully applied a Six Sigma process improvement methodology, making it compulsory for every employee who commences a project to complete a masterclass covering methodological as well as leadership and facilitation aspects. Using this model as an example, Group Operational Risk decides to adopt the same proven tactic and mandates facilitation training for any member of staff expected to direct a workshop. This training consists of two half-day sessions and contains basic and advanced components of facilitation. It prepares participants administratively, mentally and emotionally for the task ahead and ensures uniformity in the firm's approach to the workshops.

Public speaking

Public speaking deserves a special mention. A large number of candidates working in operational risk have an accounting, audit or operations background. These professions are by nature more introverted than, for example, sales and marketing. Public speaking may not be a natural strength of employees with this kind of background; so a conscious investment needs to be made in developing them to be dynamic, engaging and enthusiastic presenters. This is a valuable and transferrable skill: employees who master the art of public speaking are in great demand in any industry and will likely go further in their careers. Furthermore proficiency in public speaking is also immensely helpful in facilitation.

Build teams that excel by:

- starting with basics, training and coaching internally;
- having an observer sitting in and providing feedback to the presenter post-meeting;
- working with a coach to film the speech or presentation and then play it back, focusing on both content and delivery;
- exploring external public speaking courses;
- adding to the library of essential books, as suggested in the section on further reading.

Influencing

Those interested in psychology will acknowledge that not only is it a captivating subject, but also very useful in the corporate world. The modus operandi of operational risk employees is by *influencing*; they do not directly manage business units or support functions, but are expected to be the effective *collaborators*, *connectors* and *change agents* of culture, transforming risk management thinking and the practices of the organization. Thus, any additional knowledge on how to improve influencing skills is most welcome.

A specific area where reading the dynamics is particularly beneficial is the relationship between a second line operational risk *multiplier* overseeing a first line operational risk *champion*. This multiplier–champion pair can be dysfunctional from the start. For example, you may have encountered a first line coordinator who, like a disobedient *child*, is chronically late in completing RCSA refresh, tardy with loss event reporting and continually missing the deadline for providing commentary on their risk profile. The second line multiplier, however, acts in a *parent* capacity, always stepping in and helping their colleague out. This pair is locked in a *parent–child* relationship; with the first line getting away with poor behaviours and the second line constantly going above and beyond the call of duty. They need to recognize this dysfunction and take the relationship to a new *adult–adult* level, rebalancing their roles and responsibilities.

Another potential example is a *parent* in the first line speaking down to a *child* in the second line; perhaps scolding them for not having sufficient understanding of all the intricacies of the first line business; or maybe even asking them to come back only when they have read all the relevant policies and procedures.

For those interested in psychology, a number of excellent books explore *transactional analysis* and the famous *parent–adult–child* theory; two books have been recommended in the beginning of this chapter.

Additional areas for development

The breadth of the operational risk discipline leads to grand expectations around the general level of knowledge and skill of operational risk practitioners. Whether realistic or not, all aspects of people, systems, processes and external environment are presumed to have been mastered by the risk practitioner. Therefore, increasing the general level of knowledge of operational risk professionals will invariably bear fruit. Useful areas employees

Table 11.1 Self-development objectives for second line operational risk practitioners

Rating	Activities
Achieved Expectation	Keeps up to date on operational risk topics by reading relevant press/magazines, participating in external conferences and meetings.
	Researches, prepares and delivers at least one educational presentation to the team on a chosen operational risk topic.
Achieved Plus	Enrolls into and successfully obtains a recognized operational risk qualification or certification.
	Joins a relevant industry body or group.
	Researches, prepares and delivers a series of educational presentations to the team and first line business units support functions.
Exceeded Expectation	Authors an article published in a recognized professional/ industry magazine.
	Delivers a presentation at a public forum or external conference. Is recognized as an industry expert, takes on a role as chair of a panel, forum or committee.
	Designs and develops train-the-trainer presentations to the team and first line business units/support functions.
	Mentors a team member on public speaking/facilitation.

are encouraged to assimilate via internal (and where possible, external) courses include:

- areas of regulatory focus; for example, operational resilience, third-party, cyber, ESG;

- skills and processes helping employees to be more entrepreneurial and business-savvy, e.g. decision-making, project management and Six Sigma process improvement;

- topical know-how in the field of data, automation and traditional and generative artificial intelligence;

- financial risk management, whether credit, market or liquidity, as risk professionals frequently attend (or are members of) enterprise risk management committees, and holistic understanding of the broader risk management world is beneficial; and

- business-specific knowledge.

Encouraging employee self-development

Learning is a joint responsibility of the employee and their leader. While managing large international teams I always aimed to motivate staff to invest in their self-development. I found it useful to outline clear pointers on what 'good' looks like, encouraging staff to use their initiative to progress on their educational journey. Table 11.1 is an example of a rating scale agreed at the beginning of the year, which is subsequently incorporated into the broader performance evaluation process at year end.

Cultivating first line risk coordinators

In Chapter 3, we discussed the importance of developing a network of champions in the first line. Champions, once appointed and in situ, need to be kept continuously energized and motivated, and education plays a crucial role in achieving this objective.

What do champions need to know? Essentially, they are an extension of the second line operational risk function, so the same kinds of educational resource and opportunity should be offered to them also.

In cases where the champion is a part-time role and they have more limited time, a more concise tuition programme can be developed:

- Training on operational risk framework and tools. It is particularly powerful when this training can be delivered by the organization's second line experts, either in its entirety or in a combination with external trainers; as this explicitly reinforces the department's position as a centre of excellence. This training can cover key framework components such as losses and near misses, RCSAs, KRIs and scenarios.

- Encouraging further studying to obtain a recognized operational risk qualification.

- Providing opportunities to join external training, offering tickets to operational risk conferences (where budget permits) or extending invitations to participate in industry forums.

- Facilitation training. If the firm is already running a good programme, it is beneficial to offer it to the first line champions who inevitably will end up leading meetings and workshops.

The second line can assist by developing minimum skillset requirements for first line coordinators; and undertaking a training needs analysis, to identify gaps between the skills held and knowledge required.

CASE STUDY 11.2

A two-day training programme is developed by the second line Operational Risk department, with the aim of raising the general standard of education on operational risk and making it more comprehensive. This programme contains an overview of all framework components and how they are implemented in the organization. The team works together to add interactive elements including group work, case studies and quizzes, which all enhance the participants' experience. The course, piloted on first line champions, is delivered face-to-face, with each topic presented by a different speaker from the second line.

It receives excellent feedback. Delivery by internal personnel is praised and perceived as a strong point which immediately boosts the department's reputation. Based on this experience, subsequent sessions are scheduled regularly in various locations across the country, allowing the maximum number of attendees to benefit from the training being offered.

The educational journey: three steps towards memorable risk training

Once the second line is fully equipped with knowledge and first line champions have been well trained, it is time to launch a firm-wide campaign.

Training for the wider population of staff usually involves a combination of online modules and face-to-face sessions, since classroom-led training is widely recognized as being far more impactful than online tutorials. It is strongly recommended to include a programme for all new joiners as part of their overall induction, as well as periodic refresher sessions.

Outlined in Figure 11.3 are three suggested steps to deliver effective, memorable operational risk training.

Step 1: Design phase – high-quality materials and a theme

Education does not have to be boring, and there are many good alternatives to a set of dull training slides which merely recite Basel Committee guidelines on operational risk management. All firms have professionals whose job is to produce sleek and colourful promotional materials, ads and client presentations. Commonly, Marketing and Communications departments

Figure 11.3   Three steps for developing all-staff education

employ creative people full of ideas of what 'good' looks like when it comes to capturing an audience's attention. When developing operational risk training programmes, partner with experts and request their advice and help to design presentations for internal personnel that are not only impactful but visually appealing. This resource is not utilized nearly enough – Operational Risk departments need to reach out and speak much more to marketing, communications or other equivalent functions to take advantage of their skills and expertise. It is very fitting to mention here the brilliant work by The Bob Pike Group (included in recommended resources). The organization runs courses for all educators, from university teachers to risk professionals, on how to design and deliver impactful learning. From openers and closers to use of music and videos to strengthen the message, the courses simply excel in taking training to the next level.

In terms of strengthening the message, one practical way is to find a meaningful theme which resonates with the firm's strategy, objectives and aspirations. This makes the training more engaging, vivid and real.

CASE STUDY 11.3

An all-staff operational risk training programme is being developed in a start-up firm. The chief executive understands and embraces the value of operational risk, eloquently comparing the organization with a newly built airplane: proper management of people, systems, processes and the external environment will all support a smooth journey. The Operational Risk department partners with Marketing and agrees on an aircraft theme for the programme, with a photo of the chief executive in the cockpit and key messages from the pilot. Each training participant receives a key ring in the form of a plane as a free gift. Employees understand the analogy and connect with the theme, and the training manages to achieve its objective of reaching out with simple messages and raising awareness.

Step 2: Delivery – interactive and with a sense of humour

Once the training materials have been developed, it is important to focus on the excellence of delivery. Consider various learning styles, be they visual, auditory or kinaesthetic (learning by doing), and design a programme which incorporates a mixture of approaches. Chinese philosopher Confucius is reputed to have said: 'I hear and I forget. I see and I remember. I do and I understand.' Interactive sessions where participants apply their learning in practice maximize the degree to which the material is absorbed. Reflecting on many years of my own teaching, the delegates always quote engagement and the doing part as a very enjoyable feature of the courses I have run.

For longer one- or two-day training sessions, it is effective to use group work, splitting participants into teams. Engaging exercises can be designed for each component of the framework:

- OREs – reviewing internal or external case studies of major operational risk failures;
- RCSAs – having a go at identifying *top operational risks* and plotting them on a *heat map* to practise risk identification;
- KRIs – creating indicators for a select *top operational risk* and setting thresholds, or sharing the best metrics currently used to manage risks and discussing their attributes;
- reporting – to reinforce the message that reporting should be succinct – selecting a film or a book and summarizing it in six words.

There is still time for attendee interaction even in shorter sessions. When introducing operational risk events, ask the audience to come up with an example of a recent event for all relevant categories of the taxonomy. At the end, running a short quiz with a few simple questions on definitions, thresholds for loss reporting, roles and responsibilities works quite well.

Training should be fun, so light-hearted delivery works best. People like to laugh, and it is up to the trainer to find relevant yet humorous examples which reinforce the need for risk management. Clever use of personal stories, cartoons and images can be powerful. One video clip has two Australian comedians talking about the BP oil spill in the Gulf of Mexico; this conveys exceptionally well the need to think about risk proactively, and most participants seem to find it very amusing.

Trainers inevitably bring examples of industry disasters when talking about operational risk events. Instead of citing ordinary cases of technology failures or fines for money laundering, do some research and find more unusual events. There is a rather interesting case of a teenager taking revenge on former bosses by sending some five million emails quoting a warning from a horror film, *The Ring*, which eventually led to the collapse of the firm's servers under the weight of the email traffic.[12] I always ask the audience to guess what was in the quote.

Step 3: Feedback and continuous evolution

A training module is only as good as the audience thinks it is. It is valuable to solicit feedback after each session, via a paper form or an online survey. Key questions to consider may include:

- Was the session useful and well delivered?
- Did the training provide learnings that you can apply in your daily job?
- Do you understand your role in managing operational risk?

It is useful to leave some room for free format comments and suggestions on how to improve the training. Attendees can then come up with creative ideas and fair criticism, which should be studiously examined with the aim to continuously improve the training offering.

Tailoring the content to the audience

What about training content? While there is no universal answer and the agenda depends on each firm's individual circumstances, the emphasis should be on the relevance of the learning. Employees need to come out of the session equipped with knowledge that they can directly apply in practice.

At its simplest level, all employees need to know:

- What is operational risk?
- How is it managed?
- What is my role in the process, and what should I be doing?

All staff should be able to recognize and report operational risk events (OREs); therefore the training must provide examples of what those are and guide employees on how to do those things. If the session is delivered to a particular business or function, the content can be tailored to suit the audience, with relevant discussion around losses and near misses that can potentially happen in their area. Chapter 4 articulated such examples for Human Resources and Trading.

Training covering RCSAs, KRIs, scenarios and ORAs is more targeted to those who are taking part in these exercises, and should be carried out in a timely manner, shortly before the workshops or even as part of them.

It is imperative to incorporate executive briefings for senior management. The same concept of relevance applies, in a similar way to employees, to assist senior executives to absorb the key information while also applying the concepts. Therefore, the best learning happens when executives:

- carry out a strategic risk assessment (see Chapter 5), identifying and evaluating risks that may prevent them from achieving their objectives;

- review their departmental RCSA, outlining what keeps them awake at night and debating mitigating actions for significant risks;

- act on the operational risk assessment of a new product which has highlighted a material risk area.

An introductory methodological presentation is beneficial, especially when it is followed immediately by a participation exercise.

Online training

It may not be possible to run ongoing face-to-face sessions for all staff. Web-based refresher training can play a supportive role in delivering key messages to a larger target audience. However, a word of caution. We have all been there and done that – clicking through the pages quickly to get to the end in record time ('phew, mandatory training completed'). So it takes twice as much creativity to design an online module that stands a chance of attracting attention:

- Use the same first step as in face-to-face training, aiming for high-quality materials and a theme, to enhance attendees' visual learning experience.

- Supplement the training materials with an auditory learning element, by including personal and impactful recorded video messages. These can be from senior leaders on the importance of risk management, or from employees on what risk management means to them in their daily jobs.

- Add questions and quizzes to incorporate the *doing* part. This is one of the few advantages of online modules, where tests are easy to administer.

Well-designed activities help to engage the learners, prompting them to maintain focus and participate actively in the training.

- Place the evaluation up-front, rather than at the end of the course. A session which starts with a test of current knowledge recognizes that some employees will already have a good grasp of core material. If they pass, they do not need to proceed with the full course, thus saving them time and retaining their goodwill.

- To add variety, consider embedding pointers and/or links to the internal company website. These could contain, for example, names and (ideally) photos of second line *multipliers* and first line *champions*, making them more personal and accessible; or a template for logging operational risk losses; or other relevant information.

- Develop a sequential progressive modular training programme, which builds on the knowledge imparted during previous modules.

- If an online module is re-used as refresher, ensure that materials and evaluations are significantly amended to reflect advances in both internal processes and the external environment. Integrate new recorded messages. There is nothing worse than the same training module being offered as a refresher year after year. If staff become over-familiar with the offering they will simply switch off. In this event not only is the training called into question but also the wider reputation of the Operational Risk department.

In conclusion, training in itself will not do the job of embedding operational risk management. It needs to be supported by a robust framework with meaningful tools and the right tone from the top. Education, however, can take the firm a long way forward in achieving this objective.

Common challenges and good practices

Common challenges

Challenges that may arise when designing and delivering educational programmes are outlined below.

Limited budget

Training has cost implications. While a lot can be achieved via internal means, there are undeniable benefits from investing in targeted external courses, where relevant. Operational risk courses and conferences, as well as facilitation and public speaking programmes, can significantly enhance employee skillsets. A clear articulation of the investment being sought and the expected outcomes of the training, to help achieve senior level buy-in and approval, are therefore required.

Employees pushing back

Often, the challenge around training and education is a *'why do I need to do this?'*-type of comeback from staff. The training aids in embedding further knowledge about the responsibilities of colleagues across the firm and draws out the consequences of poor operational risk management. Understanding and managing firm's risks is an enabler to meeting strategic objectives while remaining within defined risk appetite.

Training fatigue

While in the past end-users would be responsible for seeking out their own relevant training, the ever-increasing tsunami of regulation means that many other people are out there trying to achieve mandatory training objectives for everyone in the firm. Commonly folk are now chased by Compliance (to attend new conduct and culture training), Financial Crime (it's time for your mandatory anti-money laundering refresh), Information Security (cyber risk update), Data Protection (the obligatory Global Data Protection Regulation education session), Health and Safety and many others. Operational risk is thus only part of a rather long queue. This makes it all the more important to stand out, with well-designed, memorable, engaging and meaningful learning that employees can truly benefit from. In addition, where possible, avoid organizational silos and look for synergies, developing joint modules where possible to relieve pressure on the end-user.

Apathy

At times, training workshops can be marred by apathy and/or poor attendance on the part of business units or support functions. I always believe that leading by engagement is more powerful than via punishment or penalty. Persevere and continue to deliver excellent educational programmes. Through word of mouth, employees will get to hear about them, tag along and join in.

Missed opportunities

Over the years, I have interviewed multiple second line operational risk professionals. While many came across as all-round experts, quite a few actually had experience of dealing with only one specific framework component, for example losses and near misses. They were not always proficient with other tools and could not always articulate how all the elements of the framework fitted together. When working in operational risk as an employee, be curious and strive to acquire a holistic understanding of the discipline and the surrounding business and regulatory environment. As a leader, be sure to always provide opportunities for cross-training and aim to develop a comprehensive pool of knowledge across all team members.

Good practices

Adopt entrepreneurial approach

Second line *multipliers* are key to the success of operational risk management in the organization. To encourage a more entrepreneurial approach in the second line, it is beneficial to think of it as a consultancy firm which is rewarded based on the quality of its people. Could the operational risk function take off and branch out today, if it were hypothetically to start up as an independent company? Will the level of knowledge and interpersonal skills make it profitable? Would you hire them? If not, consider what further skill development is needed.

Appoint a training coordinator

Recognizing the importance of education, appoint a training coordinator within the second line, in coordination with the relevant Learning and Development or Human Resources department. This is usually not a full-time role, but rather giving someone responsibility for thinking about the firm-wide training strategy and leading its implementation.

Embrace virtual learning

Covid-19 has taught us some valuable lessons about the effective use of virtual classrooms. What was previously an instructor-led session can now be delivered both face-to-face and virtually. Online platforms have excellent functionality, including live polls, whiteboards and break-out rooms. Other brilliant apps are available to facilitate brainstorming and group work, for example, Canva and Mentimeter. It takes some time to explore and master the features but I am really impressed with the varied offerings and online tools now available in the market.

Explore what is available on the market

When designing online training modules, it is beneficial to explore what is available off-the-shelf. Some suppliers, especially in compliance and financial crime, also develop operational risk training programmes. Because there is no standard application of the framework elements, however, any purchased solution will need to be tailored, and supplemented by relevant examples, links and policy requirements. Still, providers such as Brainshark offer platforms on which unique, tailor-made training can be developed, offering a range of excellent features to help make the module more interactive and engaging.[13]

Retain evidence

Nowadays, evidencing is key. Online modules store evidence of attendance and pass rates, making them very effective for audit and control purposes.

Celebrate success

And lastly, celebrating success. Perseverance in training will continue to increase the overall level of knowledge in the organization. This, in turn, reinforces the correct use of the different framework components, embeds the right practices and strengthens the risk culture of the firm. The progress, reflected in the maturity assessment (as described in Chapter 13), needs to be actively publicized and celebrated, to help embed operational risk management even further.

Industry benchmark

Practitioners from a wide range of financial services firms of different sizes and geographical spread joined the Best Practice Forum to participate in a live poll examining various aspects of operational risk training.

Starting with investment in their own skills and capabilities, both second line operational risk practitioners as well as embedded first line risk coordinators noted that training budgets were at reasonable levels, thus offering adequate opportunities for continuous learning (see Figure 11.4). This is a positive development, as previously educational activities were targeted primarily at second line risk resources. Inclusion of first line champions will enable them to make good progress in their learning, and develop an increasingly good grasp of the concepts, framework, and core tools.

Figure 11.4   Industry poll: investment in education of operational risk professionals

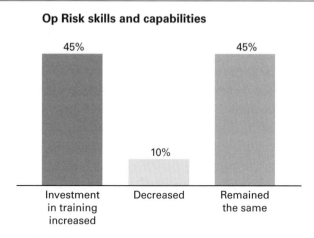

Best Practice Operational Risk Forum, 2023

Figure 11.5   Industry poll: operational risk soft skills development

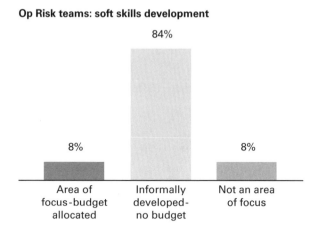

Best Practice Operational Risk Forum, 2023

Training budgets, however, were mostly used for technical areas, such as advanced operational risk management, risk reporting, ESG, cyber, operational resilience, and most recently, data science and AI. As it relates to *softer* qualities, while almost all participants (92 per cent) confirmed that some developmental activities were in place, only 8 per cent had actual spend allocated (see Figure 11.5). Given the importance of softer skills, this area warrants further investment.

As it relates to firm-wide operational risk training, participants shared good practices, including:

- Educating the board, providing purposeful briefings and ensuring that each new board member receives a good overview;
- Engaging employees via gamification, such as risk competitions at Christmas ('Riskmas competitions');
- Including operational risk module at employee induction, to ensure new starters are adequately informed;
- Speaking at all-staff meetings and Town Halls on the value of risk management;
- Delivering tailor-made departmental briefings.

Due to constant attrition and inflow of new employees at all levels, it was agreed that training must be an ongoing activity. At busy times, however, it's the education, which requires substantial time and resource investment, that was commonly descoped or delayed. Hence, members acknowledged that firm-wide operational risk training is not yet at its point of destination, and the Basel Committee's conclusion on firms needing more risk learning remains valid.

Practical workplace exercise

Review the operational risk training offering available within your firm. Consider the following questions:

1 Does the training strategy achieve the goal of developing the second line operational risk function into a centre of excellence?
2 Is the education sufficient to support first line champions?
3 What is the current level of staff knowledge and what can be done to increase it?
4 What works well? Make a note of the strong features of the current training programme.
5 What can be improved? Note down potential improvements to the current programme.

MAKE A DIFFERENCE (MAD) ACTION

Please note down one action that you will take after reading this chapter that will make a positive difference to operational risk training in your firm.

In summary, this chapter discussed the crucial importance of education at all levels of the organization, proposing an approach for developing second line operational risk experts and transferring knowledge throughout the firm via well-designed and well-developed training.

Moving on, the next chapter continues the discussion with the topic of risk culture.

Notes

1 Basel Committee on Banking Supervision (2014) *Review of the Principles for the Sound Management of Operational Risk*, www.bis.org/publ/bcbs292.pdf (archived at https://perma.cc/7V33-DWSF)

2 Basel Committee on Banking Supervision (2021) *Revisions to the Principles for the Sound Management of Operational Risk*, www.bis.org/bcbs/publ/d515.pdf (archived at https://perma.cc/E45Y-GK3N)

3 Banking Risk & Regulation (2014), Banks' non-financial risk training slammed as 'inadequate', https://www.bankingriskandregulation.com/banks-non-financial-risk-training-slammed-as-inadequate/ (archived at https://perma.cc/S2WA-Y3HT)

4 Operational Riskdata eXchange Association (ORX), managingrisktogether.orx. org/free-resources (archived at https://perma.cc/SWH8-VQGB)

5 Risk Channel, industryslice.com/RiskChannel (archived at https://perma.cc/ N59W-4HDC)

6 Thomson Reuters, www.thomsonreuters.com (archived at https://perma.cc/ SS2E-FBUS)

7 Risk.net, www.risk.net (archived at https://perma.cc/24ZN-3QN7)

8 RiskSpotlight, www.riskspotlight.com (archived at https://perma.cc/8LZ8-MW6G)

9 Institute of Risk Management, www.theirm.org/join-our-community/about-membership/ (archived at https://perma.cc/E2P6-TK6B)

10 Certificate in Operational Risk Management (CORM) www.ior-institute.org/ education/certificate-in-operational-risk-management (archived at https:// perma.cc/SUN8-QP3P)

11 Euronext Corporate Services Academy, www.corporateservices.euronext.com/ academy (archived at https://perma.cc/K399-YB7R)

12 Metro (2006) Sacked boy's revenge emails, metro.co.uk/2006/08/24/sacked-boys-revenge-emails-211474/ (archived at https://perma.cc/Z75D-F9TL)

13 Brainshark, www.brainshark.com/why-brainshark (archived at https://perma. cc/V65F-YNA3)

Risk culture   12

What this chapter covers: The chapter focuses on the least visible but most vital aspect of risk management – Risk Culture (Figure 12.1). It considers how to evaluate this key topic, and proposes ways of completing an assessment via employee focus groups and the use of metrics. The chapter outlines practical steps that can be taken to embed the right ethos and behaviours. It goes on to highlight the importance of holding meaningful risk conversations across the firm; and reflects on the implications of the *identity* of operational risk practitioners on the culture of the enterprise. The chapter also includes industry benchmark and case studies.

Understanding and measuring risk culture

Risk culture is not a new concept for operational risk practitioners. It is an integral part of the discipline, and features in Principle One of the Basel

Figure 12.1 Focus of Chapter 12: risk culture

Risk culture

Operational risk taxonomy

Governance, roles and responsibilities

Establish governance and clear roles across the Three Lines for managing operational risk.

Risk appetite and risk capacity

Define nature and types of risk accepted in pursuit of strategic objectives. Evaluate adequacy of capital resources.

Operational risk events	Risk assessments	Scenario analysis	Key Risk Indicators
Record and report risk events, act to minimize future exposure. Monitor trends against RCSAs and KRIs.	Assess risk exposure in process, business or function via RCSAs. Supplement by evaluating risks emanating from change activities via ORAs.	Identify exposure from extreme but plausible events. Mitigate through risk transfer to insurance.	Monitor risk and control performance through predictive indicators. Act if indicators breach established appetite threshold.

Reporting and decision-making

Review actual risk profile against set appetite, apply active risk management to enable achievement of strategic objectives.

Embedding and maturity assessment

Training and education

Committee's sound operational risk practices.[1] Historically, risk professionals have not only been involved in establishing and maintaining firms' risk culture, but actually often took the lead in some organizations' efforts, positively influencing ethos, values and behaviours.

DEFINITION OF RISK CULTURE

Risk culture is a social process that can be defined as an institution's values, 'norms, attitudes and behaviours related to risk awareness, risk taking and risk management'.[2]

By design, all the elements of an operational risk framework inevitably touch on themes of transparency, accountability and no blame. The effectiveness of risk management is closely linked to and largely dependent on the firm's culture. Organizations where the right values have been embedded are less likely to suffer damaging operational risk events, and stand a better chance of dealing with them effectively if they do occur.

It is, therefore, in the best interests of operational risk practitioners to be fully engaged on this topic. Two points before we move on to the main content of the chapter:

- An ample amount of literature has been published on the subject of culture. Regulators, industry bodies and consultancy firms have issued definitions, reports and guidelines which this chapter does not intend to replicate or re-interpret.

- Risk culture is undoubtedly a complex, multifaceted topic with no 'recipe book' answer. But practical steps can be taken to instil and embed the right behaviours throughout the organization.

Some form of culture assessment has become the norm within financial services firms. Boards expect it and regulators require it. As noted, for instance, by the Australian Royal Commission, 'all financial services entities should take proper steps to assess the entity's culture'.[3] A benchmarking survey of over 50 financial services firms revealed that, in general, firms' culture was measured via employee surveys or focus groups, or alternatively metrics and dashboards.[4] Interestingly, the top three methods used by organizations consisted of:

- employee exit interviews;
- employee surveys; and

- appraisals and feedback received during the performance management process.

As demonstrated by the industry benchmark survey discussed at the end of the chapter, historically, cultural efforts in most organizations were led by the Human Resources function. But operational risk teams are now actively leading and contributing to these programmes.

The five-aspects risk culture assessment model

Any measure of culture is somewhat imprecise due to the complex nature of the subject. While organizations may have different perspectives, the work undertaken by the Financial Stability Board (FSB) represents a good place to start.[5] The proposed *risk culture aspects model* described in Figure 12.2 takes into consideration FSB's framework and focuses on five components: *transparency*, *no blame*, *personal accountability*, *risk awareness* and *risk reward*. It can be argued that these aspects are indicative of the firm's cultural 'state of health', and influence the firm's ability to take the informed risk decisions necessary for achieving its strategic objectives. Organizations may add further factors that they feel are relevant to their firm.

The reasons why the five factors have been selected as particularly important to the enterprise are articulated below:

- *Transparency* plays a significant role in information flows. It allows the transmission of messages without them being modified. For example, if a KRI is reported as *Red*, it does not get downgraded to *Amber* or *Green* by the time it is escalated up the chain. Some senior managers, committees and boards do not deal well with *Red* indicators and other reports which raise alarms. As a result, true risks and issues can be demoted, leading to a lack of management focus or preventative action to mitigate potentially major problems.

- Cultivating *no blame* attitudes was discussed in Chapter 3 on operational risk events. A constructive approach to resolving problems, rather than pointing fingers, has a big influence on how employees act when things go wrong.

- *Personal accountability* is simply essential to move things forward and get things done. The institution can have transparent discussions around

Figure 12.2   Risk culture aspects model

areas of concern without attributing blame, but if no one is ready to step in and act, the issues are unlikely to get resolved. This is an area of particular regulatory focus, given the introduction of formal accountability regimes over recent years.

- *Risk awareness* has been a key theme throughout this book. It measures the extent to which employees understand risk and are aware of their own roles and responsibilities in managing it.

- *Risk reward* answers the question *what's in it for me?*. If actions or behaviours result in no personal impact – in the form of either an incentive for good risk management or punishment for poor practices – it is harder to articulate the case respectively for or against them.

CASE STUDY 12.1

A small-size corporate bank adopts the *risk culture aspects model* to run diagnostics around its existing culture, identifying its areas of strength and weakness. It creates cross-departmental employee focus groups, facilitated by the operational risk function, to gauge staff members' perceptions of how well or poorly the firm scores on a scale of 1 to 10 in each of the categories. The results, presented in Figure 12.3, are analysed and presented for discussion.

- *Risk awareness* achieves a high rating, 8 out of 10; employees recall and relate to ongoing efforts sponsored by the chief risk officer and chief executive to educate all staff on risk management. For example, the *I AM Risk Thinking* campaign encourages employees to **I**dentify, **A**ssess, **M**anage and **R**eport on **R**isk, emphasizing that it is everyone's responsibility (I AM Responsible, rather than my manager or someone in Risk department), thus developing risk thinking. This is followed by an introduction of a popular I AM Risk Thinking *mailbox* which all employees can use to informally identify particular risks or issues.

- *Transparency* also scores highly; overall, management encourages and welcomes the identification and escalation of issues across the enterprise.

- *No blame* culture varies markedly by area; while there are good behaviours in many departments, it transpires that there are pockets of poor practices within Technology and Finance.

- *Personal accountability* highlights a challenge; headcount cuts have resulted in employees becoming overstretched. While staff are eager to raise issues, they are reluctant to volunteer for additional responsibilities which add extra tasks to their already full agenda.

- Finally, *Risk reward* receives the lowest score and is not deemed functional by the focus groups. While aggressive risk taking in sales and trading is penalized, the actions and behaviours of non-revenue generating functions have no similar impact. Good or poor risk management has no bearing on compensation.

Figure 12.3   Risk culture assessment case study analysis

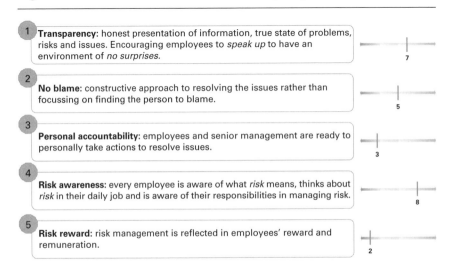

1 **Transparency:** honest presentation of information, true state of problems, risks and issues. Encouraging employees to *speak up* to have an environment of *no surprises.*   7

2 **No blame:** constructive approach to resolving the issues rather than focussing on finding the person to blame.   5

3 **Personal accountability:** employees and senior management are ready to personally take actions to resolve issues.   3

4 **Risk awareness:** every employee is aware of what *risk* means, thinks about *risk* in their daily job and is aware of their responsibilities in managing risk.   8

5 **Risk reward:** risk management is reflected in employees' reward and remuneration.   2

The study is perceived as insightful; it results in a range of tangible actions, including adopting this kind of evaluation as a matter of practice, and continuing regular culture *health checks*, via employee focus groups, on a semi-annual basis.

In this case the Operational Risk department was able to facilitate focus groups and obtain insights into employees' honest opinions due to its good standing, earning trust and a recognition of its impartiality. As highlighted later in the chapter, the *identity* of the operational risk professional, their individual personality, has a strong contributing effect on these cultural dynamics.

Metrics: culture and conduct dashboard

Culture is still widely considered as a primary root cause of major conduct failings in financial services. Often this view focuses on a firm's broader *culture* (rather than its *risk culture*).

> Numerous credible definitions of culture exist; we will use 'habitual behaviours and mindsets that characterize an organization'.[6]

But in recent years the ancillary terms *conduct* and *conduct risk* have become more prominent in supervisory publications, speeches and discussions.

> *Conduct risk* can be defined as the risk that a firm's 'decisions and behaviours lead to detrimental or poor outcomes for their customers, and the risk that the firm fails to maintain high standards of market behaviour and integrity'.[7]

Consequently the industry is undergoing a major strengthening of employees' conduct obligations, the introduction of enhanced certification and accountability regimes, and instruments such as the legally required banker's oath.[8] The concepts of *culture*, *risk culture* and *conduct* are closely intertwined; though it would be fair to say that culture and conduct have a broader social and behavioural scope than *risk culture*. Organizations are expected to create firm-specific definitions of these key terms. Both the language and the focus of these efforts vary significantly depending on the jurisdiction and the terms habitually used by the firms and their supervisors.

As with surveys and focus groups, operational risk practitioners need to actively join in the firm's efforts to create culture and conduct dashboards; after all, many of the metrics will be relevant to operational risk, and may even be already monitored by the department. Perhaps risk culture metrics are the future as they can deliver more value than occasional, discrete employee surveys. Organizations quickly suffer from survey fatigue which prevents them from being repeated often enough to keep track of changing risk cultures.

Figure 12.4 gives an example of such a dashboard. In this example, the dashboard measures the firm's performance against four pillars that have been designated as important to the organization. Some of these aspects, for example, diversity and inclusion, refer to core values that are broader than risk awareness, risk taking and risk management (which together represent *risk culture*). The indicators in this dashboard were selected, together with their thresholds, via a rigorous management process, as discussed in Chapter 7.

The dashboard is typically presented to a relevant governance committee, which could be an operational risk committee, conduct risk forum, the main risk committee, the board or all of the above. This kind of metric enables the organization to continuously monitor agreed aspects of culture and constantly drive the agenda forward.

Practical steps towards embedding risk culture

From evaluation to actions, undeniably, the operational risk function plays a key role in embedding the right ethos in the firm; so it is, to a great extent, a catalyst for positive change. Ideally, a clear tone from the top and firm-wide cultural programmes will have been established, which operational risk can participate in and contribute to. Sometimes, however, firms make minimal endeavours in this area and operational risk ends up being the *sole department* pushing the heavy load up the hill. Whichever

Figure 12.4 Example of conduct and culture dashboard

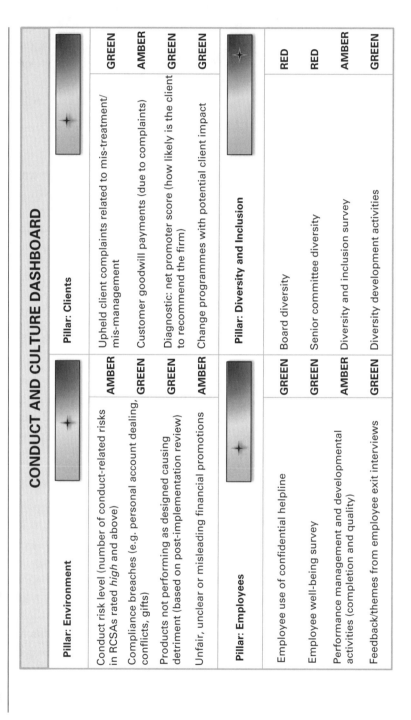

CONDUCT AND CULTURE DASHBOARD

Pillar: Environment		Pillar: Clients	
Conduct risk level (number of conduct-related risks in RCSAs rated *high* and above)	AMBER	Upheld client complaints related to mis-treatment/mis-management	GREEN
Compliance breaches (e.g. personal account dealing, conflicts, gifts)	GREEN	Customer goodwill payments (due to complaints)	AMBER
Products not performing as designed causing detriment (based on post-implementation review)	GREEN	Diagnostic: net promoter score (how likely is the client to recommend the firm)	GREEN
Unfair, unclear or misleading financial promotions	AMBER	Change programmes with potential client impact	GREEN

Pillar: Employees		Pillar: Diversity and Inclusion	
Employee use of confidential helpline	GREEN	Board diversity	RED
Employee well-being survey	GREEN	Senior committee diversity	RED
Performance management and developmental activities (completion and quality)	AMBER	Diversity and inclusion survey	AMBER
Feedback/themes from employee exit interviews	GREEN	Diversity development activities	GREEN

circumstances apply, practitioners can spearhead the following set of activities to influence behaviours across the organization.

Transparency

- Instituting incentives for transparency, such as *thank you* notes for reporting operational risk events.
- Via facilitation and challenge, helping first line business units to reflect the true state of risks, events and issues – neither under- nor overestimating them.
- By expressing opinions that are clear and independent, helping to transmit the right messages which consequently retain their true meaning (e.g. ensuring that *Red* KRIs are not diluted, when escalated upwards, by being downgraded to *Amber* or *Green*).
- Incorporating automated process workflows, for speedy dissemination and escalation of material issues to the right audience.
- Incentivizing high awareness of risks and issues.

No blame

- Developing trust with first line business units; being visible and approachable, having a known team member who serves as a liaison for every area and who can be contacted if employees have questions or doubts.
- Educating senior management on a no blame attitude; although this kind of venture does not always bear fruit, every attempt should be made.
- Setting the tone by chairing operational risk forums where issues are discussed openly and constructively.
- Documenting in policies that the firm has a no blame approach (i.e. a formal mechanism, although note that this can be less effective than establishing a no blame attitude more informally).
- Working with Human Resources to establish and analyse relevant metrics; for example, an increase in incidences of whistleblowing or the use of employee helplines may be indicative of potential problems that require focus.

Personal accountability

- Collaborating with Human Resources to document roles and responsibilities (for example, for first line risk owners, subject matter experts (SMEs) or risk champions) and ensure they align with broader statements of accountabilities.

- Developing instruments such as an RACI matrix (**R**esponsible, **A**ccountable, **C**onsulted, **I**nformed), to outline the respective roles that first and second line functions play in a process or activity.

- Embedding risk acceptance mechanisms, to alleviate pressure on front-line functions and ensure formal agreement that no further action is needed in cases where it is not cost-effective.

- Prioritizing risks, issues and actions and focusing on what is important.

- Leading by example, stepping in to moderate any cross-functional operational risk events that have no single owner, until they are fully resolved.

Risk awareness

- Conducting employee training as discussed in the previous chapter, supplemented by other educational campaigns including social media posts, flash news and newsletters.

- Using opportunities to present at senior management meetings and employee town halls; working with the chief executive to incorporate key messages into their internal presentations; developing key questions that a board should be asking itself on risk culture.

- Encouraging employees to participate in and use operational risk tools at the 'coal face'; working with RCSAs, KRIs and scenarios as a practical application is the best way of increasing understanding of the tools.

- Promoting the sharing and dissemination of lessons learnt, tips and hints; for example, via a monthly meeting of first line operational risk coordinators.

- Highlighting interdependencies, where risks can affect others in the delivery chain. Process improvement techniques including process flow charts can be very useful in achieving this aim.

Risk reward

- Joining forces with Human Resources to incorporate risk management responsibilities into employees' objectives and the performance management process.

- Considering operational risk event data in appraisals; a punitive method is quite commonly used for front-office/sales personnel, but this can be supplemented by reward mechanisms, for example, providing formal feedback on the performance of first line operational risk champions.

- Using *compare and contrast* reviews which present, for instance, logs of incidents across all departments; timely and accurate reporting can be recognized via some kind of departmental reward (e.g. a shared meal);

- Celebrating success: for example, introducing employee awards for the most improved process following an operational risk event; underscoring the importance of acknowledgement, appreciation and gratitude. To this end, one of the key messages from the 2023 Governance and Culture Reform Conference hosted by the Federal Reserve Bank of New York was on the power of recognition: 'the most emphatic and deceptively simple takeaway that emerged was that to motivate desired behaviors, it is important to appreciate organizational staff and do so publicly'.[9] Recognition is an important mechanism that is vastly underutilized.

- Agreeing reward and punishment mechanisms when embedding the use of operational risk appetite.

Role of risk conversations

Risk experts set the tone and the language of *risk conversations*. What words come to mind when picking up the phone, switching on the webcam or walking into the meeting room with business units and support functions? What topics do operational risk professionals discuss?

Compare the two dialogues illustrated in Figure 12.5. The first box, *risk administration*, focuses on the *process* and has minimal content. It does not differentiate between low and high priority items, and focuses attention mainly on the mechanical aspects of the framework; aiming to just *get things done*, regardless of whether or not they are important. These discussions are usually brief and tend to be one-way, with operational risk chasing business units to take some kind of action or complete a form.

Figure 12.5 Risk conversations

RED ZONE: Risk administration

- Have you logged the ORE? When will you log it, it needs to be reported as soon as possible?
- Have you attached the evidence? This field is blank.
- You have seven open actions. We need to review all of them.
- Your RCSA is overdue. It needs to be completed by the end of this week.
- There are only three risks raised in your RCSA. Please ensure RCSA completeness.

GREEN ZONE: Risk management

- Latest ORE highlights an issue with control X. Let's discuss how it can be improved. Can this happen to other units?
- Reviewing open actions, there is one high priority item. How is your progress in obtaining the funding needed to fix the issue? How can we help to move it forward? What is the risk in the meantime?
- Based on your RCSA, X is your top risk. How is the new product/system impacting this risk? Will it increase even further? Let's discuss.

In contrast, *risk management* discussions evolve around the *content*. They concentrate on what is important, with more time being spent on high-priority issues that matter, because they may prevent the firm from achieving its objectives or may crystallize into major incidents. These conversations are usually longer, deeper and contain a meaningful two-way exchange of opinions.

It is important for operational risk teams to stand back and reflect on their risk conversations; as their tone and content will gradually be replicated across the enterprise. If risk practitioners lead the way using a risk *administration* approach, that is how the whole risk discipline will soon be perceived: as administrative. It also affects the culture, which develops into a bureaucratic tick-box-type enterprise, with diminished faith in the second line risk function. By the same token, proper risk management discussions will send ripples through the business and will constantly repeat and reinforce themselves, teaching business units what good looks like.

Impact of the identity of operational risk practitioners

As noted in the research report on risk culture in financial services mentioned earlier,[10] 'a significant aspect of the risk culture debate closely concerns the organizational position of the risk function'.

Table 12.1 Industry study: identity of operational risk practitioner

Operational risk practitioners primarily see themselves as	% participants
Police officer	15
Consultant	52
Translator	8
Facilitator	25

Table 12.2 Industry study: skills of operational risk practitioners

What knowledge and skills do you see as most important?	% firms
Knowledge of regulatory requirements	7
Practical know-how (framework and tools)	73
Subject matter expertise (cyber, outsourcing, other)	7
Softer skills, influencing, facilitation	13

Undoubtedly, the importance of the risk profession has been increasing and the demand for practitioners is on the rise. When searching to recruit an ideal candidate, employers insist on the combination of multiple skills; including extensive experience in frameworks, knowledge of regulatory requirements, in-depth specialist knowledge, quantitative or actuarial background, and excellent communication and influencing skills. This blend makes it almost impossible to recruit the kind of superhero who possesses all the required skills and qualities. Because the operational risk discipline is still maturing, there is not yet a distinct *identity* for a typical operational risk professional.

In 2018 I conducted an industry study around this *identity* issue, to try to understand how operational risk professionals perceive themselves in their role. The results are presented in Table 12.1.

A positive result, as seen in the table, is that the majority (52 per cent) viewed themselves as consultants and trusted advisors, adopting a collaborative approach and working in partnership with the business. Around 25 per cent of respondents related to the identity of facilitators

– influencers who spend a significant proportion of their time engaging, educating and communicating with employees and senior management, for example, facilitating workshops and conducting road shows. These practitioners possess the traits of *multipliers* discussed in Chapter 3.

In cases where operational risk practitioners adopt a stance of *police officers* – emphasizing formal oversight, challenge and shareholder protection – they seem to lose some employees' trust. This, in turn, has implications for the interactions between risk management and the business, and ultimately, for the wider risk culture of the firm. We discussed these characters, also called *diminishers*, in Chapter 3.

Do risk practitioners possess the necessary skills to effectively perform the role of trusted advisors? The same study, the results of which are presented in Table 12.2, highlighted that operational risk employees may overestimate the importance of practical know-how at the expense of softer influencing, facilitation and negotiation skills.

Having stayed very close to the live debate on the necessary skills of risk professionals, I have observed that an increasing number of practitioners embrace and master the *softer* qualities; despite the progress being somewhat slow. As mentioned in Chapter 11, further investment into this important aspect would be undoubtedly beneficial.

CASE STUDY 12.2

An internal audit of an organization's culture gives rise to a follow-up project looking at the alignment of employees' expectations of the risk team compared to the firm's core values. Its aim is to explore how risk professionals are perceived by others. This project is completed via an enterprise-wide internal survey, supplemented by employee focus groups. The results highlight that, on a positive note, risk teams are *collaborative business partners*; however, most people express a desire for more engagement via an informal conversational approach. As a result, the Risk department restructures its routine tasks to free up more time for informal interactions, and takes an action to invest in the team's softer skillset.

Role of internal audit

Internal audit is a key partner which plays an important role in embedding sound practices and behaviours. As noted in the report entitled *Culture and the Role of Internal Audit* issued by the Chartered Institute of Internal Auditors, audit can be an essential contributor 'in giving confidence to boards that measures put in place to change culture and thus behaviour are actually working'.[11]

Good practices include:

- a clear mandate to audit the culture of the enterprise;
- integrating culture as part of every audit, as well as conducting thematic reviews;
- providing an engagement rating of how business units choose to interact with audit;
- producing a risk management engagement and effectiveness grid, showing the performance of each managing director relative to their peers;
- offering an opportunity for the business to voice unedited feedback on audits, which in itself provides a good insight into the firm's prevailing culture.

It is particularly powerful if the second and third lines, joined by HR, can all partner with each other on this complex subject, and think about what they can achieve with a joint, coordinated effort.

Common challenges and good practices

Common challenges

The following challenges may be encountered when embarking on the cultural journey.

Lack of the right tone from the top

Many regulatory and academic publications cite the right *tone from the top* and its significance to risk culture. In reality, at times the tone is either not right or not present. In these cases, the operational risk function is faced with the very difficult task of influencing behaviours by broadcasting the *tone from the side* (i.e. from the operational risk function itself). This is at the same time as the department is implementing framework tools, educating the units to manage risks and escalate events, to enable the firm to deal with threats that may prevent it from achieving its objectives. It is not only a challenge for the operational risk function but an inadequate substitute for the right tone from the top.

Reactive approach

Culture work is easily forgotten as long as the organization is doing fine; when there is an unwanted trigger event, the subject is brought back into focus and becomes important again. This approach is rather reactive; proactive mechanisms such as focus groups or metrics should be adopted to keep the work constantly ongoing.

Risk administration

Risk management executives may have an over-ambitious programme of work, for example enhancing risk framework tools or rolling out multiple RCSAs with tight deadlines. If this happens it raises the threat of turning the second line function into a purely administrative role, where the department concentrates on more mechanical aspects, getting things done, sometimes at the cost of quality and value-add. Conversations can easily slide into *risk administration*, affecting the risk brand and impacting the culture of the enterprise. Employees can also slip into a risk administration mindset, out of apathy or an unwillingness to focus on the content. It is important to periodically step back and listen to the words and the language being used; are the *risk conversations* good quality and adding value?

Cultural change programmes

Organizations invariably display excellence as well as flaws. Some struggle with accountability because they routinely apply a philosophy of consensus which slows down decision-making; others do not handle news of failures well. These vital aspects of the firm's mindset need to be understood; including the fact that the board and senior management are themselves an integral part of the culture. It is possible to drive change once the firm's existing state is analysed and it demonstrates a desire to move forward, making adjustments via small and progressive steps and recognizing that managing risk culture is for life. Aggressive change programmes that aim to move from *current* to *desired target* state are unrealistic; culture being a social process, both states keep changing during the intervention.

Good practices

Working with the board

Risk culture is the area where the board's engagement is key. It is good practice to develop a set of questions that a board should be constantly asking itself, to prompt good risk conversations. These may include, for example, how the board assesses the organization against the five *aspects of risk culture* described in this chapter; how it perceives the tone it is setting from the top; whether decisions are taken within the stated risk appetite; and what mechanisms are in place to ensure that new joiners absorb the desired values of the firm.

Conducting ongoing evaluation

Risk culture is 'not a static thing but a continuous process which repeats and renews itself'.[12] It is therefore good practice to conduct ongoing *health checks*, as described in the case study outlined above, where employee focus groups are run on a periodic basis rather than as a one-off effort. Changes are always occurring in the general environment in which firms operate and if the evaluation work is constant there is a better opportunity to pick them up. In general, focus groups are more useful than surveys, as they allow for more meaningful interactions and conversations around selected topics. Another powerful technique is participant observation, where, for example, an independent consultant is sitting in on risk committees, risk assessment exercises, internal audit reviews and other activities to observe behaviour at source and help the organization to conduct the assessment and interpret the results in an objective manner. This is one good reason why the help of external consultants is needed. If the organization performs and analyses the assessment, the interpretation itself is influenced by the prevailing risk culture and therefore may not be objective.

Beyond regulatory focus

Cultural change programmes often emerge due to a trigger event or regulatory criticism. Moving from rules to risk management to doing the 'right thing' displays the state of maturity of the firm. With the emergence of the terms *conduct* and *conduct risk*, many organizations commenced with an essentially supervision-driven approach, initially applying minimum regulatory standards; but subsequently have moved away from mere compliance to actively driving decision-making and outcomes.

Reflecting on the risk brand

It is good practice to consciously reflect on the *brand* of the Risk department, which plays an important role in the cultural debate. Some risk teams come up with a motto, such as, for example, *Collaborating to Safeguard*

Sustainability, emphasizing an *engaging* and *collaborative* approach combined with the *authority* of the risk function to act as a safeguard. This translates into partnering with the business to position it for success while being strong and decisive; clearly expressing an opinion when the level of risk is too high and the activity may be detrimental. The book included in recommended reading, *Brand You: Stand out from the crowd with authentic personal branding*, brilliantly emphasizes the importance of branding, noting that it is an asset, and 'if you develop it correctly, people will keep thinking and talking about you'.[13]

Industry benchmark

In 2024, Best Practice Operational Risk Forum members agreed that firms' efforts to establish a strong risk culture, which had historically been led by the Human Resources department, had now largely migrated to the Operational Risk department (see Figure 12.6). This is a positive development, as it enables a far more holistic approach to the subject of culture, going well beyond employee-related metrics. A challenging trend was noted, however, namely the proliferation of multiple overlapping culture-related activities. Often Compliance is driving *conduct* programmes, newly established Sustainability teams are leading *ESG* (and in particular, Social- and

Figure 12.6   Industry poll: leading risk culture efforts

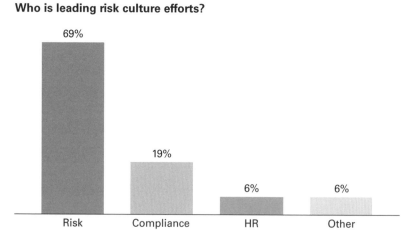

Who is leading risk culture efforts?

- Risk: 69%
- Compliance: 19%
- HR: 6%
- Other: 6%

Best Practice Operational Risk Forum, 2024

Governance-related initiatives), while Human Resources is spearheading the development of strong *corporate values*. All of these initiatives inevitably cross over. The need for coordination was yet again discussed, with operational risk professionals either planning to intervene or already stepping in to connect the dots and align various risk culture activities.

Members acknowledged that the topic of risk culture was relatively high on the board agenda. Culture assessments were becoming more common, and boards were expected to periodically receive and review such evaluations and the actions that emanated from them. Approaches varied, with some firms using annual staff questionnaires with a range of 40–60 questions; while others took the approach of leading focus groups or measuring risk culture via agreed metrics and KRIs (see Figure 12.7).

In terms of the state of the risk culture itself, participants' response was mixed. It was noted that the Covid-19 pandemic placed strain on firms' efforts to maintain their risk culture. Enforced and prolonged working from home eroded corporate cohesiveness – the attitude of 'we-ness' that unites employees and helps them to remain motivated to accomplish set goals. According to a poll conducted in December 2020 at the Best Practice Operational Risk Forum, 86 per cent of risk professionals believed that risk culture had somewhat deteriorated in their organizations. Four years on, some forum members noted marginal improvement; while others were less convinced and believed that more could still be done.

Practitioners discussed what activities could give a boost to risk culture practices in their firms. Themes such as *tone from the top* and *risk training* –

Figure 12.7   Industry poll: risk culture

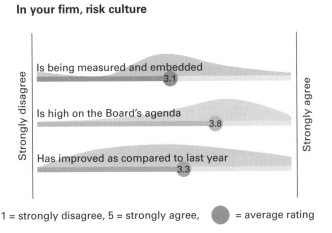

In your firm, risk culture

Is being measured and embedded — 3.1

Is high on the Board's agenda — 3.8

Has improved as compared to last year — 3.3

Strongly disagree / Strongly agree

1 = strongly disagree, 5 = strongly agree, ● = average rating

Best Practice Operational Risk Forum, 2024

Figure 12.8   Industry poll: improving risk culture

What will improve risk culture the most?

Best Practice Operational Risk Forum, 2024

which consistently feature in industry polls – were perceived as the most impactful to improving risk culture, as illustrated in Figure 12.8.

In conclusion, risk culture is not a distinct project with a clear completion date. Rather it is an ongoing social process that requires continued efforts to actively influence, maintain and enhance an institution's norms, attitudes and behaviours.

Practical workplace exercise

Reflect on the topic discussed in this chapter, considering its application in your organization:

1 How has the firm defined *culture* and what efforts and programmes are in place?

2 What is the role and involvement of operational risk teams in existing programmes?

3 Considering the five aspects of risk culture described in the chapter, where would your organization score highest?

4 What works well? Make a note of the strong elements of the firm's culture.

5 What can be improved? Note down potential improvements.

MAKE A DIFFERENCE (MAD) ACTION

Please note down one action that you will take after reading this chapter that will make a positive difference to risk culture, ethos and behaviours of your organization.

In summary, this chapter discussed the role of risk culture, the least visible but most vital aspect of risk management, and proposed practical steps operational risk practitioners can take to influence ethos and behaviours.

Having examined all the tools of the operational risk framework, the next chapter will focus on evaluating the maturity of operational risk management process in the organization.

Notes

1 Basel Committee on Banking Supervision (2021) *Revisions to the Principles for the Sound Management of Operational Risk*, www.bis.org/bcbs/publ/d515. pdf (archived at https://perma.cc/E45Y-GK3N)

2 Financial Stability Board (2014) *Guidance on Supervisory Interaction with Financial Institutions on Risk Culture*, www.fsb.org/wp-content/uploads/140407.pdf (archived at https://perma.cc/QJ3C-ZLA7)

3 Royal Commission into Misconduct in the Banking, Superannuation and Financial Services Industry, www.royalcommission.gov.au/banking/final-report (archived at https://perma.cc/4GRY-QKWP)

4 Financial Conduct Authority (2018) Discussion paper, *Transforming Culture in Financial Services*, www.fca.org.uk/publication/discussion/dp18-02.pdf (archived at https://perma.cc/U5PT-PR4Z)

5 Financial Stability Board (2014) *Guidance on Supervisory Interaction with Financial Institutions on Risk Culture*, www.fsb.org/wp-content/uploads/140407.pdf (archived at https://perma.cc/QJ3C-ZLA7)

6 Financial Conduct Authority (2018) Discussion paper, *Transforming Culture in Financial Services*, www.fca.org.uk/publication/discussion/dp18-02.pdf (archived at https://perma.cc/TS7L-WK3C)

7 Chartered Institute of Internal Auditors (2020) *Conduct Risk*, www.iia.org.uk/resources/sector-specific-standards-and-guidance/financial-services/conduct-risk/ (archived at https://perma.cc/N2BR-YVCM)

8 The Banker's Oath, www.tuchtrechtbanken.nl/en/code-of-conduct/ (archived at https://perma.cc/53NR-5RGR)

9 Dechario, T, Five Messages from the 2023 Governance and Culture Reform Conference (2023), tellerwindow.newyorkfed.org/2023/07/18/five-messages-from-the-2023-governance-and-culture-reform-conference/ (archived at https://perma.cc/Y729-TT6J)

10 Power, M, Ashby, S and Palermo, T (2013) *Risk Culture in Financial Organizations: A research report*, London School of Economics, www.lse.ac.uk/accounting/assets/CARR/documents/Risk-Culture-in-Financial-Organisations/Final-Risk-Culture-Report.pdf (archived at https://perma.cc/A8DM-5P9J)

11 Chartered Institute of Internal Auditors (2014) *Culture and the Role of Internal Audit*, www.iia.org.uk/media/598939/0805-iia-culture-report-1-7-14-final.pdf (archived at https://perma.cc/SZ4C-PE7S)

12 Power, M, Ashby, S and Palermo, T (2013) *Risk Culture in Financial Organizations: A research report*, London School of Economics, www.lse.ac.uk/accounting/assets/CARR/documents/Risk-Culture-in-Financial-Organisations/Final-Risk-Culture-Report.pdf (archived at https://perma.cc/ZX4A-FFEH)

13 Royston-Lee, D and Storey, S (2023) *Brand You: Stand out from the crowd with authentic personal branding*, Pearson

Embedding and maturity assessment

13

What this chapter covers: This chapter discusses the Operational Risk Implementation Journey, from its early stages to being fully implemented; describing a 'maturity ladder' for measuring progress and outlining the key characteristics of each phase (Figure 13.1). The chapter considers what *embeddedness* looks like and how it can be measured. It then goes on to introduce three pillars of embedded risk management and proposes a balanced scorecard with examples of metrics and indicators. The chapter includes results of live polls and an industry benchmark.

FURTHER READING

- Institute of Operational Risk (2020) *Embedding an Operational Risk Management Framework: Operational risk sound practice guidance*

  Why recommended: A succinct guide that examines the critical success factors involved in achieving an embedded operational risk management framework.

- Christian Hunt (2023) *Humanizing Rules: Bringing behavioural science to ethics and compliance*, Wiley

  Why recommended: This fascinating book takes the reader on a journey to embeddedness by arguing that rules should be made for HUMANS (that is, they need to be Helpful, Understandable, Manageable, Acceptable, Normal and Salient). If policy makers – usually second line Risk and Compliance functions – succeed in engaging with employees via a set of well-designed and articulated guidelines that work with – rather than against – the grain of natural human decision-making, that's when the rules will be bought into and followed.

Figure 13.1 Focus of Chapter 13: embedding and maturity assessment

Risk culture

Embedding and maturity assessment

Governance, roles and responsibilities

Establish governance and clear roles across the Three Lines for managing operational risk.

Risk appetite and risk capacity

Define nature and types of risk accepted in pursuit of strategic objectives. Evaluate adequacy of capital resources.

Operational risk events	Risk assessments	Scenario analysis	Key Risk Indicators
Record and report risk events, act to minimize future exposure. Monitor trends against RCSAs and KRIs.	Assess risk exposure in process, business or function via RCSAs. Supplement by evaluating risks emanating from change activities via ORAs.	Identify exposure from extreme but plausible events. Mitigate through risk transfer to insurance.	Monitor risk and control performance through predictive indicators. Act if indicators breach established appetite threshold.

Reporting and decision-making

Review actual risk profile against set appetite, apply active risk management to enable achievement of strategic objectives.

Training and education

Operational risk taxonomy

The journey to maturity: three-step maturity ladder

The journey of implementing robust operational risk management practices in an organization is as challenging as it is exciting.

At the start of the journey, the firm may be operating as a novice, experimenting in a largely ad hoc and reactive manner. In this phase business units and support functions may show a tendency to push back on the new operational risk requirements, exhibiting a natural reaction of resistance to change. They may refer to the elements of the framework as *your* processes, *your* assessments, *your* tools, implying that their role is to assist the Operational Risk department to accomplish whatever *it* requires, and consequently deprioritizing the tasks in comparison to their own activities. In turn, the operational risk function finds itself vigorously reaching out with explanations, presentations and constant follow-ups to keep the risk management ship afloat.

This initial stage is gradually replaced by an intermediate phase, which involves implementing a more structured approach and building it into the firm's routine business processes. In this phase operational risk practices are *normalized*. RCSAs, for example, become the *norm*, something that simply must be done, for multiple reasons including regulatory. This phase sees improved ownership by business units and support functions, for whom the use of the different risk framework elements – even if reluctantly at times – becomes a matter of habit.

The ultimate *embedded* stage is characterized by proactive risk management, a clear value proposition, and an enhanced risk culture in the organization. As highlighted frequently in previous chapters, the real measure of success in operational risk is when functions actively *want* to use the framework because it helps them in their decision-making. While in the first phase they may have been hesitant or sceptical, business departments now complete risks and opportunities assessments for new products – because it is useful to *them* to draw out threats and benefits. In this culture, boards and governance committees rely on reports of the firm's profile against risk appetite *to take decisions*. The framework is fit for purpose. Tools are in sync. Outputs are compared and tell a coherent story. Information is actively used to achieve measurable process improvements and reduce surprises.

Figure 13.2 Operational risk maturity ladder

EARLY STAGES
- Basic framework
- Unbalanced roles: operational risk function is doing most of the work
- Limited value-add

MANAGED
- Developed framework and tools
- Balanced roles and responsibilities
- Demonstrable value-add
- Operational risk management becomes the *norm* within the organization

EMBEDDED
- Framework and tools are fit for purpose
- Operational risk function is a trusted advisor
- Continuous, measurable value-add
- Business units *want* to apply the tools as they aid in decision-making
- Notable impact of improvements on the balance sheet

This progress can be reflected in a simple maturity ladder, as described in Figure 13.2. This version differentiates between three phases of maturity, but organizations can enhance and further develop the ladder as they see fit.

Three pillars of success: financial performance, use test, risk culture

Once a firm has embarked on its risk management implementation journey, it will want to measure its advancement across progressive levels of maturity. Measurement helps to establish a baseline, and to set targets and improvement strategies to achieve the desired stage. Maturity model can be a powerful 'diagnostic tool' and a solution for 'improving risk management system capabilities'.[1]

While firms may have widely varying views on what good risk management looks like, an approach centred around three pillars – the *financial performance*, *use test* and *risk culture* – is proposed in Figure 13.3. These three pillars work in tandem to present a coherent overall picture of *embeddedness*, defined by the Basel Framework as the level to which operational risk management practices 'have been embedded at all organizational levels'.[2] In the context of operational risk, maturity cannot be achieved without holistic engagement and use of the relevant tools by the entire enterprise. Organizations may wish to add other pillars – and even parameters within each pillar – that they feel are relevant to their firm.

Let's examine each pillar in more detail.

Financial performance

Operational risk should always be considered in the context of its impact on the firm's balance sheet and profit & loss (P&L) position. If, as discussed in

Figure 13.3 Three pillars of embedded operational risk management

Chapter 1, risk practitioners aim to sit at the strategy table and contribute to strategic decisions, P&L is often the mutual language used for these conversations. Operational risk becomes much more difficult to dismiss when it is presented in terms of hard numbers and not as 'just a risk'.

Consequently – alas, there is no avoiding it – actual operational risk losses are an indicator of embedded risk management (or the lack of it). Simply put, if there is a steady upward trend in losses year-on-year, whether in growth or during periods of business stagnation and decline, the firm should be questioning its risk management capabilities.

By the same token, the upside of risk (or positive P&L benefit emanating from good operational risk management) also has to be quantified.

The following metrics can be useful to characterize both dimensions, losses and savings:

KRI1: Operational risk losses as a percentage of revenue, operating income or operating expense.

KRI2: Actual operational risk losses compared to appetite.

KRI3: Trend, number, value of losses in new products or investments relative to product/investment performance.

KRI4: Value of financial penalties (capital add-on, fines imposed for mismanagement of risk).

KRI5: Value of any savings, including reduction in cost due to process optimization, that emanate from operational risk initiatives (measure of the upside).

These measures need to be interpreted with caution; while an increase in losses is worrying, a sharp drop also needs to be investigated, as highlighted in Chapter 4. It may be providing a false comfort and could instead be indicative of other factors – for example a change in leadership that has caused employees to simply stop reporting bad news.

Operational risk financial performance measures are not treated in a balanced way in the industry. At times, firms try to measure the embeddedness and success of their operational risk management using only numbers (such as actual losses and capital position), thus underestimating the less tangible benefits of the framework, as discussed later in the chapter. At the other extreme, financial performance is sometimes excluded altogether, resulting in operational risk not being taken seriously and not treated on a par with other risk disciplines. For this reason, financial performance metrics should constitute an important *pillar* of the risk management framework, but must also be supplemented by other tools, namely the *use test* and *risk culture*.

Use test

The importance of impact on the bottom line cannot be underestimated, but financial measures on their own cannot paint a complete picture. This is particularly true for smaller-sized firms that may have neither a large dataset of past losses nor multiple opportunities for savings. In this case the trend analysis can be less meaningful than for larger firms. The so-called *use test* – frequently referred to by the Basel Committee and regulators in various jurisdictions – goes to the heart of actively using risk tools to enhance live decision-making. The *use test* is a broad concept that encompasses many different aspects, from the risk framework and tools to responsibilities and value-add; collectively, all components covered in this book. It includes, for example:

- sophistication and fitness of the risk framework and toolset;
- clarity, usefulness and actionability of operational risk reporting;
- maturity and effectiveness of the operational risk appetite;
- responsibilities, brand and reputation of risk teams;
- roles and attitudes of functions outside the Risk department, including first line champions, subject matter experts (SMEs), and risk and control owners, as well as the board, senior management and other employees in the organization;
- the value proposition that emanates from risk management – it is impossible to truly embed risk management just by wielding a regulatory stick.

Some of the possible use test measures have been introduced in previous chapters. They may include:

KRI6: Number of material gaps emanating from gap analysis against Basel Committee Principles and other relevant requirements, as discussed in Chapter 2 (reflects the sophistication of risk framework and toolset).

KRI9: Gaps in accountability: percentage of 'orphan' RCSAs, or risks/KRIs with no owner assigned (measures whether business units have embraced their roles and responsibilities for the management of operational risk).

KRI10: Number of departments/areas without an established first line operational risk champion (similarly, presents a view on the accountability – or the lack of it).

KRI7: Number and/or monetary value of investments in control improvements resulting from the use of operational risk tools (for example, emanating from RCSAs, OREs, SAs or KRIs; which demonstrate that significant risks are taken seriously, and that budget is allocated to enhancements where needed; indicative of the risk value proposition).

KRI8: Number or percentage of internal and external audit findings which were already known and self-identified via the use of operational risk tools (for example, RCSAs, SAs, KRIs, etc; again indicative of value proposition).

Risk culture

The topic of risk culture was discussed at length in the previous chapter. Undeniably, the effectiveness of operational risk management is closely linked to and largely dependent on the firm's culture, which can either support or hinder it. Additional measures of success in this area, which supplement *financial performance* and *use test* metrics, are as follows:

KRI11: Trend in employees' views on risk culture of the organization and/ or their perception of the Risk department (obtained via employee engagement surveys, focus groups or other means).

KRI12: Number and trend of issues raised through established risk channels (e.g. risk mailbox).

KRI13: Number or percentage of material risks, ineffective controls or significant gaps with no actions or where actions are overdue (reflective of the overall strength of response or the absence of it).

KRI4: Number or percentage of risk acceptances vs actions related to risk reduction (a healthy score indicates a mature and balanced approach to risk management, including considerations of the cost-effectiveness of mitigation).

KRI15: Number of times the Operational Risk department is asked to participate in initiatives in an advisory capacity (this suggests a department that is well thought of, and seen as a reputable advisor).

The outcome-based measures proposed above can be displayed in a balanced scorecard, as described in Figure 13.4. Collectively, they evaluate the embeddedness of risk management by reflecting on *financial*, *use test* and *risk culture* aspects. These measures partially overlap and fall into more than one category, as shown here in Figure 13.4.

Figure 13.4 Operational risk balanced scorecard

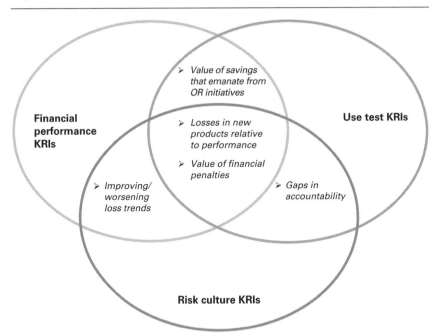

Business units' self-assessment of embeddedness

As an alternative to metrics and measures, a powerful mechanism for evaluating embeddedness is via business units' own self-assessment of how well they believe they are doing. This can be accomplished using a guided approach, where the second line operational risk function creates a questionnaire for the business with a choice of possible answers. The units then select the state they believe they are in, corroborating their responses with facts and evidence. The second line operational risk team reviews and constructively challenges the outputs.

An example extract from such a questionnaire for one component, RCSA, is presented in Table 13.1.

Self-assessment helps first line business units and support functions to understand what 'good' looks like, as well as to reflect on their own performance.

Table 13.1   Example questionnaire: self-assessment of embeddedness

RCSA aspects	Development phase: early stages	Development phase: managed	Development phase: embedded
Scope	Unclear justification of scope and/or boundaries of RCSA. No proactive risk identification.	Clearly defined boundaries of what is within and outside RCSA scope.	Scope is clearly defined, interdependencies with other RCSAs are understood.
Risk assessment	Risk profile is not in sync with actual OREs and KRIs. Risk owner(s) not explicitly defined. Control owner(s) not explicitly defined.	Risk identification and assessment is facilitated by first line operational risk champion, in coordination with risk owners.	Named risk owners proactively and regularly consider changes in risk environment, including emerging risks. There are minimal surprises from Internal Audit – risks are already known.
Control assessment	Control rating is not corroborated by evidence.	Control identification and assessment is facilitated by first line operational risk champion, in coordination with control owners.	Named control owners rate control design and effectiveness, with periodic testing of most important controls to support the assessment.
Actionability	No actions emanate from the exercise.	Tactical actions are in place, with clear owners and target dates.	RCSAs are considered in tactical and strategic decisions. Consideration is given to risk reduction and risk acceptance, demonstrating a balanced approach.

(*continued*)

Table 13.1 (Continued)

RCSA aspects	Development phase: early stages	Development phase: managed	Development phase: embedded
RCSA refresh	RCSA is updated annually, and not used in between updates.	RCSAs are referred to and reviewed during periodic risk and control meetings.	Trigger-based refresh is in place, with triggers including material ORE, change initiatives and/or KRIs.
Completion and sign-off	RCSA is filled in by the risk champion without the involvement of subject matter experts (SMEs) or unit head. There is no evidence of sign-off.	RCSA is completed by the risk champion with active participation of SMEs. RCSA is signed off by the risk champion of the business unit.	RCSA is facilitated by the risk champion in collaboration with SMEs and unit head. There is evidence that the head of the unit signed off, confirming that RCSA is a true and fair reflection of the unit's risk and control profile.

Importance of retaining evidence

We now digress slightly from the subject of embedded risk management to the ancillary topic of retaining evidence. 'Absence of evidence is *not* evidence of absence' is a quote attributed to Professor Martin Rees, the English astronomer and astrophysicist. Alas, auditors and financial services regulators would disagree; even if a firm is mature and constructive in its approach, if it is not able to produce *convincing evidence* of its operational risk management activities, this simply equates to the firm not managing operational risk at all.

In 2019, I led a study on this topic with the Best Practice Operational Risk Forum. In a live poll, practitioners opined on the strength of evidencing of operational risk management within their firms, the results of which are presented in Table 13.2.

Good evidencing involves both a disciplined approach to record retention (including the required duration and storage media) and, most importantly, agreed policies and standards on the actual content of the records themselves.

Table 13.2 Industry study: evidence of operational risk management

Strength of evidence	% respondents
Insufficient	0
Partial	19
Adequate	81
Robust	0

What is retained as proof

Effective operational risk management can be demonstrated via the following mechanisms:

- Business-as-usual operational risk tools, such as RCSAs, OREs and KRIs. The evidence may be stored in either an official system or other sources such as Excel spreadsheets, with a record of the results alongside actions and decisions taken.

- New product sign-off packs, which commonly include operational risk assessment.

- Risk consideration in change initiatives, either in the form of completed assessment(s) or the minutes of relevant committee meetings.

- Strategy documents and business plans. This area of record keeping was perceived by the forum as needing improvement from an operational risk perspective, which does not appear to be always explicitly considered in these documents.

- Risk assessments of technology changes.

Demonstrating challenge

When it comes to the role of the second line operational risk team, it is often difficult to effectively evidence all the good work the department does; in particular the *oversight and challenge* part, which will often take the form of discussion at a meeting or workshop, a phone or video call, email correspondence or all of the above.

Second line challenge can be evidenced via:

- Detailed minutes of operational risk committees or other relevant governance meetings, documenting what was discussed and agreed. It is also good practice to note options or risks that were considered and discounted (and on what basis).

- A separate second line opinion appended to first line business unit reports, thus providing a record of views from both sides.

- A presentation of common themes based on an overall analysis of OREs, RCSAs and other tools; identifying areas of weakness followed by the results of second line thematic reviews or deep dives. This documentation approach not only demonstrates a robust thought process but also generates real value-add to the firm.

Consequently, when it comes to evidence, it is better to follow Charles Dickens than astronomers such as Professor Rees, perhaps using the quote, 'Take nothing on its looks; take everything on evidence. There's no better rule.'

Common challenges and good practices

Common challenges

The following challenges may face organizations during their journey to embedding operational risk management practices.

Lack of cultural fit

At times, leaders join a firm from a different organization and immediately launch into building the blocks which proved successful in their previous place, without spending sufficient time analysing what might work in their new environment. This can lead to failure, as the maturity journey is unique to each individual firm, including its pace and sequencing, and ways of working effectively together.

Link to strategy not considered

As discussed in Chapter 1, at times operational risk domain tends to go its own way, proceeding with framework implementation in a manner and pace that are not in sync with the firm's strategy and business goals. Keeping the vital link to what matters the most – the firm's business goals – and being cognizant of the bigger picture is crucial. The guidance on embedding operational risk framework issued by the Institute of Operational Risk also emphasizes the role of risk function is in supporting 'strategic planning and objective setting'.[3]

Lack of evidence

Undoubtedly, the importance of retaining evidence has been increasing over the years. Firms with poor record retention practices are truly challenged during internal audit and external supervisory inspections. Evidence is also vital to the firm itself, in case it needs to look back and revisit prior decisions; for example, a particular new product that was approved, together with risks that have been accepted. Operational risk teams must be conscious of keeping the appropriate proof, and educating first line business units and support functions on good practices.

Good practices

Measuring embeddedness and completing maturity assessment

Over the years, I have discussed the topic of maturity assessment with multiple regulators. They considered that the firms which did not complete such an assessment struggled to articulate to their supervisors a coherent picture of their current state, together with planned areas for development. By contrast, organizations that applied healthy practices of self-reflection and evaluation came across as cognizant of their strengths and weaknesses, transparent and prepared. These practices bring benefits to the firm itself, as well as external parties such as regulators. A globally accepted standard for risk management – ISO 31000:2009 – from the International Organization for Standardization also advises firms to develop strategies to advance their risk management maturity.[4]

Progressing elements in tandem

There is no clear demarcation between the stages of operational risk maturity. The firm may be slightly more advanced in most aspects but stuck on one or two features, thus impeding its overall progress. For example, it may be progressing on target with a framework implementation project, but is not moving forward with embedding correct roles and responsibilities. In reality this often happens when a firm has to expedite the pace of deployment following regulatory criticism, perhaps having received a remediation requirement. In this case, additional efforts need to be refocused on agreeing the responsibilities with senior management and developing a system of rewards (and sometimes punishment) to progress advancement in the accountability element, alongside any enhancements being considered to the framework itself. To achieve embeddedness, different components need to progress in tandem, at a sensible pace.

Applying behavioural science

In his book *Humanizing Rules*, Christian Hunt argues that in a complex, nuanced environments (such as financial services) black-and-white rules are less effective; rather, a more human-focused approach is needed.[5] This requires reflecting on how the rules are designed, including, for example, considering whether they are *salient*, and whether employees will find what they are being asked to do *appealing*. This is a good way of thinking about the ultimate state of embeddedness, which cannot be achieved via mechanically imposed policies and frameworks. Organizations where risk teams thrive on engagement, use gamification, praise and incentives, as well as invest in clever *marketing* of operational risk tools to grab employees' attention, generally make greater progress on the embeddedness journey.

Understanding aspirations

Some firms have no aspiration to be best-in-class in their operational risk framework and tools; they do not need a Rolls-Royce and will be satisfied with a simpler model. So it is important to define the appropriate *point of arrival* for the overall journey. Requirements need to be proportionate to the size and nature of the organization. This may mean that, for some firms, not all elements of the framework will need to be fully developed. A useful tool to accomplish this proportionate outcome is presented in Figure 13.5.

In this figure, 10 desired outcomes have been articulated by the organization. The current position of each statement is outlined with crosses, while the desired state is marked with triangles. (Note: the *embedded* state remains an aspiration for many of the statements, but not all; in some cases, a lower *managed* position would be deemed acceptable.)

Industry benchmark

The Best Practice Operational Risk Forum discussed common practices related to an evaluation of the embeddedness of operational risk management.

Figure 13.5 Defining point of arrival

10. Risk teams are well regarded in the industry

9. Extensive use of scenario analysis for risk management

8. Collaboration between risk, compliance and audit

7. Integrated, actionable risk reporting

6. Training and education firm-wide

5. Fully up-to-date operational risk taxonomy

4. Embedded RCSAs (quality, actions, decisions)

3. Root cause analysis for material operational risk events

2. Full ownership of risk management in first line units

1. First line champions embedded and effective

Desired outcomes

Embedded

Managed

Early stages

Not started

X = current position on the 3-Step Maturity Ladder   ◀ = desired state on the 3-Step Maturity Ladder

Figure 13.6　Industry poll: operational risk maturity assessment

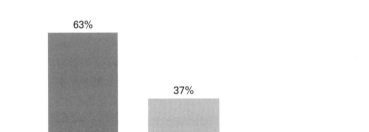

Best Practice Operational Risk Forum, 2023

As described in Figure 13.6, in 2023 63 per cent of respondents conducted a methodical evaluation of this topic in a structured way; while 37 per cent were still developing their practices. This is an improvement from previous years, driven in part by boards, internal and external auditors, and indeed regulators, who now frequently request these kinds of assessments from firms as a matter of routine.

In some firms, an assessment of the maturity of the operational risk process is also incorporated as part of the annual control attestation, a detailed process where business units and support functions review and attest on their key controls. Alternatively, operational risk maturity can be evaluated separately. Most participants (69 per cent) believed that a joint effort between first line units and the second line Operational Risk department worked best to achieve useful results from the assessment.

It terms of relevant metrics for measuring embeddedness, many firms used all three types of indicators, namely use test, risk culture and financial measures, but clearly gravitated more towards *use test* indicators (as shown in Figure 13.7).

Other firms partnered with Internal Audit, Compliance and HR to obtain supplementary measures. These included an Internal Audit evaluation of risk culture, trends (positive or negative) in people-related concerns as captured by HR, or an increase in poorly (or well) rated Compliance-led assessments.

Figure 13.7   Operational risk embeddedness: measures of success

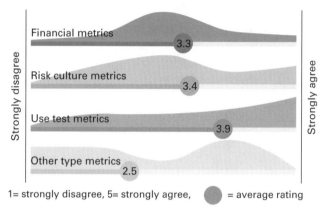

1= strongly disagree, 5= strongly agree,   = average rating

Best Practice Operational Risk Forum, 2023

It is arguably easier to identify progress in operational risk embeddedness if you are implementing a framework from scratch – i.e. right from the start of the journey – than looking back on it from a more mature perspective. Once processes are established, keeping up momentum and ensuring continued advancement in those processes and metrics – rather than deterioration – requires energy, enthusiasm and clever strategizing. This is yet another of the difficult yet exciting challenges that operational risk professionals face.

Practical workplace exercise

Consider how your organization evaluates its advancement along the stages of operational risk maturity:

1 Is there a maturity model or other mechanism in place to facilitate assessment of how well embedded your operational risk practices really are?

2 Is embeddedness defined, alongside its measures of success?

3 Is there any awareness of where the organization is on its journey and what its plans or next steps are?

4 What works well? Make a note of the strong features of the current maturity evaluation process, if they exist.

5 What can be improved? Note down how the evaluation of the operational risk implementation journey could potentially be enhanced.

MAKE A DIFFERENCE (MAD) ACTION

Please note down one action that you will take after reading this chapter that will meaningfully enhance an evaluation of the maturity of your firm's operational risk journey.

In summary, this chapter discussed the importance of evaluating the progress of implementation of operational risk management, and proposed a number of ways of measuring success.

Moving on, the next chapter will discuss the increasingly important topic of ESG, outlining practical ways of incorporating E, S and G risks into the operational risk framework.

Notes

1 Antonucci, D (2016) *Risk Maturity Models: How to assess risk management effectiveness*, Kogan Page, London

2 Basel Committee for Banking Supervision (2011) *Operational Risk: Supervisory guidelines for the advanced measurement approaches*, www.bis.org/publ/bcbs196.pdf (archived at https://perma.cc/T5QN-5SC9)

3 Institute of Operational Risk (2020) *Embedding an Operational Risk Management Framework: Operational risk sound practice guidance*, www. ior-institute.org/sound-practice-guidance (archived at https://perma.cc/8L6M-DQ2R)

4 International Organization for Standardization, ISO 31000:2009, www.iso.org / obp/ui/#iso:std:iso:31000:ed-1:v1:en (archived at https://perma.cc/35EB-GTAD)

5 Christian Hunt (2023) *Humanizing Rules: Bringing behavioural science to ethics and compliance*, Wiley

Incorporating ESG into operational risk framework

14

What this chapter covers: Environmental, Social and Governance (ESG) matters are becoming increasingly important, not only at a strategic level but also in the construct of operational risk management activities (Figure 14.1). The chapter provides an overview of ESG and suggests that the acronym needs to be deconstructed into its separate elements: E, S and G. It highlights risk management requirements and outlines the ways of incorporating E, S and G into the operational risk taxonomy, presenting practical examples of how core framework tools can be applied to manage the risks. The chapter also contains a call for action for operational risk teams to actively collaborate across silos to avoid rework and duplication. It includes examples, results of live polls and industry studies.

FURTHER READING

- Basel committee on Banking Supervision (2022) *Principles for the Effective Management and Supervision of Climate-Related Financial Risks*.

  Why recommended: Key document stipulating risk management requirements, on which national supervisors are basing their own requirements. Essential for risk management practitioners.

- European Banking Authority (2021) *Report on Management and Supervision of ESG Risks for Credit Institutions and Investment Firms*.

> **Why recommended:** In contrast to the Basel Committee's paper which focuses only on the climate-related subcomponent of the *E*, the EBA report embraces all three letters of the ESG acronym and hence represents an important comparative study text. For practitioners, it has a handy glossary and a useful set of Key Risk Indicators to consider.

Decomposing ESG into its elements: E, S and G

Without doubt, ESG considerations are becoming increasingly important for organizations and their teams, with businesses judged on their ESG performance, and risk professionals tasked with integrating ESG risks into enterprise risk management frameworks. According to McKinsey, the three-letter acronym has risen to prominence with a 'fivefold growth in internet searches for ESG since 2019'.[1] Consequently it has settled in with the myriad of other three-letter acronyms favoured by the corporate world – such as AML, GRC and BCP, among many – and has been fully embraced and adopted into the standard corporate vocabulary. The catch-all acronym 'ESG', however, combines distinct and separate matters under one umbrella. It tends to be overused and misused, creating the misnomer of *ESG risk*.

It is therefore imperative to start by taking a closer look at the three elements of the acronym. A point to note is that – similarly to risk culture, as discussed in Chapter 12 – ESG is a complex and multifaceted topic, which has received substantial coverage from government and industry bodies, policy makers and consultancy firms. It is also a highly politicized term, embraced and viewed as mission-critical by some commentators but criticized by others as 'shorthand for hype and controversy'.[2] Accordingly, some jurisdictions have been amenable to advancing ESG initiatives, while others have been less prepared to move in that direction. Without expressing opinions or entering into debates, the chapter aims to simplify ESG for the purposes of viewing it through an operational risk lens only, and considers practical ways of embedding it into the operational risk framework. This practical approach is important, as it would be fair to note that more progress has been achieved in embedding ESG into financial risk frameworks,

Figure 14.1   Focus of Chapter 14: interaction of E, S and G with operational risk framework

Embedding and maturity assessment

Risk culture

Governance, roles and responsibilities
Establish governance and clear roles across the Three Lines for managing operational risk.

Risk appetite and risk capacity
Define nature and types of risk accepted in pursuit of strategic objectives. Evaluate adequacy of capital resources.

Operational risk events	Risk assessments	Scenario analysis	Key Risk Indicators
Record and report risk events, act to minimize future exposure. Monitor trends against RCSAs and KRIs.	Assess risk exposure in process, business or function via RCSAs. Supplement by evaluating risks emanating from change activities via ORAs.	Identify exposure from extreme but plausible events. Mitigate through risk transfer to insurance.	Monitor risk and control performance through predictive indicators. Act if indicators breach established appetite thresholds.

Reporting and decision-making
Review actual risk profile against set appetite, apply active risk management to enable achievement of strategic objectives.

Training and education

Operational risk taxonomy

such as credit and market risk. By contrast, an understanding of how to integrate ESG into operational risk is still in development.

E, S and G as part of sustainability

ESG elements are often combined within the concept of sustainability. The UN's Sustainable Development Goals comprise a wide range of activities, from tackling poverty and providing access to health and nutrition, to achieving more peaceful and inclusive societies and managing the consequences of climate change.

SUSTAINABILITY DEFINITION

The European Union defines sustainability as a focus on 'development that meets the needs of the present without compromising the ability of future generations to meet their own needs'.[3]

In essence, sustainability is about responsible living, promoting prosperity while protecting the planet for future generations.

So the *E*, the environmental aspect of sustainability goals, considers effects on the environment, with climate-related risk being arguably the most researched subcategory, and often closely linked to other different environmental aspects. (Due to the prominence of climate risk, the *E* is sometimes shorthanded to *C&E*, namely 'climate-related and environmental'.) The *E* comprises multiple objectives, including the need for action to reduce greenhouse gas emissions and limit the effects of climate change. There is common agreement on the need for urgency in tackling alarming climate conditions, which for financial services firms can result (and have already resulted) in supply chain disruptions, system failures, and damage to premises and equipment. So out of the three letters of the ESG acronym, the *E* – and in particular its climate-related aspect – is a clear priority, with companies, regulators and politicians all focusing with determination on the subject.

In turn, the *S* – the 'Social' aspect of sustainability – refers to the impact that firms can have on society and the quality of life. It urges organizations to address topics such as diversity and inclusion, employee health and well-being, and workplace safety. Risks can arise from inadequate labour standards and poor safety protocols, from mental health issues for employees caused by discrimination and from dealing with suppliers that apply unacceptable practices such as child labour.

Last but not least, governance – the G aspect – refers to 'the governance factors of decision making',[4] which encompass business ethics, compliance practices of anti-bribery and anti-corruption, firms' policies and procedures, and the wider responsibilities of the board and other stakeholders. Poor application of the G can result in conflicts of interest, fraud and money laundering, among a range of adverse outcomes, and can lead to high profile corporate scandals.

Use E, S and G as separate elements

Considering the three letters of the acronym, while each of the topics is undeniably significant, it is apparent that they are rather different in nature. Hurricanes and heatwaves driven by climate change have no direct correlation with corporate diversity and inclusion scores, or bribery and corruption practices. In fact, McKinsey has noted that 'ESG represents an odd and unstable combination of elements'.[5] Similarly, the Bank for International Settlements (BIS) paper on 'Deconstructing ESG Scores: How to invest with your own criteria'[6] argues that there is no such thing as *ESG investment*, as it is nearly impossible to create a portfolio aligned with *all three* ESG values. Investors should separate and align their portfolios with E, S *or* G factors individually. Consequently the debate continues as to whether the combination of E, S and G in a single term is meaningful or, whether, as Jonathan Guthrie noted in the *Financial Times*, 'ESG is a category error that needs unbundling'.[7]

Unfortunately, in the meantime, the inconsiderate bundling has ballooned, creating a world of *'esg-ness'*. As an example in the operational risk space, the publication of the top five non-financial risks for 2023 highlighted:

1 Cyber risk;

2 ESG (inclusive of climate risk);

3 Geopolitical risk;

4 Third-party risk;

5 Resilience and business continuity.[8]

From a practical perspective, the second top risk, which includes 'the risks associated with a diverse range of issues such as climate change, greenhouse gas emissions, deforestation, biodiversity, customer and employee relations, labor, human rights, supply chains, board management practices, diversity, equity and inclusion, compliance, and more',[9] is not something that is easily manageable.

Therefore, it is recommended to approach the acronym with due care, using E, S and G separated into its three elements:

E, S and G   NOT   ESG

I have been running courses on this topic for several years and have often felt the need to pause and discuss the importance of decomposing the acronym. Often participants enter the course with a preconception about 'ESG risk' which they feel they need to identify, assess, manage and report on.

> There is a multitude of E, S and G-related risks stemming from E, S and G-related factors; rather than a single, all-inclusive *ESG risk.*

E, S and G: understanding risk management

Sustainability is often a key part of many firms' strategies, as the financial services sector in particular is expected to play a vital role in transitioning to a greener economy. While the *strategic* agenda is being set and debated, firms also recognize that there are *risks* emanating from E, S and G factors, which can materialize through the traditional risk categories such as credit, market and operational risk, potentially impacting the firm's P&L. Consequently, risk management frameworks should actively embrace the topic, while risk management professionals need to establish adequate identification, assessment, management and reporting practices.

Scope of risk management activities

The essence of regulatory requirements related to risk management can be demonstrated using the Basel Committee principles for the effective management and supervision of climate-related financial risks,[10] which outline common sense practices such as:

- Identifying, assessing, managing and reporting on material climate-related financial risks;
- Conducting scenario analysis to assess the resilience of business models;

- Incorporating relevant considerations within risk appetite;
- Embedding through policies, procedures and internal controls;
- Enhancing accountability, via assigned climate-related responsibilities and robust governance; and
- Ensuring risk data aggregation capabilities account for climate-related risks.

Note that the Basel Committee principles in fact only address the *E* letter of the acronym, and, in particular, its climate-related subcomponent. In contrast, the 'Report on Management and Supervision of ESG Risks'[11] from the European Banking Authority (EBA) focuses on *all three letters* of the acronym. In a similar vein are the EBA's 'Guidelines on the Management of ESG Risks',[12] establishing prerequisites across the whole spectrum of E, S and G factors. While the risk management requirements are similar in nature in these publications, there is a notable deviation in scope, which is reflective of a divergence in scope among firms on this topic. Some organizations centre their efforts on *climate risk*, while others divide their focus equally between *E, S and G risk matters*. The scope depends on the jurisdiction and the focus of the firms' supervisors and policy makers.

Defining E, S and G risks

The EBA report proposes the following definition of ESG risks:

> *ESG risks* are 'the risks of any negative financial impact on the institution stemming from the current or prospective impacts of ESG factors on its counterparties or invested assets'.[13]

This definition is geared more towards financial risks, as it takes into account counterparty default or a reduction in the value of assets. In fact, in operational risk, negative impacts can emanate from the firm's own practices, and can be broader than merely financial. I will therefore propose an alternative definition.

ALTERNATIVE DEFINITION OF E, S AND G-RELATED RISKS

E, S and G-related risks are the risks of negative impacts stemming from an organization's E, S and G-related practices, or from the current or prospective impacts of E, S and G factors on its counterparties or invested assets.

Inadvertently, by bundling the three letters together, the EBA's definition may have helped spark the 'esg-ness' in risk management. But now we have ascertained that E, S and G come separated into their different elements, we can conclude that each of the letters individually needs to be viewed through a risk lens.

E, S and G interaction with operational risk framework elements

As outlined in Figure 14.1 at the start of the chapter, E, S and G risk management arguably touches on *all the aspects* of the operational risk framework. This will be explored further below, starting with the supporting elements, outlined on the perimeter in Figure 14.1.

Risk culture

Risk culture is a pertinent topic here as E, S and G factors affect the long-term sustainability of the firm (as well as the planet more broadly), and therefore have a deep connection to the values, beliefs and overall culture of the firm. Consequently, risk managers who are likely already involved in – or even leading – the firm's culture-related efforts can help promote particular behaviours, engaging employees in sustainability initiatives and encouraging a culture of awareness and responsibility.

In this context, it is appropriate to consider the triangle pictured in Figure 14.2, which explores a firm's motivation when approaching this topic.

- The initiative may be viewed merely through a *compliance lens*, aiming to meet minimum requirements, close audit comments or remove a capital add-on. In this case, the overall programme will be regulatory-driven, likely led by the second line (Risk or Compliance function),

Figure 14.2   The Triangle: firm's motivation in addressing E, S and G without considering the wider opportunities or conducting strategic board conversations on how E, S and G fits into the institution's business model.

- Alternatively, the programme can be regarded as an *opportunity*. As an example, the asset management industry thrives on proactively developing products to meet the demand for E, S and G investments as a result of changing consumer behaviour. In this case, the lead direction for the initiative would likely be provided by the business. However, if product *opportunity* is the only angle that matters, E, S and G will be viewed narrowly as a front office activity, with intellectual capacity being applied primarily to new fund development, while the firm's own practices and behaviours may conflict with E, S and G priorities. For example non-eco-friendly facilities, excessive printing, the use of plastic cups or poor diversity and inclusion scores might not be addressed. It is therefore important that the product *opportunity* aspect is in sync with the firm's *values and beliefs*, which brings us to the third vertex.

- *Values and beliefs* motivate E, S and G programmes in organizations that are genuinely interested in the topic. Those firms are likely to be industry leaders that advocate widely for E, S and G matters, joining industry groups and leading activities to achieve a positive impact. In these firms, employees are likely to be hearing about E, S and G matters directly from the CEO and the board, who will be sponsoring the programme, and the discussions will revolve around being a leader in the space rather than a follower; setting industry standards and making a real impact for the benefit of future generations.

Organizations that excel in embedding E, S and G into their wider strategy – in addition to their risk management activities – are making use of the full triangle. All three motivations are combined in a coherent way to build a meaningful, value-added programme. In these cases, cultural education is beneficial, linking all the incentives together. If a firm has no genuine belief in the subject, its approach to E, S and G may be largely operational or even hypocritical, reflecting back a poor organizational culture.

Operational risk taxonomy

Taxonomy is an essential starting point in defining how E, S and G elements are tackled. Linking the three letters in a meaningful manner leads to coherent and effective risk analysis, management and reporting. The opposite is also true – if the letters are not integrated or are connected sub-optimally,

Table 14.1   Industry study: integrating E, S and G into the corporate risk taxonomy

Firm 1	Firm 2	Firm 3
Strategic	Strategic and Business	Credit
Credit	Credit and Investment	Traded market
Market	Market	Operational
Non-Financial	Operational	Financial Crime
Liquidity	People	Conduct
	Legal and Compliance	Pension
	Reputational	Technology
	Information	*ESG*
	Climate	

this will inevitably cause confusion and duplication. The proposals for integrating E, S and G into the operational risk taxonomy are discussed in the respective sections of this chapter.

It is equally relevant to consider the wider *corporate risk taxonomy*, which usually sits above the operational risk taxonomy. Let's review three examples of how three different organizations approached this task, as set out in Table 14.1.

In this example:

- Firm 1 perceives that E, S and G-related risks materialize into the traditional risk types of strategic, credit, market, non-financial and liquidity, and therefore makes no amendments to its existing risk taxonomy; this approach is recommended.

- Firm 2 singles out *climate risk* as a stand-alone risk type, which is elevated and added into the risk taxonomy in its own right; this approach may be viable in certain circumstances.

- Firm 3 incorporates *ESG* as a catch-all entry; as previously discussed, this approach should be avoided due to the breadth and diversity of components that fall under the E, S and G banner.

Training and education

As E, S and G is a relatively new discipline, end-user education is vital for achieving embeddedness in organizations. An industry survey run in 2022[14] revealed that more than 35 per cent of respondents noted that no training on this subject was conducted at all. Yet ensuring a solid understanding of E, S and G is an excellent opportunity for collaboration across departments, whereby joint sessions might include a Sustainability team introducing the key concepts, the CEO or a member of the executive team explaining how these fit into the firm's overall strategy, and then respective risk professionals – credit, market, operational – joining in to cover the risk management aspects. The Operational Risk department can also run topical training sessions, for example including a spotlight on the treatment of E, S and G matters when performing its routine ORE or RCSA processes. There is no doubt the seriousness of E, S and G could make it a rather dry and humourless topic. Involvement of operational risk professionals, masters of training and education, as discussed in Chapter 11, can help to make the narrative interesting for stakeholders, increase enjoyment and get more people engaged in the programme.

Embedding and maturity assessment

Embedding and maturity assessment should also consider E, S and G factors, which can be important for maintaining competitive advantage and pursuing business opportunities as well as managing risks. In some jurisdictions there is also regulatory prioritization of this topic, with the European Central Bank (ECB) for example outlining 'material exposures to physical and transition risk drivers of climate change' as a prioritized vulnerability for review in their list of priorities for 2024–2026.[15] Thus a firm's existing maturity assessment, while applying the same methodology described in Chapter 13, can be expanded in scope to address the question of whether E, S and G integration into the operational risk framework works. There is also the opportunity for this to be addressed at an enterprise risk level, with integration into the operational risk framework being one of the components of the overall evaluation of E, S and G.

Next, we'll examine the *governance arrangements* and *risk reporting*, as shown in Figure 15.1, stretching above and below the main toolset.

Governance, roles and responsibilities

Risk professionals – credit, market, liquidity and operational – can work together, guided by the CRO, to agree a fit-for-purpose approach. This may include:

- Updating the enterprise risk management framework with references to E, S and G components, with an outline of how the topic is handled across the various risk disciplines.

- Amending Terms of Reference (TORs) of governance committees, from the Risk committee to Operational and Credit risk committees, to explicitly include responsibilities relating to the management of E, S and G-related risks (the recommended approach); alternatively, establishing a dedicated risk oversight committee for E, S and G matters (this is less desirable, as the existing risk governance structure should already be fit for purpose and able to accommodate new topics).

- Revising the organizational structure and role profiles, to reflect the firm's approach to the Three Lines. This will largely depend on the stance taken with the Sustainability (or ESG) team. (We'll refer to this as the Sustainability team throughout the rest of this chapter, as terminology varies widely between firms.) It is helpful if the Sustainability team:

  o Owns E,S,G risk policy and methodology;

  o Coordinates overall E, S and G risk exposure assessment;

  o Aggregates information and coordinates risk reporting and risk appetite development across the risk disciplines;

  o Provides firm-wide training and education;

  o Performs horizon scanning for new E, S and G-related emerging risks;

  o Develops expertise and serves as subject matter expert on the topic, partners with relevant industry bodies and commissions appropriate research.

- If this team is functional, the role of the Operational Risk department becomes much easier and pleasurable to execute. Therefore due consideration should be given to the clarity in the allocation of tasks early on in the programme.

- Even if E, S and G is not forming part of operational risk activities, it is beneficial to consider what other governance committees may require revision. For example, the TORs of New Product/New Business committees or similar governance bodies may merit revision.

Reporting and decision-making

The aim here is to ensure that E, S and G risks are taken into account in risk-related reporting.

The operational risk report, discussed in Chapter 10, should not change, but rather should include periodic thematic updates on E, S and G risks, on a frequency agreed by the board and documented in the relevant TORs. This is a point of contention, as often new reports covering E, S and G risks are created from scratch, duplicating existing information. Documenting what is reported by the Sustainability team vs Risk department is also useful. There is a broader reporting challenge which requires a development of an E, S and G reporting framework aligned with international standards where applicable, for example the Global Reporting Initiative (GRI) or the Sustainability Accounting Standards Board (SASB). This matter is outside immediate operational risk responsibilities, but still useful to bear in mind.

Let's now proceed to examining the three components of the acronym – E, S and G – as well as remaining core operational risk elements – in more detail.

The E in ESG

This section explores how the *E* element can be integrated into an existing operational risk framework, placing particular focus on the climate-related subcomponent.

Operational risk events

OREs are discussed in detail in Chapter 4. The process of identifying and gathering OREs should already be in place, enabling the firm to record incidents such as the following:

- An employee submits a fraudulent expense report and claims $5,000;
- An ATM is destroyed, repaired at a cost of $50,000;
- A processing error results in a loss of $75,000;
- System failure leads to a major technology outage, resulting in customer harm and a regulatory fine of $350,000.

A subset of these events is of interest. Specifically, the ATM destruction needs to be further investigated to determine why it occurred; was it due to an act of vandalism (not climate-related), or due to torrential rain leading to a flood (climate-related)? Similarly, what was the cause of system failure? Was it due to human error (not climate-related), or as a result of increased humidity due to a wetter winter (climate-related)?

At times, this process may necessitate the 5 Whys technique discussed in Chapter 4, with continual asking of the *why* question, to drill down into the problem and understand its true origin:

- Why did the incident occur? Due to system failure.

- Why did the system fail? Due to a malfunction of a hardware part.

- Why did the part malfunction? It was damaged by moisture.

- Why was there moisture? Due to too much humidity in the data centre.

- Why was there humidity in the data centre? We have experienced an unusually wet winter leading to a rise in humidity, which the cooling unit failed to control.

Here, at last, we arrive at the true cause, namely an excessively wet winter impacting humidity levels; and consequently we are able to attribute the event to climate-related drivers.

This type of investigation is needed to determine whether events that have materialized are relevant to the E category. It is recognized that the main challenge lies in potential data gaps. While the operational risk event database may be complete with *descriptions* of what went wrong, it may be missing the *causes* of the events. Working with organizations in my consultancy capacity, in many cases we have had to embark on an interesting journey of trying to locate an individual who remembered the historic event and could talk about its cause.

In the example given above, the database would be updated to show that the event was *caused* by a climate-related driver.

INCORPORATING E INTO OPERATIONAL RISK TAXONOMY

The environmental (and specifically climate) aspect is not a separate risk type but a cause, or driver, of traditional operational risks materializing.

OREs caused by climate-related drivers will most obviously materialize in the *Damage to Physical Assets* Basel taxonomy category, which by definition already includes natural disasters. Additional impacted categories may include:

- *Business Disruption and System Failure*, as outlined in the earlier example, for a relevant subset of events;

- *Employment Practices and Workplace Safety*, for accidents related to unsafe working conditions as a result of flood or fire (or similar events);

- Third-party risk covering failures of service providers resulting from natural disasters, as part of *Execution, Delivery and Process Management*; and

- *Clients, Products and Business Practices*, specifically climate-related lawsuits, regulatory non-compliance or inadequate product features/ product mis-selling.

Suggested impacted taxonomy categories are highlighted in Figure 14.3. Primary categories are circled; secondary categories are marked with an arrow.

It is fair to note that not all categories are in scope; internal and external fraud, general execution errors and similar events are less relevant here.

In the same way, where a firm is using its own tailor-made taxonomy, relevant impacted categories would also need to be ascertained.

As we are discussing potential lawsuits and regulatory non-compliance, it is pertinent to consider broader climate-related risks which go beyond rain and heatwaves, splitting them into physical, transition and liability.

Climate-related risk drivers are comprised of three components, namely physical, transition and liability.

- *Physical risk* accounts for acute events such as storms, heavy rain and heat waves as well as longer-term chronic shifts in climate.

- *Transition risk* encompasses the process of transitioning to a greener economy. It includes, among other things, changes in regulation, changes in consumer behaviour, technological developments or decreases in the value of particular investments resulting in stranded or uninsurable assets.

- *Liability risk* arises from climate-related legal actions, which might be incurred for failing to mitigate or adapt to the impact of climate change.

Figure 14.3 Mapping of *E* to operational risk taxonomy

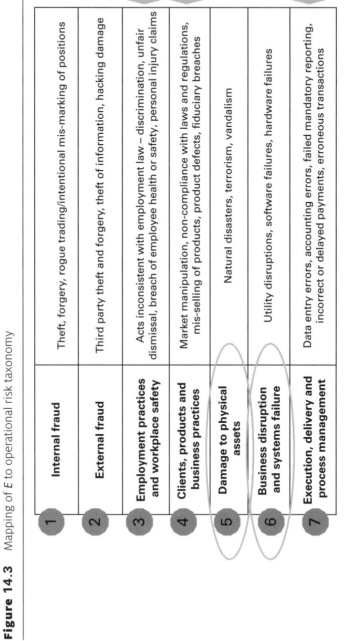

1	Internal fraud	Theft, forgery, rogue trading/intentional mis-marking of positions
2	External fraud	Third party theft and forgery, theft of information, hacking damage
3	Employment practices and workplace safety	Acts inconsistent with employment law – discrimination, unfair dismissal, breach of employee health or safety, personal injury claims
4	Clients, products and business practices	Market manipulation, non-compliance with laws and regulations, mis-selling of products, product defects, fiduciary breaches
5	Damage to physical assets	Natural disasters, terrorism, vandalism
6	Business disruption and systems failure	Utility disruptions, software failures, hardware failures
7	Execution, delivery and process management	Data entry errors, accounting errors, failed mandatory reporting, incorrect or delayed payments, erroneous transactions

The topic therefore encompasses issues that stretch beyond weather-related forces.

To enable the quick detection of climate-related OREs, the Basel Committee suggests incorporating a *flag* to mark the events with 'root causes stemming from climate-related risk drivers'[16] into a database or spreadsheet; or alternatively, if the organization is using a *causal* taxonomy in addition to a *risk* taxonomy (see Chapter 1), then the *causal* taxonomy can be amended accordingly.

A note on the need for reflection to determine that climate risk is not a separate operational risk sub-type. This is a point of contention in the industry, and opinion is divided, as was discovered by the Best Practice Operational Risk Forum. Some 40 per cent of respondents treated climate as a *cause*, while 50 per cent approached it as a *risk in its own right*, and added it into their taxonomy; the remaining 10 per cent were undecided.

Adding climate as a *risk* will inevitably cause duplication with existing risks, events, KRIs and scenarios. In contrast, treating climate as a *cause* is supported by multiple regulatory publications. This includes the EBA, who in their review of good practices for climate-related and environmental risk management noted that 'institutions broadly recognize C&E risks as risk *drivers* that materialize in *existing risk categories*'.[17] ORX, the industry body that authored the reference operational risk taxonomy, also concurs, stating that climate constitutes a *causal factor* and therefore does not require a new event category.[18]

In conclusion, analysis of past losses is essential for understanding the level of organizational exposure to climate risk. If, as mentioned in Chapter 4, a firm does not have a clear understanding of its loss profile, it will be significantly less equipped for effectively managing its forward-looking risks.

INCORPORATING E INTO OPERATIONAL RISK EVENTS

✓ Perform a look-back of existing OREs, and detect and analyse relevant events;

✓ If there is uncertainty about the relevance of the event (where the cause is either unknown or not clearly defined), supplement with any available details;

✓ Create an action plan for addressing data gaps, potentially aligning with existing risk data remediation projects;

> ✓ Establish the means to spot relevant events promptly in the future, by either adding a climate 'flag' or amending a causal taxonomy;
>
> ✓ Carry out training and education to increase end-user awareness.

Operational risk assessments

Let's consider another core tool of the framework, namely risk assessments. RCSAs were addressed in Chapter 5, and this section builds on the principles and methodology established there.

Risk and control self-assessment (RCSA)

As is the case for any risk assessment, the first step is to create a pre-reading pack including supplementary information. This preparatory pack needs to include:

- Relevant ORE analysis, as discussed above, providing a factual view on the frequency and severity of events stemming from climate-related drivers.
- Relevant external loss data: where internal data is insufficient or of suboptimal quality, it can be supplemented with pertinent external loss data.
- Previous RCSA or other risk assessment results.
- Additional external research that may be relevant. This can be, for example:
  - Climate-related peer lawsuits, as an aid for evaluating *liability* risk;
  - Regulatory priorities and/or penalties for non-compliance, for *transition* risk;
  - Predictions on the risk of flood, wildfire and other threats to premises and facilities (such as branches and headquarters); these can be available from government registers, externally produced hazard maps and footprints, or other sources, and are essential for a better understanding of the firm's exposure to *physical* risk.

There are obvious challenges related to the use of external research on the physical risk side. Firstly, such data may not be available and/or accessible for a given jurisdiction; and secondly, there are often disputes on whose responsibility it is to source and analyse such information. The debate often revolves around the role of the central Sustainability team vs the Operational Risk department vs Facilities, and in particular on where the knowledge and capability to address these matters should reside. From a practical perspective, it is essential that the teams agree their approach and relative responsibilities early on, with the recommendation being for the Sustainability team to lead on sourcing and evaluating such data together with the Facilities department. This may necessitate partnering with contacts in academia to persuade them to launch, and perhaps even sponsor, forward-looking research for those jurisdictions where it is not readily available.

Once the preparatory pack is ready, an RCSA workshop can be conducted with relevant units. It can be top-down, with the CEO and executive team at the table; or bottom-up, with subject matter experts (SMEs) from the Business, Legal, Compliance, Facilities, IT, Procurement/Third-party and other relevant areas, facilitated jointly by the Sustainability team and the Operational Risk department. This is a *thematic* risk assessment, focusing on a particular theme (in this case, climate risk). During the workshop, physical, transition and liability risk drivers are examined and any material operational risks emanating from the assessment are identified and categorized in line with the operational risk taxonomy. Some examples of risks that might be identified during this exercise are presented in Table 14.2.

Table 14.2   Examples of operational risks stemming from climate-related drivers

	Cause	Resulting operational risks
Physical risk	Acute or chronic events, e.g. wildfires, flood/precipitation, severe storm, sea level rise, wind and soil erosion	**1. Damage to premises:** Branches or headquarters **2. Health & Safety:** Workplace safety/staff injury resulting from physical hazard **3. Third-party risk:** Failure of a critical third-party service provider
Transition risk	Policy and regulatory	**4. Regulatory risk:** Inability to identify or correctly apply requirements
	Change in consumer behaviour	**5. Product risk:** Defects in sustainability-related features
Liability risk	Market sentiment	**6. Legal risk:** lawsuits for environmental impact of firm's activities

Figure 14.4 Example results of climate-related risk assessment

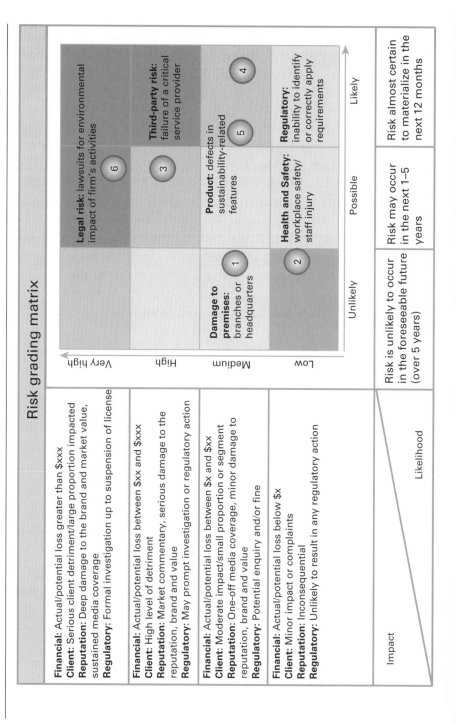

Following this step, risks are evaluated based on the existing methodology and using the materiality matrix previously described in Figure 5.6. The results of the assessment are presented in a heatmap in Figure 14.4.

In this example, the organization's risk profile is quite contained, as it has determined that its own facilities are less exposed to *physical* risk. However, *transition* and *liability* risks such as regulatory, legal and product, are more significant, and so is *physical* risk emanating from dependency on critical third-parties, and their possible lack of resilience to climate-related drivers. Against this background, areas are identified for further deep dive and action, including running a scenario analysis as described further in this chapter.

As noted in Chapter 5, heat maps are imprecise, and it is important to understand their limitations. Despite these constraints, they are a very useful tool in determining which areas are more material and thus in agreeing priorities for subsequent exploration, remediation or risk transfer.

In other cases the firm's geographical footprint may be more complex, with facilities spread out across counties and continents. In this case, a more granular *physical* risk analysis would be beneficial:

- Hazards can be split into sub-types (e.g. flood, fire, hurricane, etc);
- Subsequently each facility – such as office buildings, recovery site, third-party locations (e.g. data centre) – can be assessed against each type of hazard;
- Based on the assessment, actions can be developed with a view to enhancing operational resilience, improving staff awareness and revisiting insurance cover.

Lastly, the risk assessment may also include developing a more sophisticated understanding of physical risk exposure via the use of probabilistic models, such as the catastrophe models widely used in the insurance industry.

Risks and opportunities assessment

As argued in Chapter 6, risk management as a discipline benefits from taking a balanced stance and focusing on the *upside* as well as the *downside* of risks. Climate-related risk assessment is no different and can be executed via a *risks and opportunities* assessment. The objective of this exercise is to tease out the opportunities, and ways in which they might be increased, in addition to minimizing the material risks. An example of this balanced view of *risks and opportunities* is presented in Figure 14.5.

Figure 14.5 Example climate risks and opportunities assessment

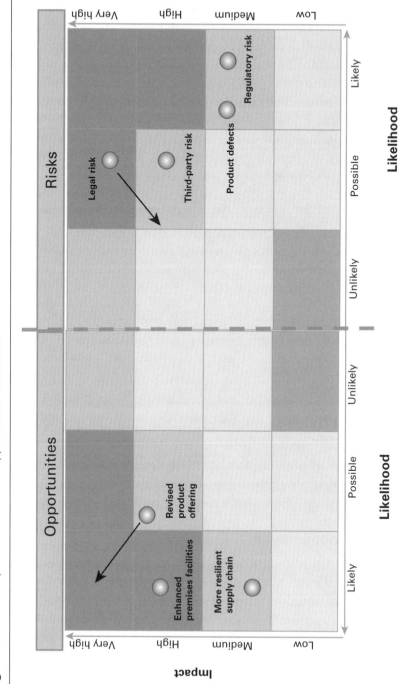

In this illustration, the organization considers a range of opportunities:

- A revised product offering, including designing a range of products that will create a competitive edge.

- The opportunity to make its own premises and facilities more eco-friendly by using renewable energy; reducing waste and recycling furniture; decreasing paper consumption; and consolidating premises or data centres using a more efficient architecture – all vital in reducing the firm's own carbon emissions.

- Increasing the resilience of the supply chain, achieved via supplier diversification, creating some redundancy in critical supply chain elements and enhancing contingency plans.

Opportunities are neither required nor overseen by most regulators and thus, sadly, are often omitted from the assessment, especially if the latter is tackled with a compliance 'tick-box' mindset. Needless to say, however, they are extremely beneficial from a business point of view, so an approach that takes into account both risks and opportunities is strongly recommended.

To summarize, key activities related to risk assessments involve the following.

INCORPORATING *E* INTO OPERATIONAL RISK ASSESSMENTS

✓ Conduct a pilot thematic workshop with relevant units, facilitated by the sustainability and operational risk teams, to identify material risks caused by climate-related drivers;

✓ Update relevant policies and procedures;

✓ Carry out training and education for end-users;

✓ Subsequently embed risk identification as part of the regular RCSA cycle;

✓ Furthermore, consider adopting a *risks and opportunities* approach.

Scenario analysis

As a tool, scenario analysis is worthy of special mention in the climate context, as it lends itself very well to considering extreme but plausible events at both short and longer-term time horizons. Scenario analysis is thus an

Figure 14.6   Climate-related scenario example

CAUSE	SCENARIO STORY LINE	CONSEQUENCE
•Dependence on multiple critical service providers •Control framework is being put in place to meet internal and regulatory requirements •Slow progress in implementation	*Failure of critical third-party service provider*: the firm failed to embed a robust third-party management process, complete risk assessment, incorporating climate-related considerations. Critical supplier of cloud service solutions suffers a flood due to extreme weather event, which results in extended downtime and inability to meet the SLA. *Assumed control failures:* 1) Climate-related assessment of critical third-party service providers X 2) Service substitutability X	•Client harm and loss of business •Investigation •Regulatory fine

excellent tool for exploring the operational risk impacts of climate-related factors. An example is presented in Figure 14.6.

In this example, the organization is using a bow-tie *cause, event* and *impact* methodology, as described in Chapter 8, to review and enhance its existing scenario related to third-party failure. Climate-related considerations are added to the story line, which helps the firm to acknowledge that it does not in fact possess sufficient knowledge around the exposure of critical third parties to climate risk drivers. This results in the development of an action plan to carry out a review of all critical service providers, to ensure that due diligence and climate-related exposure assessments have been completed in line with policy. The firm also commits to revisiting its substitutability arrangements.

If the organization is already conducting scenario analysis as described in Chapter 8, then it may not need to develop story lines from scratch. Scenarios are common for categories such as *Damage to Physical Assets and Business Disruption and Systems Failure*. Therefore, the objective is to build on the existing framework, strengthening the suite of scenarios, developing further plausible assumptions and delving into areas that may not have been fully explored.

Scenarios can be selected from the RCSA risks for a further deep dive. For example, if lawsuits have been specifically identified as an area of concern, they can be further explored to consider what action or inaction may lead to directors of the firm being sued. Additionally, this process presents a perfect opportunity to re-evaluate the adequacy of the firm's insurance cover and other risk transfer mechanisms. The Institute of Risk Management

(IRM) supports a scenario approach for understanding the firm's exposure to climate-related risk drivers, noting that this methodology can help in a number of ways.[19] From a regulatory standpoint, the Basel Committee specifically cites the need for scenario analysis to 'assess the resilience of... business models and strategies... and determine the impact of climate-related risk drivers on... overall risk profile'.[20]

In conclusion, scenario analysis creates great value-add, with both *risk measurement* and *risk management* benefits emanating from it.

Risk appetite and Key Risk Indicators

The suggested approach to tackling operational risk appetite was outlined in Chapter 9. We have mentioned throughout this chapter that E, S and G risks materialize in existing operational risks; and therefore, no brand new appetite statements are necessary. Using the same approach as we suggested for scenario analysis, existing statements and monitoring metrics can be enhanced instead.

Let's take a look at the example of an appetite statement for third-party risk described in Table 9.2:

> The firm relies on third parties in delivering core business activities and services to its clients. It is willing to accept moderate level of risk working with contracted third-parties to gain access to new technological platforms, improve flexibility and efficiency. Clients and regulators expect the firm to manage these arrangements effectively. *The firm aims to limit disruptions by conducting robust third-party due diligence and performing monitoring and oversight by a dedicated Outsourcing team.* The firm has identified single points of failure and where feasible, developed a substitution plan in case of critical provider failure or unavailability. Where substitution is not viable, the firm has enhanced oversight and actively takes part in third-parties' testing of their resilience and recovery capabilities.

> Elevated level of risk and breaches to appetite are escalated to the board and require action according to the firm's Response Framework. The firm accepts that occasional minor disruptions may occur.

The appetite remains valid overall; however, the statement in italics can be improved by incorporating key climate-related considerations, so it reads: *The firm aims to limit disruptions by conducting robust third-party due diligence, which includes due diligence around third-party exposure to climate factors and performing monitoring and oversight by a dedicated Outsourcing team.*

This addition cites a specific new activity, namely, working closely with critical third parties to understand their own exposure to climate-related risks. This kind of provision needs to be put in place, to mitigate the risk of third-party failures.

Respectively, appetite monitoring will benefit from a new KRI (in addition to the ones mentioned in Table 9.3), for example:

KRI: % of critical providers with inadequate climate risk assessments or where assessments have not been completed.

With these small additions, the process of appetite setting and monitoring remains unchanged.

The S and the G in ESG

Now that we have considered the *E*, let's turn our attention to the remaining two letters of the acronym. As evidenced by an Airmic survey,[21] the top three responses to the question about *non-climate* E, S and G aspects of concern were:

- Diversity, equity and inclusion (80.4%);
- Employee mental health (63%);
- Regulatory compliance, including sanctions (63%).

These are all familiar themes, which fall under the Social (*S*) and Governance (*G*) headings.

The essence of S

When considering the *S* factor, it is imperative to bear in mind that 'the social aims of ESG are vaguer than the environmental ones'[22] and that 'references to definition of social factors are generally more difficult to identify'.[23] Areas of focus in these domains stretch from human rights to community relations. The rating agency S&P, which uses E, S and G factors as contributors in arriving at its overall opinion on a company's creditworthiness, comments on such things as:

- General Motors being 'in the second week of a nationwide strike that has seen some 46,000 employees down tools',[24] noting that 'labour issues fall under the social aspect';[25]

- Walmart Inc, the US superstore chain, announcing it 'will stop selling handguns, as well as ammunition for handguns and short-barrel rifles',[26] opining that it had become 'a more palatable choice for socially minded investors'.[27]

Due to how broad these topics are, and in the absence of a coherent standardized taxonomy, the firm needs to outline its own vision of what is included in the *S*, how that connects to its strategy and values, and, in turn, how the firm defines the relevant risks.

From a practical perspective, without reinventing the wheel, social risks can be extracted from the existing operational risk framework. A potential mapping of social risks to the operational risk taxonomy can be as follows:

- *Employment Practices and Workplace Safety*, as a primary category, covers human capital management as well as safe working conditions;
- Under *Execution, Delivery and Process Management*, the risk of third parties/service providers failing to apply robust employment and safety practices.

Therefore, social risks may be defined as follows:

> Social risks evolve around human capital management, including but not limited to well-being, equality, safety and labour standards, as well as suppliers' relationship with their workforce.

PRACTICAL TIP: 'HANDLING *BOUNDARY* EVENTS'

There are *boundary* events that span across *E* and *S* elements. An example would be a health and safety incident (a social matter, or *S*) caused by a flood because of torrential rain (a climate-related risk driver, or *E*). In this particular case, the suggestion is to capture it under the *E* banner.

Dependent on the firm's size, nature and business model, it may be fitting to apply a wider definition of *S*, in which case additional categories may be impacted:

- Product defects and inadequate product introduction, as part of *Clients, Products and Business Practices*, as it can be argued that social responsibility includes a conscientious and reliable customer product and service offering;

- Privacy and data security, under *External Fraud*, as keeping personal data safe provides customer protection, and is part of social responsibility, especially for retail businesses.

Consequently, the example definition given above may need to be expanded:

> Social risks evolve around human capital management by the organization and its suppliers, as well as product and data responsibility to its customers, investors and stakeholders.

A potential mapping of S to the taxonomy is highlighted in Figure 14.7 with the primary categories circled and secondary categories marked with an arrow.

The firm can go even further and add risks emanating from its community interactions, for instance under-achievement of strategic goals related to community aid programmes. The definition will then stretch across operational and strategic risks. Where relevant, the composition of S and its risks can be reconciled with relevant jurisdictional guidance, such as UN Sustainable Development Goals or the European Pillar of Social Rights Action Plan. Each firm needs to decide on how widely or narrowly it is willing to interpret the S element, and, in turn, social risks.

INCORPORATING S INTO THE OPERATIONAL RISK TAXONOMY

The social element is neither a *cause* nor a *risk* in its own right, it is a *lens* through which we view traditional operational (and, potentially, strategic) risks.

The social element bears some similarity with *conduct* risk discussed in Chapter 1, which is best interpreted as an *overarching term* to identify a multitude of risks that may result in poor customer outcomes. The social element (like governance, as we will see later) is also an *overarching term* that will benefit from being mapped to specific taxonomy categories. Indeed, the similarity goes beyond mere taxonomy mapping, as the concepts of *conduct*, *social* and *governance* matters are closely interlinked. For example, the issue of poor employee working conditions is both a social and a conduct matter; bribery is both a conduct and a governance issue.

Figure 14.7 Mapping of S to operational risk taxonomy

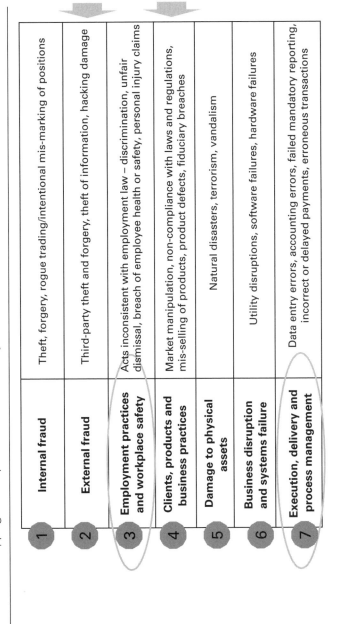

1	**Internal fraud**	Theft, forgery, rogue trading/intentional mis-marking of positions
2	**External fraud**	Third-party theft and forgery, theft of information, hacking damage
3	**Employment practices and workplace safety**	Acts inconsistent with employment law – discrimination, unfair dismissal, breach of employee health or safety, personal injury claims
4	**Clients, products and business practices**	Market manipulation, non-compliance with laws and regulations, mis-selling of products, product defects, fiduciary breaches
5	**Damage to physical assets**	Natural disasters, terrorism, vandalism
6	**Business disruption and systems failure**	Utility disruptions, software failures, hardware failures
7	**Execution, delivery and process management**	Data entry errors, accounting errors, failed mandatory reporting, incorrect or delayed payments, erroneous transactions

The beauty of mapping S into the operational risk taxonomy lies in the fact that it enables us to extract relevant data such as OREs, risks and KRIs, and thus to understand the exposure to S via the existing framework, without needing to create a brand new stand-alone framework and process. For example, information can be obtained on past losses related to employment lawsuits, and analysis conducted on their materiality and frequency of occurrence. Similarly, forward-looking people-related risks can be filtered out, and their significance evaluated. This analysis paints a picture of the company's social risk profile. Organizations may supplement it with further metrics/KRIs that they feel are relevant to their firm.

PRACTICAL TIP: DO NOT 'OVER-MAP'

Approach the mapping of S to the operational risk taxonomy with caution, and do not 'over-map' S to multiple taxonomy categories. If we are not careful, everything can be interpreted as a social matter.

In my experience of consultancy and training on this topic, some perceived social as a separate risk category, and added it as such into the operational risk taxonomy. This treatment of S is not advisable, as it will inevitably result in overlaps and double counting.

On the opposite side of the spectrum, some organizations I've worked with questioned whether they in fact needed to highlight separately the social element and social risks. They felt that S was something they already did, and that it already fitted organically into their frameworks and activities. To a large extent they are right, as many components of the S element refer to activities led by the corporate HR department, risk management or others. Many of the practices that make up S have been mentioned throughout this book, including, for example, the Conduct and Culture Dashboard presented in Figure 12.4. While considering the key pillars that fall under the conduct and culture heading, the firm may have already outlined core employee- and customer-related measures. It may already have dashboards with well-thought-out KRIs being presented to governance committees. There is most likely already a process through which the firm monitors topics such as diversity and inclusion, and employee mental health. Given this, it is essential to understand existing practices, and not fall into the trap of the Sustainability team creating a *social dashboard*, only to find out that HR and/or the Risk department already report on similar information under a slightly different banner. Hence the call for action for operational risk professionals.

CALL FOR ACTION

Collaborate with HR, Sustainability and other relevant units to:

- Map *S*-related risks to the operational risk taxonomy, and extract and analyse relevant information, if not done already;

- Review any existing activities that fit under the social banner;

- Agree a joint approach to risk management and risk reporting, avoiding duplication and instead building on existing practices;

- Jointly, consider how the organization can make improvements on the *S* element.

After all, whichever way *S* is approached, it is less about frameworks and definitions and more about the value-add it brings to the organization. *S* can be used as an opportunity to focus on important social activities and consider what and how the firm can do better; and what, in turn, will make the firm better.

Understanding G

Just as the *S* element is potentially very broad in scope, the *G* element is even more so. As noted by the *Financial Times*, 'governance is a catch-all title within a catch-all acronym'.[28] Like the *S* examples cited earlier, here are some examples of the kind of governance topics that the rating agency S&P would comment on:

- The fact that Facebook Inc was facing 'growing calls from shareholders for greater transparency and risk oversight';[29] S&P noted that 'poor corporate governance practices have stood at the core of some of the biggest corporate scandals'.[30]

- A 2020 report, 'WeWork slipping into 'negative spiral' as IPO hopes dim',[31] concluded that 'companies like WeWork have been scrutinized for their lack of leadership accountability and oversight, as well as conflicts of interest'.[32]

From these and other examples, the spirit of governance is clear; the challenge lies in the practical application and mapping of G into the taxonomy – yet again to avoid creating a separate framework but still understanding the risk profile.

Applying an analogous approach, governance risks can be extracted from the current operational risk framework, and mapped as follows:

- *Clients, Products and Business Practices*, as a primary category, with relevant risks of bribery and corruption, tax evasion, illicit financial flows, conflicts of interest and regulatory non-compliance;

- Under *Execution, Delivery and Process Management*, the potential risk that third parties or service providers commit acts of bribery and corruption, tax evasion or similar offences.

Again, there is an opportunity to apply a wider definition, and add other taxonomy categories:

- Under *Execution, Delivery and Process Management*, the risk of possible financial misstatements or disclosures, or incorrect books and records, since in financial services, balance sheet accuracy and transparency relies heavily on robust governance practices; and

- Under *Business Disruption and Systems Failure*, the risk of failure of a core system, based on the argument that good governance ensures responsible investment in and oversight of technology.

A potential mapping of G to the taxonomy is highlighted in Figure 14.8, with primary categories circled and secondary categories marked with an arrow.

INCORPORATING *G* INTO THE OPERATIONAL RISK TAXONOMY

Similarly to *S*, the governance element is neither a *cause* nor a *risk* in its own right, it is a *lens* through which we view traditional operational, balance sheet (asset-liability management) and, potentially, strategic risks.

Given that G is even broader than S, it is equally important not to over-map it to taxonomy categories. In one rather extreme case, a firm I worked with took the view that governance is a cause of the *majority* of operational risk events. Therefore, its G included:

- Mundane errors: Failure to apply four-eyes principles was viewed as poor governance;

Figure 14.8 Mapping of G to operational risk taxonomy

1	**Internal fraud**	Theft, forgery, rogue trading/intentional mis-marking of positions
2	**External fraud**	Third party theft and forgery, theft of information, hacking damage
3	**Employment practices and workplace safety**	Acts inconsistent with employment law – discrimination, unfair dismissal, breach of employee health or safety, personal injury claims
4	**Clients, products and business practices**	Market manipulation, non-compliance with laws and regulations, mis-selling of products, product defects, fiduciary breaches
5	**Damage to physical assets**	Natural disasters, terrorism, vandalism
6	**Business disruption and systems failure**	Utility disruptions, software failures, hardware failures
7	**Execution, delivery and process management**	Data entry errors, accounting errors, failed mandatory reporting, incorrect or delayed payments, erroneous transactions

- Fraud: Inability to detect/prevent incidents was perceived as a governance flaw;
- Model risk: Errors or poor calibration signalled a failure of governance.

Their list of G went on and on. This is a very broad interpretation that would likely be both costly and unwieldy to implement, and might even serve to mask more important governance risks. If this approach is chosen, the organization needs to seriously consider what benefits this stance is intended to bring.

In a similar way to S, G is less about definition and more an opportunity to bring focus to the topics that should be already ingrained in the corporate DNA, such as good ethos, culture and corporate governance framework. In one sense, E, S and G could just as easily be transposed to read as 'G, S and E'. This is based on the premise that all practices, whether good or bad, originate from the tone set at the top and from the conscientious (or not) application of governance arrangements in their broad sense. Corporate governance frameworks, if not fit-for-purpose, result in operational as well as balance sheet risk exposures. The G element encourages to ensure, via robust reporting mechanisms and close two-way communication between the Board and the lower-level executive committees, that the Board is fully aware of the situation at the coalface. To help organizations evaluate their practices, the Organization for Economic Cooperation and Development (OECD) issued principles to help firms 'evaluate and improve the legal, regulatory, and institutional framework for corporate governance',[33] which is a valuable benchmark in this area.

Effective cross-functional coordination is also vital for addressing governance-related risks. Almost certainly, the Compliance department will be leading on policies, education, and reporting related to anti-bribery and corruption, prohibition of engagement in illicit activities and management of conflicts of interest. Corporate Secretariat, Legal and Risk teams will be building and assessing the effectiveness of governance arrangements. The Operational Risk department may already be extracting and reporting on relevant risks and KRIs; and a plethora of other activities may already be under way. It is therefore essential that existing information is examined to point to existing governance-related risk management, to avoid the creation of a whole separate industry of G-related reports. Hence the call for action.

CALL FOR ACTION

Collaborate with Compliance, Corporate Secretariat and Sustainability teams, or with other relevant units, to:

- Map *G*-related risks to the operational risk taxonomy, and extract and analyse relevant information, if not done already;

- Jointly examine how the *G* topic is addressed in the firm, what activities are in place and what information is available;

- Agree a joint approach on reporting, avoiding duplication and instead building on existing practices;

- Consider what the organization can do better on the *G* element.

Common challenges and good practices

Potential challenges related to integrating E, S and G into the operational risk framework can include the following.

Lack of involvement

Operational risk professionals are very busy individuals. On several occasions when discussing the E, S and G topic, risk managers mentioned that, thankfully, the corporate Sustainability team was handling the integration, including its incorporation into the operational risk framework, so at least this task was off their table. This delegation is undesirable. Without active engagement from operational risk SMEs, who are clearly the most familiar with their own framework, other units end up taking the critical decisions on E, S and G integration, which usually leads to sub-optimal results. Operational risk professionals need to claim a seat at the E, S and G table, and take the lead in integrating E, S and G risk management into their own framework.

Focus on optics

In circumstances where the E, S and G programme is compliance-focused, senior management will usually demand quick results. This leads to emphasizing *quantity over quality* – for optics purposes, lengthy reports are developed from scratch, repeatedly mentioning the ESG acronym to create an impression of multiple ESG-related activities (whether strategic or related to risk management). Producing siloed reports, without thoughtfully examining existing practices and aligning components to existing activities, creates duplication and adds little value.

Inconsiderate use of the acronym 'ESG' and taxonomy mapping

One of the key challenges is in the bundling of E, S and G components, resulting in 'ESG risk' being considered as a top operational risk. In numerous industry surveys on top operational risks, the label 'ESG risk' repeatedly comes up. As discussed in this chapter, the term 'ESG risk' is a misnomer. Risk practitioners need to be more considerate in their use of the acronym and its elements. A related challenge is in the incorrect mapping to the risk taxonomy – or even the complete absence of any mapping – resulting in the appearance of new *social* and *governance* risks in the taxonomy. Gaining knowledge on E, S and G topics, reading regulatory literature and obtaining relevant qualifications will increase the overall level of awareness among operational risk practitioners and reduce inconsiderate usage.

Reliance on existing tools

Management of E, S and G-related operational risks relies on the existing framework components. If the tools are not well designed or are performing sub-optimally, adding new requirements will bring existing challenges to the fore, potentially leading to push-back and complaints from the first line. Rather, E, S and G can be used as an opportunity to make thoughtful revisions, thus enhancing the overall framework.

Good practices

Developing accountability

In some jurisdictions, accountability regimes have prompted the appointment of a named individual responsible for the management of climate-related risks. This has resulted in more timely discussions on roles and responsibilities in this area, which have subsequently enabled the programmes to progress at speed. Defining roles and responsibilities, especially between the Sustainability department and the risk teams, helps to avoid grey areas and ensure effective implementation.

SWOT analysis applied to E, S and G

Operational risk practitioners excel in facilitating different types of assessments. One tool that lends itself well to E, S and G is SWOT analysis – identifying Strengths, Weaknesses, Threats and Opportunities. Risk practitioners can aim to get involved in the firm's broader strategic E, S and G programme, and lend their facilitation skills in running SWOT workshops.

Reputational risk assessment

Reputational risk can be treated as a consequence of other risk types (mostly operational risk) materializing. In this case it can be evaluated in the risk assessment process as part of the risk grading matrix. An alternative approach is to view reputation as an asset, conducting a separate reputational risk assessment of the risks stemming from E, S and G factors. This is usually a three-step process, which includes identifying key stakeholders, developing material reputational risk scenarios and finally assessing what scenarios will cause the most significant (whether positive or negative) stakeholder reactions. Reputational risk assessment in the E, S and G area is beneficial, as reputational damage invariably features as one of firms' primary concerns.

Programme transparency and collaboration

E, S and G is usually an extensive, multi-year commitment, led as a strategic programme at a corporate level. Ideally, the programme is well established, with cross-functional representation from all relevant units, from Business to HR to Operational Risk, collaborating effectively, breaking the silos, acknowledging existing practices and connecting the dots. During the education programmes I run on the E, S and G topic we usually discuss whether it is actually *essential* – or merely *desirable* – for Operational Risk to be involved in the broader programme. The unanimous response is that it is *essential* good practice for the Operational Risk department to be an integral part of the E, S and G programme, at least at the beginning or even throughout.

Industry benchmark

The Best Practice Operational Risk Forum has discussed the topic of E, S and G integration into the operational risk framework many times over the years, each time noting some, albeit slow, advancement in implementation. In 2022, 10 per cent of respondents confirmed significant progress, 40 per cent acknowledged it being on the way, 30 per cent had commenced work and 20 per cent had not yet started.

Participants reflected on numerous challenges with this integration process, which perhaps explain the slower than expected advancement:

- 37% listed other pressing priorities, with the pace being slowed by the pandemic years and the subsequent challenging macro-economic and geopolitical environment. This resonated with a 2022 KPMG survey, which showed that during times of economic uncertainty, CEOs had to reprioritize, with as many as '50 percent... pausing or reconsidering their existing or planned ESG efforts'.[34]

- Methodological difficulties were noted by 27% of participants. In particular, climate risk management requires investment in the development of the approach, and enhanced knowledge and skills in the Operational Risk department. Here, operational risk is somewhat lagging, with more progress achieved in credit and market risk areas. The Basel Committee acknowledges the challenge, commenting that 'publicly available information regarding climate-related operational risks is scarcer than for other risk types, and therefore the whole risk category would benefit from more data and research'.[35]

- On this note, 18% raised concerns related to data quality and reliability; in particular, loss data may not clearly flag past climate-related losses, making it difficult to analyse the frequency and severity of relevant events.

- Lastly, 18% mentioned unclear roles and responsibilities, especially between Sustainability teams and the Operational Risk department, with ongoing debates on who should lead activities such as the thematic assessment, risk reporting or training and education.

The results of the live poll are presented in Figure 14.9.

Figure 14.9 Industry poll: challenges of ESG integration

What are E, S and G integration challenges?

18%	27%	37%	18%
Poor/ insufficient data	Methodological difficulties	Other priorities	Unclear roles and responsibilities

Best Practice Operational Risk Forum, 2022

Given other priorities, operational risk professionals reflected on their time spent on E, S and G risk management. The majority (67 per cent) dedicated less than 5 per cent of their time to E, S and G matters; 33 per cent spent from 2 to 20 per cent; none spent over 20 per cent of their time.

Despite the challenges, there is growing interest in the topic, with increasing numbers of practitioners signing up for relevant educational courses. Operational risk professionals need to continue to meaningfully embed E, S and G factors into their framework, working in collaboration with other units and assertively claiming a seat at the corporate E, S and G table.

Practical workplace exercise

Reflecting on the content of this chapter, review how your firm integrates E, S and G factors into its operational risk framework, considering the following:

- Does the scope include all the three letters of the acronym or the climate-related component only?

- In the operational risk context, is *climate* treated as a *risk* or as a *cause* of other risks materializing?

- Has the exposure to risks stemming from E, S and G-related drivers been ascertained via the use of operational risk tools, as described in this chapter?

- Is the Operational Risk department collaborating well with the Sustainability and other teams?

- What works well? Make notes of the progress made and features that work well and deliver value.

- What can be improved? Note down potential future enhancements.

MAKE A DIFFERENCE (MAD) ACTION

Please note down one action that you will take after reading this chapter that will meaningfully enhance the integration of E, S and G-related risks into the operational risk framework in your organization.

In summary, this chapter focused on practical ways to address the pertinent topic of managing the risks emanating from E, S and G factors, focusing on the effective integration of those risks within the operational risk framework.

The next chapter will discuss operational resilience, a subject that has also achieved a significant degree of focus from firms and regulators, and outline its links with operational risk management.

Notes

1. McKinsey (2022) *Does ESG really matter – and why?*, www.mckinsey.com/ capabilities/sustainability/our-insights/does-esg-really-matter-and-why (archived at https://perma.cc/PF65-CNPL)
2. The Economist (2022) *ESG should be boiled down to one simple measure: emissions*, www.economist.com/leaders/2022/07/21/esg-should-be-boiled-down-to-one-simple-measure-emissions (archived at https://perma.cc/4EL8-VR46)
3. United Nations, Department of Economic and Social Affairs, eur-lex.europa.eu/EN/legal-content/glossary/sustainable-development.html (archived at https://perma.cc/2G78-K6K7)
4. S&P Global (2020) *What is the 'G' in ESG?*, www.spglobal.com/en/research-insights/articles/what-is-the-g-in-esg (archived at https://perma.cc/HV7L-HRTC)
5. McKinsey (2022) *Does ESG really matter – and why?*, www.mckinsey.com/ capabilities/sustainability/our-insights/does-esg-really-matter-and-why (archived at https://perma.cc/PF65-CNPL)
6. Bank for International Settlement (BIS) (2020) *Deconstructing ESG scores: How to invest with your own criteria*, www.bis.org/publ/work1008.pdf (archived at https://perma.cc/74J8-PEL2)

7 Guthrie, J (2022) *ESG is a category error that needs unbundling*, *Financial Times*, www.ft.com/content/c8b11672-4847-44ae-b132-788cb2383a2c (archived at https://perma.cc/AN6D-86G5)

8 Center for Financial Professionals (CefPro) (2023) *Non-Financial Risk (NFR) Leaders*, www.cefpro.com/nfr-leaders/#1452775774465-27c1e69f-9d41 (archived at https://perma.cc/QSV6-BQ58)

9 Center for Financial Professionals (CefPro) (2023) *Non-Financial Risk (NFR) Leaders*, www.cefpro.com/nfr-leaders/#1452775774465-27c1e69f-9d41 (archived at https://perma.cc/QSV6-BQ58)

10 Basel committee on Banking Supervision (2022) *Principles for the effective management and supervision of climate-related financial risks*, www.bis.org/bcbs/publ/d532.pdf (archived at https://perma.cc/87UK-J6MW)

11 European Banking Authority (2021) *Report on Management and Supervision of ESG Risks for Credit Institutions and Investment Firms*, www.eba.europa.eu/sites/default/documents/files/document_library/Publications/Reports/2021/1015656/EBA%20Report%20on%20ESG%20risks%20management%20and%20supervision.pdf (archived at https://perma.cc/H6U8-8WD8)

12 European Banking Authority (2024) *Draft Guidelines on the management of ESG risks*, www.eba.europa.eu/sites/default/files/2024-01/c94fd865-6990-4ba8-b74e-6d8ef73d8ea5/Consultation%20papaer%20on%20draft%20Guidelines%20on%20ESG%20risks%20management.pdf (archived at https://perma.cc/7PG2-CNUD)

13 European Banking Authority (2021) *Report on Management and Supervision of ESG risks for Credit Institutions and Investment firms*, www.eba.europa.eu/sites/default/documents/files/document_library/Publications/Reports/2021/1015656/EBA%20Report%20on%20ESG%20risks%20management%20and%20supervision.pdf (archived at https://perma.cc/H6U8-8WD8)

14 Center for Financial Professionals (CefPro) (2022) *ESG State of Play: Banks' Compliance and Automated Reporting Trends*, www.workiva.com/resources/esg-state-play-banks-compliance-and-automated-reporting-trends (archived at https://perma.cc/MHP7-MLC7)

15 European Central Bank, *ECB priorities 2024–2026*, www.bankingsupervision.europa.eu/banking/priorities/html/ssm.supervisory_priorities202312~a15d5d36ab.en.html (archived at https://perma.cc/NM7L-6B73)

16 Basel committee on Banking Supervision (2022) *Frequently asked questions on climate-related financial risks*, www.bis.org/bcbs/publ/d543.pdf (archived at https://perma.cc/JWP6-BJ4C)

17 European Banking Authority (2022) *Good practices for climate-related and environmental risk management*, www.bankingsupervision.europa.eu/ecb/pub/pdf/ssm.thematicreviewcercompendiumgoodpractices112022~b474fb8ed0.en.pdf (archived at https://perma.cc/E47Z-JPAM)

18 Operational Risk e-Xchange Data Association (ORX) (2022) *Climate and Operational Risk: The ORX Approach*, 5992322.fs1.hubspotusercontent-na1.net/ hubfs/5992322/Website/Resources/Member%20reports/2022/ORX%20 Climate%20Operational%20Risk%20-%20The%20ORX%20Approach%20 2022.pdf (archived at https://perma.cc/NB95-53YK)

19 IRM, *Climate Change Risk Management Guidance*, www.theirm.org/ media/2516912/climate-change-risk-management-guidance-report.pdf (archived at https://perma.cc/VTG9-V7AD)

20 Basel committee on Banking Supervision (2022) *Principles for the effective management and supervision of climate-related financial risks*, www.bis.org/ bcbs/publ/d532.pdf (archived at https://perma.cc/87UK-J6MW)

21 Airmic (2022) *Risk and resilience in a perfect storm*, www.airmic.com/system/ files/technical-documents/Airmic%20survey%20report%202022%20A%20 Perfect%20Storm.pdf (archived at https://perma.cc/N755-GZAF)

22 Guthrie, J (2022) *ESG is a category error that needs unbundling*, *Financial Times*, www.ft.com/content/c8b11672-4847-44ae-b132-788cb2383a2c (archived at https://perma.cc/AN6D-86G5)

23 European Banking Authority (2021) *Report on Management and Supervision of ESG Risks for Credit Institutions and Investment Firms*, www.eba.europa. eu/sites/default/documents/files/document_library/Publications/Reports/ 2021/1015656/EBA%20Report%20on%20ESG%20risks%20manage- ment%20and%20supervision.pdf (archived at https://perma.cc/H6U8-8WD8)

24 S&P Global (2019) *General Motors faces a new breed of strike*, www.spglobal. com/marketintelligence/en/news-insights/latest-news-headlines/54431339 (archived at https://perma.cc/BDW7-7EHB)

25 S&P Global (2020) *What is the 'S' in ESG?*, www.spglobal.com/en/research- insights/articles/what-is-the-s-in-esg (archived at https://perma.cc/Q3TD- XGV7)

26 S&P Global (2019) *Walmart's halt on gun, ammo sales could woo socially minded consumers, investors*, www.spglobal.com/marketintelligence/en/ news-insights/latest-news-headlines/54330232 (archived at https://perma. cc/2WNX-QTMK)

27 S&P Global (2020) *What is the 'S' in ESG?*, www.spglobal.com/en/research- insights/articles/what-is-the-s-in-esg (archived at https://perma.cc/Q3TD- XGV7)

28 Guthrie, J (2022) *ESG is a category error that needs unbundling*, *Financial Times*, www.ft.com/content/c8b11672-4847-44ae-b132-788cb2383a2c (archived at https://perma.cc/AN6D-86G5)

29 S&P Global (2018) *Shareholders push Facebook for change, Facebook pushes back*, www.spglobal.com/marketintelligence/en/news-insights/latest-news- headlines/shareholders-push-facebook-for-change-facebook-pushes-back- 44261008 (archived at https://perma.cc/32XD-GSX5)

30 S&P Global (2020) *What is the 'G' in ESG?*, www.spglobal.com/en/research-insights/articles/what-is-the-g-in-esg (archived at https://perma.cc/HV7L-HRTC)

31 S&P Global (2020) *WeWork slipping into 'negative spiral' as IPO hopes dim*, www.spglobal.com/marketintelligence/en/news-insights/latest-news-headlines/54444907 (archived at https://perma.cc/N8MC-Y6Y2)

32 S&P Global (2020) *What is the 'G' in ESG?*, www.spglobal.com/en/research-insights/articles/what-is-the-g-in-esg (archived at https://perma.cc/HV7L-HRTC)

33 Organization for Economic Co-operation and Development OECD (2023) *Principles of Corporate Governance*, www.oecd-ilibrary.org/sites/ed750b30-en/index.html?itemId=/content/publication/ed750b30-en (archived at https://perma.cc/6JMV-DBPL)

34 KPMG (2022) *Great ESG expectations*, kpmg.com/xx/en/home/insights/2022/08/kpmg-2022-ceo-outlook/esg-and-diversity-trends.html (archived at https://perma.cc/FR9Q-4TFD)

35 Basel Committee on Banking Supervision (2021) *Climate-related risk drivers and their transmission channels*, www.bis.org/bcbs/publ/d517.pdf (archived at https://perma.cc/9ULC-F84Z)

Operational resilience

15

What this chapter covers: The chapter introduces the topic of Operational Resilience, a subject that has achieved a prominent degree of focus from firms and regulators in recent years, particularly due to technology disruptions, third-party failures and in the light of the Covid-19 pandemic. The chapter confirms that resilience has close links with the operational risk discipline and presents a call for action for operational risk teams to reach out, get involved and actively collaborate with resilience experts, to achieve a joined-up approach which is much needed in this space. The chapter includes industry benchmarks and the results of live polls which support the call for action.

FURTHER READING

- Basel Committee on Banking Supervision (2021) *Principles for Operational Resilience*

  Why recommended: Key document on operational resilience, on which national supervisors often base their own requirements. Essential for risk management practitioners, in addition to local regulatory guidance.

- Australian Prudential Regulation Authority (APRA) (2023) Prudential Standard CPS230, Operational Risk Management

  Why recommended: An especially positive feature of the Australian approach is the inclusion of operational resilience requirements in their core operational risk management principles, emphasizing the close links between the two disciplines. In addition, the standard contains useful examples of how critical operations and tolerances for disruption can be articulated, which is helpful for both risk and resilience practitioners.

- Bank of England (2021) *Impact Tolerances for Important Business Services,* and Financial Conduct Authority (2021) *Building Operational Resilience*

  Why recommended: These documents by UK regulators provide valuable insights on how to achieve the key elements of an operational resilience framework *in practice.*

Operational resilience: a step up from its predecessor

Business continuity planning (BCP) has always been a part of the agenda of financial services firms, and an important component of the sound practices for the management of operational risk. And in a similar way to operational risk, it has always faced the challenge of being perceived as a rather administrative domain. Traditional business continuity activities, by way of illustration, included completing a periodic business impact analysis, refreshing and testing the arrangements on an annual basis, and requesting employees to print and duly store a copy of the plan at home.

With increasing digitalization and reliance on technology, over the years the risk of serious disruptions has led to business continuity gaining more focus and upping its game. To combat what the Bank for International Settlements (BIS) calls 'vulnerabilities brought about by technological change and an increasingly hostile cyber environment',[1] firms have augmented the depth of their recovery capabilities and doubled the frequency of their testing.

Subsequently the Covid-19 pandemic somewhat refocused what was primarily a technology-related resilience discussion to include broader considerations on firms' preparedness, including their most important asset: their people. Covid-19 proved that many firms could quickly adapt and transfer their entire business operation to a home-working environment, support their employees and maintain service continuity. This was an extraordinary achievement. Indeed the European Banking Authority has recognized publicly that 'banks proved their resiliency', and accordingly assessed operational resilience in the second quarter of 2020 as merely a medium-level risk, with a stable trend.[2]

But despite the undoubted accomplishment, is it too early to claim victory? Four years on in 2024, the European Banking Authority warned that

Table 15.1   Operational resilience is a step up from its predecessor, business continuity

Response	% of responses
Yes, a significant step up	62
Yes, somewhat	29
Same, a different name	9

information and communication technology (ICT) risks, IT security risks and cyber-related risks remain highly relevant, and that the 'volume and frequency of cyber-attacks is unabatedly high'.[3] In Australia, after 'a cyber attack at its biggest port operator… brought supply chains to a standstill',[4] as reported by Reuters, the government released its 2023–2030 Cyber Security Strategy, which includes the aim of becoming a 'resilient region'.[5] In the US, following a highly disruptive ransomware attack, the Commodity Futures Trading Commission proposed new cybersecurity rules for brokerages and swaps dealers, to 'bolster that foundational framework to promote operational resilience in the face of increasingly sophisticated cyber-attacks and heightened technological disruptions'.[6]

Is the resilience dialogue therefore shifting again, towards primarily combating technology-related threats? And is operational resilience now clearly seen as a prominent area of focus, which requires continued attention?

In 2024, I ran a LinkedIn poll for my network of risk and resilience professionals asking whether operational resilience was a step up from its predecessor, business continuity. The results presented in Table 15.1 demonstrate that the vast majority of respondents (91 per cent) agreed, and out of these 62 per cent perceived resilience to be a *significant* step up; while only a minority (9 per cent) viewed it as merely a *name change*.

OPERATIONAL RESILIENCE DEFINITION

While multiple definitions exist, the Basel Committee defines operational resilience as the ability to 'deliver critical operations through disruption', which enables a firm to 'identify and protect itself from threats and potential failures, respond and adapt to, as well as recover and learn from disruptive events'.[7]

It can easily be argued that operational risk management supports the operational as well as financial resilience of an institution. The *identification and protection* aspects of the above definition, in particular, are based on prudent and proactive risk management: recognizing, examining and mitigating threats and vulnerabilities. By assuming that disruptions are inevitable and will eventually occur, post-event detective and corrective controls help firms to respond, recover and learn from incidents. Resilience implies building strength, not just the ability to continue as before. Resilience requirements go further than business continuity, as will be seen below, and therefore operational resilience certainly represents a welcome addition and a step forward from business continuity:

Operational Resilience ≠ Business Continuity

And, as noted by the Basel Committee in its 2021 Principles for Operational Resilience:[8]

Operational Resilience ❯ Outcome of
Operational Risk Management

So, the topics of risk and resilience are indeed interconnected. Indeed historically, in many organizations the role of the Operational Risk department included overseeing – or even leading – its business continuity efforts. It is important to further explore these connections, especially as industry polls demonstrate that operational risk professionals appear to be struggling to find their optimum role in this stepped-up resilience domain (also see Chapter 16).

Integrating operational risk and resilience

The operational resilience lifecycle can be described in Figure 15.1. Let's review some of these sub-components in more detail.

Maintain robust frameworks (Step 1)

Operational resilience relies on and converges core organizational frameworks, including ICT/cyber and third-party risk – these being prominent operational risk sub-categories – as well as business continuity planning, a key control that mitigates operational risk failures. These frameworks collectively build a foundation of solid risk and control management, and

Figure 15.1   Operational resilience lifecycle

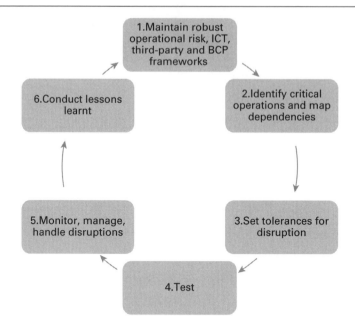

hence enable the firm's preparedness to withstand disruptions. If these frameworks are in place and functioning, the job is already half done.

There are many areas within these frameworks where risk and resilience professionals can cooperate effectively. These include defining governance arrangements, preferably using existing structures such as the operational resilience forum, mentioned in Chapter 1, in addition to the risk committee and the board for effective oversight of resilience. They also include agreeing roles and responsibilities across the Three Lines, as well as putting continuous effort into ensuring that the frameworks operate effectively, via monitoring, conducting control testing and thematic reviews.

Critical operations and their dependencies (Step 2)

As a further significant step to becoming resilient, an organization needs to achieve a shift in its mindset, developing a view of the firm from 'outside-in', in other words how a customer would see it. From the client's perspective, when an expected service is not delivered or a commitment is not met, the question of whether the process broke down within the firm's operations, technology or due to third-party failure is neither important nor visible. It is

Figure 15.2   Critical operation dependencies

only the availability of the end product – the fact of the failure – that matters. In this light, it is becoming increasingly important for firms to understand their end-to-end mission-critical services, and all their related dependencies, in order to make a solid commitment to clients that these services will continue to be delivered even during a disruption. In addition to policies and frameworks, this necessitates harnessing an end-to-end customer-centric mentality; one in which employees look out beyond their own narrow silos to the overall impact on the end-client. This is presented in Figure 15.2.

Arguably, this is one of the enhancements that operational resilience brings compared to business continuity, in which a departmental approach is often applied. A departmental approach tends to be more siloed, with every unit outlining their own requirements, rather than a holistic, end-to-end view driven by the perspective of what is important to the *end-customer*. Against this background, there are number potential areas for collaboration between risk and resilience functions.

Identifying critical operations

While the terminology may differ, mission critical services (referred to as *critical operations* throughout the rest of this chapter) are the essential core services of the firm, the disruption of which would have a material impact on the operation of the firm, its customers or even the economy more broadly. Critical operations are dependent on people, facilities, technology, information and third parties – and these interconnections need to be carefully identified and documented. Fortunately the laborious task of defining critical operations and mapping their dependencies may have already been accomplished, at least in part, in the implementation of the operational risk framework. This is especially so if, as discussed in Chapter 5, process risk self-assessments (PRSAs) have been applied across the enterprise, enabling an end-to-end view of key processes.

But it may be that it is resilience colleagues, instead, who initiate the journey of documenting and inventorying the resources that deliver and support the firm's critical operations. Indeed many organizations have made good progress in this area as part of enhancing their financial resilience and complying with regulatory requirements around recovery and resolution planning. Financial resilience regulations in many jurisdictions preceded the issuance of operational resilience rules. That said, both form part of the same resilience continuum, with incidents and disruptions at the business-as-usual end of the scale, and resolution at the extreme end of the spectrum. Resolution and day-to-day resilience have many features in common, including the notion of critical operations and their dependencies.

Irrespective, it is crucial that operational risk teams also benefit from the work of resilience teams on the identification and mapping of critical operations. This is to ensure that future risk assessments are conducted on an integrated basis, and take into account the dependencies identified in the mapping process. Additionally, as noted in Chapter 5, cross-functional process mapping exercises can help to optimize effectiveness and increase process efficiency.

Developing a customer-centric mentality

In additional to formal policies and process maps, the topic of resilience has an equally (if not more) important *softer aspect*. Employees on the ground need to improve their understanding of how what they do impacts the whole critical operations supply chain and the firm's external customers. If staff can visualize this kind of interconnectedness, it enables more thoughtful and robust preventative action, and speedier, more coherent responses. Do employees have a solid understanding of their firm's critical operations, and do they apply a customer-centric mentality? And if not, what training and education needs to be provided by risk and resilience colleagues to enhance it? Operational risk teams are already in the habit of delivering staff education, which provides an excellent opportunity to incorporate resilience components, rather than creating two separate training programmes. Additionally, at a practical level, it is beneficial to link the OREs discussed in Chapter 4 to critical operations, by adding a dedicated field in the ORE reporting form presented in Appendix 2. Staff will be asked to consider whether the incident they are logging has in fact resulted in a disruption of a *critical operation*. This should demonstrate either a solid understanding of critical operations, or the absence of it (for example if employees repeatedly question the meaning of the field 'what are critical operations?'). In this way, a need for further training can be identified.

Consequently, areas for active teamwork between operational risk and resilience colleagues should include the review – or even restructuring – of existing RCSAs to extract meaningful risk information on critical operations, as well as jointly enhancing a customer-centric mentality among employees.

Tolerance for disruption and testing (Steps 3 and 4)

Another opportunity for collaboration presents itself when setting tolerances for disruption and testing resilience capabilities. Tolerances articulate the maximum level of disruption the organization is willing to accept, including the duration of the disruption, and need to be determined in connection to the firm's risk appetite. (Regulatory guidance differs across jurisdictions on how these two concepts interact; namely, whether tolerance is *within* the risk appetite or if it applies at the extreme end after the appetite has been *exceeded*.) Risk and resilience professionals need to work together to ensure that risk appetite, discussed in Chapter 9, especially relating to ICT/cyber and third-party risk, is not in contradiction with the firm's tolerances. Tolerances represent another step beyond business continuity, recovery time objectives (RTOs) and recovery point objectives (RPOs) – which are usually set at the lower level of the tolerance range and tend to express desired outcomes that are achieved with high probability.

Additionally, setting and testing tolerances requires firms to think through a range of severe but plausible scenarios. As outlined in Figure 15.3, this creates a meaningful overlap between the operational risk and resilience universes.

Story lines in the operational risk space may well touch on themes such as fraud, regulatory non-compliance or employment lawsuits. While these are important topics to explore, they do not necessarily impact a firm's resilience capabilities.

In turn, major breakdowns of external infrastructure might be considered in order to proactively develop contingency measures and review potential alternative means of operating. These kinds of scenarios may not be required for operational risk capital purposes, as a firm can hardly

Figure 15.3   Operational risk and resilience scenarios

Operational Risk
- Internal/external fraud
- Execution, e.g., payment errors
- Regulatory non-compliance
- Employment lawsuits

Overlap
- Cyber attack
- Third-party failure
- People unavailability
- The *E* in E, S and G, e.g., climate-related disaster
- Technology failure

Operational resilience
- Failure of external infrastructure
- Failure of correspondent

be expected to hold capital against the risk of external failures such as unavailability of the power supply or the national payments network.

Consequently, the area of overlap consists of several topics of mutual interest. These might include:

- Cyber attacks, leading to data theft, corruption or system unavailability;

- Third-party failures;

- People unavailability;

- The E component of ESG, for example climate-driven disasters resulting in the destruction of premises; and

- Legacy technology failures.

Risk and resilience scenarios are aiming for different outputs: expected financial loss in the case of operational risk; and estimated disruption in terms of, for example, duration, transaction volume or data loss in addition to potential expenditure in the case of operational resilience. Nevertheless, there are common themes that are relevant for both domains. By working together, the two teams can align their scenario story lines, enriching the whole experience on both sides and providing benefits for the firm overall.

In Chapter 8, the importance of using scenarios for *risk management* purposes was discussed, including taking actions to improve the control environment. This approach and philosophy are even more crucial for resilience purposes, where firms – in particular, boards and senior management – should be prioritizing their investment decisions on the basis of identified weaknesses that can threaten their ability to provide important business services. Developing scenario story lines, jointly running workshops with stakeholders to avoid duplication, and using operational risk structure, techniques and expert facilitation are all viable areas for conducting group work for risk and resilience colleagues.

Monitor environment, manage disruptions and learn lessons (Steps 5 and 6)

In order to remain within tolerances on an ongoing basis, it is critical to be able to avoid and recover from disruptions within set time frames and parameters, and to proactively identify and manage threats and vulnerabilities. As discussed in Chapter 1, each firm must decide how operational resilience fits into its taxonomy, enabling transparent and meaningful information flows across the organization. An example of a resilience dashboard is presented in Figure 15.4. This dashboard displays essential risk and control indicators by critical operation, based on their dependencies, which enables the firm to manage risk proactively.

Back to the topic of shifting mentality, organizations need to apply a critical operations lens to these reports, displaying the kind of information which enables an end-to-end view. This is a challenging task, because in reality departments tend to both operate and report in silos.

Figure 15.4 Operational resilience reporting dashboard

Critical Operation: X					
People		+	**Facilities**		+
Metric 1	**AMBER**	Remedial action:	Metric 1	**GREEN**	
Metric 2	**GREEN**		Metric 2	**GREEN**	
Technology and Information		+	**Third Parties**		+
Metric 1	**AMBER**	Remedial action:	Metric 1	**RED**	Remedial action:
Metric 2	**AMBER**	Remedial action:	Metric 2	**AMBER**	Remedial action:

Another area for potential interaction between resilience and risk was described in Chapter 4, Operational risk events. Organizations can look to implement a *single notification route* for material disruptive events, whether IT-related or not. The channel used for reporting of operational risk *material events* can clearly be followed for swift escalation, enabling firms to respond more quickly to an event as well as communicate promptly with customers, employees and regulators. Also, as mentioned earlier, the ORE process can be enhanced to establish a closer link to critical operations.

And last but not least: *lessons learnt* that are useful for operational resilience purposes may already exist in the operational risk space, for example, from OREs. The structure, format and rigour of the risk event management process can be replicated for resilience purposes, and in fact, implemented on an enterprise-wide basis.

So there are numerous areas where collaboration can be improved, including enhancing reporting capabilities to effectively monitor and manage threats and vulnerabilities; jointly developing response protocols and channels for the escalation of threats; and instituting a structured 'lessons learnt' process for operational resilience.

CALL FOR ACTION

In conclusion, this is a call for action for operational risk professionals to reach out and engage with operational resilience colleagues to:

- Treat operational resilience as an outcome of operational risk management, recognizing the strong links between the two disciplines;

- Collaborate on all aspects of the resilience lifecycle to ensure alignment;

- Focus on ICT/cyber and third party as significant operational risk sub-categories that pose an increased threat to resilience; and conduct control testing, deep dives and thematic reviews in these areas;

- Engage with the board to deliver a transparent view on resilience, and assist in prioritizing and targeting investments to enhance it;

- Continuously develop your own expertise, by studying relevant regulatory and industry developments.

Finally, a few observations on particular areas of regulatory focus on resilience.

Continued regulatory focus on operational resilience

There are many commonalities among the different regulatory approaches to operational resilience, including agreement that there is a clear need for enhancement in this area. As noted by the Basel Committee, 'further work is necessary to strengthen banks' ability to absorb operational risk-related events, such as pandemics, cyber incidents, technology failures and natural disasters'.[9] This creates a strong case for continued collaborative teamwork between risk and resilience professionals in the foreseeable future.

Many national supervisors have adopted – or are closely basing their requirements on – the Basel Committee Principles issued in 2021. The challenge for operational risk and resilience professionals in global firms lies in integrating and converging various different national nuances:

- In the EU, the Digital Operational Resilience Act (DORA)[10] is a notable piece of legislation that explicitly focuses on the technological aspect, concentrating on the resilience of critical ICT. Topics of particular focus in DORA include incident reporting, digital operational resilience testing and third-party requirements, where standards have certainly been elevated. With DORA coming into effect in 2025, there is urgency for firms in its implementation.

- This focus on the ICT aspect of resilience is also apparent in the US, where regulatory authorities have adopted a consolidated regime for systemically important organizations via the jointly issued Sound Practices to Strengthen Operational Resilience.[11] This document specifically lists recommended practices for cyber risk management, with references to frameworks such as the National Institute of Standards and Technology Cybersecurity Framework (NIST),[12] and the Federal Financial Institutions Examinations Council (FFIEC) Cybersecurity Assessment Tool.[13] These tools serve to underscore the prominence of technology-related resilience in the regulatory domain.

- In the UK, the focus has been on holistic resilience, whether technology-related or more broadly. In many ways the UK and its regulators can be thought of as introducing measures to ensure operational resilience ahead of the Basel Committee on Banking Supervision (BCBS) and other regulators. While this encouraged early focus on this important topic, it has also resulted in a partial disconnect with the BCBS approach, with, for example, the UK considering:

o *Important Business Services* while the BCBS discuss *critical operations*;

o *Impact tolerances* (the maximum tolerable level of disruption for the PRA and the point at which the disruption would cause intolerable harm to consumers for the FCA) while the BCBS refer to an overall risk appetite for tolerance and disruption.

Nevertheless, joint regulatory papers[14,15] published in the UK have proved valuable in providing a level of insight into how firms might strengthen their operational resilience by including useful examples of scenarios that can be used for setting and testing tolerances for disruption. Arguably, the strength of the UK contribution is its ability to answer the question *what might this look like in practice*, while its weakness is its detachment from operational risk management, which is mentioned only in passing.

• In contrast, the approach adopted by the Australian Prudential Regulation Authority (APRA) is to include operational resilience requirements in its operational risk management principles,[16] instead of issuing them in a separate document. This approach serves to emphasize the close links between the two disciplines. The Australian guidelines also helpfully stipulate what activities, at a minimum, must be defined as *critical operations* (for example, payments, deposit-taking and management, custody, settlements and clearing). This directive approach is particularly beneficial as many organizations operating under less prescriptive regimes found it challenging to calibrate the level of granularity at which critical operations should be defined. *Tolerance levels*, another somewhat ambiguous concept, are also explicitly articulated in the APRA requirements, requiring firms to focus on the *maximum period of disruption time, maximum extent of data loss and minimum service level during the disruption*.

Clearly, then, various different international guidelines already contain strong and effective features which can help practitioners and enhance their practices. Inevitably, organizations that adopt these approaches and practices, and continue to invest in building sound resilience capabilities – with risk and resilience practitioners working hand-in-hand – will emerge stronger than their peers, and better prepared to withstand any subsequent disruptions.

Industry benchmark

In 2024, Best Practice Operational Risk Forum members ranked top operational risks in order of significance (see Figure 15.5). The poll highlighted operational resilience as a prominent theme. Seven out of nine risks were interconnected and revolved around technology, presenting a net of potential technology-related threats to organizational resilience.

- *Cyber risk* remains a major threat to resilience, and is predicted to remain prominent in the risk charts for the foreseeable future. It is closely linked with *third-party risk*, due to an increased reliance on service providers to deliver technology-related services. In turn, *Generative AI*, a new entrant on the risk charts in 2024, has appeared due to growing concerns in a number of areas, including intellectual property/copyright and exploitation by malicious actors to create sophisticated cyber attacks.

- When it comes to *change and execution*, this is largely technology-driven, whether migrating to the cloud, replacing legacy technology, integrating

Figure 15.5   Industry poll: top operational risks 2024

Rank Top Operational Risks 2024

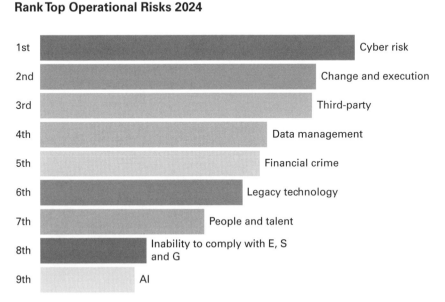

Best Practice Operational Risk Forum, 2024

new with old or outsourcing to a third-party. Poor change and integration could, in turn, cause *legacy technology failure*, resulting in potential customer and market detriment.

- With increased digitalization and reliance on systems, the amount of *data* being used by firms continues to increase significantly. Whether residing on new or legacy systems, data mis-management can result in breaches, loss and corruption.

- All risks have a *people* component, related to *skill set, succession and well-being*. A prominent feature of that people component is key person dependency in the area of IT support, where the demand for skilled professionals far exceeds the available talent pool.

- Arguably, two remaining risks, *financial crime*, an inherent risk in financial services, and *inability to comply with E, S and G requirements* due to increasing regulatory and societal pressures, have less impact on operational resilience.

On a more basic level – despite the high level of awareness and preparedness observed over the course of the Covid-19 pandemic, when resilience was at the forefront of everyone's mind – familiarity with continuity planning has declined since then, as demonstrated in Figure 15.6. In 2023, only a small portion (12 per cent) of risk and resilience practitioners attending an operational resilience industry conference were confident that the majority of staff in their firms were closely familiar with BCP, implying yet again the need for ongoing training and awareness sessions, walk-throughs and simulations.

Figure 15.6   Industry poll: employee familiarity with BCP

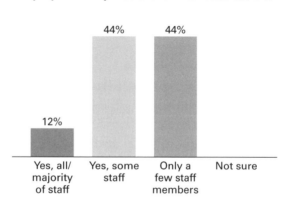

Employees in my area are familiar with the BCP

Operational resilience industry conference, 2023

At the same industry conference, confidence in firms' business continuity planning was also mixed, with 43 per cent feeling that their BCP plan provides clear guidance and addresses a variety of scenarios; while the remaining 57 per cent admitted that more work was needed, and that plans were of limited scope and would benefit from further guidance. This especially applied to technology-related topics covering cyber attacks, data corruption or system unavailability. On a positive note, 78 per cent of respondents confirmed that they were able to reach their staff promptly in an emergency situation, as updated employee lists are continuing to be well maintained.

Overall, these discussions clearly reflect the fact that resilience remains a prominent topic for financial services firms. Displaying agility, leadership and situational awareness, operational risk professionals must collaborate with resilience colleagues to embrace the evolving risk landscape, reaching across the silos to achieve effective risk management; and as an outcome, build more resilient organizations.

Great momentum was achieved during the Covid-19 pandemic, with risk and resilience clearly working in closer collaboration than ever before. There is no doubt that carrying forward this momentum and energy will be hugely beneficial for organizations in future years.

MAKE A DIFFERENCE (MAD) ACTION

Please note down one action that you will take after reading this chapter that will meaningfully enhance the integration of risk and resilience practices in your organization.

In summary, this chapter discussed the importance of operational risk practitioners getting involved in firms' operational resilience activities, searching for synergies and implementing joint solutions.

Moving on, the final chapter will reflect on the future of the operational risk discipline and how key operational risk priorities can be rebalanced so that risk practitioners remain well positioned to face new challenges.

Notes

1 Bank for International Settlements (2020) FSI Briefs, *Covid-19 and Operational Resilience: Addressing financial institutions' operational challenges in a pandemic*, www.bis.org/fsi/fsibriefs2.pdf (archived at https://perma.cc/H3WC-4EB5)

2 European Banking Authority (2020) Risk dashboard data as of Q2 2020, www.eba.europa.eu/sites/default/documents/files/document_library/Risk%20 Analysis%20and%20Data/Risk%20dashboard/Q2%202020/933053/EBA%20 Dashboard%20-%20Q2%202020.pdf (archived at https://perma.cc/VL9T-7STP)

3 European Banking Authority (2020) Risk dashboard data as of Q3 2023, www.eba.europa.eu/sites/default/files/2024-01/8039a4ea-6e61-45a9-a746-058fd070c34a/EBA%20Dashboard%20-%20Q3%202023.pdf (archived at https://perma.cc/U4WG-WQPW)

4 Kaye, B (2023) *Australia beefs up cyber defences after major breaches*, Reuters, www.reuters.com/technology/cybersecurity/australia-goes-cyber-offensive-with-sweeping-resilience-plan-2023-11-22/ (archived at https://perma.cc/X8EQ-9LEP)

5 Australian Government, *2023–2030 Australian Cyber Security Strategy*, www.homeaffairs.gov.au/about-us/our-portfolios/cyber-security/strategy/2023-2030-australian-cyber-security-strategy (archived at https://perma.cc/9BLP-3Y4V)

6 Beyoud, L (2023) *Ion hack spurs new cybersecurity push for swaps dealers, brokers*, Bloomberg, www.bloomberg.com/news/articles/2023-12-13/us-regulator-floats-cybersecurity-plan-in-response-to-ion-hack?leadSource=uverify%20wall (archived at https://perma.cc/T9XM-H3ZE)

7 Basel Committee on Banking Supervision (2021) *Principles for Operational Resilience*, www.bis.org/bcbs/publ/d516.pdf (archived at https://perma.cc/CFM7-KSKT)

8 Basel Committee on Banking Supervision (2021) *Principles for Operational Resilience*, www.bis.org/bcbs/publ/d516.pdf (archived at https://perma.cc/CFM7-KSKT)

9 Basel Committee on Banking Supervision (2021) *Principles for Operational Resilience*, www.bis.org/bcbs/publ/d516.pdf (archived at https://perma.cc/ CFM7-KSKT)

10 Digital Operational Resilience Act (DORA), www.digital-operational-resilience-act.com/DORA_Articles.html (archived at https://perma.cc/QY6D-DWL5)

11 Office of the Comptroller of the Currency OCC (2020) *Sound Practices to Strengthen Operational Resilience*, www.occ.gov/news-issuances/news-releases/2020/nr-occ-2020-144a.pdf (archived at https://perma.cc/XLT7-EUGJ)

12 National Institute of Standards and Technology (NIST), Cybersecurity Framework, www.nist.gov/cyberframework (archived at https://perma.cc/4T4J-KVGT)

13 Federal Financial Institutions Examinations Council (FFIEC), Cybersecurity Assessment Tool, www.ffiec.gov/cyberassessmenttool.htm (archived at https:// perma.cc/Y9Z6-SFTZ)

14 Bank of England (2021) *Impact Tolerances for Important Business Services*, www.bankofengland.co.uk/-/media/boe/files/prudential-regulation/policy-statement/2021/march/ps621.pdf (archived at https://perma.cc/KA6X-S7DH)

15 Financial Conduct Authority (2021) *Building Operational Resilience*, www.fca. org.uk/publication/policy/ps21-3-operational-resilience.pdf (archived at https:// perma.cc/DNZ7-FF4W)

16 Australian Prudential Regulation Authority (APRA) (2023) *Prudential Standard CPS 230, Operational Risk Management*, www.apra.gov.au/sites/ default/files/2023-07/Prudential%20Standard%20CPS%20230%20 Operational%20Risk%20Management%20-%20clean.pdf (archived at https:// perma.cc/MC59-68KY)

Reflections on the future of the operational risk discipline

16

What this chapter covers: The chapter reflects on the topical challenges facing operational risk management, and considers the role of the second line risk management function in technical areas such as third-party and cyber risk. It argues that the operational risk discipline is in fact not disintegrating as some commentators have suggested, and that risk professionals are adding significant value as *connectors*: collaborating, reaching across silos and streamlining processes. The chapter also examines the risks and opportunities associated with generative AI, and encourages risk professionals to invest time exploring this subject. Finally, it reflects on how key operational risk priorities can be rebalanced to enable risk practitioners to remain well positioned to face new challenges. The chapter is largely based on a series of recent live polls which reflect the industry's stance on the subjects under discussion.

FURTHER READING

There is no specific reading suggested for this particular chapter, other than daily news stories, which are an essential source of information given that new challenging topics are constantly emerging. Twenty years ago, while attending a strategic leadership programme at Oxford University, I took part in a fascinating discussion on whether a modern leader could truly be effective without being well informed. The conclusion was that was simply not feasible. Since then, I have made an effort to closely follow the news daily, including preferred sources such as the Risk Channel (noted in Chapter 11) which focus on *risk angles* in particular. I would recommend to find and follow your own preferred news sources, with a view to staying right up to date in a fast-changing world.

Think sharper, act smarter

In this final chapter, we will reflect on some of the challenges that operational risk professionals are currently facing. These challenges arise against the backdrop of a complex and evolving risk landscape which is also highly interconnected. This landscape features growing dependency on third parties, constantly increasing cyber risk and a new emerging threat emanating from generative artificial intelligence (GenAI); overlaid with climate issues and ongoing geopolitical tensions. The World Economic Forum's Global Risks Report 2024 highlights 'a predominantly negative outlook for the world over the short term that is expected to worsen over the long term', noting that 'the majority of respondents... anticipate some instability and a moderate risk of global catastrophes'.[1]

In early 2024, I ran a LinkedIn poll for my network of risk professionals asking for opinions on whether the year 2024 would be *more challenging* for operational risk teams. The majority (82 per cent) of respondents agreed, as indeed they had a year earlier, when 84 per cent of surveyed risk practitioners in my LinkedIn poll affirmed that the year 2023 would be more challenging than 2022. Justin Trudeau, the Prime Minister of Canada, once noted that 'the pace of change has never been this fast, yet it will never be this slow again',[2] highlighting that year on year the bar is being raised ever higher. In this testing environment, when demands are continuing to increase while budgets and resources (at best) remain at the same level, operational risk professionals must think sharper and act smarter. There is less room for *risk administration* and more impetus for value-added *risk management*.

Of course this shift might have been achieved already in cases where the operational risk discipline has reached its ultimate *embedded* stage, characterized by proactive risk management and an enhanced risk culture, as described in Chapter 13; allowing operational risk teams more time and resource to focus on new challenges. Yet judging from the industry work I do, risk professionals on the front line are telling a different story: namely that embedding operational risk and empowering the first line has far from reached its crux and is still very much work in progress.

On this basis, time dedicated to new challenges must be carved out of a day that is already filled to the brim with the usual *embedding* activities. So we will consider some areas where thinking sharper and acting smarter will be beneficial for the operational risk managers, helping them to re-prioritize their work and improve their effectiveness, by making greater use of tools such as AI and by collaborating more actively with other units.

Third-party and cyber: establishing the optimum second line role

We start by examining the role of the Operational Risk department in third-party and cyber risk management, two prominent risk sub-types, which, alongside the topic of operational resilience discussed in Chapter 15, appear to create the most tension for operational risk teams when it comes to roles and responsibilities.

It does appear that the second line is struggling to find its optimal position in confronting cyber risk, third-party and operational resilience, as presented in Figure 16.1. Only 9 per cent of Best Practice Operational Risk Forum members rated the role of the Operational Risk department as 'spot-on', with the rest considering either enhancement or an even a more radical re-think.

Third (and nth) party risk management

Over the past decade, many organizations have increased their engagement with suppliers in order to gain access to specialist expertise, streamline their processes and improve productivity. Consequently, firms' dependency on third parties has also grown, especially as core information technology services are now often outsourced to external cloud providers rather than hosted in-house; and the sub-outsourcing chains have become ever more complex. It is therefore not surprising that the associated risks have also

Figure 16.1   Industry poll: role of second line risk in cyber, third-party and resilience

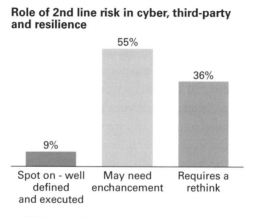

Role of 2nd line risk in cyber, third-party and resilience

Best Practice Operational Risk Forum, 2023

increased. Since 2022, *third-party risk* has appeared prominently in the top five operational risks for the financial services sector, as assessed by the Best Practice Forum. And external statistics are pointing to a need for more focus on this area, as illustrated by the following examples:

- The European Central Bank reported that in 2022 banks under its supervision lost 148 million euros 'due to unavailability or poor quality of outsourced services',[3] a 360% increase from the previous year;

- The 2023 Mid-Year Cyber Claims Report[4] reveals that 28.9% of cyber insurance claims were caused by vendor breaches, signalling the evolving tactics of bad actors in targeting companies' suppliers by using them as a gateway.

Regulators are aiming to strengthen industry practices in this area, producing directives such as the European Banking Authority guidelines on outsourcing,[5] which outlines requirements for supplier management throughout the chain of third and fourth parties. Also worth noting in this area are the EU Digital Operational Resilience Act (DORA),[6] which zooms in on critical information communication technology (ICT) arrangements; and the Australian Prudential Regulation Authority requirement to manage the risks associated with the use of service providers as a core operational risk management principle,[7] which clearly reinforces this topic as an integral part of operational risk management. Third-Party Risk Management (TPRM) has risen to prominence, with organizations increasingly recruiting TPRM specialists to embrace, comprehend and control the vast spectrum of risks in this area.

Against this background, it is paramount for operational risk professionals to exhibit leadership qualities and assert their own place in the TPRM arena.

A good foundation can be laid by reinforcing the message that the *first line units* are the ultimate owners of *their own third-party arrangements*, which are simply an extension of any arrangements they would have otherwise made for themselves; while the specialist TPRM team owns the firm's third-party policy, developing the firm's expertise in TPRM risks and working closely with business owners to ensure that robust controls are in place. In this kind of structure the Operational Risk department focuses mainly on meaningful second line activities such as scenario analysis, thematic reviews, risk appetite and metrics. An example of allocated responsibilities is presented in Table 16.1.

Table 16.1   Example responsibilities in third-party risk management

First line units/business owners	Central function (TPRM)	Second line operational risk
Own and manage third-party relationships	Owns the outsourcing/third-party risk framework	Provides oversight and challenge to the central function and business owners
Own and manage controls and mitigation measures	Maintains a centralized register of third-party arrangements	Reviews/signs off on particular arrangements (notably critical arrangements)
Conduct due diligence and monitoring	Provides training and guidance to business owners	Facilitate development of risk appetite and supporting metrics/KRIs
Raise incidents, carry out lessons learnt	Conducts control testing to check that arrangements are managed in a compliant manner	Conducts thematic reviews and facilitates scenario analysis and ORE lessons learnt
Report on KRIs/pre-defined metrics	Performs horizon scanning for new and emerging risks	Reports on the overall level of third-party risk

In reality, the roles are often neither clearly laid out, documented or explicitly agreed in the way set out in the table. For example the business owners may push back on being assigned the added duty of managing third-party arrangements (despite them being *their own* arrangements); while the central TPRM function and operational risk teams may dispute the boundary of responsibility between them. In some cases a central function may not exist, and the Operational Risk department is asked to step in and assume both roles, TPRM as well as second line oversight. In my consultancy experience, as well as from running industry forums, third-party risk management always comes up as an area of challenge. And, as reflected by the Best Practice Forum, if this challenge is not addressed promptly and decisively, it may distract all parties from actual, much needed *risk management*. This conundrum is reflected in Figure 16.2, which represents a poll from the Best Practice Forum where only 17 per cent of respondents were confident that their firm's third-party risks were fully understood, enabling their

Figure 16.2   Industry poll: understanding the third-party risk landscape

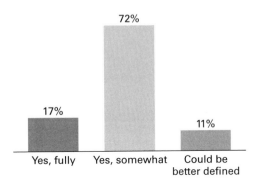

Third-party risks are well understood

Best Practice Operational Risk Forum, 2023

Figure 16.3   Industry poll: board-approved appetite for TPRM

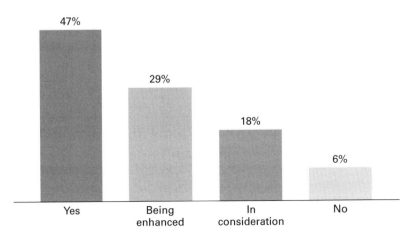

There is a board-approved risk appetite for TPRM

Best Practice Operational Risk Forum, 2023

organization to answer the vital '*so what?*' question, take necessary actions, enhance the supervision of their third-party arrangements and perhaps even exit some relationships.

On a more positive note, more firms do engage with their boards early on in the establishment of third-party relationships, developing an appetite statement and monitoring metrics, examples of which were discussed in Chapter 9. The Best Practice Forum poll highlighted in Figure 16.3 shows that 47 per cent of respondents have made good progress in this area; despite not yet having full transparency. Board engagement is particularly important if third-party risks are *not fully understood*, because in these cases an honest conversation is needed at an early stage; to agree a plan, resources and budget that enable the necessary transparency for effective decision-making. The risk appetite framework can be a very effective tool here, and KRIs can be progressively enhanced as the firm's third-party practices mature.

Ultimately, this chapter is less a step-by-step guide on how to manage the risks associated with service providers and instead addresses how operational risk practitioners might respond to the new challenges that are coming their way, such that they remain relevant and current.

Hence the call for action for operational risk teams to find their seat at the third-party risk management table, early in the process, to ensure their firm is well positioned to manage its supplier risk.

CALL FOR ACTION

Advance the effectiveness of third-party risk management by:

- Recognizing that third-party risk is a significant area requiring focus (where firm engages service providers);

- Directing organizational efforts towards *actual risk management* and away from distracting debates on roles and responsibilities; this may require influencing, bringing clarity and seeking to pacify the conflict between various parties;

- Engaging with the board and advocating for third-party risk as a topic to be prioritized;

- Identifying emerging threats in collaboration with TPRM; and

- Continuously developing their own expertise in the TPRM arena.

The fact is that operational risk professionals are a new breed of leaders who are mastering the arts of facilitation and dealing with audiences at all levels of the firm, while at the same time giving the benefit of their considerable technical expertise. They can have a positive influence and make a remarkable difference in all sorts of difficult situations. And third-party risk management is a good example of the kind of area where these skills are much needed.

Cyber-risk management

With successful attacks occurring every 0.65 seconds[8] in the US alone, cyber risk has been topping the risk charts for several years. And it is not going away in the next decade – Protiviti predicts cyber risk will occupy the top position in 2034,[9] and the World Economic Forum places it in eighth place over the same time horizon.[10]

In my experience of leading second line cyber risk teams which are accountable to the board and the regulators, I am acutely aware of how prominent and complex this area is. On the one hand, detailed technical standards such as the National Institute of Standards and Technology (NIST) Cybersecurity Framework (version 2.0, highly praised by the industry, issued in 2024)[11] need to be both studied and then rigorously applied as the basis of firms' organizational controls around cyber risk. On the other hand, relative simplicity is also needed to ensure board conversations are distilled down to the crucial questions. Is the organization exposed? Is it taking too much risk? What needs to be done? There is also a close connection to third-party risk, as discussed above, as a firm's cyber defence strategy must also extend to its service providers.

In a similar way to third-party risk, a live debate concerns the role of second line operational risk professionals. What constitutes the optimum second line capability to provide meaningful oversight and challenge, before major gaps in the firm's cyber controls emerge?

To this end, I have been leading industry discussions on the role of operational risk, investigating whether the recruitment of cyber experts into the second line Operational Risk department, in addition to first line experts, is a *must* for effective oversight. The results of a poll I ran with Best Practice Forum are presented in Table 16.2. This shows that a majority of respondents (59 per cent) opted for the duplication of expertise, while the remaining portion disagreed.

This question is directly linked to ongoing industry deliberations on the future of the operational risk discipline. Two options present themselves:

- Further specialization into niche areas of operational risk sub-types: whether cyber, third-party, model or other risk sub-categories, with diminishing use of generalists and ultimately the disintegration of operational risk as a discipline; or

- Further recognition of the uniqueness of operational risk generalist skills, and their extended use in a board advisory capacity.

Table 16.2   Is the recruitment of cyber experts in the second line Operational Risk department, in addition to first line cyber experts, a *must* for effective oversight?

Response	% of responses
Yes, absolutely	59
Not necessarily	35
No, ineffective to duplicate	6

Passionate about the operational risk discipline, and an active supporter of many experienced individuals working in this field, I am certain that operational risk professionals have a uniquely brilliant set of skills. The discipline brings a combination of a *curious mind*, a focus on the *risk angle* and the ability to *distil complex matters* into simple statements, coupled with the *soft skills* associated with dealing with people. The value of such professionals is immense, and it is no surprise that the number of CROs with an operational risk background is on the rise; whereas previously CROs came exclusively from a financial risk background, such as credit or market risk.

Returning to the particular topic of cyber risk, while IT experts are typically situated in the first line, tasked with ensuring cyber security by design, effective second line oversight can be provided by focusing on *material risks* and *key controls*. This can be achieved via a combination of mechanisms which are particularly useful in smaller-size firms. These may include accessing third-party professional firms to carry out benchmarking and cyber maturity assessment; working with insurance brokers to transfer the risk as well as identify the best cyber controls and the worst new trends; and studying the respective frameworks with a view to challenging the IT departmental RCSA and picking up on obvious gaps. It is reassuringly clear from studying formal industry frameworks such as the NIST that they are still intuitive in their construction of the key cyber controls.

In my opinion, therefore, the recruitment of cyber experts into the second line is not necessarily the answer; great generalist skills, like those displayed by the operational risk professional, and the ability to tease out and summarize material risks, are wholly complementary to detailed IT expertise, enabling the overall control framework to operate very effectively with combined collective efforts.

Figure 16.4   Industry poll: is cyber a people risk?

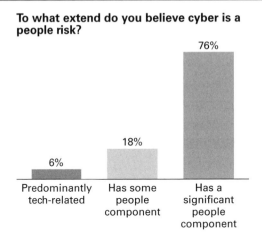

To what extend do you believe cyber is a people risk?

- Predominantly tech-related: 6%
- Has some people component: 18%
- Has a significant people component: 76%

Best Practice Operational Risk Forum, 2023

Another note on cyber risk is that it is not entirely about IT. In fact, a large proportion of the risk revolves around the human element. More than three-quarters of Best Practice Forum members concurred that cyber risk has a significant people component, as demonstrated in Figure 16.4.

As Sabine Lautenschläger, a member of the Executive Board of the ECB noted, 'we must keep in mind that cyber risk does not invariably arise from the technology itself but also from how we use it. It is people who are behind the hacking. And often, it is people who leave doors unlocked and gates wide open for cyber criminals to sneak in. People play a big role when it comes to cyber resilience'.[12] This clear statement signifies that effective and continuous employee education, working with the board and bringing the 'people' element of the risk to the fore, is very much needed. These are all areas where operational risk professionals excel.

CALL FOR ACTION

Find your perfect place in cyber risk management by:

- Collaborating with IT experts to achieve a perfect complement of generalist and specialist skills;
- Accessing available expertise (whether external, group level or other);

- Teasing out material risks and key controls;
- Assisting and encouraging the board to have essential conversations on cyber risk;
- Progressively enhancing your own skills.

Is operational risk disintegrating?

Deliberations on the role of operational risk teams in third-party and cyber risk bring us neatly to the broader question hinted at earlier: whether operational risk as a discipline is starting to disintegrate. The new ORX reference taxonomy, mentioned in Chapter 1, with its 16 distinct sub-categories replacing the original seven categories defined by the Basel Committee, brought along with it a variety of specialist functions, which provide oversight of the respective risk sub-types. Some examples are outlined in Table 16.3.

These units, staffed with skilled professional resources, can sometimes be protective of their territory, often firmly making the point that it is *their role* to oversee the relevant risk sub-type. For example these specialist units may:

- Design their own risk assessments, using different methodologies and templates which are different in terminology, grading scales and approach compared to the operational risk assessments;
- Suggest their own processes for incident logging, which differ to OREs and exist alongside them; or
- Conduct training and education in parallel to operational risk teams.

Table 16.3   Example second line specialist functions

Operational risk sub-type	Specialist oversight unit
Financial crime, Conduct, Regulatory	Compliance Function
Cyber/Information security	Information Security Unit
Third-party	TPRM
Data management	Data Protection Officer
Legal risk	Legal department

If this situation is not addressed, it may leave operational risk teams with solely oversight of *employment practices* and a portion of the *execution, delivery and process management* sub-categories, as most other risk categories would have already been 'taken', distributed across the various specialist units.

Proliferation of risk assessments and incident logging methodologies is a particular and growing concern, as these processes are burdensome for end-users, who are left both confused and struggling under an ever-increasing load of risk assessments. Different grading scales for rating risks add to the confusion, leading to a bad data foundation and sub-optimal decision-making. Conversely, the best way forward is to collaborate with other departments to align methodologies, streamlining where possible and incorporating all risk assessments into the RCSA framework. The industry Best Practice Forum discussed whether this kind of alignment was a priority, and 75 per cent of members confirmed that it was on their agenda. In particular, members reflected on areas where they had achieved success in aligning these tools and approaches, as presented in Table 16.4.

Table 16.4 Alignment successes

Alignment successes	% of respondents
Adopted risk management software which serves as one true source for risks, controls, incidents and metrics	27
Agreed a common risk assessment methodology, with the same rating bands, impact and likelihood scales for all risk assessments	21
Combined multiple risk assessments (i.e. incorporated *conduct* and *financial crime* risk assessments into RCSAs)	21
Implemented one single risk taxonomy throughout the firm	16
Aligned governance of issues between Operational risk, Compliance and Internal Audit	5
Adopted a common risk-acceptance process across all second line units	5
Achieved joined-up reporting of *top 10 risks* between Risk and Compliance	5

It stands to reason that alignment and collaboration are recurring themes in this book. Indeed operational risk professionals can serve as vital *connectors*, reaching across the silos and bringing different areas together. After all, the kind of risks mentioned in this section are all operational risk sub-types, and it is sensible and meaningful to adopt a coherent and joined-up approach to their management.

CALL FOR ACTION

Strive for alignment and collaborate with other units to:

- Agree on common terminology, methodology and data sources;
- Jointly listen to the voice of first line business and support units, who may be subject to multiple risk assessments;
- Jointly develop a plan to streamline the assessments and other practices where possible.

AI

A fascinating topic – and one impossible to ignore – artificial intelligence (AI) represents a *must-examine* area for operational risk professionals, both in terms of understanding the risks it poses and exploring the opportunities it provides. This applies to AI in general and, more particularly, generative AI, as will be seen below.

The use of AI skyrocketed during 2023 with the introduction of ChatGPT (generative pretrained transformer), a chatbot from OpenAI, which according to Reuters achieved a record by reaching 100 million monthly active users in January 2023, just two months after launch, making it 'the fastest-growing consumer application in history'.[13] On a personal level, my first encounter with ChatGPT came during an educational course I ran in early 2023. I split participants into groups and asked them to discuss and note down what they perceived to be the core *future skills* of operational risk professionals, expecting a lively debate on this exciting topic. Interestingly, one group promptly typed the question into the ChatGPT app and transposed the response onto their flip chart. This way of approaching a task by consulting ChatGPT, which at the time I may have perceived as unconventional, now seems a rather *conventional* response, whether we like it or not, and neatly demonstrates the app's widespread use.

Traditional application of AI in financial services

According to IBM, 'Artificial intelligence, or AI, is technology that enables computers and machines to simulate human intelligence and problem-solving capabilities.'[14]

AI has been in use in financial services for over a decade. Proprietary algorithms developed to perform a specific task are most commonly applied in algorithmic trading, telephone banking and pattern analysis to recognize money laundering and fraud. From a risk management perspective, the risks are largely addressed under *model risk* management, as each proprietary model must be rigorously assessed for fitness. Indeed model risk management in itself has been an area of growing regulatory focus, due to the complexity of models and the technical expertise needed to carry out model validation.

Technological developments, including AI, have been of great interest to the Best Practice Operational Risk Forum over the years. As is clear from the industry poll highlighted in Figure 2.8 in Chapter 2, back in 2020 companies' technological skill levels were extremely varied, and the use of AI in operational risk management was still at its inception. It has progressed somewhat since then. For example, algorithms are now embedded into GRC software platforms which compare data, draw conclusions and make recommendations, providing prompts for users to revisit relevant risks in the event of a material ORE. Others prompt to re-evaluate control ratings in cases where analysis demonstrates sub-optimal control performance or the occurrence of multiple incidents. At the same time, it is important to recognize that there is still a vast range of technological sophistication among financial services firms, and to note that a number of organizations still manage operational risk via Excel spreadsheets. Admittedly this is a declining trend, but even so operational risk systems are not yet generally seen as a top priority investment. More progress would be beneficial in this area, to take full advantage of benefits of technological advancement.

Generative AI

Generative AI is characterized by a broad range of capabilities, its ability to generate new content and respond to almost any question asked. We will use IBM's definition, which presents generative AI as 'deep-learning models that can generate high-quality text, images, and other content based on the data they were trained on'.[15]

An advantage – which is simultaneously a threat – of open GenAI apps such as ChatGPT is their easy accessibility. There is general consensus on the corresponding risks, which are broader and more complex than in the more conventional, proprietary AI case. They include:

- **Increased cyber risk:** The exploitation of generative AI by malicious actors to create sophisticated scams and attacks is a worry for 99% of business and IT professionals according to Information Systems Audit and Control Association (ISACA); while 74% believe that 'cybercriminals are harnessing AI with equal or even greater success than digital trust professionals'.[16]

- **Misinformation and disinformation:** This was a new entrant that shot straight into the number one risk position as cited by the Global Risk Report 2024,[17] acknowledging the ease of access to AI which has 'already enabled an explosion in falsified information'.

- **Disclosure of confidential information/privacy concerns:** Users may input sensitive data which later turns out to have been inadvertently memorized and mistreated by the AI, posing a threat to privacy. This angle of GenAI continues to attract significant government and regulatory attention: an inquiry into ChatGPT by Italy's Data Protection Authority reportedly found data privacy violations.[18]

- **Legal and regulatory:** This includes 'identifying any legal or regulatory obligations that need to be met or may be breached by the use of AI',[19] as noted by the Monetary Authority of Singapore in their proactive paper 'Emerging Risks and Opportunities of Generative AI for Banks'.

- **Traditional model risk**, including bias and fairness, also needs to be addressed.

More widely there are also societal concerns around dependency on AI, including the potential for over-reliance leading to diminished analytical ability and intuition. To this end, one of the top risks in 2024 noted by Edward Segal in Forbes is 'inability to connect with others',[20] as social skills may be reducing with the ever-increasing amount of time being spent by individuals on their personal technological devices.

Job displacement is also frequently cited, with predictions that GenAI will perform better than human experts in many fields; in my opinion, however, AI will boost productivity rather than substitute smart, creative and intuitive individuals.

That being said, there are things to consider in terms of use of GenAI in operational risk management:

- It is simply too good to ignore;

- Its responses can be used as ideas and thought about – to the extent that any other sources or inputs are normally subject to review and consideration;
- Good *prompt management helps*, including practising asking questions and specifying what good looks like;
- It will not replace skilful and intuitive operational risk professionals, but rather will help them to produce better outputs;
- The risks associated with its use need to be well understood and carefully managed.

The application of GenAI in operational risk management – which tends to be more qualitative and text-based compared to other quantitative risk disciplines – can be extensive, and has the potential to save a great deal of time for operational risk practitioners. Use cases might include educational video clips and creative images to bring examples to life. Other more secure/private use cases might include:

- Conducting ORE pattern analysis to search for similar root causes;
- Reviewing control library to identify the multitude of controls performing the same task despite being worded differently, to standardize and simplify RCSAs;
- Proposing story lines for scenario analysis; and the list goes on.

It is no surprise, then, that following the launch of ChatGPT many organizations have developed and adopted their own private versions of the app, which provide arguably the same benefits in a more secure environment.

In December 2023, the Best Practice Operational Risk Forum evaluated the progress made by firms with respect to GenAI, deliberating whether the risks associated with its use outweighed the opportunities. As presented in Figure 16.5, the jury was still out on this question, as the assessment was either still in progress or had not even started in some organizations.

As ISACA noted, 'a mere 10% of organizations have formal, comprehensive policies in place governing the use of AI technology, and 29% have no policy, and no plans to implement one at all'.[21] This finding resonated with the Best Practice Forum, in the sense that the majority have either not yet firmed up their overall stance on generative AI or are still in the process of deliberation, as presented in Figure 16.6.

In one way, against this background, inaction represents action, and non-prohibition signifies permission: employees may already be using a public version of ChatGPT and sharing proprietary information without specific internal guidance or a full understanding of the risks involved. There is clearly a need for rapid mass education. ISACA notes that 'just 7% of organisations are providing all employees with AI training'.[22] Similarly, only a minority of firms had adequate knowledge of AI as a topic within operational risk management, as presented in Figure 16.7.

Figure 16.5 Industry poll: integrating Generative AI into operational risk management

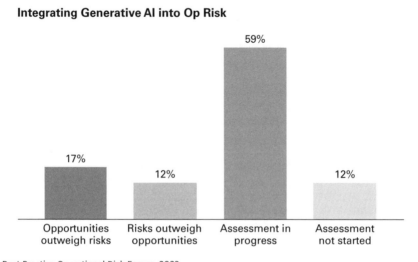

Integrating Generative AI into Op Risk

Best Practice Operational Risk Forum, 2023

Figure 16.6 Industry poll: overall stance on Generative AI

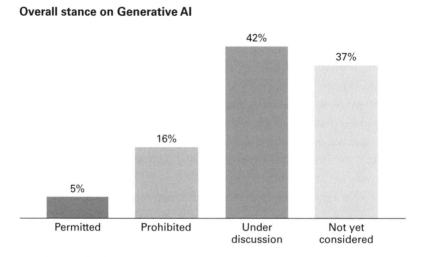

Overall stance on Generative AI

Best Practice Operational Risk Forum, 2023

Figure 16.7   Industry poll: knowledge of risk teams on AI

Skills and knowledge of Op Risk teams: AI

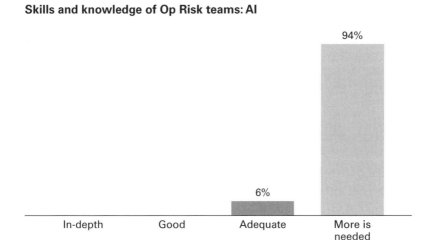

Best Practice Operational Risk Forum, 2023

In conclusion, it is recommended that operational risk professionals not only continue to actively explore AI as a tool for their own use, but also add their voice to the firm-wide programmes tasked with deliberating on AI applications.

CALL FOR ACTION

Accelerate the organizational pace of decision-making on GenAI by:

- Conducting your own research;
- Joining firm-wide projects tasked with developing the firm's stance on AI; lending expertise and facilitating the assessment of risks and opportunities;
- Engaging with the board to ensure risks are understood;
- Progressively enhancing your own expertise.

Call for action to call for action

Throughout this book, and especially in the three final chapters, the reader may have noticed multiple *calls for action* being put out to operational risk professionals. This paradigm reflects a dramatically elevated ask from modern risk practitioners. While 20 years ago operational risk teams were primarily expected to report on loss data and carry out capital computations, nowadays many boards are seeking their independent opinion on the level of third-party and cyber risk; requesting their view on the firm's risk culture; and reaching out for advice on how to proceed with generative AI. This elevated role is of course an honour for operational risk professionals, but at the same time is a heavy load to carry. Maintaining a trusted advisor position in such a broad field requires deep knowledge of every topic residing under the operational risk umbrella. And we should bear in mind that these asks are *on top* of what are perceived to be the core operational risk duties, embedding and integrating operational risk management into the firm's day-to-day practices, and continuously educating and empowering first line business and support units.

In my experience of working with different organizations, operational risk professionals are overwhelmed with work. A saying attributed to Benjamin Franklin goes, 'If you want something done, ask a busy person'. And so it is that requests for help, or *calls for action*, keep coming to operational risk professionals due to their unique skillsets and ability to execute effectively.

In reality, it is not feasible to satisfy all requests. So *prioritization* becomes critical. And prioritization was the word of the day when the Best Practice Operational Risk Forum discussed 2024 priorities.

Similarly to previous years, the perpetual topic of *embedding* and increasing ownership of risk in the first line yet again topped the chart. This has been the case as long as I can remember running these surveys with the industry. Exercising prudent decision-making, by managing risks that may prevent first line areas from achieving *their own objectives,* seems intuitively the right thing to do. Yet participants agreed that this remains a challenge, and noted that operational risk teams spend a large proportion of their time working on the front line, constantly seeking to embed risk practices.

In contrast, engaging with the board and assisting with decision-making came third on the priority list. This is reflected in Figure 16.8.

Figure 16.8 Industry poll: top operational risk priorities 2024

Top operational risk priorities 2024

1st	Continue educating and empowering 1st line
2nd	Focus on topical areas (e.g. AI, Cyber, Third-party, E, S and G)
3rd	Engage with Board/ExCo, act as advisor for making better decisions
4th	Carry out assurance/themed reviews
5th	Further develop Risk team's skills and capabilities of risk
6th	Collaborate with other units (e.g. compliance) to streamline
7th	Upgrade/invest in risk system(s)

Best Practice Operational Risk Forum, 2024

Participants reflected whether the right proportion of time was being spent working bottom-up at the coalface, as opposed to top-down with the Board. Inevitably, situations will come up that require honest discussion on the few top initiatives achievable in a year. In the current rapidly evolving environment, operational risk professionals should perhaps be looking to rebalance their day, and reinvent themselves as board advisors, spending more time at a strategic level, advising and prioritizing. So that is the final call for action for operational risk professionals – to make a systematic inventory of all the calls for action that come into the department, and then spend time with the Board agreeing the areas of focus and accepting what can and will not be achieved during the year.

In turn, day-to-day embedding activities can gradually be delegated to the first line risk champions described in Chapter 3. As the risk champions make progress in their learning, and develop increasingly excellent relationships with the people they are working with, this will also enable second line operational risk professionals to spend more value-added time with the board. This is a vitally important point of this chapter – and indeed, the whole book. Effective operational risk management of the future will be achieved via the first line business units owning risk management, well supported by embedded risk champions, and second line operational risk practitioners lending their valuable expertise at the strategic level.

MAKE A DIFFERENCE (MAD) ACTION

Please note down one action that you will take after reading this chapter that will meaningfully enhance your department's preparedness to face future challenges.

Notes

1 World Economic Forum (2024) *The Global Risks Report 2024*, www3. weforum.org/docs/WEF_The_Global_Risks_Report_2024.pdf (archived at https://perma.cc/7JUW-AY38)

2 World Economic Forum (2018) *Trudeau: 'The pace of change has never been this fast'*, www.youtube.com/watch?v=fTl1YNTNb0g (archived at https://perma.cc/T37C-D2A7)

3 Reuters (2023) *Euro zone banks lose millions of euros to poor IT outsourcing*, www.reuters.com/markets/europe/euro-zone-banks-lose-millions-euros-poor-it-outsourcing-2023-11-15/ (archived at https://perma.cc/EJ5M-E5LS)

4 Resilience (2023) *2023 Mid-Year Cyber Claims Report*, 4526209.fs1. hubspotusercontent-na1.net/hubfs/4526209/Claims%20Report/Resilience_2023MidYearClaimsReport_Final10162023%20(1).pdf (archived at https://perma.cc/96GX-2FJB)

5 European Banking Authority (2019) *EBA Guidelines on Outsourcing Arrangements*, extranet.eba.europa.eu/sites/default/documents/files/documents/10180/2551996/38c80601-f5d7-4855-8ba3-702423665479/EBA%20revised%20Guidelines%20on%20outsourcing%20arrangements.pdf?retry=1 (archived at https://perma.cc/CPJ3-WP58)

6 Digital Operational Resilience Act (DORA), www.digital-operational-resilience-act.com/DORA_Articles.html (archived at https://perma.cc/36UR-9XHG)

7 Australian Prudential Regulation Authority (APRA) (2023) *Prudential Standard CPS230, Operational Risk Management*, www.apra.gov.au/sites/default/files/2023-07/Prudential%20Standard%20CPS%20230%20Operational%20Risk%20Management%20-%20clean.pdf (archived at https://perma.cc/KX5K-Y6GN)

8 Comparitech (2024) 300+ Terrifying Cybercrime and Cybersecurity Statistics (2024 EDITION), www.comparitech.com/vpn/cybersecurity-cyber-crime-statistics-facts-trends/ (archived at https://perma.cc/CB6Q-3W6V)

9 Protiviti (2023) *Executive Perspectives on Top Risks for 2024 and 2034*, www.protiviti.com/uk-en/survey/executive-perspectives-top-risks (archived at https://perma.cc/NFC6-QS33)

10 World Economic Forum (2024) *The Global Risks Report 2024*, www3.weforum.org/docs/WEF_The_Global_Risks_Report_2024.pdf (archived at https://perma.cc/7JUW-AY38)

11 National Institute of Standards and Technology (NIST) (2024) *The NIST Cybersecurity Framework 2.0*, nvlpubs.nist.gov/nistpubs/CSWP/NIST.CSWP.29.pdf (archived at https://perma.cc/Y3H3-ZRJW)

12 Bank for International Settlements (BIS) (2018) *Sabine Lautenschläger: Cyber resilience – objectives and tools*, www.bis.org/review/r180319c.htm (archived at https://perma.cc/X29Y-T87T)

13 Reuters (2023) *ChatGPT sets record for fastest-growing user base – analyst note*, www.reuters.com/technology/chatgpt-sets-record-fastest-growing-user-base-analyst-note-2023-02-01/ (archived at https://perma.cc/ES32-PKZE)

14 IBM, *What is artificial intelligence (AI)?*, www.ibm.com/topics/artificial-intelligence (archived at https://perma.cc/F4MA-26SJ)

15 IBM (2023) *What is Generative AI?*, research.ibm.com/blog/what-is-generative-AI (archived at https://perma.cc/XE3T-W3SW)

16 Information Systems Audit and Control Association (ISACA) (2023) *New Study: Business and IT professionals are worried about the exploitation of generative AI by bad actors*, www.isaca.org/about-us/newsroom/press-releases/2023/new-study-business-and-it-professionals-are-worried-about-the-exploitation-of-generative-ai (archived at https://perma.cc/JX3C-MUQQ)

17 World Economic Forum (2024) *The Global Risks Report 2024*, www3.weforum.org/docs/WEF_The_Global_Risks_Report_2024.pdf (archived at https://perma.cc/7JUW-AY38)

18 BBC (2024) *ChatGPT: Italy says OpenAI's chatbot breaches data protection rules*, www.bbc.co.uk/news/technology-68128396 (archived at https://perma.cc/L8V5-GMS3)

19 Monetary Authority of Singapore (MAS) (2023) *Emerging Risks and Opportunities of Generative AI for Banks*, www.mas.gov.sg/-/media/mas/news/media-releases/2023/executive-summary---emerging-risks-and-opportunities-of-generative-ai-for-banks.pdf (archived at https://perma.cc/UK6Q-A8SM)

20 Segal, E (2023) *The 9 biggest risks and threats that companies will face in 2024*, Forbes, www.forbes.com/sites/edwardsegal/2023/12/03/the-8-biggest-risks-and-threats-that-companies-will-face-in-2024/ (archived at https://perma.cc/U8FX-TNNU)

21 Information Systems Audit and Control Association (ISACA) (2023) *New Study: Business and IT professionals are worried about the exploitation of generative AI by bad actors*, www.isaca.org/about-us/newsroom/press-releases/2023/new-study-business-and-it-professionals-are-worried-about-the-exploitation-of-generative-ai (archived at https://perma.cc/JX3C-MUQQ)

22 Information Systems Audit and Control Association (ISACA) (2023) *New Study: Business and IT professionals are worried about the exploitation of generative AI by bad actors*, www.isaca.org/about-us/newsroom/press-releases/2023/new-study-business-and-it-professionals-are-worried-about-the-exploitation-of-generative-ai (archived at https://perma.cc/JX3C-MUQQ)

APPENDIX 1

Operational Risk Champion: role description

- Risk management is the responsibility of **each and every employee**.
- The **head of each Business Unit** is ultimately accountable for ensuring that robust risk management practices are embedded within the respective Business Unit.
- The role of **Risk Champion** is to assist the head of the Business Unit in ensuring that risks are identified, assessed, managed and reported.

The position

The Risk Champion is the Subject Matter Expert and the main liaison point between the second Line Risk Function and the Business Unit, facilitating the implementation and embedding of the use of risk management tools and techniques within the Unit, supporting the Head in continuous development and enhancement of the business unit's risk management practices.

Responsibilities

The Risk Champion's responsibilities include:

- ensuring all staff in the department are familiar with the operational risk event (ORE) identification and reporting process; and that there is clear understanding of what constitutes an event and what course of action should be followed;
- ensuring OREs are reported when they occur; with root causes analysed and actions taken to prevent reoccurrence;

- ensuring the unit's RCSAs are conducted; acting as a central liaison between second line risk department and the business unit in planning and organizing the RCSA workshops;
- ensuring the RCSA is fit for purpose and is a true reflection of the business unit's risk profile;
- raising the awareness of the unit's risk profile, ensuring all employees are familiar with and able to articulate the unit's top risks and mitigating actions;
- assisting the business unit head in the development of key risk indicators and the establishment of appropriate thresholds;
- identifying the business unit's risk training needs, and flagging new employees to the second line risk department for the provision of training;
- maintaining contact with other Risk Champions, to share information about relevant OREs, RCSA risks and lessons learnt;
- developing risk procedures/desk instructions relevant for the business unit as necessary;
- coordinating with second line risk department to implement any new risk-related initiatives, processes and/or tools;
- participating in other risk initiatives as appropriate.

APPENDIX 2

Example operational risk event reporting template

Reporting business/function
Date of discovery
Date of occurrence (if known)
High-level description *Enter a clear and succinct description of the transaction/event that allows those who are not familiar with it to quickly understand the problem.*
How was ORE discovered? *Provide an explanation as to how the ORE was discovered and the area that identified it.*
Root cause (if known) – why did it occur? *Provide an explanation about the primary root cause of the event and any control breaks that contributed to the ORE occurring.*
Actual or estimated cost *Consider any direct out-of-pocket costs of the event and any additional costs to resolve the issue (e.g. legal fees, consultancy costs to investigate/solve the problem); if a near miss, a rough estimate of potential exposure client/ reputational/regulatory impact.* *If the value is unknown, say so, detailing steps being taken to determine the exposure.*
Resolution target date

(continued)

(Continued)

Remedial action *Highlight action steps already taken and any further plans to close the issue and prevent reoccurrence, including the person responsible for completion and target resolution date.*
Event category *Select the most appropriate taxonomy category from the menu.*
Suspicious activity report filed (Y/N) *Refer to Compliance Manual.*
Status of loss: Pending/Incurred (paid)/Reserved/Recovered *If needed, discuss with finance, establishing a reserve or writing the amount off.*
Cost centre/Reference accounting entries
Conduct (Y/N) *Highlight whether or not the event has a conduct element.*
Operational resilience (Y/N) *Highlight if the event has resulted in a disruption of a critical operation.*
Department head sign-off

APPENDIX 3

ORA template

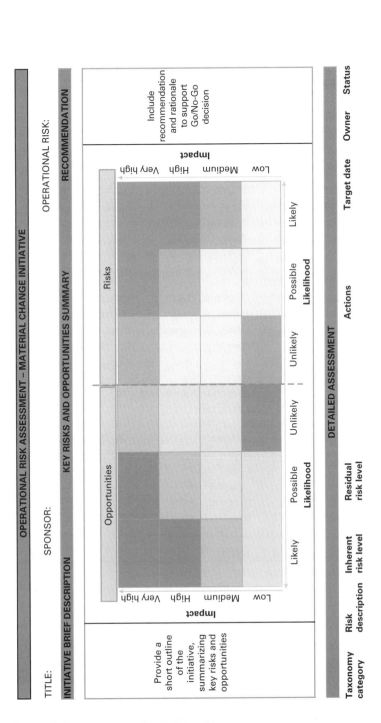

APPENDIX 4

Table of 50 Key Risk Indicators

No.	Risk or theme	KRI description	Why useful?
1	Change management	% of overdue and at-risk projects within active project portfolio	Presents overall health of change portfolio – overdue and 'at-risk' projects vs on-track ones
2	Change management	Number of change activities where post-implementation reviews (PIRs) highlighted material issues	Post-implementation reviews measure the success of project discipline; metrics tracks unsuccessful/ poorly implemented projects
3	Change management	% of employees in business areas undergoing change meeting or exceeding their expectations compared to the rest of the firm	Indicator of change fatigue, measures employee productivity levels in business areas undergoing change
4	Conduct and culture	Number of exceptions to the New Product Approval (NPA) process, where product went live prior to formal governance approval	Monitors new products traded/sold to the client by-passing new product governance

(continued)

(Continued)

No.	Risk or theme	KRI description	Why useful?
5	Conduct and culture	Number of products that do not meet the target market	Identifies products that appeal to clients outside of the primary target market (based on complaints, incidents and annual product reviews)
6	Conduct and culture	% of operational risk events not reported within timeline required by the policy	Helps identify poor risk management/risk culture issues in terms of not being open and transparent in reporting events quickly
7	Conduct and culture	% of staff background checks with 'high-risk' observations/ high-risk social media profiles	Where periodic screening of existing employees is performed, including social media screening, flags 'high-risk' observations
8	Conduct and culture	Number of new accounts proposed by relationship managers and not approved	Monitors instances of potential account opening outside of the appetite, where subsequent approval was not granted
9	Conduct and culture	Number of exceptions in product sales quality identified by quality assurance (QA) process	Monitors inappropriate sales identified via a spot-check quality assurance review
10	Cyber	Remediation of critical vulnerabilities outside of the SLA	Monitors the speed of remediation of most important (critical) vulnerabilities that could be exploited
11	Cyber	Number/% of unmanaged devices detected on network	Predictive indicator measures organization's exposure to cyber risk; can also monitor % of network devices not meeting configuration standards

(continued)

(Continued)

No.	Risk or theme	KRI description	Why useful?
12	Cyber	Number/% of employees who failed phishing tests	Reflects on the overall level of staff awareness and identifies repeat offenders within staff, who continue to click on internally created educational phishing emails
13	Cyber	Number/% of patches not updated within SLA	Predictive KRI; measures system health via timely installation of patches; can be narrowed down to critical systems
14	Cyber	Number/% increase in intrusion attempts/ malware alerts	Continuous monitoring of the volume of alerts, identifying spikes
15	Cyber	Number of table-top exercises to test response to a cyber incident conducted against plan	Monitors preparedness by ensuring periodic tests are conducted as planned; additional KRI can measure number of open actions emanating from the tests
16	Data breach	% completion of mandatory information security training	Monitors adherence to mandatory employee training process
17	Data breach	Volume of attempts: staff sending emails/ files to personal email addresses	Monitors email traffic focusing on attachments, identifying potential policy breaches
18	Financial crime	% of new accounts opened with exceptions	Identifies non-standard accounts requiring additional approvals and sign-offs
19	Financial crime	Open activity monitoring alerts not actioned within x days	Control indicator; monitors how promptly the alerts are investigated and resolved

(continued)

(Continued)

No.	Risk or theme	KRI description	Why useful?
20	Financial crime	Suspicious activity reports (SARs) – increase/decrease in cases reported	Monitors changes in volume and highlights spikes
21	Internal fraud	Number of systems that permit staff to process payments or transactions single-handedly	Highlights exceptions where segregation of duties is not enforced, presenting a higher risk of error and/or internal fraud
22	Internal fraud	Critical systems with user access not re-certified on time	Control indicator of system re-certification process; focusses on user access to ensure joiners/transfers/leavers are acted upon in a timely manner, preventing unauthorized access
23	Internal fraud	% of movers or leavers with privileged access where access is removed outside of timescales	Identifies exceptions where leavers' access was not removed in a timely way
24	Internal fraud	Whistleblowing – % increase/decrease in cases reported	Monitors unusual spikes and falls in the use of whistleblowing process
25	Internal fraud	Premises access – unusual working patterns	Highlights unusual access to facilities, for example after hours or on weekends
26	Internal fraud	Number/% of staff that did not take mandatory leave	Monitors compliance with mandatory leave policy; applied to identified staff in scope, which can include trading, payments and others

(continued)

(Continued)

No.	Risk or theme	KRI description	Why useful?
27	Internal fraud	Trading policy breaches – trades in breach of trader's mandate	For trading business, monitors trades that have been erroneously or deliberately entered in breach of the prescribed mandate
28	Legal & regulatory	Horizon scanning: number of new regulatory initiatives/ consultations with potential significant impact in the next 6 months	Monitors regulatory developments and potential volume of change expected in the near future
29	Legal & regulatory	Timeframe pressure: deals requested to be completed in less that x days	Monitors potential increase in legal risk due to sub-optimal deal execution as a result of time pressure
30	Legal & regulatory	Litigation: value at risk of active legal claims	Provides insight into potential value of settlement for legal claims
31	Model risk	Number of models that have not been validated/validation overdue	Identifies potential areas of model risk
32	Model risk	Results of blind test of HR algorithms for bias	Measures the success or failure of independent testing for bias of existing HR algorithms
33	Outsourcing/ third-party risk	Frequency of extreme weather events in critical supplier location	Monitors the average number of months between weather events that disrupt the business of the supplier
34	Outsourcing/ third-party risk	Number/% of supplier resiliency assessments overdue or with exceptions	Monitors timeliness and outcomes of proactive assessments of third-party resilience arrangements

(continued)

(Continued)

No.	Risk or theme	KRI description	Why useful?
35	Outsourcing/ third-party risk	Number/% of material exceptions to standard contract clauses	Identifies a proportion of providers with non-standard legal contracts that require additional attention
36	Outsourcing/ third-party risk	Number/% of critical providers without defined exit plan/not easily substitutable	Assesses reliance on a critical supplier which cannot be substituted
37	People	Number/% of non-permanent staff in service over 12 months	Monitors long-term contract staff, indicating difficulties in filling open positions or a need to raise a permanent vacancy
38	People	Number/% of offers for preferred candidates rejected	Provides a view on the firm's attractiveness as an employer, and the risk of inability to recruit key staff
39	People	Percentage of managers that have received training on managing remote and hybrid teams	Highlights areas that demand greater attention, before problems materialize
40	People	Average spend on activities to promote employee wellbeing, as a % of operating income	Ensures that wellbeing remains at the top of senior management's agenda
41	People	Number and trend of employees logging over 60 hours per week for over 1 month	Employee burnout indicator, important with the transition to remote or hybrid working. Working long hours should prompt workload review

(*continued*)

(Continued)

No.	Risk or theme	KRI description	Why useful?
42	Technology failure	End-of-Life hardware [software] as a % of overall hardware [software]	Predictive KRI; monitors reliance on software/hardware that is approaching the end of the service contract and needs to be replaced
43	Technology failure	Average time to mitigate the highest impact technology incidents impacting service level agreements (SLA)	Provides a view to the firm's ability to recover quickly without significant internal or external impact
44	Technology failure	Number of complex tests completed to stress business strategies	Predictive KRI; measures the success of operational resilience testing/planning
45	Technology failure	% change requests not signed off or signed off with exceptions	Monitors technology change management process, ensuring robust governance is applied
46	Technology failure	Number of critical systems that failed periodic disaster recovery test	Raises awareness of systems that failed to recover within stipulated recovery time objective (RTO)
47	Transaction processing	% staff with 2+ years' experience vs total staff	'Experience' indicator, valuable for complex processing units [e.g. derivatives, corporate actions]
48	Transaction processing	Processing volume vs operations staff capacity	Monitors capacity and potential for over-stretching leading to risk of error

(continued)

(Continued)

No.	Risk or theme	KRI description	Why useful?
49	Transaction processing	Number of cash/ stock breaks outstanding >30 days at month end	Monitors effectiveness of reconciliation and investigation process via number of 'aged' discrepancies
50	Transaction processing	% straight-through processing rate	Assesses rate of transactions without manual intervention

INDEX

Looking for another book?

Explore our award-winning
books from global business
experts in Risk and
Compliance

Scan the code to browse

www.koganpage.com/risk-compliance

More books from Kogan Page

ISBN: 9780749478612

ISBN: 9781398605022

ISBN: 9781398614871

ISBN: 9781398610613

www.koganpage.com